# History, Heritage

## An Introduction

### (Third Edition)

### Andrew Pickering

Copyright © 2013, 2014, 2016 Andrew Pickering

All rights reserved. No part of this publication may be reproduced or transmitted in any form or by any means, electronic or mechanical including photocopying, recording or any information storage or retrieval system, without prior permission in writing from the publishers.

The right of Andrew Pickering to be identified as the author of this work has been asserted by him in accordance with the Copyright, Designs and patents Act 1988.

First published in 2014 by the History, Heritage and Archaeology Press, an imprint of Ape or Eden Books. Devizes, England.

**APE OR EDEN**

# Contents

Contents ................................................................................... iii

Preface to the First Edition ........................................................ 1

Part 1 HISTORY ........................................................................... 2
1 Historical theories and interpretations ................................... 2
    *What is History?* ...................................................................... 2
    *Historical evidence* ................................................................. 3
    *Historical questions and approaches* ................................... 4
    *Categorisation and classification* ......................................... 5
    *The narrative approach* ......................................................... 7
    *Whig history* ........................................................................... 8
    *Historical concepts and theories* .......................................... 8
    *Chance in history* ................................................................. 10
    *Intentionalist interpretations* ............................................. 14
    *Structural interpretations* ................................................... 14
    *Historical determinism* ....................................................... 14
    *Profound causes - the 'Frontier thesis'* .............................. 15
    *Metanarratives* .................................................................... 16
    *Marxist interpretations* ...................................................... 16
    *History and progress* .......................................................... 19
    *'From above' and 'from below' interpretations* ................ 21
    *Psychoanalytical interpretations* ....................................... 23
    *Women's history* ................................................................. 24
    *Some conclusions* ............................................................... 27
2 Historical approaches and methods ..................................... 30
    *Introduction* ......................................................................... 30
    *Historical relationism* .......................................................... 31
    *History as a social science* .................................................. 32
    *Narrative history* ................................................................. 33
    *Literary and heroic history* ................................................. 34
    *Is History a science?* ............................................................ 36

*Social and economic history* ............................................................. *42*
*The Annalists* ..................................................................................... *45*
*The history of the mentalities* ........................................................ *45*
*Cultural history* ................................................................................ *49*
*Psychoanalytical history* ................................................................. *51*
*New economic history* .................................................................... *52*
*The history of the marginalised* ..................................................... *52*
*History and anthropology* ............................................................... *54*
*Some conclusions* ........................................................................... *55*

## Part 3 HERITAGE ............................................................................. 59
## 3 Heritage and its management .................................................... 59
*What is heritage?* ............................................................................ *59*
*Heritage history* ............................................................................... *61*
*The Society for the Protection of Ancient Buildings* .................... *65*
*The National Trust* ........................................................................... *69*
*The Royal Commission on Ancient Monuments* .......................... *70*
*Historic England* .............................................................................. *75*
*The English Heritage Trust* ............................................................. *76*
*The Heritage Lottery Fund* .............................................................. *76*
*National Amenity Societies* ............................................................. *79*
*The Georgian Group* ........................................................................ *80*
*The Victorian Society* ...................................................................... *82*
*The Council for British Archaeology (CBA)* .................................... *85*
*World Heritage Sites* ........................................................................ *88*
*The Heritage Alliance* ...................................................................... *91*
*The Heritage Trust* ........................................................................... *91*
*The Heritage Industry* ...................................................................... *92*
*Intangible cultural heritage (Marja Haas)* ...................................... *93*

## 4 Heritage and its interpretation ................................................. 104
*Museology* ..................................................................................... *104*
*Interpretation* ................................................................................ *107*
*Display* ........................................................................................... *117*
*Visitor experiences in museums* .................................................. *119*

Research surveys ................................................................ 120
Evaluating displays and exhibitions..................................... 121
Access ................................................................................... 122
Open Air Museums ................................................................ 124
Industrial Archaeology (Claire Gore) .................................. 137
Museum Education................................................................ 149
The abuse of cultural heritage............................................. 151
CASE STUDY: heritage and hidden history.......................... 157

## Part 3 ARCHAEOLOGY ......................................................... 166
5 Archaeological methods and practices ................................. 166
What is Archaeology? .......................................................... 166
Archaeology and Planning Guidance.................................. 167
Some important developments .......................................... 172
Non-intrusive Archaeology ................................................. 175
Field-walking ....................................................................... 175
Geophysics............................................................................ 178
Excavation ............................................................................ 185
Tools and technology: attributes........................................ 186
CASE STUDY: 'Otzi' the Iceman ........................................... 187
The investigation of domestic buildings ........................... 192
Structure and fittings.......................................................... 192
Documentary sources.......................................................... 196
Experimental archaeology................................................... 198
CASE STUDY: The Kon Tiki Expedition ................................ 203
CASE STUDY: The Brendan Voyage...................................... 209
CASE STUDY: The Overton Down earthwork ...................... 216
Experiential approaches to the past.................................. 224
6 Archaeological theories and interpretations ....................... 241
Prehistory ............................................................................. 241
Hawkes' 'ladder of inference'............................................. 243
Social organisation .............................................................. 244
CASE STUDY: The socio-economic organisation of Britain in the Late Iron Age - evidence for warriors and warfare ......................... 246

Models for identifying territories ..................... 259
Social Organisation: archaeological indicators ............................... 260
Trade and Exchange ..................... 262
CASE STUDY: The expansion of Rome and the resurgence of Britain's continental trade c. 100 – 50 BC ..................... 263
Religion and ritual ..................... 276
Explanations for cultural change ..................... 278
Ethnoarchaeology ..................... 279
CASE STUDY: Southern Britain's Late Iron Age Slave Trade ............. 280

## Part 4 PROFESSIONAL PRACTICE ..................... 288
7 Practice ..................... 288
Interpreting and evaluating sources ..................... 288
Official documents ..................... 289
Private papers and personal writings ..................... 290
Newspapers ..................... 291
Novels ..................... 292
Oral accounts and personal histories ..................... 292
Maps ..................... 294
Cartoons and posters ..................... 295
Statistics ..................... 296
Photographs ..................... 297
Primary and secondary sources ..................... 298
How to read sources ..................... 299
Context ..................... 300
Hypotheses ..................... 300
Counterfactual method ..................... 301
Regressive method ..................... 302
Essay planning ..................... 302
Cause and effect ..................... 304
Essay writing ..................... 313
Report writing ..................... 314
Referencing: Harvard and MHRA ..................... 316
Referencing: bibliographies ..................... 316

*Referencing: footnotes and endnotes* ............................................. *318*
*Book reviews* ................................................................................ *320*
*Literature review* ......................................................................... *323*
*The Peasants' Revolt, 1381: literature review (Claire Gore)* ............ *324*
*Presentations* ............................................................................... *331*
*PowerPoint presentations* ........................................................... *334*
*Poster presentations* ................................................................... *335*
*Archaeological drawing* ............................................................... *335*
*Personal development plans* ....................................................... *337*
*Careers in the heritage sector* .................................................... *337*
8 Projects ........................................................................................ 341
*Desktop survey* ............................................................................ *341*
*Local history* ................................................................................ *343*
*Family history* .............................................................................. *344*
*Oral history* .................................................................................. *348*
*Archaeological experiments* ........................................................ *351*
*CASE STUDY: Understanding ancient spears and spear-throwers* .... *358*
*Architectural survey* .................................................................... *363*
*Investigations and dissertations* .................................................. *365*
*CASE STUDY: A history of a house in Wells, Somerset* .................. *370*
*Research* ...................................................................................... *376*

# Glossary ............................................................................. 394
# Bibliography ...................................................................... 402
# Further reading ................................................................. 410

# Preface to the First Edition

History, Heritage and Archaeology are the component parts of the Plymouth University degree I manage at Strode College in Street, Somerset. Inspired by the example of a Plymouth University Foundation degree launched at Truro College, the programme delivered at Strode College is unique and reflects the interests and expertise of its module leaders. It is for students studying this programme that this book is principally intended but I hope undergraduates studying one or more of these subjects elsewhere and, of course, the general reader, will find it both useful and interesting. The material it contains has been gathered from various places including projects I have undertaken in recent years, and notes compiled in the delivery of the modules I teach. Each section endeavours to introduce some, but by no means all, of the key concepts, methods, approaches and interpretations associated with its theme. They include case studies which explore a few of these in some depth. I fully expect members of my team and some of our students to identify limitations in terms of what this book contains, just as I will be reviewing and, no doubt, revising sections during the course of the next academic year. Hopefully we won't discover too many mistakes but I think it is likely that this volume will become the first of two or more editions!

I wish to thank a number of people who have contributed to the course that prompted the compilation of this book. First, the excellent team I have had the pleasure of working with since we started up back in 2009: landscape archaeologist Katherine Dray, medievalist Sean McGlynn, and experimental archaeologist Eddie Daughton. We are very ably supported in our work by various colleagues in the college, particularly Shirley Theedom, Wendy Cavill, Shonagh Butler, Jane Stoodley, Philippa Piper, Margaret Baker, and Angela Leavens. Our Principal, James Staniforth, shares our faith in the development of Higher Education in a Further Education context and, as a Cambridge History graduate, follows our activities with particular interest.

I am very grateful to our colleagues at Plymouth University, especially Chris Groucutt and Liz Tingle, not least for their support in our recent application to deliver the programme at Level 6 / 'Bachelor' level in

September 2014. The effort and willing engagement of our past and present external examiners, Kristen Doern (Bath Spa University) and Andrew Jackson (Bishop Grosseteste University, Lincoln) is also much appreciated.

We are very lucky in delivering this degree programme in a county that has an exceptionally rich and diverse history and archaeological record. Furthermore Somerset has a superb County Heritage Service and numerous other well-run and innovative heritage centres and independent heritage organisations. My thanks go to all those who have engaged with us over the last few years, attending and speaking at our heritage conferences, providing work placements for our students, and, in particular, joining our employers' forum to guide and advise us in the development of our modules. These include, among others, Bob Croft, Richard Brunning, Jane Hill, Natalie Watson, Charlie, Nancy and Arthur Hollinrake, Sonja Power, John Smith, Andrew Tizzard, Susan Strong, Mary Claridge, and Estelle Gilbert. I am especially grateful to Helen Mansfield, the Somerset Heritage Service's Learning Manager, for her willingness to share her expertise regarding the communication of information in a museum setting, and for involving us in the exciting developments planned for the Somerset Rural Life Museum in Glastonbury.

Most importantly I acknowledge with gratitude the many students who have enrolled on the course over the last few years, without whom this volume would not exist. In every sense this book is for them.

## Preface to the Second Edition

As anticipated this book is a new edition of the original volume. The most significant change is the reordering of some of the material and the addition of a fourth section entitled 'Professional Practice'. Some of the new material introduces topics which we will be exploring in our new BA (Hons) 'top-up' programme when we launch it later this year (2014). I am grateful to Maureen Wincott of Bournemouth University who contributed the final Case Study in the book. Dr. James Gregory of Plymouth University kindly provided many of the addresses and much of the information for web-based academic research, covered in Chapter 7.

## Preface to the Third Edition

This third version of *History, Heritage and Archaeology: an introduction* contains several entirely new sections and updated versions of others. The 'heritage' world is constantly changing and I am sure I have neglected some important developments. This does not aim to offer a comprehensive coverage of the subject but to serve as a useful reference tool and guide to further reading. To help whet appetites for independent research and learning, I have added some recent examples of student work, and I am most grateful to Claire Gore and Marja Haas for their permission to include, in part or whole, their work in a wide range of heritage projects. Other additions include career advice, dissertation guidance, and an extensive guide to on-line history, heritage and archaeology resources.

**Andrew Pickering**

*Programme Manager (History, Heritage and Archaeology)*
*Strode College and Plymouth University, 2016*

# Part 1 HISTORY

## 1 Historical theories and interpretations

### What is History?

'The study of history, then amounts to a search for the truth.'
(G. R. Elton (1969) *The Practice of History*, p. 70)

Not all historians believe an objective historical 'truth' can be attained. It has been argued that, ultimately, history is interpretation. It is an idea of what the past may have been like and, probably, an explanation for why it was as it was. History is not the past but a collection of views of the past. The point has been made succinctly by the historian Keith Jenkins: 'Let us say you have been studying part of England's past - the sixteenth century [...] Let us imagine that you have used one major text-book: Elton's England under the Tudors. In class you have discussed aspects of the sixteenth century, you have class notes, but for your essays and the bulk of your revision you have used Elton. When the exam came along you wrote in the shadow of Elton. And when you passed, you gained [...] a qualification for considering aspects of "the past". But really it would be more accurate to say you have [a qualification] in Geoffrey Elton: for what, actually, at this stage, is your "reading" of the English past if not basically his reading of it?'[1]

History, therefore, is a view of the past seen through subsequent layers of interpretation, building up across generations of historians like the layers of sediment obscuring the ruins of an ancient culture. As historians look to the past, they encounter, analyse and revise the interpretations of their predecessors. Consequently, it can be argued that history is **historiography**[2] since it is all to do with the evaluation of previous interpretations in the fashioning of new ones or, in the case of a 'counter-revisionist' interpretation, the restoration of older

---

1   Jenkins (1991), p.7
[2] For technical terms and historical references printed in **bold**, see the Glossary section at the end of the book for definitions and explanations.

arguments. As E. H. Carr in *What is History?* stated: 'The historian is part of history. The point in the procession at which he finds himself determines his angle of vision over the past'[3]. Perversely, however, hindsight provides historians with the argument that, despite this, they 'in a way know more about the past than the people who lived it'[4].

Such postmodernist arguments are fine to a point, but more traditional-minded historians are deeply critical of views that suggest that history is simply subjective storytelling based on incomplete and problematic evidence. Some history, in the view of Richard Evans, can / should only be read one way: 'The gas chambers were not a piece of rhetoric. Auschwitz was indeed inherently a tragedy and cannot be seen as either a comedy or a farce.'[5]

**Postmodernism** is the term that has been applied over the past 50 years to ways in which the 'modern' ideas of the twentieth century in academic disciplines, including philosophy, literature and history, have been challenged. A central theme in 'postmodern' history is the theory that the pursuit of an objective truth about the past is misguided. Just as 'postmodern' literary critics have argued that literary criticism reveals more about the critic/reader than the author, 'postmodern' history theorists argue that historians should focus on the processes by which written history is formed. Hence it encourages a laudably critical, but gloomily sceptical, reading of historical sources.

### Historical evidence

> '...agreement among historians is remarkably difficult to achieve, and historical events are open to a multiplicity of interpretations.'
> (A. Green and K. Troup (1999) *The Houses of History*, p. 6)

The problem every historian confronts, even when they are dealing with relatively recent historical events, is that the evidence they rely upon is likely to be fragmentary, incomplete and contradictory. Everything surviving from the past that indicates some aspect of human activity is potential evidence for the historian. Thus the range

---

3   Carr (1964), p.36
4   Jenkins (1991), p.13
5   Evans (1997), p.166

of evidence is vast for all periods of history, and for all periods, it survives in fragmentary form. Some forms of evidence are more ephemeral than others. Some types of evidence were intentionally saved for posterity; others were thrown away as rubbish.

As a consequence of these factors, each historian's conclusions are influenced by the selection of evidence used and the interpretation of that evidence. Furthermore, each generation of historians has access to a different range of evidence as some is lost and more is discovered.

Because of the fragmentary nature of evidence, historians need to be alert to the fact that they will never know everything about what happened in the past. This is what makes the subject so interesting: it may be concerned mostly with the lives of dead people but, as an academic discipline, it is full of life. Academic history is often described as 'organic' - it is continually developing, often in surprising ways. The academic historian, like the designer of a modern car, builds a new history which is based on a critical reflection of the old and the availability of new techniques and new materials.

## Historical questions and approaches

Historians approach sources with their own agenda. They all interrogate their sources, but the questions they ask are not always the same. These questions are shaped, in part, by what the historian is looking for. For example, the historian interested in gender issues is likely to ask different questions of the evidence for witch-hunting in early modern Europe from those of an historian interested in the history of religion.

Each historian's approach to the evidence is also determined, to a degree, by who they are: their ethnicity, sex, creed, and so on. For example, the feminist historian of such subjects as witch-hunting is, typically, female, and the **'subaltern'** studies of colonial and post-colonial India, typically, are those of Indian historians. Furthermore, the age in which the historians live is as likely as anything else to fashion their outlook and the questions they ask. The emergence of social history, for example, is very much associated with the emergence of the politics of socialism. In recent decades, many historians have adopted inter-disciplinary approaches and sometimes academics in other fields - sociologists, psychologists, anthropologists, etc. - have applied their subject-specific expertise to the construction of new histories.

As a result, modern history comprises a great range of approaches and perspectives, reflecting the diversity of the historians who write it. These include (among others): political history, social history, economic history, cultural history, **gender history**, the history of class relations, history 'from above', history 'from below', local history, comparative history, **total history**, the history of mentalities.

## Categorisation and classification

Arguably, the one thing that binds historians together is their common objective in trying to make sense of the past. Since human life in the past was as complex as it is in the present, and the evidence is fragmented, this is a tall order. In trying to simplify things, historians have a habit of categorising the past by, for example, 'inventing' ages of history - the early medieval period, the later medieval, the early modern, the modern, and so on. As soon as they do so, they open themselves to criticism, as other historians reveal such things as periodisation to be nothing more than the artificial constructs of the historical community.

Even the most conservative of historians, suspicious of any 'simple' model of explanation for human behaviour and historical events, engages in the business of categorising and classifying the past. The periods into which the history of western Europe is divided are the convenient constructs of historians. In English history, for example, it is widely accepted for the sake of convenience that the medieval period ended on the battlefield at Bosworth in 1485. The Tudor dynasty ushered in a new historical epoch - 'the early modern period'. Every historian knows that this is a gross over-simplification of the very gradual historical processes that resulted in new modes of political, social and economic organisation, but it is convenient and helps historians give shape to a very complex past. These inventions classify historians themselves as they come to be tagged with labels such as 'medievalist', 'early modernist' and 'modernist' to reflect the spheres of their particular interest.

The habit of dividing the past into centuries poses a problem: while the passing of a century can influence history by creating a '*fin de siecle*' / 'turn of the century' mentality, many historical 'periods', such as reigns, straddle centuries. While, with the benefit of hindsight, the sixteenth century might 'look' different to the fifteenth, there were few, if any, fundamental differences in the world of the late 1490s and that of the early 1500s. A 'short' twentieth century has been identified by some historians which starts with the First World War (1914-18), a decisive historical turning point, and ends with another - the collapse of the Soviet Union in 1991. Arguably the historical 'era' in which we are now living began in the year 1991, not 2000.

In turn, people in the past are 'tagged' by historians. Diverse swathes of humanity are categorised with simple labels, for example 'peasants', '**proletarians**', 'subalterns', 'radicals', 'reactionaries', 'protestants', and so on. It is tempting but erroneous for the historian to think of these as homogenous groups in which all individuals shared broadly the same outlook, values and life experience.

Much of the jargon used by historians would have been unfamiliar to the people they describe. For example, people living in the period between the demise of the classical civilisations and the Renaissance had no idea that they were living in the 'Middle Ages'. Furthermore, they would not have recognised their economic and political structures as the 'feudal system'. Detailed studies of feudalism defy a simple definition of the concept: historians of the impact of the Norman Conquest speak of a pre-1066 English version and a distinct Norman model. In both cases, it was still evolving; the term 'bastard feudalism' has been coined to describe the system in its fifteenth-century death throes.

Historians spend a lot of time arguing over semantics, and it is right to question how far other historians have oversimplified or applied misnomers to the complexities of the past. Historians who are anxious not to exaggerate the phenomenon, or who prefer to find 'rational' explanations for seemingly irrational behaviour, reject the loaded term 'witchcraze' to describe witch-hunting in Europe in the early modern period as inappropriate since it implies that some kind of irrational mania was the root cause of the phenomenon.

## The narrative approach

Traditionally, history writing was preoccupied with the writing of a narrative of the major political and cultural events in history and the life stories of the (mostly) men who precipitated these events. Description, as opposed to analysis, was its focus. Students soon learn that descriptive/narrative writing does not earn marks; however, as Ludmilla Jordanova has pointed out, description is of some value in the wider world of historical writing: 'Fine historical writing uses detail to further understanding. Perhaps "description" is misleading because it implies low-grade intellectual activity: simply recounting what is there. In fact, description is exceptionally telling because it selects pertinent details and thus, when well done, moves effortlessly into analysis. A brief yet vivid story or description can be an extremely effective distillation of a broader historical point. It makes what is past lively, immediate and interesting, and helps readers build up mental pictures.'[6]

In modern academic writing, analysis is the focus, whereas 'popular' histories continue to focus on 'the story'. If that story is a life history, probably the widest read form of history in the western world at the present time, it is likely to be told with a hefty amount of amateur psychoanalysis as the biographer explains the actions of their chosen personality.

In constructing narratives of the past, historians analyse evidence, choose what to discuss and what to leave out, and draw their own conclusions about how and why it developed as it did. Much modern academic writing focuses on historical themes rather than chronologies. Comparative studies provide opportunities for historians to contrast geographical areas, societies, and individuals which may or may not have been contemporaneous. Anthropologists have helped historians understand the past by observing human activities in modern societies.

Analysis invites interpretation. Interpretation leads to controversy and

---

6 Jordanova (2006), p.98

historical debate. The secure certainties of the past, at least in modern democracies, are no longer accepted as they once were. Students, almost from the day they start studying history, are encouraged to question evidence and to recognise the possibility of alternative interpretations.

## Whig history

Certain early British historians, taking an essentially narrative approach in their writing have come to be known as 'Whig' historians. The term **'Whig history'** is often used to denote a triumphalist view of the past, one firmly wedded to the notion of progress. The term 'Whig' referred to the staunchly Protestant 'whiggamores' of late seventeenth-century Scotland and England who paved the way for the Glorious Revolution of 1688 and championed the values of political and civil liberty. No longer used as a term of contemporary political reference, unlike its counterpart 'Tory', it now refers to outmoded optimistic views of the past that celebrate the forming of the institutions of modern Britain. Consequently, the Whig historian 'adopted a nationalistic self-confidence that combined a patriotic sense of national qualities and uniqueness with an often xenophobic attitude towards foreigners, especially Catholics'.[7]

Whig historians traced the evolution of these institutions through a series of constitutional struggles and triumphs that extended at least as far as the *Magna Carta* in the reign of King John. In so doing, their history was influenced by Darwin's theory of evolution. For Whig historians like **Macaulay**, Britain's political crises of the seventeenth century were part and parcel of the heroic struggle for political and religious liberty, rather than Hugh Trevor-Roper's subsequent cynical view of it as a desperate attempt by the old rural elite to restore their former status.

## Historical concepts and theories

Since historical concepts and theories are so central to modern studies of history, it is worth considering the value of the theoretical approach.

---

7 Black in *History Review* (1995), p.32

This is what historians Jeremy Black and Donald MacRaild have said on the matter: 'Concepts help us to order and clarify. They help historians to distinguish between essential and particular features of history. Concepts can also simplify historical problems, or at least our view of them. There are, of course, pitfalls. History is not easy, and there is rarely one answer to a problem (as the propensity of historians to "debates" suggests). Nor are concepts - created in the modern world and not used by the actors themselves - necessarily responsive to nuance.

Historians invariably do simplify [...] selection, ordering and choice are all in the historian's vocabulary; but definitions imply simplification. A better term is "clarifying". Theory need not be jargon, and it can be enlightening. Historians should be open-minded about new ideas, for they may improve our insights into the past. To test ideas in the light of theoretical developments is to show humility and insight: this is the sign of a good historian.'[8]

History without theory is **'empirical'** - it relies entirely upon the objective 'truth' some consider inherent in every piece of historical evidence. The problem with the strictly empirical approach is that as soon as the historian starts up a dialogue with the past through the questioning of the evidence, their personality comes to shape the history that is subsequently written. If subjectivity cannot be taken out of history, a compelling argument to which many subscribe, then the historian might as well accept this and begin to interpret the evidence on their own terms. Historians, like other people, are defined to a considerable extent by their points of view. In history, these are their theories. Arguably, all historians theorise, but some do it with more conviction than others. Consequently, it stands to reason that 'Historians need to be able not just to recognise and name specific theoretical perspectives, but to have some idea of the properties of theories in general'[9]

Empirical approaches to history are based on the assumption that theories / hypotheses / interpretations should be assessed according to how far they 'stand up' to the evidence. Consequently, 'empiricists'

---

8 Black and MacRaild (2000), p.168
9 Jordanova (2006) , p.57

rely on the principle that reliable evidence about the past exists. In the twentieth century, the discipline became preoccupied with the skills deployed by the historian in the finding and reading of the evidence. It was widely accepted that only through the most careful analysis of a source would the historian avoid the numerous pitfalls that could lead to misinterpretation.

## Chance in history

> 'Nothing is inevitable until it happens.'
> (A. J. P. Taylor in *The Daily Telegraph*, 7 January 1980)

According to John Tosh, 'Historians spend most of their time explaining change - or its absence'.[10] In this respect, medieval monkish chroniclers had it easy: for them all things were ordained by God and both the predictable and unpredictable events that unfurled were all the consequence of divine providence. If there was any human agency involved in why things happened, it was to do with divine punishment for human sinfulness. Human history was placed in the context of an inexorable march towards the end of the world and the Last Judgement.

When God is taken out of the picture, historians have a stark choice: they can either accept that everything is the product of chance and random circumstances, or they can devise their own determinist theories and explanations that may or may not be part of the Creator's great plan. **Determinist explanations** certainly exist, but it is appropriate to start by pointing out that plenty of historians reject such explanations entirely. This is explained by John Tosh:

> *'These grounds for rejecting theories of history are closely related to another argument which has often been given heavy emphasis: that theory denies not only the "uniqueness" of events but also the dignity of the individual and the power of human agency. Traditional narrative shorn of any explanatory framework gives maximum scope to the play of personality, whereas a concern with recurrent or typical aspects of social structure and social change elevates abstraction at the expense of real living individuals. Worst of all*

---

[10] Tosh (1984), p.129

*from this viewpoint are theories ... whose insidious effect is to confer an inevitability on the historical process which individuals are powerless to change, now or in the future; all theories of history, the argument goes, have determinist elements, and determinism is a denial of human freedom. The polar opposite of determinism is the rejection of any meaning in history beyond the play of the contingent and the unforeseen - a view held by many historians in the mainstream of the discipline. A. J. P. Taylor delights in informing his readers that the only lesson taught by the study of the past is the incoherence and unpredictability of human affairs: history is a chapter of accidents and blunders."*[11]

These 'accidents and blunders' make for a situation which, some would argue, is far too complex and unique to be explained away by the convenient theories of social scientists. In the view of one modern historian, it is in the historian's very nature to question theoretical models in any explanation of past events: 'the critical attitude to minutiae has become in the end the powerful agent of selection. It now attracts to history persons of a cautious and painstaking disposition, not necessarily endowed with any aptitude for theoretical synthesis.'[12]

In any case, evidence in support of any theory is likely to be found with a little imagination and if the historian looks hard enough. After all, as Aileen Kraditor has pointed out in the case of American historical studies, the range of source material is vast and often contradictory: 'If one historian asks, "Do the sources provide evidence of militant struggles among workers and slaves?" the sources will reply, "Certainly". And if another asks, "Do the sources provide widespread acquiescence in the established order among the American population throughout the past two centuries?" the sources will reply, "Of course".'[13]

For some, theoretical models of explanation are not just wrong, they are also dangerous. They prepare the ground for and justify experiments in social engineering. This, after all, was the experience of Nazi-occupied Europe which was slave to the creed of '**Social**

---

11 Tosh (1984), p.132
12 M. M. Postan, quoted in Tosh (1984), p.133
13 in Tosh (1984), p.130

**Darwinism**[1].

Divine explanation aside, that chance to some degree plays a role in history is undeniable. Natural disasters such as volcanoes, floods and epidemics, have been powerful factors in shaping the course of history. The chance outcomes of battles in which, for example, a stray arrow kills a leader, have had serious consequences. Seven types of chance in history have been identified by Gilbert Pleuger:

> 'The place of chance in history can be differentiated. Firstly, there is that chance which is the sudden activity of an aspect of nature. It can be weather (serious drought, unusual precipitation and flood), or geomorphological disaster (earthquake or volcano), or disease. The Black Death, 1349, and the 1590s plague in Spain are examples of the latter. Secondly, war and battle condenses and accelerates relationships and magnifies the consequences of the minor and the unpredictable act, because in a battle or war there is less opportunity for action to counter the unexpected and unpredictable.
>
> The death of Gustavus Adolphus while in dense fog at the battle of Lutzen, 1632, is a well known example. Thirdly, if historians allow a place to the potency of individual action they need also to allow that a man may act unpredictably, irrationally or in a way inappropriate to his needs and wishes, because of misjudgment or confusion. Napoleon III's paralysis of decision in January 1871 during the Franco-Prussian war may be seen as an illustration. Fourthly, situations of even, pivotal, balance within and between states and societies or institutions may magnify beyond normal proportions the consequences of singular events and individual acts. The attempt of Charles I to arrest the Five Members, 1642, may be seen in this way as also the actions of Boris Yeltsin, symbolized by the picture of him on a tank, during the days of the attempted coup in August [1991]. Similarly, and fifthly, when social and institutional inertia is reduced and society, its government and economy, have less stability the actions of individuals have greater decisiveness. This is a tenable, if unfashionable, view of German history between 1928 and 1932.
>
> Sixthly, if we accept any kind of stratification of type of event and relationship a change at one level may, in the unusual circumstance,

influence not only "its" level but be important in other levels. It can now be seen, for example, that the minor administrative decision to place a maximum price for Castilian grain in 1539 had consequences far beyond the agrarian and significantly influenced Spain at the economic, demographic, social and military levels. Seventhly and lastly, the form of chance that receives more explicit recognition in historical accounts, is the accident. The deaths of William III in 1702 and Sir Robert Peel in 1850, after riding accidents, are examples.'[14]

Jeremy Black, who has written extensively on the theory and practice of history, has highlighted the importance of chance in history by commenting on the activities of war-gamers:

> 'Military history is the most obvious field in which it is dangerous to adopt the perspective of hindsight. War-gamers devote their time to an entirely reasonable pastime, asking whether battles, campaigns and conflicts could have had different results. Could the Jacobites have won, the British have defeated the American Revolutionaries or the Confederates triumphed in the American Civil War? Recent work has thrown doubt on any determinist technological approach to the history of warfare, and the role of chance and contingent factors of terrain, leadership quality, morale, the availability of reserves and the unpredictable spark that ignites a powder magazine, appear crucial when explaining particular engagements. War is not always won by the big battalions and the determinist economic account that would explain success in international relations in terms of the economic strength of particular states [...] is open to serious question.'[15]

Since the outcome of campaigns has had such a huge impact in history, these are very important considerations. The war-gamer perhaps is presented with something approaching a real opportunity to set up scientific experiments for testing claims of inevitability in history. However, the complexities of a military struggle as vast as, say, the English Civil War, probably make this a forlorn hope.

---

14 Pleuger in *History Review* (1992), pp.22-3
15 Black in *History Review* (1995), p.33

## Intentionalist interpretations

In evaluating the British policy of appeasement in the 1930s, historians need to consider the situation facing the Prime Minister Chamberlain and his government. How far was Hitler in control of German foreign policy? Did he have a pre-planned foreign policy with clear aims? A. J. P. Taylor argued that Hitler was an opportunist who capitalised on Chamberlain's blunders, whereas Hugh Trevor-Roper believed he had a master-plan that could be traced back to the pages of his 1920s autobiography *Mein Kampf* ('My Struggle'), his 'blueprint' for future war. Trevor-Roper's argument that the Second World War was the realisation of this master-plan can be defined as an intentionalist interpretation in which history is driven by human agency: in this case, Hitler.

## Structural interpretations

The discipline of sociology has had a great impact upon the work of historians. Sociologists have studied the social structures that help determine the behaviour of both the 'socialised' and the 'deviant'. **Structuralist** historians have fused the sociologists' interest in structures with the new interest of twentieth-century historians in social and economic history. The culture of the societies they investigate is regarded as having a 'super-structure' of ideas, such as religious and folkloric beliefs, and institutions, such as political and legal structures, which are determined by the base structure. For **Marxist** historians, this is the economic system upon which society is based (see Marxist interpretations below).

## Historical determinism

Social historians and sociologists interested in the past have looked for underlying historical trends in their analyses. These are the dynamic forces - the historical processes such as the struggle between classes - that have shaped history.

Black and MacRaild have explained how Keith Thomas provided a determinist interpretation for such things as witchcraft beliefs and witch hunts: 'Keith Thomas's major study of belief, Religion and the

Decline of Magic (1971) was heavily influenced by the [**Annalist**] School [...] Thomas argued: 'One of the central features was a preoccupation with the explanation and relief of human misfortune'. In this respect, by painting an image of a people locked in fear of their world, [writers like Thomas] shared Braudel's social determinism - the idea that the world was shaped by forces extraneous to humankind.'[16]

The identification of such profound forces in the present and the past has led sociologists, political philosophers and historians into the forming of 'scientific' theories to explain historical change. They have aimed 'to uncover the dynamic of history - that which gives it motion'[17].

## Profound causes - the 'Frontier thesis'

The French Annalist historians advocated a 'total' history that considered the influence of profound causes as well as specific events in the formulation of interpretations regarding why things happened as they did in the past. In his investigation of the emergence of the institutions of the USA, Frederick Jackson Turner declared in 1893: 'Behind institutions, behind constitutional forms and modifications, lie the vital forces that call these organs into life and shape them to meet changing conditions'[18]. In Turner's interpretation, these 'vital forces' were unique and conditioned by the drive to extend the frontier of white settlement: 'The peculiarity of American institutions is the fact that they have been compelled to adapt themselves to the changes of an expanding people - to the changes involved in crossing a continent, in winning a wilderness, and in developing at each area of this progress out of the primitive economic and political conditions of the frontier into the complexity of city life.'[19]

Although Turner would be criticised for neglecting the European roots of American civilisation and for failing to undertake a comparative study of other 'frontier' histories, his perception of the profundities of historical causation were hugely influential.

---

16 Black and MacRaild (2000), p.79
17 Black and MacRaild (2000), p.134
18 in Marwick (1970), p.70
19 in Marwick (1970), p.70

## Metanarratives

The 'Frontier thesis' is an excellent example of what might be described in some interpretations as a 'metanarrative', that is, a major text (e.g. the Bible, the Communist Manifesto), a scientific principle (e.g. Darwinism / Social Darwinism) or myth (e.g. Aryan supremacy, witchcraft) used by a society to help explain its past and present, and to help unite that society in a common purpose.

## Marxist interpretations

> 'Some would argue that ... the very heart of human activity is dominated by an oscillation between two opposites, the idea and the economic prerogative.'
> (Marwick (1970), *The Nature of History*, p. 73)

The most influential determinist explanation concerning the historical process is that of the political philosopher, Karl Marx. In the mid-nineteenth century; Marx, together with Friedrich Engels, developed a theory which was concerned with the conflict between opposing forces. This was to become the foundation of the principle that in history the force that leads to change is the struggle between social classes. Since this struggle was to do with the nature of the provision of human material needs (food, shelter, clothing), Marx concluded that, though other things such as scientific discoveries, are important, the driving force in history is economics (economic determinism). Until society developed a system that was satisfactory for all (communism) this struggle would continue. Only when all inequality was destroyed, and hence society became classless, would this struggle cease. Since Marxist history is to do with change, the establishment of the classless, communist society could be described as the end of history.

Marxist history is essentially a positivist approach since it works on the principle that the historical dynamic inevitably drives society towards the communist resolution of the class struggle. Marx and Engels identified three stages through which all human society must pass before it developed the economic structure - communism - that ended class conflict:

Stage 1: the Ancient - the slave-driven economies of classical Greece and Rome.

Stage 2: the Feudal - the lord and serf system of obligations associated with the medieval period.

Stage 3: the Bourgeois - the capitalist system in which cash payments, rather than obligations, became the 'nexus' (link) in the relationship between the classes (i.e. 'bourgeois' entrepreneurs and 'proletarian' workers).

The final epoch, communism, would emerge from the overthrowing of the capitalist system and the destruction of the concept of class by giving the producers (the workers) communal ownership of everything they produced. Until this stage, the mode of production was bound to lead to tension and conflict: slaves would rebel against slave-owners, serfs against lords, workers against employers. As the highly stratified world of medieval Europe was reduced to two powerful classes - the 'bourgeoisie' and the 'proletariat' - the stage was set for a final violent showdown: the revolution(s) that would eliminate the bourgeoisie and its capitalist system for good.

Consequently, for Marxist historians, economics largely determines the nature of society, including its cultural as well as political aspects, at every point in the past.

In Marx's opinion, everything was influenced by the economic structure of the epoch in which people live: 'The mode of production of material life conditions the process of social, political and intellectual life. It is not the consciousness of men that determines their existence but their social existence that determines their consciousness.'[20]

Thus Marx challenged the conventional view that the ideas of men and women shaped their destinies. Consequently, historians of beliefs that resulted in such episodes as the witch hunts of early modern Europe and the Holocaust of the twentieth century argue over the extent to

---

20 Karl Marx, from the preface to *Contribution to the Critique of Political Economy* (1859)

which ideas determined events or whether they were the product, like every other part of the social 'super-structure', of the economic base upon which it was founded.

Marxist analyses, focusing on class struggle, have been directed at most of the major themes of modern historical studies including the nature of Norman feudalism, the English Revolution / Civil War and other seventeenth-century crises, and the causes of nineteenth-century imperialism.

Having identified what he believed to be the natural law of history, Marx was able to claim that future developments could be predicted. These lofty philosophical claims, of course, are anathema to historians who believe that history is the product of chance and coincidence. For postmodernists, the difficulty, even impossibility, of arriving at an objective 'truth' in the historical interpretation of evidence, prevents historians from finding universal laws equivalent to the natural laws of science.

Ludmilla Jordanova explains why Marxist interpretations have a much lower profile now than they did in the recent past:

*'Until about 20 years ago, most people would have come up with Marxism if asked to name a theory important to the practice of history. Now there appear to be few attempts to develop Marxian historiography further. We could interpret this shift in a number of ways. It could indicate disenchantment with the world view that Marxism represented. It could suggest that its key elements have already been incorporated where they are useful. Perhaps just fragments of Marxism remain alive. It is possible that, because of cultural shifts, historians have lost interest in the leading themes of Marxism, such as class struggle and the nature of production, because they ceased to be apt for the world we now inhabit. Intellectual fashions do change, as a result of which theories fall out of favour, less because of explicit criticisms than because they are no longer vital and relevant.'*[21]

Conversely, John Arnold has claimed that 'Practically all historians

---

21 Jordanova (2006), p.57

writing today are marxists (with a small 'm').' This does not mean they are necessarily left-wing in their personal politics but 'one key element of Marx's thought has become so engrained in historians' ideas that it is now practically taken for granted: the insight that social and economic circumstances affect the ways in which people think about themselves, their lives, the world around them, and thus move to action.'[22]

## History and progress

Most modern historians are less convinced than many of their 'positivist' Whig predecessors regarding the optimistic view that history is essentially the story of human progress. This revision of old ideas has been summarised by Lawrence Stone:

> *'Today we are uneasily aware that for long periods of time, as long as a century or more, Europe has in fact stagnated or regressed. The first, longest, and most tragic of such intermissions lasted from about 1320 to 1480, and covered the whole of Europe with the exception of Italy. During this dismal period, governmental authority crumbled as local warlordism grew, tax yields declined, and the state became a prey of aristocratic factions. Worse still, a **Malthusian crisis**, followed by recurrent attacks of devastating bubonic plague, prolonged Anglo-French war, and erratic monetary manipulation combined drastically to reduce both the population and the production and trade of Europe. Population shrank even faster than production so that real income per capita rose and the poor were probably economically better off than ever before, or than they were to be again until the mid-nineteenth century. But the psychological impact of living in a contracting world, with a horribly low expectation of life, was very high indeed. As Huizinga showed many years ago, the fifteenth century was an age of melancholy and morbid introspection.'[23]*

The subsequent **Renaissance** and **Reformation**, and the emergence of modern capitalism in place of medieval feudalism, could have heralded a lasting pattern of progress, but they did not. Instead, for Europe the

---

[22] Arnold (2000), p.85
[23] Stone (1981), p.133

seventeenth century is perceived as another age of stagnation or regression - an age of crises:

> 'In [...] Germany, there raged for thirty years a war as destructive of civilian lives and property as any of this [twentieth] century, and much of the area was left in ruins [...] Even England, which, thanks to the improvement in agricultural productivity and the extraordinary prosperity of its colonial trade after 1660, was only mildly affected by the Great Depression, saw its population stagnate, its trade endure a prolonged crisis of readjustment from 1620 to 1660, and its output of iron, lead and tin level off [...] the mid-seventeenth century saw a crisis in the growth of the nation state [...] the 1640s were the decade during which major upheavals occurred in England, Ireland, Scotland, France, Sweden, Catalonia, Portugal and Naples, there was a coup in Holland, and Germany endured the final, desperate, convulsions of the Thirty Years War.'[24]

In his consideration of the English Civil War, Britain's greatest crisis of the seventeenth century, Stone has shown how historians can arrive at radically different interpretations regarding whether a major historical event should be perceived as a human triumph or a disaster, an example of progress or regression.

> 'What happened in England in the middle of the seventeenth century? Was it a "great rebellion" as Clarendon believed, the last and most violent of the many rebellions against particularly unprepossessing or unpopular kings, that had been staged by dissident members of the landed classes century after century throughout the Middle Ages? Was it merely an internal war caused by a temporary political breakdown due to particular political circumstances? Was it the Puritan revolution of S. R. Gardiner, to whom the driving force behind the whole episode was a conflict of religious institutions and ideologies? Was it the first great clash of liberty against royal tyranny, as seen by Macaulay, the first blow of [...] Whiggery, a blow which put England on the first bourgeois revolution, in which the economically progressive and dynamic elements in society struggled to emerge from their feudal swaddling clothes? This is how Engels saw it, and how many historians of the

---

24 Stone (1981), p.134

1930s, including R. H. Tawney and C. Hill, tended to regard it. Was it the first revolution of modernization, which is the Marxist interpretation in a new guise, now perceived as a struggle of entrepreneurial forces to remould the institutions of government to meet the needs of a more efficient, more rationalistic, and more economically advanced society? Or was it a revolution of despair, engineered by the decaying and backward-looking elements in rural society, the mere gentry of H. R. Trevor-Roper, men who hoped to recreate the decentralised, inward-looking, socially stable and economically stagnant society of their hopeless, anachronistic dreams?'[25]

## 'From above' and 'from below' interpretations

Historians argue about the influence of the elite and the masses on events. This is especially true of social history, such as that of witchcraft beliefs in the early modern period, but also underpins many of the debates surrounding 'political' events such as revolutions. Arthur Marwick, for example, has commented on 'from below' interpretations of the British government's policy of appeasement in the late 1930s: 'Much was once made of "pacifist" British public opinion which is supposed to have deterred Britain's Conservative Government from taking the action it really believed to be desirable: the labours of D. C. Watt and some early work of my own have, I hope, done something to dispel this nonsense - "public opinion" and government formed a confused continuum in which pacifism was one element, but never a dominant one.'[26]

It is often difficult to divorce the attitude of the elite from that of the masses. For example, the enthusiasm with which Neville Chamberlain was greeted in 1938 on his return from securing the Munich agreement with Hitler was share by both the king, George VI, and his people. Similarly, the fundamental beliefs in magic, witchcraft, and the devil, upon which witch-hunting in early modern Europe relied, 'were universal concepts that were not 'class-bound', although the support for such beliefs 'from above' may well have been a crucial element in the persecution of ordinary people by their neighbours (i.e. 'from

---

25 Stone (1981), p.182
26 Marwick (1970), p.275

below').

Historians, however, are generally alert to the likelihood that the mentality of one socio-political group of people in the past was likely to be significantly different from that of another. Indeed, the conflict between different classes could be a significant force in the creation of opposing mentalities. This, according to Brian Levack, appears to have been the case in the history of the decline of witch-hunting:

> 'The persistence of superstitious beliefs among the peasantry may have actually contributed, in a somewhat ironic way, to the triumph of scepticism among the elite. One of the tactics that sceptics like Nicholas de Malebranche, Laurent Bordelon and Cyrano de Bergerac used to win support for their views was to ridicule the beliefs of the silly rustic shepherds and other peasants who continued to claim that witches were active in their communities. The same tactics of ridicule and satire, it should be noted, were later used by William Hogarth and Francisco Goya in the paintings and engravings they made on the theme of witchcraft and superstition. The effect of this ridicule was to encourage those who occupied the upper strata of society, even those who were not well-educated, to give at least lip-service to the new scepticism, so as to confirm their superiority over the lower classes. Scepticism, in other words, became fashionable. During the late seventeenth and early eighteenth centuries the barriers that separated the aristocracy and the wealthy from those who occupied the lower strata of society began to widen throughout Europe. In order to put as much distance as possible between themselves and the common people, the landowners and members of the professions, especially those who were upwardly mobile, did all they could to prove that they shared nothing with their inferiors. Knowledge of the latest scientific discoveries may have been one way to establish one's social and intellectual credentials; but scepticism regarding witchcraft, since it involved the expression of open contempt for the lower orders, was far more effective. The decline of witch beliefs among the wealthy and educated elite may have had as much to do with social snobbery as with the development of new scientific and philosophical ideas.'[27]

---

27 Levack (2006), p.269

The 'subaltern' studies of the Indian experience of British colonialism are also, by definition, history 'from below'. 'From above' interpretations favour a narrative approach, particularly that of the biography of the 'great men' and women of history. 'From below' interpretations are more likely to highlight the place of structures, such as those of class or mentality, in the shaping of past events. Black and MacRaild have provided an interesting account of the dilemma faced by a structuralist historian who set out to write a biography: 'When Ian Kershaw was first approached to write a biography of Hitler, he was dubious about the utility of such an exercise, because, as a structuralist historian, he was more interested in wider aspects of the Third Reich and German history than in the Fuhrer himself.

As Kershaw approached the task, he found himself battling to understand "the man who was the indispensable fulcrum and inspiration of what took place, Hitler himself", while trying simultaneously to 'downplay rather than to exaggerate the part played by the individual, however powerful, in complex historical processes'.[28] This juxtaposition of seemingly contradictory forces illustrates well the tension inherent in writing historical biography.'[29]

## Psychoanalytical interpretations

Biographical approaches to history invite psychoanalytical explanations. The histories that identify 'great men' as the movers and shakers in the shaping of the past are bound to consider the psychological make-up of the leading protagonists. Ludmilla Jordanova has provided a contemporary perspective on the state of play regarding acceptance in historical circles of this approach:

> 'Although still regarded with suspicion in some quarters, it has become an accepted part of the historian's theoretical armoury, especially in the United States, where many large history departments include a psychohistorian on the staff, and where special training courses are available to scholars who want to use psychoanalysis in their research but have no wish to develop clinical skills. Yet most people, and scholars are no exception, think

---

26 Kershaw (1998)
29 Black and MacRaild (2000), p.104

*psychoanalytically without being particularly aware of doing so.*

*Many of the explanations we give of behaviour in everyday life owe much to what are now commonplace assumptions about how the unconscious works. Since a significant proportion of historical explanation rests on such assumptions, psychoanalysis has found its way into historical practice. However, many historians still have little direct knowledge of psychoanalytical thinking or of the significant differences between its principal traditions: Freudian, Jungian, Kleinian and Lacanian. There have been attacks on psychoanalysis in history, as there have been on psychoanalysis in general.'*[30]

For the study of such issues as the Holocaust and early modern witch-hunting, psycho-historians have engaged in investigations into collective psychology to understand why such phenomena could, at best, be greeted with widespread indifference and, at worst, with enthusiasm. Consequently, **psycho-history** can be as much to do with 'from below' interpretations as it is with those 'from above'.

## Women's history

'Research during the last 15 years or so has resulted in a major new discovery. It now appears that, contrary to all assumptions, there were women in English history.'
(K. Charlesworth and M. Cameron (1986) *All That... The Other Half of History*, Pandora, quoted in K. Sayer (1994) 'Feminism and History', in Modern History Review, November, p. 7)

Karen Sayer has explained why, in the words of Virginia Woolf, 'women have no history':

*'Until relatively recently, despite notable exceptions, history was written by and for men, especially white academic men. This was, and still is, the structural problem, built into the production of knowledge, that Virginia Woolf attacked. Those who write history have decided what is significant, so that women have been excluded and hidden [...] The prevalent view was that historians should only*

---

30 Jordanova (2006), p.57

*be concerned with change and with major political and economic movements. As women did not play a decisive role in such processes, because women were supposed to be wives and mothers who did not take part in national decision-making, industry etc., they were not believed to be a legitimate subject of history.'*[31]

Since the 1960s, great strides have been taken in writing the story of groups hitherto 'hidden from history'. Not surprisingly, the bulk of the work on women's history has been done by women historians, typically those of a 'feminist' persuasion. A pioneering social historian, Joan Thirsk, on this point, has commented that:

*'It is not usual to distinguish the work of women historians from those of men, though it is always instructive to do so. Their different lives make for different viewpoints and yield different insights; hence, in practice, they frequently choose distinctive themes for investigation, have their own styles in research and presentation, and rank their objectives and priorities differently. In the fields of local and family history especially, their insights are likely to be original and influential, since much of women's energy is devoted to creating and maintaining families and sustaining communities. But other signs of their individuality are likely to stem from their stronger sympathy for animate creatures than for inanimate things, and their keen observation of social relationships.'*[32]

Sayer has identified three stages in the development of writing about the history of women:

*'Stage 1: pre-1960s writings about the lives of exceptional women, i.e. women who in their lifetimes made an impact in a 'man's world' but who had since been largely forgotten. For example, the playwright, poet and novelist Aphra Behn (1640-89), and the late seventeenth-century English traveller and writer Celia Fiennes.*

*Stage 2: women's contribution history - the re-exploration of major themes involving a search for the women who contributed to historical developments previously associated with men. For*

---

31 Sayer (1994), p.5
32 in Hey (1996), p.498

*example, the work of Dorothy Thompson who revealed the role of women in Chartism in the 1830s and 1840s.*

*Stage 3: **feminist / women-centred history** - included a transfer of focus from the subjects deemed important by traditional, male-orientated history, to those of particular relevance to the lives of women. For example, the history of contraception, which is of peripheral interest in traditional male-dominated histories, might now take centre stage. The last quarter of the twentieth century saw a plethora of publications exploring 'new' avenues of history, such as Reay Tannahill's* Food in History *(1973) and her companion volume,* Sex in History *(1980). More conventional subjects, such as the industrial revolution, were now written about in relation to their impact upon the lives of women. Hence the emergence of titles like Jane Rendell's* Women in an Industrialising Society: England 1750-1880 *(1990).'*

Since the 1970s, universities have offered women's studies courses. Modern studies have focused on the differences of the experiences of women in historical situations and how these were influenced by such factors as their race, class, religion and sexuality. Historians of the lives of women have come to focus particularly upon the central issue of gender which, unlike biological sex, is a social construct, and changing roles across time and place. Gender studies focus on how the lives of men and women are formed by the societies in which they live. Restricted opportunities and cultural assumptions are identified as key elements in their life experience and the forming of their mentalities.

Feminist historians of witch-hunting have focused on gender relations in their exploration of the phenomenon and found in these the root cause of the persecution. Anne Llewellyn Barstow, concerned with present and future gender relations, has drawn parallels between witch-hunting in the early modern period with modern forms of violence against women and pornography. Having catalogued certain instances in which accused women seem to have been subjected to severe sexual abuse by their interrogators, including intimate examination, sexual mutilation and rape, she has concluded:

'It appears that jailers, prickers, executioners and judges, all could take their sadistic pleasure with female prisoners. And so could respectable ministers and judges. At a public session in New England, Cotton Mather, while working to control a seventeen-year-old girl possessed of demons, uncovered her breasts and fondled them [...] These men took advantage of positions of authority to indulge in pornography sessions, thus revealing that they wanted more from witch hunting than the conviction of witches: namely, unchallengeable sexual power over women [...] In the witch hunts, the policy of forcing a witch's confession may have been a cover for making a socially approved assault on her body [...] given the low opinion of women in European society, there was little social pressure to restrain the court officials from taking their pleasure with the victims.'[33]

## Some conclusions

In response to the cynicism of Keith Jenkins and other 'postmodernists', Black and MacRaild have written a spirited defence of the theories in history that underpin historical interpretation:

'In general, it is not wrong to use theory in history. All thought is structured insofar as the human mind orders information in some way or another. Historians who claim to subscribe to no theory may in fact be said to be antitheoretical: that is their 'theory'. Theory grows from within the historian and is externalised as soon as he or she begins to select particular evidence. The quest for covering laws to explain historical phenomena such as the Industrial Revolution might seem either grandiose or simplistic, depending on perspective, but, as Alex Callinicos (Theories and Narratives, 1995) has suggested, there is not a single historian who does not acquire understanding "inferentially by a process of interpreting data according to a complex system of rules and assumptions".

The postmodernists award ideas primacy in historical explanation. Since Marx, however, much more emphasis has generally been placed on materialist notions. The fixity of explanation that this implies (objectivity, truth, fact) has been challenged by post-modernists. However, too many of their criticisms are based on old-fashioned, stereotypical images of how historians work. In fact, the

---

33 Barstow (1994), pp.132-3

*rise of Marxism, the Annales school of historians, and gender, social and cultural history have long since consigned the over-confident, narrow, male-centred and political focus of much nineteenth-century historical writing to the margins of what is now a wider and more vibrant discipline.'*[34]

This thesis reminds us that historians are very much the product of the age in which they live and of the political, social, economic and cultural climate of their time. Perhaps the most telling characteristic of any history is the language in which it is written. Just as language and its use changes across time so do the approaches of historians to the past. This is evident, for example, in the historiography of women's history outlined above.

**A. J. P. Taylor** was the great populist historian of the English speaking world in the second half of the twentieth century. He was an exceptionally popular lecturer, a TV personality, and prolific writer of books, learned papers and newspaper articles. He wrote extensively about the history of the history he helped shape - that of the era of the Second World War - as an outspoken critic regarding the policy of appeasement, and as a member of the Homeguard. His initial writings about Germany in this period, such as *The Course of German History* (1945), were negative to the point of being Germanophobic. He considered National Socialism the natural product of a Germanic culture that could be traced back across hundreds of years. The triumph of Nazism was no mere conspiracy but the expression of the will of the masses. The same was true of the antisemitism that led to the policy of racial extermination. He was furious over the establishment of West Germany by the Allies at the end of the war and warned against the imminent danger of an emergent Fourth Reich. Such convictions perhaps should not surprise us. In the opinion of his biographer Robert Cole, 'He seemed to take Germany and the Germans personally, and perhaps what he had witnessed in this quarter century was justification'.[35] As a socialist, he advocated a foreign policy that gravitated towards the Soviet Union instead of the USA in this period.

Taylor's great adversary over the origins of the Second World War

---

34 Black and MacRaild (2000), p.167
35 Cole (1993), p.75

debate was the right-wing historian Sir Hugh Trevor-Roper. Trevor-Roper is also associated with the historiography of early modern witch-hunting in Europe. His interest in, and views on this subject were greatly influenced by his experience of the Second World War. Raisa Maria Toivo has explained the links Trevor-Roper and others were making between the history of their own times and that of 400 years before:

> 'In the aftermath of the Second World War, with the experience of systematic genocide and totalitarianism, new developments in sociological and political analysis began to emerge, such as the logics of persecution and victimology. The history of ethnic minorities and of ideological crimes also assumed greater prominence. As a consequence there was a general reassessment of the historical significance of the witch trials. The study of the persecutions both before and during the war and the study of early modern witch hunts seemed mutually supportive. Furthermore, in the post-war period the term "witch hunt" became a common descriptor for contemporary persecutions, such as the **McCarthyite campaign** against suspected communists and political purges in the Soviet Union.'[36]

In this case, the age in which the historian lived influenced both his choice of subject matter, witch-hunting, and his method, a comparative approach. Despite Taylor's arguments, the prevailing view at the time was that the persecution of the Jews was imposed from above as a political device by the Nazi leadership. The same elite, 'from above' explanation was provided by Trevor-Roper for the witch-hunts. These examples reveal both how history is made and why it changes from one generation to the next. This is not something to deplore but something to celebrate - debate is the life-blood of the discipline; without it history would be as dead as the people it endeavours to understand.

---

36 Toivo in Barry and Davies (2007), p.90

# 2 Historical approaches and methods

## Introduction

Interpretations are partly shaped by the ways in which the historian investigates the past. Some of these have already been touched upon in the sections dealing with such concepts as Marxist history, gender studies and history from below. This chapter will develop your knowledge and understanding of the different approaches and methods historians have adopted in their study of the past and how these have developed across the last couple of hundred years.

The approaches an historian adopts are highly subjective and influenced by the historian's interests and own life experience. Historians are likely to approach the past 'at a different angle' from their predecessors and, in so doing, may well end up writing a very different account of that past. A 'from below' approach to the Crusades that focuses particularly on the role of women, for example, is likely to result in a very different kind of history to a more traditional 'from above' and male-orientated approach. One historian, studying the impact of the Norman Conquest for example, may set out to demonstrate how this resulted in fundamental changes in the way of life in England, whereas another may be determined to reveal how much of the old Anglo-Saxon world survived the invasion: they are likely to write two very different accounts of the past. Such concepts were introduced in the previous chapter and they are further explored here as the evolution of modern history writing is explained.

The methods historians employ also shape the history they write. Some historians adopt a broadly scientific methodology by forming and testing a hypothesis. For example, an historian of British appeasement in the 1930s may set out to test the hypothesis that this policy was the outcome of structural issues. Another historian, however, convinced by the importance of the role of 'human agency' (i.e. individuals) in such matters might be less sensitive to the possibility that human actions are largely determined by factors beyond their control. Similarly, the Marxist historian, convinced that economic relationships are at the heart of history, is perhaps more inclined to carefully analyse statistical evidence for the crises in seventeenth-century Britain than the historian of religious radicalism. Some historians, such as those involved in studies of witch-hunting in early modern Europe, have adopted a method that takes a regional approach to the past and produced accounts, rich in local detail, that reassess the extent to which the experience of certain historical phenomena varied from place to place. Such alternative methodologies and their place in the history of history writing are further explored in this chapter.

## Historical relationism

To a degree, modern historical approaches and methods have their origins in the Romantic movement of the late eighteenth and early nineteenth centuries. Ironically perhaps, historical fiction, specifically the historical novels of Sir Walter Scott, who strove to recreate faithfully the character and culture of the medieval world, were a big influence on the thinking of the most influential of the early nineteenth-century historians, **Leopold von Ranke**. Ranke, together with Barthold Niebuhr, was a pioneer of the approach known as **'genetic (or 'historical') relationism'** which championed the principle of exploring past events and individual actions in relation to past values and conditions. To this end, Ranke relied on primary sources 'to show what actually happened'[37]. In so doing, he contributed to a new rigorous methodology that would remain the keystone upon which future historical writing would be based. For these reasons Ranke is regarded as 'the founder of the modern discipline of history'.[38]

Ranke judged such things as memoirs far too unreliable. He was wary of the inclination to judge the past and considered it the historian's job to discover what happened in the past without passing judgment. Under Ranke's influence, by the end of the nineteenth century, historians had developed a systematic approach to their work. This has been summarised by Anna Green and Kathleen Troup as a three point process: 'the rigorous examination and knowledge of historical evidence, verified by references; impartial research, devoid of a priori beliefs and prejudices [i.e. those based on a presumed historical 'law']

---

37 Ranke quoted in Stern (1956), p.57
38 Marwick (1970), p.38

fill; an inductive method of reasoning, from the particular to the general.¹³⁹

In Ranke's day history writing was, and perhaps still is, predominantly the history of political events. Considering the importance and drama of politics, together with the abundance of evidence for the subject, this is not surprising.

The central importance of politics in history is summed up by E. A. Freeman's famous remark: 'History is past politics'⁴⁰. The diplomatic history of modern times has received particular attention as historians have mined diplomatic archives to understand why catastrophes, such as wars, occurred. Public concern regarding the outbreak of the Second World War, and the debate regarding Britain's policy of appeasement in the 1930s, helped fuel the writing of influential historians such as A. J. P. Taylor, just as the recent war in Iraq is destined to merit the attention of future historians. Historians of English history of the seventeenth century are likely to focus their attention on constitutional developments in that epoch of change.

While Ranke focused on 'top-down' history - diplomacy and politics - a Frenchman, Auguste Thierry, in writing his *History of the Norman Conquest of England* (1825) envisaged 'the destiny of peoples and not of certain famous men, to present the adventures of social life and not those of the individual'⁴¹. In so doing he broadened the scope of history writing and laid the foundations for the social histories that appeared in the early twentieth century.

## History as a social science

The historian / proto-sociologist / philosopher Auguste Comte (1798-1857) identified history as a social science. He was concerned with the possibility that certain scientific laws fashioned human society. These laws, he suspected, not only explained the past but helped predict the future. As in the natural sciences, he advocated the forming and testing of hypotheses as the key approach to unlocking the truths of

---

39 Green and Troup (1999), p.3
40 Freeman quoted in Tosh (1984), p.67
41 Thierry quoted in Marwick (1970), p.41

the past. This approach that links the 'social sciences' to the natural, or what Comte called the 'positive', sciences is termed 'positivism'. As explained in the previous chapter, positivist thinking was at the core of the work of the later nineteenth-century German political theorist and historian, Karl Marx. For Marx, the 'law' that shaped history was that of economic relationships and class struggle: 'The history of all hitherto existing society is the history of class struggles' (*The Communist Manifesto*). In the opinion of Arthur Marwick, the great contribution of Marx and Comte and their followers was that they inspired a new breed of historian: one that did not merely compile facts but endeavoured to explain their interconnections.[42]

The Marxist approach to history is, essentially, a structuralist one. 'Structuralists' work on the assumption that the 'great men' of history were, like everyone else, the product of the environments into which they were born. Social, economic and cultural structures fashioned their politics as much as, or more than, their unique personalities. Consequently, structuralist approaches focus on these when explaining the major events of the past, such as the Crusades or the Holocaust, more than the individuals who helped perpetrate such things. Modern historians are as wary of ascribing past triumphs to 'hero' figures as they are of condemning 'scapegoats' for past calamities.

## Narrative history

Whether or not they took on board Rankean ideas regarding documentation or subscribed to Comte's positivism, the historians of the nineteenth century were largely concerned with the writing of narrative history. Although this approach fell out of favour in more recent times, the establishment of a sound narrative remains a fundamental task of the historian. In its simplest form, history writing is story-telling, though the writing of narrative history is not a 'simple' activity. Historians, adopting this perfectly valid approach to the past, dedicate their time and energy to research the reconstruction of past events on the basis of the surviving evidence, all of which is limited and at least some of which is problematic. This activity is of particular importance for historians studying subjects for which the source

---

42 Marwick (1970), p.45

material is relatively slight and the narrative of events is less certain. For medieval historians, their main business is likely to be the close examination of early narrative histories: the monastic chronicles. Every scrap of additional evidence, such as a law code, a list of fortifications or a property evaluation, is hugely important to the historian trying to verify the accuracy of the chronicles and 'filling in the gaps'. A chronological approach is often favoured by historians who are most concerned with political and diplomatic history.

Green and Troup have summarised the views of historian Allan Megill (1995) who distinguished certain categories or 'levels' of narrative history: '[...] these levels range from the micronarrative of a particular event; a master narrative which seeks to explain a broader segment of history; a grand narrative "which claims to offer the authoritative account of history generally"; and finally a metanarrative which draws upon some particular cosmology or metaphysical foundation, for example, Christianity.'[43]

The pre-eminence of narrative history has been overtaken in modern times by 'problem-orientated' history that is largely concerned with issues of causation. Not all historians have welcomed this development. Lawrence Stone in the late 1970s complained that the 'story-telling function [of history) has fallen into ill-repute among those who have regarded themselves as in the vanguard of the profession, the practitioners of the so-called "new history" of the post-Second-World-War era'.[44]

## Literary and heroic history

Auguste Comte's contemporary, Thomas Babington Macauley, declared 'I shall not be satisfied unless I produce something which shall for a few days supersede the last fashionable novel on the tables of the young ladies'.[45] Macauley's importance in the evolution of modern historical writing lies in his concern for its literary quality. Sometimes, as Arthur Marwick has explained, his laudable ambition of writing appealing, popular history took precedence over hard historical fact:

---

43 Green and Troup (1999), p.204
44 Stone quoted in Green and Troup (1999), p.210
45 Macauley quoted in Marwick (1970), p.46

'By the standards of historical scholarship established since the early nineteenth century, Macauley sometimes falls short as a historian. In his search after effect he sometimes cheated, his rendering of the past was less "truthful" than, given the resources available to him, it could have been. One notorious example of this is the passage in the first volume of the History ['History of England', 1848-55] describing the speech in which William III bade farewell to the States of Holland before setting out for Britain. Macauley writes:

"In all that grave senate there was none who could refrain from shedding tears. But the iron stoicism of William never gave way; and he stood among his weeping friends calm and austere, as if he had been about to leave them only for a short visit to his hunting-grounds at Loos."

Macauley had no reliable source for this fanciful description. In fact it is a direct plagiarism (conscious or unconscious) from the Odes of Horace, the description of Regulus making his farewell to the Senate.'[46]

Another very influential writer from this period, in Britain at least, was **Thomas Carlyle**. In his great moralising, polemical works he highlighted the roles of the 'heroes' of history. In so doing, he helped foster a vogue for history writing based upon the lives of the 'great men' of history that remains popular to the present day. Probably the most widely read history is biography. Individuals from the past such as Henry VIII and Adolf Hitler are of enduring interest and have inspired literally hundreds of books. By definition, biography provides a very singular way of observing the past. The 'great' men and women of history inevitably attract particular attention due to their high profile in their own lifetimes and the relative abundance of evidence they left to posterity. Sometimes biographers attempt to psychoanalyse their subjects. Much has been written, for example, about the significance of Hitler's vegetarianism, tee-totalism, and affection for children and dogs. Historians, however, cannot interview and observe their subjects on a psychiatrist's couch, and the paucity of evidence severely limits such approaches. The less available the evidence, the more the debate

---

46 Marwick (1970), p.47

regarding an individual's personality is likely to rage.

Medieval English kings such as John and Richard III have both their apologists and detractors. In any case, historians more convinced by structural explanations for historical events are less likely to seek solutions to problems in history in the personality traits of its leading protagonists. For them, 'psycho-history' is a mere distraction.

John Richard Green (1837-83) took a very different approach to the past to most of his contemporaries by emphasising social, as opposed to political, developments:

> 'The aim of the following work ['Short History of the English People', 1874] is defined by its title; it is not a history of English kings or English conquests, but of the English people [...] I have preferred to pass lightly and briefly over the details of foreign wars and diplomacies, the personal adventures of kings and nobles, the pomp of courts, or the intrigues of favourites [...] I have devoted more space to Chaucer than Cressy, to Caxton than to the petty strife of Yorkist and Lancastrian, to the Poor Law of Elizabeth than to her victory at Cadiz, to the Methodist revival than to the escape of the Young Pretender.'[47]

## Is History a science?

By the start of the twentieth century, historians confidently asserted that 'history is a science, no less and no more' (J. B. Bury, 1902, quoted in Marwick, p. 55). Historical sources, in their opinion, needed to be approached with scientific rigour, laws shaped the past, and, as in the natural sciences, the truth of the past could be discovered. Lord Acton, Regius' Professor of Modern History at Cambridge (1895-1902), commented, optimistically: 'the long conspiracy against the knowledge of truth has been practically abandoned, and competing scholars all over the civilised world are taking advantage of the change [aiming to] meet the scientific demand for completeness and certainty'.[48]

---

[47] Green quoted in Black and MacRaild (2000), p.58
[48] from a note sent to the contributors of 'The Cambridge Modern History' in 1896

In the following passages, J. B. Bury, Lord Acton's successor as Regius Professor, outlines the case for the scientific approach to the past.

'It has not yet become superfluous to insist that history is a science, no less and no more [...] All truths (to modify a saying of Plato) require the most exact methods; and closely connected with the introduction of a new method was the elevation of the standard of truth. The idea of a scrupulously exact conformity to facts was fixed, refined and canonised; and the critical method was one of the means to secure it. There was indeed no historian since the beginning of things who did not profess that his sole aim was to present to his readers untainted and unpainted truth. But the axiom was loosely understood and interpreted, and the notion of truth was elastic. [...] So long as history was regarded as an art, the sanctions of truth and accuracy could not be severe. [...] Though we may point to individual writers who had a high ideal of accuracy at various ages, it was not till the scientific period began that laxity in representing facts, came to be branded as criminal.

And here [...] I may remind you that history is not a branch of literature. The facts of history, like the facts of geology or astronomy, can supply material for literary art; for manifest reasons they lend themselves to artistic representation far more readily than those of the natural sciences; but to clothe the story of human society in a literary dress is no more the part of an historian as an historian, than it is the part of an astronomer as an astronomer to present in an artistic shape the story of the stars. [...] The national movements of Europe not only raised history into prominence and gave a great impulse to its study, but also partially disclosed where the true practical importance of history lies [...] It is of vital importance for citizens to have a true knowledge of the past and to see it in a dry light, in order that their influence on the present and future may be exerted in right directions. For, as a matter of fact, the attitude of men to the past has at all times been a factor in forming their political opinions and determining the course of events [...]

It seems inevitable that [...] the place which history occupies in national education will grow larger and larger. It is therefore of supreme moment that the history which is taught should be true, and that can be attained only through the discovery, collection, classification and interpretation of facts - through scientific research [...] We want [...] recognition that it is a matter of public concern to promote the scientific study of any branch of history that any student is anxious to pursue. Some statesmen would acknowledge this; but in a democratic state they are hampered by the views of unenlightened taxpayers [...] The universities themselves have much to do; they have to recognise more fully and clearly and practically and preach more loudly and assiduously that the advancement of research in history, as in other sciences, is not a luxury [...] but is a pressing need, a matter of inestimable concern to the nation and the world.

Beyond its value as a limiting controlling conception, the idea of the future development of man has also a positive importance. It furnishes in fact the justification of much of the laborious historical work that has been done and is being done today. The gathering of materials bearing upon minute local events [...] the patient drudgery in archives of states and municipalities, all the microscopic research that is carried on by armies of toiling students [...] this work, the hewing of wood and the drawing of water, has to be done in faith - in the faith that a complete assemblage of the smallest facts of human history will tell in the end. The labour is performed for posterity - for remote posterity [...]

Every individual who is deeply impressed with the fact that man's grasp of his past development helps to determine his future development, and who studies history as a science not as a branch of literature, will contribute to form a national conscience that true history is of supreme importance, that the only way to true history lies through scientific research, and that in promoting and prosecuting such research we are not indulging in a luxury but doing a thoroughly practical work and performing a great duty to posterity [...]

I may conclude by repeating that [...] if, year by year, history is to become a more and more powerful force for stripping the bandages of error from the eyes of men, for shaping public opinion and advancing the cause of intellectual and political liberty, she will best prepare her disciples [...] but by remembering always that, though she may supply material for literary art or philosophical speculation, she is herself simply a science, no less and no more.'⁴⁹

In 1903, the well-known, early twentieth-century British historian, George Macauley Trevelyan, Macauley's grand-nephew, taking the 'history as art / literature' position, wrote a sturdy riposte to Bury's claims that history is a science:

'The last fifty years have witnessed great changes in the management of **Clio**'s temple [Clio - the Greek goddess (muse) of History]. Her inspired prophets and bards have passed away and been succeeded by the priests of an established church; [...] doctrine has been defined; [...] and the tombs of the aforesaid prophets have been duly blackened by the new hierarchy. While these changes were in process the statue of the Muse was seen to wink an eye. Was it in approval, or in derision? Two generations back, history was a part of our national literature, written by persons moving at large in the world of letters or politics [...] Of recent years the popular influence of history has greatly diminished. History was, by her own friends, proclaimed a 'science' for specialists, not 'literature' for the common reader of books.

[...] Until quite recent times, from the days of Clarendon down through Gibbon, Carlyle and Macaulay to Green and Lecky, historical writing was not merely the mutual conversation of scholars with one another, but was the means of spreading far and wide a love and knowledge of history, an elevated and critical patriotism and certain qualities of mind and heart. But all that has been stopped, and an attempt has been made to drill us into so many Potsdam Guards [reference to German scientific historians - Niebuhr, Ranke and Hegel] of learning.

The functions of physical science are mainly two. Direct utility in practical fields; and in more intellectual fields the deduction of laws of "cause and effect". Now history can perform neither of these functions.

In the first place it has no practical utility like physical science. No-one can buy a knowledge of history, however profound, invent the steam-

---

49 J. B. Bury, 1902, quoted in Stern (1970), pp.210-23

engine, or light a town, or cure cancer, or make wheat grow near the Arctic Circle. For this reason there is not in the case of history, as there is in the case of physical science, any utilitarian value at all in the accumulation of knowledge by a small number of students.

In the second place history cannot, like physical science, deduce causal laws of general application. All attempts have failed to discover laws of "cause and effect" which are certain to repeat themselves in the institutions and affairs of men.

The law of gravitation may be scientifically proved because it is universal and simple. But the historical law that starvation brings on revolt is not proved; indeed the opposite statement, that starvation leads to abject submission, is equally true in the light of past events [...] An historical event cannot be isolated from its circumstances, any more than the onion from its skins, because an event is itself nothing but a set of circumstances, none of which will ever recur.

To bring the matter to the test, what are the "laws" which historical "science" has discovered in the last forty years, since it cleared the laboratory of those wretched "literary historians"? [...] Not only can no causal laws of universal application be discovered in so complex a subject, but the interpretation of the cause and effect of anyone particular event cannot rightly be called "scientific". The collection of facts, the weighing of evidence as to what events happened, are in some sense scientific; but not so the discovery of the causes and effects of those events. In dealing even with an affair of which the facts are so comparatively well known as those of the French Revolution, it is impossible accurately to examine the psychology of twenty-five million different persons, of whom - except a few hundreds or thousands - the lives and motives are buried in the black night of the utterly forgotten. No-one, therefore, can ever give a complete or wholly true account of the causes of the French Revolution. But several imperfect readings of history are better than none at all; and he will give the best interpretation who, having discovered and weighed all the important evidence obtainable, has the largest grasp of intellect, the warmest human sympathy, the highest imaginative powers. Carlyle, at least in his greatest work, fulfilled the last two conditions [...]

I conclude, therefore, that the analogy of physical science has misled many historians during the last thirty years right away from the truth about their profession. There is no utilitarian value in knowledge of the past, and there is no way of scientifically deducing causal laws about the action of human beings in the mass. In short, the value of history is not scientific. Its true value is educational. It can educate the minds of men by causing them to reflect on the past. If historians neglect to educate the public, if they fail to interest it intelligently in the past, then all their historical learning is valueless except in so far as it educates themselves. What then, are the various ways in which history can educate the mind?

The first, or at least the most generally acknowledged educational effect of history, is to train the mind of the citizen into a state in which he is capable of taking a just view of political problems. But, even in this capacity, history cannot prophesy the future.

[...] History should not only remove prejudice, it should breed enthusiasm. To many it is an important source of the ideas that inspire their lives. With the exception of a few creative minds, men are too weak to fly by their own unaided imagination beyond the circle of ideas that govern the world in which they are placed [...]

One may aspire to the best characteristics of a man of Athens or a citizen of Rome; a Churchman of the twelfth century, or a Reformer of the sixteenth; a Cavalier of the old school, or a Puritan of the Independent party; a Radical of the time of Castlereagh, or a public servant of the time of Peel [...] Another educative function of history is to enable the reader to comprehend the historical aspect of literature proper [...] For example, the last half dozen stanzas of Browning's "Old Pictures in Florence", the fifth stanza of his "Lovers' Quarrel" and half his wife's best poems are already meaningless unless we know something of the continental history of that day. The value and pleasure of travel, whether at home or abroad, is doubled by a knowledge of history.

In this vexed question whether history is an art or a science, let us call it both or call it neither. For it has an element of both. It is not in guessing at historical "cause and effect" that science comes in; but in collecting and weighing evidence as to facts [...]

To my mind, there are three distinct functions of history, that we may call the scientific, the imaginative or speculative, and the literary. First comes what we may call the scientific, if we confine the word to this narrow but vital function, the day-labour that every historian must well and truly perform if he is to be a serious member of his profession - the accumulation of facts and the sifting of evidence [...] Then comes the imaginative or speculative, when he plays with the facts that he has gathered, selects and classifies them, and makes his guesses and generalisations. And last, but not least comes the literary function, the exposition of the results of science and imagination in a form that will attract and educate our fellow countrymen. For this last process I use the word literature.

[...] Writing history well is no child's play. The rounding of every sentence and of every paragraph has to be made consistent with a score of facts [...] some of them perhaps discovered or remembered by him at the last moment to the entire destruction of some carefully erected artistic structure. In such cases there is an undoubted temptation to the artist to neglect such small, inconvenient pieces of truth. That, I think, is the one strong point in the scholar's outcry against "literary history", but ... in history, as it is now written, art is sacrificed to science ten times for every time that science is sacrificed to art [...] If, as we have so often been told with such glee, the days of "literary history" have gone never to return, the world is left the poorer ... but if we confess that we lack something, and cease to make a merit of our chief defect, if we encourage the rising generation to work at the art of construction and narrative as a part of the historian's task, we may at once get a better level of historical writing, and our children may live to enjoy modern Gibbons, judicious Carlyles and skeptical Macaulays.'[50]

## Social and economic history

In his not altogether successful efforts to write a social history of England (*English Social History*), Trevelyan is identified with the emergence of social history as an academic discipline in its own right. To the dismay of subsequent social historians, he defined social history

---

50 G. M. Trevelyan, 1903, quoted in Stern (1970), pp.227-45

as 'history with the politics left out'[51]. Social history provided an alternative approach to the events-led view of the past.

The rise of the labour movement and socialism stimulated a new interest in the lives of ordinary working people. Their contribution to, and exploitation by, the economic systems they enabled, became valid subjects for a new generation of left-wing historians. The great pioneers of this approach in Britain were the social reformers, Sidney and Beatrice Webb, who founded the London School of Economics in 1895. In 1894, they published their influential *History of Trade Unionism*, which was followed by *Industrial Democracy* in 1897. In the USA, such approaches were termed the 'New History'. More recently, these approaches have become known as 'history from below'. Where, traditionally, the major developments of the past were deemed to be the consequence of the initiatives of the elite and the ruling class, modern historians are likely to identify popular culture as a crucial factor. 'From above' and 'from below' factors set the parameters of debate for many subjects, including the Holocaust, witch-hunting, appeasement in the 1930s and the Crusades. The changing nature of society has often been linked to political development; the crises of the seventeenth century in England, for example, are associated with the rise of the gentry and the political tension that ensued.

At much the same time, economic histories appeared, notably *War and Capitalism* by a German historian, Werner Sombart, in 1913. This explored the role of war in the process of industrialisation. The most influential early advocate of using statistics in the pursuit of historical truths, such as the standard of living in industrialised Britain, was the English historian, J. H. Clapham (1873-1946). The recognition of the place of counting in historical studies gave rise to a new journal, *The Economic History Review*, first published in 1926. In another age of great technological progress, the 1950s and 1960s, a 'new' economic history emerged, sometimes termed as 'econometrics or 'cliometrics' (after Clio, the muse of History in Greek mythology).

A further alternative to the nineteenth-century diplomatic and constitutional histories was the emerging 'intellectual history' of the new century, evident in the titles of such works as Friedrich Meinecke's

---

51 quoted in Black and MacRaild (2000), p.59

*The Doctrine of Raison d'Etat and its Place in Modern History* (1924). Many historians, subsequently, have emphasised the importance of ideas in the past. Religion was, of course, the focus of the Crusades, and belief in the possibility of people making pacts with the devil seems to have helped generate the witch-hunts of the early modern period. However, historians with a more 'materialistic' perspective debate the extent to which ideas can override circumstances in the shaping of history.

Researchers interested in the influence of ideas have to grapple with the fact that, until recent times, writings indicating philosophical understanding for any given period were usually produced by members of the social elite. It would be unwise, for example, to assume that the German priests who wrote the most famous witch-hunting manual *Malleus Maleficarum* in the fifteenth century accurately reflected the common mores of the age in which they lived.

In the following passage Arthur Marwick offered some interesting explanations for the appearance of new approaches to history in the early twentieth century.

> 'It may seem strange that historical studies in the early years of the twentieth century should simultaneously try to face in two different directions: in the direction of economics and in the direction of ideas [...]. However, this turning in different directions was all part of the same internal revolution within historical studies: the bad old men of the dying generation had ignored both economic and intellectual factors, so the brave young men of the present must explore one or other or both. The turning to economic history, which had its origins deep in the nineteenth century, obviously makes sense in the context of a developing technological civilisation. The fashion for intellectual history was essentially a more temporary one, associated with the tide of philosophical doubt which swept the Western world in the aftermath of the First World War, washing away much of the older faith in the existence of solid historical "facts". "Everything is relative" and "It's all in the mind, anyway" were the cant phrases which affected and reflected thinking at all levels of intellectual activity.'[52]

---

52 Marwick (1970), pp.72-4

# The Annalists

In 1929, two French historians, Marc Bloch and Lucien Febvre, launched a new journal entitled *Annales d'histoire sociale et economique*. In it they championed a broader vision of history, later dubbed 'total history' or, more recently, 'holistic history' (Jordanova 2006) that tapped into the associated disciplines of geography, psychology, economics and sociology. They helped initiate an academic culture of integration across subjects. It is not unusual now for sociologists and social-psychologists to write texts on such historical topics as sixteenth- and seventeenth-century witch-hunting. The 'Annalists', as they came to be called, contested the traditional preoccupation with political narrative and the history of 'great men'. Sometimes they tackled a long time-span ('longue duree') in order to identify historical developments that occurred over long periods of time. In trying to explain why things happened they sought 'profound causes' and considered such things as geography and climate upon the actions of men. Theirs was likely to be a macro, as opposed to a micro, history. This approach is exemplified in the title of their most famous publication - Marc Bloch's *Feudal Society* (1940).

## The history of the mentalities

Another great contribution of the Annalists was their recognition of the importance of understanding the 'mentalité' of people in the past. John Tosh has explained how the history of collective mentality is distinct from the history of ideas: 'while the history of ideas deals with formally articulated principles and ideologies, the history of mentality is concerned with the emotional, the instinctive and the implicit - areas of thought which often have found no direct expression at all. And it is social historians rather than intellectual historians who have made the running in this new field.'[53]

The Annalists argued that, in terms of people's ideas and emotions, the past was indeed a foreign place. The collective mentality of the past was the product of specific time and place and it would be naive to

---

53 Tosh (1984), p.86

assume that people in the past shared the same psychological make-up of people in the present. Gaining access to the 'collective mentality', however, is difficult for any but the most literate of societies. However, it is sometimes possible, even when the people concerned wrote no record of their own. A more recent exponent of Annalist values, Emmanuel Le Roy Ladurie, wrote an immensely influential book, *Montaillou* (1978) that reconstructed the lives of around 250 people living in a village in the Pyrenees between 1294 and 1324. His account was based upon the court records of the local bishop, Jacques Fournier, subsequently Pope Benedict XII, who kept the detailed records of the Inquisition which was investigating the Albigensian heresy in the region during that period. This 'micro-historic' approach has been much emulated. Ladurie's work was anticipated a few years earlier by Alan Macfarlane's *Witchcraft in Tudor and Stuart England* (1970), which also used the detail of court records of two counties to explore the beliefs and experiences of people subjected to witch-hunting in seventeenth-century England.

The Annalists' 'total history', inevitably, focused on history 'from below'. Marc Bloch's famous works on the feudal system focused on the peasants instead of lords and kings, and Febvre's first great account of the French Revolution, published in two volumes, was entitled *The Peasants of the North during the Revolution* (1924). Inclined to the left politically, his writing was informed by the Marxist concept of the central place of class struggle in history. History 'from below' developed throughout the twentieth century, flowering in the 1960s, with a new enthusiasm for such things as women's history, oral history, historic demography, and labour history.

As Tosh has pointed out, local studies can shed a good deal of light on issues of national significance: 'as a result of the many county studies undertaken in recent years, historians now have a more sophisticated understanding of the inter-relationship between religious, economic and political factors in the origins of the English Civil War.'[54]

Emmanuel Le Roy Ladurie and others demonstrated that communities with a relative abundance of evidence were worthy of special attention. Alan Macfarlane's examination of witchhunting in Suffolk

---

54 Tosh (1984), p.91

and Essex was so illuminating precisely because, for those counties, the record of trials was especially complete. Detailed studies of localities in Norman England for which substantial records survive can be used as a guide for the wider experience of conquest. Equally, local studies can reveal regional variations - the experience of British colonialism, for example, varied widely from continent to continent and place to place.

Marc Bloch emphasised the importance of the comparative and regressive approaches to history. Comparison is a central activity of the historian - all historians, to a greater or lesser extent, are 'comparativists'. At a micro level historians compare and contrast evidence to try to ascertain the 'truth' of the past; at a macro level they compare and contrast societies that might be far apart in terms of time and / or place. Anthropological approaches, for example, endeavour to illuminate the past through the study of human behaviour in societies that can be observed in the present, or have been observed in the recent past. For historians interested in the principle of historical 'laws' in the explanation of why things change, Marxist historians for example, the identification of the common experience of diverse societies is a fundamental approach in the testing of their hypotheses. This is sometimes described as 'universalising comparison'. Equally importantly, comparative studies can undermine the temptation of historians to generalise about the past.

Historians of early modern witch-hunting have found in the detail of witchcraft beliefs and the scale of witch-hunting at a local level plenty of evidence to challenge the view that there ever was some kind of universal European 'witchcraze'; historians of the Crusades recognise the great diversity of motives that inspired those involved, just as each Crusade itself was a unique phenomenon. This, the opposite of 'universalising', is known as 'individualising comparison'. The two are not necessarily mutually exclusive: the historian is often concerned with trying to establish whether either the differences or the similarities 'outweigh' the other.

With a keen interest in such things as place names, folklore, linguistics and maps, Bloch was able to see how the past resonated in the present. He recognised how the evidence of modern customs, for example, could enable the historian to 'regress', to draw conclusions regarding the origin of such customs. This technique is especially associated with the work of modern archaeologists and anthropologists.

The importance of the Annales historians in developing new approaches to historical writing has been amply described by Black and MacRaild:

> 'In 1924 [ ...] Bloch published his seminal work - The Royal Touch, one of the classics of this century. It is a study of mentalites, ideas and beliefs - a classic Annales subject area. In it Bloch examines a belief, held in France and England down to the eighteenth century, that the king could cure the skin disease scrofula ('the king's evil') just by touch. In three ways, The Royal Touch was path-breaking. First, it did not conform to rigid periodic boundaries and crossed the traditional divisions between medieval and early modern where necessary. Secondly, it was perhaps the first truly comparative history. By using comparison Bloch was formalising what he believed to be the way forward for all history. Finally, it was a study of 'religious psychology', an attempt to give meaning to the dominant beliefs and actions of real people. As such it shattered the mould of standard political histories of the medieval period.
>
> At this time, Febvre too was developing his interest in ideas, plainly influenced by psychology. Martin Luther (1928), for example, was far from just a biography, but was, instead, a study of "social necessity", of the links between men and groups. The new trend was set.'[55]

The work of the French Annalists represented a revolution in approaches to the writing of history and yet it would be many decades before its impact was felt elsewhere. In the following passages Black and MacRaild explain how and why the approaches adopted by historians can be regarded as being culturally determined:

> 'In America, the Annales, like Marxism have been taken on board only slowly and patchily. This has been explained by American historians' liberal approach to the past, which mirrors the [...]

---

55 Black and MacRaild (2000), pp.70-71

*political culture of that country, and by the absence in America of the social chaos that has pierced European culture and self-confidence since 1914. In Germany, the Annales "mentalities" approach did not take off till the 1970s, although many German historians were preoccupied with the modern period and the cataclysmic events of 1914-18 to 1945, the rise of Hitler and the spectre of genocide.*

*In Britain, the pre-eminence of traditional political history (especially in the 1950s and 1960s) was tellingly discussed by Peter Burke, in "The French Historical Revolution" (1990). Britain at this time, Burke suggested, was a good example "of what Braudel [the most famous "second generation" Annalist historian] used to call a 'refusal to borrow'". Despite the importance of the major works by Annales historians, they were met by an underwhelming response in Britain [...] Prior to the 1970s, the Annates works were only rarely translated.'*[56]

## Cultural history

The Annalist inspired 'history of mentalites' is also known as 'cultural history'. For some, archaeologists in particular, 'cultural history' specifically identifies the 'material culture' of the past - the artefacts and artistic works that help to define societies. For most historians, however, it is seen as an approach that is concerned with the history of popular ideas.

Intellectual historians have tended to focus on 'elite' ideas, such as those informing science and the fine arts, whereas cultural historians focus on the popular culture of the past. This covers all manner of things as diverse as the histories of leisure, food, pop music, sex, crime, and witchcraft. In their investigations, cultural historians combine social history, anthropological and sociological approaches when explaining past modes of behaviour. A. Cazorla-Sanchez , the author of the following extract, argues in favour of this approach:

*'The past, we are often told, is a foreign country. We may add that History is a passport that allows us to visit that country. The trip will*

---

56 Black and MacRaild (2000), p.82

sarily be short, so everything that we learn has to be understood as just a small part of what actually happened. Our experience in the past will be fragmentary. Like any traveller, we have to avoid seeing what we expect to see, leaving behind our prejudices and pre-formed opinions. Since nobody can completely accomplish this, and we always perceive reality through the prism of our own experience, every successive visit to the past will reveal different things. This doesn't imply that we cannot make well documented and soundly reasoned History, only that the past continues to change as we change.

[...] This is where Cultural History makes its entry. Historians realise that one of the main problems in trying to understand the past is sometimes not what we do not know but what we do. This is only an apparent paradox. If we are studying a problematic question, let's say the United Kingdom's Appeasement policy in the 1930s, we know what happened afterwards (its ultimate failure and the outbreak of World War" and all the horror that followed), something that the people whom we are studying (Britons in the late 1930s) could not - and for the good reason that our past was their future. Our understanding of the past is fogged and distorted by the subsequent events that eventually resulted in our present, and we should be careful not to make easy assumptions, based on a supposedly superior knowledge, about our ancestors.

A good way to avoid this risk is to try to re-construct what people and different groups thought at the time and why; what was their relationship with others, the problems and things that surrounded them and in what was their perception of reality, of their present. Here is where History takes as much as it can from Sociology and becomes New Cultural History. Notice that this new approach does not limit itself to describing the ideas and conditions of the Past, as traditional Social History does, or the coining of great ideas and tendencies, which is the focus of traditional Intellectual History. What New Cultural history attempts is far more ambitious and difficult, and perhaps for this reason more interesting ... it wants to know why people did what they did by understanding what they thought and how those ideas came into being. Be ready, for this trip is no visit to old ruins and yellowed documents but to our ancestors' minds [...] and your own mind.'[57]

---

[57] Cazorla-Sanchez in *History Review* (2008)

## Psychoanalytical history

Sigmund Freud fashioned the modern science of psychology in the first half of the twentieth century, and this science has informed historical writing ever since. Febvre declared his investigation into sixteenth-century views on religion (*Le Probleme de l'incroyance au XVI siecle*, 1947) an exercise in 'historical psychology'. In Marwick's opinion 'no historian today could discuss the French Revolution, or any similar topic without acquainting himself with the discoveries of the individual and social psychology'[58]. The application of psychoanalysis to the explanation of the past has been described as 'the most powerful of interpretive approaches to history' by historian and psychoanalyst Peter Loewenberg[59]. As an example Green and Troup have summarised a contemporary psychoanalytical explanation for the rise of the Nazis:

> 'Wilhelm Reich attempted to blend history, in the form of historical materialism, with group psychoanalysis. In The Mass Psychology of Fascism, written in the early 1930s, Reich synthesized the theories of Freud and Marx. He argued that Nazism, like all political movements, was grounded in the psychological structure of the German masses, in particular of the lower middle class. This group was anxious due to their increasing poverty in the face of depression and German war debts. Lower middle class fathers were authoritarian, and able to sexually repress their children on account of the correspondence of familial and economic structures: that is, the family lived and worked together. These psychically damaged children therefore became submissive, and were relieved to rely on an authoritarian Fuhrer in later life. At the same time they craved authority, and so acted in an authoritarian manner towards those below them. This is, of course, a simplified account but it serves to show how Reich enriched his analysis of a concrete historical situation with psychoanalytic insights.'[60]

'Psycho-historic' approaches have some validity in exploring the actions of groups of people. The 'crowd mentality' and 'mass

---

58 Marwick (1970), p.59
59 Green and Troup (1999) p.59
60 Green and Troup (1999), p.62

psychology' that psychologists can observe in the contemporary world can help historians in their analysis of the behaviour of those that persecuted Jews in the 1940s and 'witches' in the 1640s.

## New economic history

Post-Second World War approaches to history - the 'New Economic History' - relied heavily on statistical analysis and other methods developed by the new discipline of 'social science' - 'sociology' as it was termed by Augustus Comte in the mid-nineteenth century. As historians came to recognise the full importance of economic developments in the shaping of politics, more attention was paid to such things as prices and wages. For a time, it seemed to some that the computer would become the principle tool in solving the riddles of the past.

Some of these 'New' historians, 'demographers', chose to specialise in the study of data related to population studies (demography). Like the research historians who are occupied just trying to complete the record of past events, demographers are fully employed in their reconstruction of past-populations from incomplete and difficult evidence. Historians pursuing explanations for historical phenomena, such as early modern European witch-hunting and the settlement of the American West, have explored the significance of population expansion.

## The history of the marginalised

In the twentieth century, many historians approached the past with the specific intention of recovering for posterity the history of minority and marginalised groups that traditionally have been largely written out of, or misrepresented by, history books. The 'New History' of the late nineteenth and early twentieth centuries was largely focused on the experience of ordinary working people. Since then, other marginalised groups have received a great deal of attention. For example, the history of black communities in predominantly white contexts has been much explored, and a fair amount of work has been done on the history of homosexuality.

Historians are now concerned, for example, with the impact of the Norman Conquest on the lives of women, and the role of women in the Crusades, British empire-building, and the forging of the American West. Women, so often confined to the sidelines in the most studied historical subjects of the past, take centre stage in some of the most high-profile subjects of the present, such as the European witch-hunts of the early modern period. Similarly, students of the American West are encouraged to pay as much attention to Native Americans as white settlers, and other minorities that were persecuted with the Jews in the era of the Holocaust have received attention. British imperialism is studied extensively from a non-British perspective. It is recognised that around one fifth of 'cowboys' in the American West were African-Americans and not the white stereotype of mid-twentieth century Hollywood movies.

The history of imperialism benefits from a canon of historical writing derived from the experiences of the colonised instead of the more usual traditional colonialists' perspective. The following passage outlines one such post-colonial perspective:

> *'At the other end of the postcolonial spectrum of historical writing are the subaltern studies historians of India who employ contemporary methodology and theory to re-interpret the experience of colonialism. The fundamental perspective of subaltern studies is very simple: "that hitherto Indian history had been written from a colonialist and elitist point of view, whereas a large part of Indian history has been made by the subaltern classes"[...]. The subaltern are those of inferior rank, whether of class, caste, age, gender or in any other way. Arguing that Indian history had largely been written from the perspective of the elite, the subaltern studies historians reject the conventional nationalist history of India which "seeks to replicate in its own history the history of the modern state of Europe".'*[61]

Similar revisions of the forging of the American West were made by historians in the second half of the nineteenth century. Like women's history courses in many British university departments, Native American studies are now delivered in US universities.

---

61 Green and Troup (1999), p.283

## History and anthropology

Just as twentieth-century historians employed the approaches of statisticians and sociologists, they also harnessed the methodology and discoveries of anthropologists. The term anthropology was coined by the naturalist Francoise Peron in his study of Tasmanian Aboriginal peoples at the start of the nineteenth century. In trying to understand past mentalities, some historians have explored more recent and contemporary societies. The approach is of central importance to archaeology. However, just as archaeologists are aware of the danger of presuming that the lifestyles and beliefs of modern Australian aborigines have anything in common with their ancestors from 40,000 years ago, historians have questioned the validity of explaining witch-hunting in sixteenth-century Europe by drawing parallels with witchcraft beliefs in twenty first century Africa. Although problematic, anthropology at least has alerted historians to the vast range of human experience and outlooks that are shaped by cultural and environmental factors, and historic processes.

Commenting on the fascinating business of exploring different cultures in place and time, John Tosh has concluded: 'For historians encountering a past society through the medium of documentary sources there is - or ought to be - the same sense of "culture shock" that the modern investigator experiences in an exotic or "primitive" community.'[62]

Anthropological approaches to the study of witch-hunting in early modern Europe were pioneered by G. L. Kittredge in 1929 and more thoroughly explored by G. Parrinder in 1958. The major works associated with the approach are Keith Thomas' *Religion and the Decline of Magic* (1971) and Alan Macfarlane's *Witchcraft in Tudor and Stuart England* (1970).

They drew on the findings of E. E. Evans-Pritchard's anthropological study of tribal life in *Africa, Witchcraft, Oracles and Magic among the Azande* (1937), to help explain the witchcraft and witch-hunting phenomena in the early modern era. Most importantly, the findings of

---

62 Tosh (1984), p.87

the anthropologists raised the historians' awareness of the interconnectedness of material conditions and popular beliefs.

More recent historians, however, are less convinced of the effectiveness of an anthropological approach:

> 'anthropology [...] is simply not designed to explain change over long timespans, arguably still one of the major objectives of the historian. Moreover, even early modern England was a more developed society than those which have traditionally formed the subject matter for anthropologists. It had a complex and increasingly dynamic economy, a complex social structure and a fair degree of social mobility, a developed church, and a developed state judicial system. One must express sympathy and admiration of Macfarlane and Thomas's approach, and for their major achievement in constructing a totally new perspective on the history of witchcraft: nevertheless, it is probably instructive that few historians have followed them in their pursuit of anthropological comparisons [...] comparing tribal societies studied by anthropologists in the first half of the twentieth century like is not being compared with like.' [63]

## Some conclusions

In their excellent guidebook for students of history, Studying History, Black and MacRaild summed up their chapter on historiography by citing Peter Burke's conclusions in New Perspectives on Historical Writing (1991) regarding the differences between 'Old' and 'New' approaches to history:

'History of the "traditional paradigm" is concerned with politics; the new history, which "has come to be concerned with virtually every area of human activity", is not.

Traditional historians "think of history as essentially a narrative of events", although new historians do not entirely dismiss the narrative form, greater weight is given to structures than was previously the case.

---

63 Sharpe (2001), p.39

*Traditional historians focus on "a view from above ... concentrated on the deeds of great men", whereas new historians favour "history from below", the view of the common person.*

*Traditional history is shaped around documents (empiricism); new history draws upon a much wider range of sources, including non-textual types, such as oral and visual material.*

*Traditional approaches fail to account for a variety of questions which historians must ask, whereas new history does not.*

*The traditional paradigm stresses the singular power of the authorial voice, privileging the historian's objectivity and balance. New history, however, stresses the variety of voices and viewpoints in the past and acknowledges the subjectivity of the author.*

*Traditional historians have emphasised the uniqueness of their subject; newer approaches stress intellectual interplay through inter- and multi-disciplinary approaches.*[64]

Much modern academic history is as concerned with the history of the history writing as it is with the narrative of events. For example, much has been written about how nineteenth and early twentieth century views of the Crusades, in which they were perceived as noble, chivalric and romantic endeavours, reflected the age in which they were formulated. The nineteenth century was the great age of imperialism in which western Europe imposed its values and political systems upon other continents, and Europeans were generally convinced that they were doing the wider world a favour in the process. It was also a period when northern Europeans, in their art and literature, celebrated their medieval 'Gothic' ancestry. More recently, anti-colonial attitudes have led to a revision of the 'heroic' crusade tradition. All major subjects have generated books that are exclusively concerned with historiography.

The 'postmodern' preoccupation with historiography and how the views of historians are shaped by the age in which they write as much

---

64 Black and MacRaild (2000), pp.84-5

as, or more than, the history they write about, is a cause of concern to some. These concerns have been eloquently expressed by Richard J. Evans in an article entitled *Postmodernism and the study of history* from which the following is an extract:

'In order to understand any aspect of history, it seems generally agreed, we have first to understand what historians have written about it. But what if that was all we needed to understand? What if the past itself was unrecoverable in any meaningfully objective sense, what if historians, instead of merely interpreting and reinterpreting it, simply made it up as they went along? What if, in other words, there was no difference between history and fiction?

This, or something much like it, is the argument put forward, with varying degrees of emphasis, by a growing number of literary theorists, critics, and indeed historians themselves, as they contemplate the discipline of history and how it is written and researched. The ideas they are advancing can roughly be grouped under the convenient label of "postmodernism". For most of the twentieth century, so the argument goes, we lived in a culture of "modernism", grounded in a strong belief in science and progress. In historical studies, this was expressed in the belief that history was a science, and used a particular range of theories and techniques to analyse the documentary and other remains left behind by the past in order to achieve an objective assessment of what happened and why.

[...] In the postmodernist world, meanings are shifting and uncertain, truth unobtainable, objectivity a meaningless concept [...] History, in other words, is ultimately not about the past, it's about historians. [...] If we do not believe that we can establish the truth about the past, how can we for example refute the obnoxious exponents of "Holocaust denial", who deny that millions of Jews were killed by the Nazis in the Second World War? Moreover, if oppressed minorities want to improve their position in society, they are hardly going to do so by writing only about and for themselves: they are going to have to dissect the mechanisms and institutions which oppress them, and convince society as a whole that these should be changed. Some wide-ranging view of history, indeed some concept of objectivity, is necessary for this.

*When we have discounted the more extreme statements of postmodernists about history, what is left? If we distinguish in this, as in other areas, between extremists and moderates, the answer is quite a lot. The postmodernist emphasis on culture and identity has given rise to a great deal of new and important historical work [...] In the light of moderate postmodernist criticism it is no longer possible to maintain a simple view of economic or social causation in history, and this too is leading to a lot of rethinking of major historical topics. But postmodernism is not just relevant to traditional historical subjects, it has also redirected our attention to the marginal and the apparently insignificant, much to the benefit of historical knowledge. Finally it has forced all historians to think again about what they are doing when they study the past, and that perhaps is its most important contribution of all.'*[65]

---

65 Evans in *History Review* (1998)

# Part 2 HERITAGE

## 3 Heritage and its management

### What is heritage?

Unlike history and archaeology, heritage is not a 'discipline'; it has no particular mode of analysis or enquiry. Ben Cowell has provided a simple definition: 'an ongoing concern for the tangible and intangible remains of the past, for the benefit of present and future generations'.[66] According to Don Henson, 'Heritage is not a thing, it is a relationship where we use things from the past for various purposes in the present.'[67] He considers it a 'set of active processes' ('seeing, experiencing, understanding, using') whereby we create our (and, presumably, other people's) heritage according to our 'various purposes'. UNESCO's definition for 'cultural heritage' highlights the concepts of inheritance: 'the entire corpus of material signs – either artistic or symbolic – handed on by the past to each culture and, therefore, to the whole of mankind. As a constituent part of the affirmation and enrichment of cultural identities, as a legacy belonging to all humankind, the cultural heritage gives each particular place its recognisable features and is the storehouse of human experience.'[68]

The tangible remains of the past identified by Cowell include structures, landscapes, and portable antiquities. The intangible remains comprise oral traditions and languages, performance, rituals and festive events, social practices, knowledge, and traditional arts and crafts. Such things define 'cultural heritage', the focus of this book - things conceived and made by humanity. Nature of course plays its part in cultural heritage but only in as much as it relates to the human cultural experience.

Conceivably, Cowell has suggested, the modern 'obsession' with

---

[66] Cowell (2008), p.10
[67] Henson (2012). P.74
[68] UNESCO (https://en.unesco.org)

heritage in the UK is a reaction to present circumstances. This, broadly, was the conclusion of Horace Walpole who commented at the time of the first flowering of this 'obsession': 'Our empire is falling to pieces; we are relapsing to a little island. In that state, men are apt to imagine how great their ancestors have been; and when a kingdom is past doing anything, the few, that are studious, look into the memorials of past time; nations, like private persons, seek lustre from their progenitors, when they have none in themselves.'[69]

For a range of reasons we value our cultural heritage. In an excellent account of why it matters, Don Henson summarised the findings of the Archaeology Forum, representing many different organisations engaged in the subject, in 2005, concerning the value of archaeology. These included:

- *a core contribution to local identity and sense of who we are;*
- *a sense of place and common cultural perspectives;*
- *links people with continuity and change in their surroundings and society;*
- *a major contribution to tourist income and heritage led regeneration.*[70]

His own thoughts on the matter, have led him to the following conclusion:

> *'Getting to know the past has many benefits. It helps us make sense of the present and provides a sense of permanence and stability that reassures us in times of change. It can help us to validate the present by providing it with an origin or example to follow. But, it can also be used to subvert the present by finding alternative ways of doing things in the past that might be better than what we do now. The past gives us our cultural identity and our sense of difference from other people. But, it can also give us a strong sense of a common humanity. We all have pasts, and the farther back in time we go the more of that past is shared between people today. The past gives us lessons about how to do things, and a lot of fun arguing over whether these are the right lessons or not. The past can enrich our*

---

69 Horace Walpole, 1778 in Cowell (2008)
121 Henson (2012), p.62

lives through its beauty, the sense of wonder it provides or the thrill of touching something made thousands of many years ago. The past is also an escape from a troubled present and a source of comfort for.'[71]

## Heritage history

Classical precedents for the modern enthusiasm for preserving aspects of the past include Emperor Hadrian's rebuilding of the Parthenon (Rome). Ironically, in England the imminent Henrician Reformation and the subsequent destruction of so many magnificent medieval ecclesiastical buildings seems to have prompted an early intervention by the state in the preservation, at least by record, of aspects of England's heritage. One of Henry VIII's personal chaplains, John Leland, was commissioned to visit and record the contents of monastic libraries in 1533, the year in which Anne Boleyn became England's new queen, and just three years before the dissolution of the lesser monasteries by act of parliament. Hundreds of the invaluable books he listed subsequently ended up in the royal collections.

When he passed through Somerset Leland (no doubt eager to please a royal master who was of Welsh ancestry and the head of a family that his father, Henry Tudor / Henry VII[72], had overtly linked to the mythical King of Britain - Arthur) left a fascinating account of his detour, between abbey visits, to 'Camelot' – South Cadbury hillfort.

> 'Right at the south end of South Cadbury church stands Camelot. This was once a noted town or castle, set on a real peak of a hill, and with marvellously strong defences. It has just two entrances up very steep tracks, one on the north-east, the other on the south-west. The distance around the foot of the hill on which this fortress stands is more than a mile. Near its summit there are four ditches or trenches, each separated by an earthern rampart. Above these ditches right on the hilltop is a large open space which I would reckon to be twenty acres or more; in various parts of it one may observe the foundations and rubble of walls. There used to be a

---

[71] Henson (2012), pp.63-4
72 Henry VII named his first born son Arthur.

*quantity of blue-grey stone which has been removed by the inhabitants of the nearby villages. This area has often been ploughed, and produced many good yields.*

*Roman coins of gold, silver and copper have been turned up in large quantities during ploughing there, and also in the fields at the foot of the hill, especially on the east side. Many other antiquities have been found, including at Camelot, within living memory, a silver horseshoe. The only information local people can offer is that they have heard that Arthur frequently came to Camelot. The old Lord Hungerford owned this Camelot, but now it has passed to Hastings, Earl of Huntingdon, by his mother. Several villages in that area have the name Camelot as an affix, such as Queen Camel, and others. The hill and ditches are now good for rearing sheep. The land on the south-west and west sides of Camelot all lies in a vale, so that from one or two directions it may be seen from a great distance.*[73]

In 1560, at the start of the reign of Elizabeth I, legislation was passed, in defiance of the emerging puritan opposition to the moderate *via media* ('middle way') of the Elizabethan religious settlement, forbidding the 'defacing of Monuments of antiquity, being set up in the churches or other public places for memory, and not for superstition'.

The so-called 'English renaissance' was the context in which a new enthusiasm for the collection of antiquities and curiosities took off — the foundation of the museums revolution of the nineteenth century. The large collection put together by the enigmatic Elias Ashmole (1617-92), lawyer, politician and alchemist among other things, evolved into the great Ashmoleon Museum founded in Oxford in 1683. In so doing Ashmole effectively introduced the term 'museum' into the English language. By 1800 over 100 significant collections were held in private hands in England.

Other influential seventeenth century antiquarians included William Camden (1551-1623) who published in 1586 *Britannia* – a massive county by county work of history and topography. He was an eminent member of a 'college' (i.e. society) of 'antiquaries', established in Elizabeth's reign. This was the precursor for the eighteenth century

---

73 Leland in Chandler (1993), pp.416-7

Society of London Antiquaries (founded 1717) that has been active ever since. Its members, Fellows of the Society of Antiquaries, identify themselves by the acronym 'FSA'.

John Aubrey (1626-97), best known for his potted biographies collected in the nineteenth century under the title *Brief Lives*, remains a crucial source for archaeologists and prehistorians investigating the remains of henges, stone circles and suchlike at Stonehenge, Avebury and other ancient sites. These he visited and recorded in words and sketches in various unpublished manuscripts, notably *Monumenta Brittanica* and *Wiltshire Antiquities*. In 1563 he joined the Royal Society for Improving Natural Knowledge (established in 1560) and, in the same year, treated its benefactor, Charles II, to a guided tour of Avebury. Another member of the Royal Society was Ralph Thoresby (1658-1725) - a Leeds cloth merchant who accumulated a substantial private collection of antiquities.

William Stukeley (1687-1765) was a member of both the Royal Society and the Society of Antiquaries. While his inclination to explain them as druidic remains is problematic, Stukely's observations and, especially, his detailed sketches of ancient sites are of inestimable value to modern antiquarians. When he visited Avebury he witnessed the on-going destruction of colossal menhirs by 'stone killer' Tom Robinson, an eighteenth century housing developer, and made it his mission to record what still remained before it too was gone. His findings were recorded in his *Stonehenge, a Temple Restor'd* and *Palaeographia Britannica or discourses on Antiquities in Britain.*

The popularity of the 'Grand Tour' of Europe for the sons of wealthy Georgian families stimulated the interest in collecting ancient artefacts and helped cultivate a taste for exotic and dramatic landscapes. When the French Revolution (1789) and the Napoleonic Wars (ending 1815) effectively ended the era of the Grand Tour abroad, the attention of the educated elite became all the more focused on Britain's own heritage. The enthusiasm for the picturesque underpinned the late eighteenth century **'Romantic Movement'**, while the growing interest in Britain's indigenous medieval heritage, as opposed to the imported Classical, gave rise to the fascination with the 'Gothick' in all of the arts, most notably, architecture.

English antiquarians, quite literally, began to dig deeper in the search for their cultural inheritance. By the start of the nineteenth century excavation for antiquarian goals had become commonplace. Of particular interest were the countless burial mounds that littered the landscape. Sir Richard Colt Hoare of Stourhead in Wiltshire (1758-1838), alone was responsible for the excavation (and destruction) of 379 round barrows.

In 1753, based on three private collections, the British Museum was founded by act of Parliament. It was the world's first national public museum. It was based upon the vast collection (71, 000 objects) of Sir Hans Sloane (1660–1753) bequeathed to the nation in return for £20,000 payable to his heirs. In 1759 the collection was moved to its present location in Bloomsbury, London. Here it used to attract around 5000 visitors each year; today the figure is closer to 6 million.

The ground-breaking **Great Exhibition** of 1851 - part trade fair, part celebration of British culture and that of her colonies - played an important role in the development of heritage sensibilities in Victorian Britain. Held at London's purpose-built Crystal Palace, made of iron and glass and designed by Joseph Paxton, it attracted around 6 million visitors at a time when the total population of England and Wales was less than 28 million. It was a huge success in promoting England as 'the workshop of the world' and the world's leading industrial power, and its profits funded the setting up of a new national public museum in its locality (subsequently nicknamed 'Albertopolis') in 1852: the South Kensington Museum. Among the new could be found spectacular examples of the old in the Great Exhibition, including the magnificent early eighth century Tara Brooch, found in Ireland the previous year.

The South Kensington Museum evolved into three distinct museums: the Victoria and Albert Museum, the Science Museum and the Natural History Museum. These became the models for the plethora of civic museums established throughout the country in the second half of the nineteenth century. Typically these local museums housed collections of fine art, archaeological finds, historic artefacts, and plant and animal specimens.

# The Society for the Protection of Ancient Buildings

The **'Gothic' restoration** of medieval churches – the routine destruction of post-medieval features to be replaced, at worst, by *faux*-medieval that had as much to do with the architect's imagination as the traces of earlier structures in the fabric of the existing church. Provoked by the restoration of Burford Church in Oxfordshire and the plans to restore Tewkesbury Minster, the remarkable William Morris (1834-1896), artist, craftsman, poet and revolutionary, formed the Society for the Protection Ancient Buildings (SPAB) in 1877, nicknamed by its founders 'Anti-Scrape'. Inspired by the arguments of art critic and philosopher John Ruskin, author of *The Stones of Venice*, SPAB, supported by prime ministers Gladstone and Disraeli among others, promptly launched a campaign to protect the west front of St Marks, Venice. Further to its function as a pressure group SPAB provided free architectural advice and helped raise money for essential repairs to historic buildings. One of its early members and activists was the novelist, trained as an architect, Thomas Hardy who worked hard to protect churches in the 'Wessex' region of his fiction.

To this day all applicants for membership of SPAB must agree to the principles of William Morris's and the organisation's original manifesto:

'A society coming before the public with such a name as that above written must needs explain how, and why, it proposes to protect those ancient buildings which, to most people doubtless, seem to have so many and such excellent protectors. This, then, is the explanation we offer.

No doubt within the last fifty years a new interest, almost like another sense, has arisen in these ancient monuments of art; and they have become the subject of one of the most interesting of studies, and of an enthusiasm, religious, historical, artistic, which is one of the undoubted gains of our time; yet we think that if the present treatment of them be continued, our descendants will find them useless for study and chilling to enthusiasm. We think that those last fifty years of knowledge and attention have done more for their destruction than all the foregoing centuries of revolution, violence and contempt.

For architecture, long decaying, died out, as a popular art at least, just as the knowledge of mediaeval art was born, so that the civilised world of the nineteenth century has no style of its own amidst its wide knowledge of the styles of other centuries. From this lack and this gain arose in men's minds the strange idea of the restoration of ancient buildings; and a strange and most fatal idea, which by its very name implies that it is possible to strip from a building this, that, and the other part of its history - of its life that is - and then to stay the hand at some arbitrary point, and leave it still historical, living, and even as it once was.

In early times this kind of forgery was impossible, because knowledge failed the builders, or perhaps because instinct held them back. If repairs were needed, if ambition or piety pricked on to change, that change was of necessity wrought in the unmistakable fashion of the time; a church of the eleventh century might be added to or altered in the twelfth, thirteenth, fourteenth, fifteenth, sixteenth, or even the seventeenth or eighteenth centuries; but every change, whatever history it destroyed, left history in the gap, and was alive with the spirit of the deeds done midst its fashioning.

The result of all this was often a building in which the many changes, though harsh and visible enough, were, by their very contrast, interesting and instructive and could by no possibility mislead. But those who make the changes wrought in our day under the name of restoration, while professing to bring back a building to the best time of its history, have no guide but each his own individual whim to point out to them what is admirable and what contemptible; while the very nature of their task compels them to destroy something and to supply the gap by imagining what the earlier builders should or might have done. Moreover, in the course of this double process of destruction and addition, the whole surface of the building is necessarily tampered with; so that the appearance of antiquity is taken away from such old parts of the fabric as are left, and there is no laying to rest in the spectator the suspicion of what may have been lost; and in short, a feeble and lifeless forgery is the final result of all the wasted labour. It is sad to say, that in this manner most of the bigger minsters, and a vast number of more humble buildings, both in England and on the continent, have been dealt with by men of talent often, and worthy of better employment, but deaf to the claims of poetry and history in the highest sense of the words.

For what is left we plead before our architects themselves, before the official guardians of buildings, and before the public generally, and we pray them to remember how much is gone of the religion, thought and manners of time past, never by almost universal consent, to be restored; and to consider whether it be possible to restore those buildings, the living spirit of which, it cannot be too often repeated, was an inseparable part of that religion and thought, and those past manners. For our part we assure them fearlessly, that of all the restorations yet undertaken, the worst have meant the reckless stripping a building of some of its most interesting material features; whilst the best have their exact analogy in the restoration of an old picture, where the partly-perished work of the ancient craftsmaster has been made neat and smooth by the tricky hand of some unoriginal and thoughtless hack of today. If, for the rest, it be asked us to specify what kind of amount of art, style, or other interest in a building makes it worth protecting, we answer, anything which can be looked on as artistic, picturesque, historical, antique, or substantial: any work, in short, over which educated, artistic people would think it worth while to argue at all.

It is for all these buildings, therefore, of all times and styles, that we plead, and call upon those who have to deal with them, to put protection in the place of restoration, to stave off decay by daily care, to prop a perilous wall or mend a leaky roof by such means as are obviously meant for support or covering, and show no pretence of other art, and otherwise to resist all tampering with either the fabric or ornament of the building as it stands; if it has become inconvenient for its present use, to raise another building rather than alter or enlarge the old one; in fine to treat our ancient buildings as monuments of a bygone art, created by bygone manners, that modern art cannot meddle with without destroying.

Thus, and thus only, shall we escape the reproach of our learning being turned into a snare to us; thus, and thus only can we protect our ancient buildings, and hand them down instructive and venerable to those that come after us.'[74]

These principles are summed up by the modern organisation as the following:

'Repair not Restore
*Although no building can withstand decay, neglect and depredation entirely, neither can aesthetic judgement nor archaeological proof justify the reproduction of worn or missing parts. Only as a practical expedient on a small scale can a case for restoration be argued.*

Responsible methods
*A repair done today should not preclude treatment tomorrow, nor should it result in further loss of fabric.*
Complement not parody
*New work should express modern needs in a modern language. These are the only terms in which new can relate to old in a way which is positive and responsive at the same time. If an addition proves essential, it should not be made to out-do or out-last the original.*

Regular maintenance
*This is the most practical and economic form of preservation.*

Information
*To repair old buildings well, they must be understood. Appreciation of a building's particular architectural qualities and a study of its construction, use and social development are all enlightening. These factors also help us to see why decay sets in and how it may be put right.*

Essential work
*The only work which is unquestionably necessary (whether it be repair, renewal or addition) is that essential to a building's survival.*

Integrity
*As good buildings age, the bond with their sites strengthens. A beautiful, interesting or simply ancient building still belongs where it*

---

[74] Manifesto of SPAB http://www.spab.org.uk/what-is-spab-/the-manifesto/ accessed 22/1/13

stands however corrupted that place may have become. Use and adaptation of buildings leave their marks and these, in time, we also see as aspects of the building's integrity. This is why the Society will not condone the moving or gutting of buildings or their reduction to mere facades. Repairs carried out in place, rather than on elements dismantled and moved to the work-bench, help retain these qualities of veracity and continuity.

Fit new to old
When repairs are made, new material should always be fitted to the old and not the old adapted to accept the new. In this way more ancient fabric will survive.

Workmanship
Why try to hide good repairs? Careful, considered workmanship does justice to fine buildings, leaving the most durable and useful record of what has been done. On the other hand, work concealed deliberately or artificially aged, even with the best intentions, is bound to mislead.

Materials
The use of architectural features from elsewhere confuses the understanding and appreciation of a building, even making the untouched parts seem spurious. Trade in salvaged building materials encourages the destruction of old buildings, whereas demand for the same materials new helps keep them in production. The use of different but compatible materials can be an honest alternative.

Respect for age
Bulging, bowing, sagging and leaning are signs of age which deserve respect. Good repair will not officiously iron them out, smarten them or hide the imperfections. Age can confer a beauty of its own. These are qualities to care for, not blemishes to be eradicated."[75]

## The National Trust

Where SPAB led others followed. When it was formed in 1895, the National Trust for Places of Historic Interest and Natural Beauty readily

---

75   http://www.spab.org.uk/what-is-spab-/spab-s-purpose/
Accessed 22/1/13

adopted SPAB's abiding repair without restoration principle. The Trust was formed by Canon Hardwicke Rawnsley, Robert Hunter and Octavia Hill who had all, in various ways, been involved in campaigns to protect open spaces threatened by modern developments such as the building of railways. As a newly registered company, the National Trust was endowed with the responsibility of looking after just five acres of land on the cliff tops at Dinas Oleu in Wales. The first building it acquired was Alfriston Clergy House in Sussex which came into the Trust's hands in 1896. In 1899 it took over Wicken Fen in Cambridgeshire, now recognised as Britain's oldest nature reserve. The Trust now cares for 618,000 acres of land and has around 2000 tenants. It owns and manages 73,000 archaeological sites, over 60 pubs and inns, 49 churches, and 59 villages. With around 4 million members, the Trust is the largest voluntary sector conservation group in Europe. Around 56,000 people each year work as volunteers on behalf of the organisation. One in ten of the UK's museums are maintained by the National Trust.

The Trust's mission is, and always has been: 'promoting the permanent preservation for the benefit of the nation of lands and tenements (including buildings) of beauty or historic interest and as regards lands for the preservation (so far as practicable) of their natural aspect features and animal and plant life'.[76]

From the start the National Trust acted as an advisory body, even a pressure group, getting involved in discussions regarding development issues including the developments carried out by local authorities and the heated debate concerning the proliferation of advertising hoardings. In 1919 the Trust joined forces with SPAB in opposition to plans to pull down 13 historic churches in the City of London.

## The Royal Commission on Ancient Monuments

The forming of the Society for the Protection of Ancient Buildings in 1877 owed a good deal to the failure of the state to protect the built heritage by law. When the first Ancient Monuments Protection Act was passed in 1882 Britain was decades behind equivalent initiatives taken

---

76  The National Trust Acts 1907 – 1971, 2005, p.3

in France and Scandinavia. In Britain the protection of birds by act of parliament (the Wild Birds Protection Act, 1880) predated the protection of monuments. As detailed in the extracts below, the Act established the principles of the 'scheduling' of ancient monuments, a state appointed inspectorate, the compulsory purchase of monuments, state-funded maintenance, and punishment by fines or imprisonment of those damaged monuments on the list.

'Where the Commissioners of Works have been constituted guardians of a monument, they shall [...] maintain such monument, and shall, for the purpose of such maintenance, [...] have access to such monument for the purpose of inspecting it. And of bringing such materials and doing such acts and things as may be required for the maintenance thereof. [...] The cost of maintenance shall, subject to the approval of Her Majesty's Treasury, be defrayed from moneys to be provided by Parliament.

The Commissioners of Works, with the consent of the treasury, may purchase [...] any ancient monument to which this Act applies [...]

Any person may by deed or will give, devise, or bequeath to The Commissioners of Works all such estate and interest in any ancient monument to which this Act applies [...] and it shall be lawful for the Commissioners of Works to accept such gift, devise, or bequest if they think it expedient so to do.

The Commissioners of her Majesty's Treasury shall appoint one or more inspectors of ancient monuments, whose duty it shall be to report to the Commissioners of Works on the condition of such monuments, and on the best mode of preserving the same, and there may be awarded to the inspectors so appointed such remuneration and allowances for expenses, out of moneys provided by Parliament, as may be determined by the Commissioners of Her Majesty's Treasury [...]

If any person injures or defaces any ancient monument to which this Act applies, such person shall, on summary conviction, be liable, at the discretion of the court by which he is tried, to one of the following penalties; (that is to say) (1.) To forfeit any sum not exceeding five pounds, and in addition thereto to pay such sum as the court may think just for the purpose of repairing any damage which has been caused by the offender; or (2.) To be imprisoned with or without hard labour for any term not exceeding one month. [...]'[77]

However, as Ben Cowell has observed, the maximum penalty meant 'that technically Stonehenge could have been demolished for as little as £5 [or a month in prison] under the Act.'[78]

The first Inspector of Ancient Monuments was the remarkable pioneering archaeologist and founder of the museum of archaeology and anthropology that takes his name, now located at Oxford University, General Augustus Henry Lane-Fox Pitt Rivers (1827-1900). Although he was successful in adding monuments to the list (13 in the first year, 23 by 1890), his efforts were undermined by the voluntary nature of the Act whereby there was no provision for compelling owners of monuments to have them scheduled. Those that were, typically, were prehistoric earthworks: monuments that were being destroyed at an alarming and increasing rate due to modern farming technology that enabled deeper ploughing. As for historic buildings, these remained unprotected by law. Historical documents fared better with the establishment of the Public Records Office in 1838 and the Historic Manuscripts Commission in 1869.

In 1908 the Royal Commission on Ancient and Historical Monuments (RCAHM) was created for the purpose of surveying and producing a record of all existing monuments dated earlier than 1700 AD and to publish the record in various ways as a first towards protecting and maintaining them by increasing public and parliamentary awareness. This task was itself monumental and after 50 years only a fifth of the country had been fully surveyed for inclusion in the record. To this day the Commission survives for Scotland (RCAHMS) and Wales (RCAHMW) but in England, the Royal Commission on Historical Monuments (RCHME), as it came to be called, merged with English Heritage (EH) in 1999.

In 1913 the Ancient Monuments Consolidation and Amendment Act

---

77  http://heritagelaw.org/AMA-1882- Accessed January 2013

78  Cowell (2008), p.87

united independent organisations and the state's Office of Works in establishing an Ancient Monuments Board which included experts from SPAB and the National Trust. Most importantly the act introduced the principle of the compulsory purchase by the state of ancient monuments and the board acted as the advisory body in identifying endangered monuments that warranted purchase.

By 1931, when a new, stronger, Ancient Monuments Act was introduced, over 3000 monuments were scheduled, either by consent or, in the event of landowners objecting, by act of parliament. However inhabited historic buildings remained unprotected by the terms of the Ancient Monuments Act. Many were saved for the nation by the National Trust but many more were demolished or developed almost beyond recognition. The Town and Country Planning Act of 1932 was the first piece of planning legislation to have any significant effect on the preservation of historic buildings. Its opening clause, 'Scope of Planning Schemes', addressed the issue directly:

> *'A scheme may be made under this Act with respect to any land, whether there are or are not buildings thereon, with the general object of controlling the development of the land comprised in the area to which the scheme applies, of securing proper sanitary conditions, amenity and convenience, and of preserving existing buildings or other objects of architectural, historic or artistic interest and places of natural interest or beauty, and generally of protecting existing amenities whether in urban or rural portions of the area.'*[79]

Thus the County Councils could place Building Preservation Orders (BPOs) on buildings that they considered to be of special historic significance and thereby protect them against demolition or development. What constituted such a building was an issue that was tackled by the National Buildings Record (NBR), an independent body, set up in 1941 to collect photographic and other records of historic buildings at risk from enemy action across Britain. In 1963 NBR was transferred to the RCHME and a new National Monuments Record (NMR), including the NBR's massive collection of Second World War

---

79  http://www.legislation.gov.uk/ukpga/1932/48/enacted
Accessed January 2013

aerial photographs taken by the RAF, was created.

The extensive damage to certain cities bombed during the war left planners with a choice regarding whether to repair and rebuild damaged streets or to demolish the ruins and surviving structures with a view to a total redevelopment of sites. Even before the Blitz, the Modern Archaeological Research Group (MARS), a society of radical left-wing architects established in 1933, had produced a Plan for London that advocated the demolition of large parts of the city to be replaced by a futuristic assemblage of 'hubs' of houses, work premises and recreational centres, built in modern materials – glass, concrete and steel - enclosed by a ring road. In some cases urban planners seized the opportunity to revolutionise their city centres in modernistic and utilitarian ways, often at the expense of preserving the character and fabric of the old. In Bath 19000 properties were damaged or destroyed in a handful of Luftwaffe bombing raids in 1942. In the aftermath a fresh battle was fought by modernist planners and the newly formed Bath Preservation Trust in the debate regarding the city's architectural future.

In 1944 a new Town and Country Planning Act introduced the listing of buildings, a statutory obligation for local authorities from 1947. Buildings on the list were categorised by grades of 1-3 with grades 1 and 2 being subject to statutory levels of protection (1 being the highest). Since then the grades have been redefined as grades I, II and II* and all receive measures of statutory protection.

Categories of listed buildings

- *Grade I buildings are of exceptional interest, sometimes considered to be internationally important; only 2.5% of listed buildings are Grade I*
- *Grade II\* buildings are particularly important buildings of more than special interest; 5.5% of listed buildings are Grade II\**
- *Grade II buildings are nationally important and of special interest; 92% of all listed buildings are in this class and it is the most likely grade of listing for a home owner.*[80]

---

80  http://www.english-heritage.org.uk/caring/listing/listed-buildings/ Accessed January 2013

English Heritage had over 374,000 buildings in its list by 2013. Of these 15% predate 1600, 19% predate 1700, 31% predate 1800, 32% predate 1900 and just 3% are younger, virtually all dating from the period 1900-1944.

The listing initiative was another massive undertaking and it took over 20 years to complete the initial national survey was completed in 1966. The Historic Buildings and Ancient Monuments Act of 1953 introduced grants to assist with the maintenance of buildings on the list.

A new organisation, very much in the tradition of SPAB, emerged in 1975. SAVE Britain's Heritage was established 'by a group of architects, journalists and planners' as 'a strong, independent voice in conservation, free to respond rapidly to emergencies and to speak out loud for the historic environment.' Like SPAB it acts as a pressure group and one that raises public awareness and funds in its struggle against the development of such historic structures as London's late nineteenth century Smithfield General Market, considered by the organisation 'the finest parade of market buildings in Europe', culminating in an EH backed conservation victory in 2008.[81]

## Historic England

The Historic Buildings and Monuments Commission for England (subsequently 'English Heritage' and, since April 2015, 'Historic England') was created in 1984 'to secure the preservation and enhancement of the man-made heritage of England for the benefit of future generations, and to directly manage the sites and monuments taken into state care since the 1880s.' It presently has over 400 sites open to the public, 11 million visitors each year, just under 750,000 members, over 445,000 free educational visits a year, 10 million photographs, plans and surveys publicly accessible, and each year gives out around £24 million in grants each year and advises on 17,000 planning applications. Since it was formed twentieth-century listing was introduced – Jodrell Bank Observatory, the Royal Festival Hall and, later, Centre Point, both in London, and Park Hill council estate in

---

81   http://www.savebritainsheritage.org/news/campaign
Accessed January 2013
133   imagesofengland.org.uk

Sheffield are now listed. In 1998 it created the Buildings at Risk Register listing buildings that are threatened due to owners' inability to afford their maintenance. Since 2000 4,000 volunteers have photographed all the listed buildings and structures in England leading to an online digital library of 370,000 entries.[82] The Historic England on-line database with maps and detailed descriptions, the National Heritage List for England (NHLE) was launched in May 2011, providing access to up to date information on all nationally designated heritage assets.[83]

## The English Heritage Trust

This trust was set up as a new charity in April 2015. It looks after the 400+ state-owned historic sites and monuments in England and opens them to the public under licence from Historic England. Through English Heritage membership fees, entry ticket sales, and commercial enterprise, it aims to be completely self-funding by 2023.

## The Heritage Lottery Fund

The Heritage Lottery Fund (HLF) is a non-departmental public body accountable to Parliament via the Department of Culture, Media and Sport and administered by the National Heritage Memorial Fund (NHMF) which was given in 1994 'the responsibility of distributing a share of money raised through the National Lottery for Good Causes, to heritage across the UK'. In its own words:

*'The Heritage Lottery Fund (HLF) sustains and transforms a wide range of heritage through innovative investment in projects with a lasting impact on people and places. As the largest dedicated funder of the UK's heritage, with around £375 million a year to invest in new projects and a considerable body of knowledge, we are also a leading advocate for the value of heritage to modern life. From museums, parks and historic places to archaeology, natural environment and cultural traditions, we invest in every part of our heritage. Since 1994, HLF has supported over 34,000 projects allocating £5.2 billion across the UK.'*[84]

---

83 http://www.english-heritage.org.uk/ Accessed January 2013
84 http://www.hlf.org.uk/ Accessed January 2013

This initiative has massively increased the amount of public spending on the protection and maintenance of aspects of both the 'tangible' and 'intangible' national heritage. A wide range of grants are available under the following schemes:

### 'Your Heritage (£3,000 to £100,000)

*This is our general small grants programme for all types of heritage projects. It is a flexible programme particularly designed for voluntary and community groups and first-time applicants.*

### Heritage Grants (Grants of over £100,000)

*This is our open programme for grants over £100,000, for any type of project related to the national, regional, or local heritage in the UK.*

### Young Roots (£3,000 to £50,000)

*This programme is for projects led by young people. It aims to involve 11-25 year-olds in finding out about their heritage, developing skills, building confidence and promoting community involvement.*

### All Our Stories (Grants from £3,000 to £10,000)

*All Our Stories is an opportunity for everyone to get involved in their heritage. With our funding and support you could plan activities that help you explore, share and celebrate yours.*

### Townscape Heritage Initiative (£500,000 to £2,000,000)

*Townscape Heritage Initiative makes grants that help communities to regenerate Conservation Areas displaying particular social and economic need.*

### Parks for People (£100,000 to £5million)

*Parks for People is for projects related to historic parks and cemeteries in the UK.*

**Landscape Partnerships (£250,000 to £2million)**

This programme supports schemes that are led by partnerships of local, regional and national interests, which aim to conserve areas of distinctive landscape character throughout the UK.

**Skills for the Future (£100,000 to £1million)**

Skills for the Future funds projects which provide training placements to meet skills shortages in the heritage sector, and fully support trainees to learn practical skills.

**Grants for Places of Worship (£10,000 to £250,000)**

The Grants for Places of Worship programme is for projects that involve urgent structural repairs to places of worship that are at risk. As part of a repair project we can also fund work to encourage greater community use and engagement.

**Catalyst (Various)**

The Catalyst grants initiatives form part of a broader partnership initiative between HLF, DCMS and Arts Council England (ACE).[85]

The HLF is probably correct in its own claims that it does not merely protect existing 'heritage' but actually plays a key role in redefining it in the present and for the future:

'Our projects have not only revitalised hundreds of museums, parks, historic buildings, landscapes and wildlife sites, but also given new meaning to heritage itself: people from every walk of life are now involved with the heritage that inspires them, making choices about what they want to keep and share from the past, for future generations.'[86]

---

85   http://www.hlf.org.uk/HowToApply/programmes/
Accessed January 2013
86   http://www.hlf.org.uk/ourproject
Accessed January 2013

# National Amenity Societies

A number of independent societies have emerged since the late nineteenth century, all designed to preserve the artistic and architectural output of past times. In 1968 the Town and Country Planning Act necessitated the notifying of the recognised specialist groups regarding plans for the partial or complete demolition of listed buildings. These groups have come to be termed 'National Amenity Societies' and they have provided advice and guidance on planning proposals for thousands of listed buildings and registered gardens.

They meet in a Joint Committee of the Societies six times a year. In Scotland the Scottish Civic Trust and the Scottish Architectural Heritage Society are the equivalent organisations. At present there are seven National Amenity Societies:

## Ancient Monuments Society

Concerned with the study and conservation of historic buildings of all ages and types. Publishes a list of total demolition applications each year. In working partnership with the Friends of Friendless Churches which owns 34 disused but historically important places of worship in England and Wales.

## Council for British Archaeology

The CBA is concerned with historic buildings and sites of all periods and with promoting appreciation of their archaeological significance. The CBA's special focus is on Grade II buildings, on vernacular and industrial buildings, and on multi-period buildings where an informed understanding of the building's archaeological and historic interest is important.

## The Garden History Society

Promotes the protection and conservation of historic parks, gardens and designed landscapes, and advises on their restoration.

## The Georgian Group

Concerned with architecture from the late seventeenth century to the early nineteenth century but with a watching brief over earlier and later Classical buildings.

## Society for the Protection of Ancient Buildings

The oldest conservation society in the English-speaking world, founded in 1877 by William Morris and others. Concerned with pre-1700 buildings and technique and philosophy of repair. Runs National Maintenance Week.

## The Twentieth Century Society

Concerned with buildings from 1914.

## The Victorian Society

Concerned with Victorian and Edwardian buildings 1837 - 1914.[87]

## The Georgian Group

Founded in 1937, originally as a sub-group of SPAB, the Georgian Group, in its own words, 'exists to protect and preserve Georgian buildings, monuments and landscapes.' This was at a time when 'Masterpieces of eighteenth century urban architecture, such as Norfolk House in St James's Square and the Adam Brothers' Adelphi by the Thames, were being destroyed at an alarming rate, and at the whim of their owners, to make way for new developments. Outside our towns, country houses were suffering just as badly. An astonishing one in six of them – many Georgian, and many home to exquisitely-crafted interiors – were pulled down in the twentieth century.'

Among its achievements it was largely the work of the Georgian Group

---

[87] http://www.jcnas.org.uk/ Accessed January 2013

that saved magnificent buildings such as Carlton House Terrace in The Mall in London which seemed destined to be replaced by a department store. The group was also 'critical in introducing conservation areas in the 1960s and thus giving the first formal protection to groups of buildings, such as the superb Georgian terraces in London, Liverpool, Bath, Exeter and Newcastle.'

As a statutory amenity society it is consulted, by law, in regard of around 7000 planning applications in England and Wales each year. As a registered charity it is heavily reliant on its members for funds. The organisation faces many challenges: 'Outright demolitions are still among them; often we are a lone voice speaking up for unlisted buildings, even for Grade II buildings that are not high on anyone else's agenda. Alternatively, we may be faced with plans for over-intensive development in the grounds of country houses, or unsympathetic alterations to churches, or extensions that swamp the host building. Then again we may be asked to look at plans to subdivide buildings in ways that obscure, or even destroy, historic features. Besides that there is the unthinking erosion of architectural detail and, in another league again, brand new buildings that in our view diminish the special qualities of a Georgian neighbourhood.'

The Georgian Group maintains that 'Preserving our Georgian heritage is not just about short-term campaigns but about the longer-term work of educating and informing.' To this end it has a programme of education and activities committed to:

- *improving visual awareness*
- *giving children access to Georgian buildings*
- *providing conservation advice to householders*
- *running practical skills masterclasses and specialist study courses*
- *arranging visits to Georgian buildings and gardens both here and abroad*
- *curating exhibitions*
- *holding academic symposia*
- *disseminating primary research through our highly-regarded Journal*
- *publishing best practice guidance on matters ranging from*

*window repair to enabling development.*[88]

## The Victorian Society

The Victorian Society, founded in 1958, lists its aims as:

- **Conserving**: *to save Victorian and Edwardian buildings or groups of buildings of special architectural merit from needless destruction or disfigurement.*

- **Involving**: *to awaken public interest in, and appreciation of, the best of Victorian and Edwardian arts, architecture, crafts and design;*

- **Educating**: *to encourage the study of these and of related social history and to provide advice to owners and public authorities in regard to the preservation and repair of Victorian and Edwardian buildings and the uses to which they can, if necessary, be adapted*[89]

The society has helped save many national monuments including the Albert Memorial in London and the Albert Dock in Liverpool. More often it is concerned with 'local churches threatened with closure or good houses flattened to make way for undistinguished offices.' Its work is guided by the principle that 'Victorian and Edwardian buildings are part of our collective memory, and central to how we see ourselves as individuals, communities and as a nation.'

The history of the Victorian Society was summarised by Dr William Filmer-Snakey in a short paper in its magazine, *The Victorian*, in 1998:

'The catalyst for the foundation of the Victorian Society was Anne, Lady Rosse, the granddaughter of Edward Linley Sambourne, who had inherited the remarkably-preserved family house at 18 Stafford Terrace, Kensington, after the death of her bachelor brother Roy in 1946. On Guy Fawkes Night in 1957 she summoned a group of 32 of

---

[88] http://www.georgiangroup.org.uk Accessed April 2013
[89] http://www.victoriansociety.org.uk/ Accessed April 2013

her friends, who included John Betjeman and Nikolaus Pevsner, to consider the possibility of founding a Society for the preservation and appreciation of Victorian architecture and the arts. No doubt encouraged by the cocktails of legendary strength mixed by her butler, it was agreed that a Society should be founded, and the deed was done at a second meeting at 18 Stafford Terrace on 24 February 1958. From the start it was agreed that, despite the chosen name, the Society would also have within its remit the Edwardian period, up to the outbreak of the First World War. John Betjeman became the first secretary.

The founding of the Society took place against the background of an almost universal dislike of Victorian things, and the widespread destruction of Victorian buildings as the post war reconstruction continued apace. Threats to two particularly important buildings provided the Society with early battlegrounds. The first was Euston Station and the famous Arch that stood in front of it. The second was JB Bunning's wonderful Coal Exchange in the City of London. In both cases the battle was lost, but only after long struggles which increasingly attracted not just public attention but also public support for the fledgling Society.

It is for these campaigns that the early years are best remembered, but the Society's early members were always interested in much more than just the big buildings. Right from the start they championed those normal nineteenth-century buildings which, although not necessarily great architecture in themselves, nevertheless gave character and attractiveness to the surrounding area. John Betjeman's famous enthusiasm for suburbia found practical expression in the Battle for Bedford Park. By the early 1960s Jonathon Carr's groundbreaking planned suburb of the 1870s and 80s, with its houses by Norman Shaw, was a run-down area of bedsits, threatened with demolition and piecemeal redevelopment. One of the Society's earliest successes came when Tom Greeves, having enlisted Betjeman's support, finally managed to persuade the Ministry of Housing to list 356 houses in the area. This prevented further demolitions and laid the foundations for its revival: these days it is west London's most desirable suburb (and the home of the Victorian Society!).

Right from the start, the Society strove to avoid over-emphasis on London. Throughout the UK, the great Victorian cities were under perhaps even greater threat than the capital. Predating the current political trend for regionalisation by some forty years, Regional Groups were set up, initially in Liverpool and Manchester, to carry out casework and mount their own campaigns; we now have eight such groups, giving the Society its distinctive federal character.

After the initial failures at Euston and elsewhere, the tide gradually began to turn in our favour. When British Rail wanted to knock down St Pancras Station in 1966, the station was instead listed at Grade I. In Liverpool the Albert Dock was saved and converted.

The Jewellery Quarter in Birmingham was made a Conservation Area in 1981. As the shortcomings of the brave new planning of the 1960s became all too apparent, people began to regret the loss of the terraced streets and of the communities that had lived in them. Victorian art event became part of the 1960s with Biba taking up Art Nouveau designs and Oz magazine finding inspiration in the work of Beardsley.

As the Society's message got through and its influence grew, so the Society changed. In the first place its membership grew from an initial 28, to 1824 in 1970 and 3200 in 1980. The work of the Secretary quickly became too great for a volunteer and the post was made salaried. Casework similarly soon required the employment of the professional officer, initially one for the whole country, then a second for the north and now with a third to concentrate on churches. The Society also began to be taken seriously by the government. In 1964 it presented the Minister of Transport with a list of 60 railway stations worthy of protection. In 1969, following the passing of the Town and Country Planning Act, it was given a legal role in the listed building consent system when the Secretary of State directed that all applications involving demolition should be refereed to the Society for comment. In 1973 this role was partly supported by a grant from government funds.'

## The Council for British Archaeology (CBA)

The Council was founded in 1944 for the 'safeguarding of all kinds of archaeological material and the strengthening of existing measures for the care of ancient and historic buildings, monuments, and antiquities' and to improve public education about archaeology.'[90]

The CBA's mission was clarified in its Strategic Objectives document for 2010-2015:[91]

### CBA Strategic Objectives 2010-15

'Our vision is Archaeology for all: by 2020 everyone will know how they can enjoy, understand and care for the historic environment – and why it matters.

### Making Archaeology Matter

At the Council for British Archaeology we believe passionately that what archaeology can do is fundamental to society. We are dedicated to Making Archaeology Matter.

Archaeology matters, because most of human history has no written record, only physical remains.

Archaeology matters, because appreciating this legacy contributes to our sense of who we are in our communities and as a nation.

Archaeology matters, because it benefits the economy through tourism and heritage-related regeneration.
And archaeology matters, because it enriches our lives: millions of people enjoy discovering the past. Archaeology is exciting and fun.

### Scope

The practice of archaeology is now stretched to maintain its

---

[90] new.archaeologyuk.org Accessed April 2013
[91] An updated version for 2016 has not yet appeared at the CBA website.

achievements as never before – in responding to development, in universities, museums and in local and national government. Yet public interest in archaeology has never been stronger. And historic remains continue to need care and reveal new stories.

With a large public membership and an unrivalled network of national and regional groups across the UK, the CBA is the one organisation that can enable people to protect and celebrate their archaeological heritage.

**Strategic aims**

Over the next five years we plan to double our membership and strengthen our role as archaeology's public champion. We are an environmental charity whose only allegiances are to archaeology and the public.

**Strategic Plan 2010–15**

Our Strategic Plan 2010–15 presents themes and objectives to take us towards 2020 – Archaeology for all.

**Themes**

1) Participate (support people)
2) Discover (support knowledge)
3) Advocate (support stewardship)
4) Sustain (support resources)

**Objectives**

Increase participation

1) Support innovative projects to enable wider public participation in discovering and protecting the UK's historic environment
2) Increase the number of people with skills to work with volunteers and young people, to facilitate their active engagement in archaeology
3) Broaden the opportunities for both young and older people

to build archaeological skills and make their contribution
4) Develop the Festival of British Archaeology to inspire and increase public participation in archaeology
5) Identify and break down barriers to joining archaeology

Enhance discovery

1) Initiate an online Hub of Archaeological Learning as a one-stop shop for educational resources and a network for learning
2) Broaden the range of the CBA's publications to provide high quality, accessible material of interest to public and professional audiences
3) Expand the range of high quality content in CBA's British Archaeology magazine to reach out to a broader audience
4) Develop and enhance the benefits and resources available to Young Archaeologists' Club members
5) Extend user involvement with the CBA's web-based resources

Strengthen advocacy

1) Raise awareness at all levels of the public benefits of engaging with archaeology and the historic environment
2) Champion community archaeology and public engagement across the UK
3) Facilitate and empower more local involvement in protecting the historic environment
4) Develop a distinctive new role in the national heritage protection systems in England and in Wales to reflect the CBA's core mission
5) Build capacity amongst our members and UK-wide partners to champion and engage with the historic environment through events, training, and online resources

Develop sustainability

1) Campaign for action to ensure sustainability for the historic environment and to combat the effects of climate change

2) Launch and sustain a Development Campaign to secure the long-term future of the CBA's charitable activities
3) Expand CBA and YAC membership by at least doubling our numbers by 2015
4) Expand our financial reserves to cover at least three months trading costs
5) Work with the CBA's UK network to enhance our collective capacity and the benefit we offer, whilst raising the public profile for the CBA's achievements'

## World Heritage Sites

In 1954 the decision of the Egyptian government to go ahead with plans to build the colossal Aswan Dam threatened the immediate destruction of ancient monuments including the Abu Simbel temple sites. These and other structures were saved from complete destruction by funds raised from 50 countries by UNESCO (United Nations Educational, Scientific and Cultural Organization) that enabled there dismantling and reconstruction elsewhere. This initiative gave rise to the creation of World Heritage Committee, subscribing to the set of principles defined by the Convention Concerning the Protection of the World Cultural and Natural Heritage in 1972.

The World Heritage mission is to:

- encourage countries to sign the World Heritage Convention and to ensure the protection of their natural and cultural heritage;
- encourage States Parties to the Convention to nominate sites within their national territory for inclusion on the World Heritage List;
- encourage States Parties to establish management plans and set up reporting systems on the state of conservation of their World Heritage sites;
- help States Parties safeguard World Heritage properties by providing technical assistance and professional training;
- provide emergency assistance for World Heritage sites in

immediate danger;
- support States Parties' public awareness-building activities for World Heritage conservation;
- encourage participation of the local population in the preservation of their cultural and natural heritage;
- encourage international cooperation in the conservation of our world's cultural and natural heritage.[92]

Sites nominated by signatory states that meet certain criteria are added to the World Heritage Site list at the discretion of the committee and its associated panels:

'The Committee considers a property as having outstanding universal value [...] if the property meets one or more of the following criteria. Nominated properties shall therefore:

1) represent a masterpiece of human creative genius;
2) exhibit an important interchange of human values, over a span of time or within a cultural area of the world, on developments in architecture or technology, monumental arts, town-planning or landscape design;
3) bear a unique or at least exceptional testimony to a cultural tradition or to a civilization which is living or which has disappeared;
4) be an outstanding example of a type of building, architectural or technological ensemble or landscape which illustrates (a) significant stage(s) in human history;
5) be an outstanding example of a traditional human settlement, land-use, or sea-use which is representative of a culture (or cultures), or human interaction with the environment especially when it has become vulnerable under the impact of irreversible change;
6) be directly or tangibly associated with events or living traditions, with ideas, or with beliefs, with artistic and literary works of outstanding universal significance. (The Committee considers that this criterion should preferably be used in conjunction with other criteria);

---

92  http://whc.unesco.org/en/about/ Accessed January 2013

7) contain superlative natural phenomena or areas of exceptional natural beauty and aesthetic importance;
8) be outstanding examples representing major stages of earth's history, including the record of life, significant on-going geological processes in the development of landforms, or significant geomorphic or physiographic features;
9) be outstanding examples representing significant on- going ecological and biological processes in the evolution and development of terrestrial, fresh water, coastal and marine ecosystems and communities of plants and animals;
10) contain the most important and significant natural habitats for in-situ conservation of biological diversity, including those containing threatened species of outstanding universal value from the point of view of science or conservation.'[93]

Sites on the list are defined as either 'cultural heritage sites' or 'natural heritage' sites. These conform to the following definitions:

'For the purposes of this Convention, the following shall be considered as "cultural heritage"; - monuments: architectural works, works of monumental sculpture and painting, elements or structures of an archaeological nature, inscriptions, cave dwellings and combinations of features, which are of outstanding universal value from the point of view of history, art or science; - groups of buildings: groups of separate or connected buildings which, because of their architecture, their homogeneity or their place in the landscape, are of outstanding universal value from the point of view of history, art or science; - sites: works of man or the combined works of nature and of man, and areas including archaeological sites which are of outstanding universal value from the historical, aesthetic, ethnological or anthropological points of view.

For the purposes of this Convention, the following shall be considered as "natural heritage": natural features consisting of physical and biological formations or groups of such formations, which are of outstanding universal value from the aesthetic or

---

[93] Operational Guidelines for the Implementation of the World Heritage Convention (2008) pp. 20-21

scientific point of view; geological and physiographical formations and precisely delineated areas which constitute the habitat of threatened species of animals and plants of outstanding universal value from the point of view of science or conservation; - natural sites or precisely delineated natural areas of outstanding universal value from the point of view of science, conservation or natural beauty.'[94]

By the end of 2012 962 properties in 157 of the 190 states that had ratified the World Heritage Convention were listed as World Heritage sites. Of these 745 were cultural, 188 were natural, and 29 were mixed properties.

## The Heritage Alliance

The Heritage Alliance represents over ninety-five non-governmental and voluntary organisations working in the heritage sector. It proclaims itself 'The voice of the independent heritage movement in England'. Originally called 'Heritage Link' it was established in 2002. In its *Heritage Alliance Manifesto 2014-15* it defined England's heritage as one of the country's greatest national assets as 'a source of national pride' and 'the envy of the world'. As 'an engine of economic growth', England's heritage 'is already at the heart of planning for a sustainable future', creating wealth and jobs and boosting 'the identity of places'. It exists in part to work against 'the continuing destruction of ancient monuments'. The Alliance outlined four proposals for the consideration of all political parties:

- Create a positive tax regime for maintenance and conservation
- Put heritage at the heart of sustainable development
- Attract more investment into heritage
- Secure the protection of our heritage

## The Heritage Trust

Founded 2011 the mission of the Heritage Trust is 'to promote

---

94 Operational Guidelines for the Implementation of the World Heritage Convention (2008) p. 13

knowledge, understanding and the preservation of aspects of world art, culture, traditions and sites of historical importance that are under threat from damage, neglect, development, vandalism, theft or natural disasters.'

In 'Preserving the Past for the Future' it aims to create collaborative and active global research networks, disseminate the results of its own work and the work of others, and advance educational activities and publications.

One interesting initiative is its 'Cared for Rating' of sites and properties. This accreditation scheme awards a site a maximum of five stars for how well the site is cared for. This includes such things as parking facilities, wheelchair access, signage, rest areas, and general maintenance.[95]

## The Heritage Industry

By the end of the Twentieth Century the mass involvement of people in heritage, and its commercial role, not least as a key element in the UK's booming leisure and tourism industry, had led to the recognition that the management of our heritage is an 'industry' in its own right. Public funding, which necessitates 'selling' the heritage product (the excavation, the museum, the visitor centre, the TV documentary etc.) as effectively as possible, keeps the practitioners in their posts! The popularisation of heritage in the interests of this industry is all about increased accessibility and the education of the general public. These are the primary objectives of most heritage 'providers' – museum managers, custodians of monuments and so on. Ultimately, their aim is to capture the attention and interest of the public, to 'entertain' in the broadest sense of the word. This of course troubles many of those engaged in heritage, particularly those who are more concerned with the research end of heritage rather than its popularisation: commercial interests can go hand-in-hand with the 'dumbing down' of the information and, at worst, an imagined version of the past that suits popular tastes but is not an accurate portrayal. The term 'disneyfication' has been coined for the worst examples of the phenomenon. Numerous heritage centres in the UK are more or less

---

[95]

successful in striking the right balance; the pioneering Jorvik Centre, revealing through reconstruction the history of Viking York and the archaeological works that discovered it, has thrilled, intrigued and informed millions of visitors since its opening in the early 1980s.

The five main areas of employment for heritage experts are:

- National agencies and organisations such as English Heritage, the National Trust, the Council for British Archaeology
- Local authorities
- Archaeological field units and other types of contractor; amenity groups
- Museums and historic sites
- Colleges and universities

Although heritage tourism is big business, many heritage practitioners are comparatively poorly paid. Don Henson has warned budding archaeologists that: 'It is important to realise that archaeology is not well paid. In 2008, the average professional full time archaeologist was paid a salary of £23,310 while the national UK average salary was £29,999. The lowest quarter earned less than £16,500 and the highest quarter more than £28,000.' [96]

Many of those working in heritage, some at an expert level, do so for very little remuneration or for nothing at all. The sector has a vastly higher proportion of volunteers than most others in the modern British economy.

## Intangible cultural heritage (Marja Haas)

*In this fascinating essay[97] a Level 6 History, Heritage and Archaeology student, Marja Haas, considers the extent to which intangible heritage is preserved in modern contexts. Her focus is on initiatives taken in Scotland. She begins with the UNESCO definition for 'intangible cultural heritage'.*

---

[145] Henson (2012), p.44
[97] Marja Haas, submission for *History, Heritage and Archaeology* Module SHHA 302, Strode College in partnership with Plymouth University, 2015-2016.

For the purposes of this discussion, preservation will be considered as synonymous with 'safeguarding' as used by UNESCO,[98] in order to avoid confusion. In addition, the definition of intangible heritage will be that termed Intangible Cultural Heritage (ICH) by UNESCO and is deemed to include 'traditions or living expressions inherited from our ancestors and passed on to our descendants, such as oral traditions, performing arts, social practices, rituals, festive events, knowledge and practices concerning nature and the universe or the knowledge and skills to produce traditional crafts.[99] ICH can simply be described as the customs and traditions that identify or contribute to the unique character of any given community and applies equally on a local, regional and national level. However, ICH does not usually apply multi-nationally and in this respect it can be seen as those practices which are the opposite of globalisation which, together with intolerance, pose threats to ICH which may result in the destruction and disappearance of ICH.[100] As will be illustrated by this discussion, there are a number of practices that are in active use in the UK including (but not necessarily limited to) preservation by record and safeguarding by education and/or funding. However, safeguarding ICH is not a simple task and is faced by a number of challenges including those of distortion and suppression, which will be discussed to present a balanced discussion.

Preservation by record, as evidenced by examples such as oral history and film, is a widespread practice that many are familiar with. In recent years there has been a marked increase in the interest in and practice of creating sound recordings (and associated transcriptions) of memories by interview and this methodology is supported by both The Oral History Society[101] (OHS) and the Heritage Lottery Fund[102]

---

[98] 2003 saw the advent of the UNESCO Convention for Safeguarding Intangible Cultural Heritage. See 'Intangible Cultural Heritage' UNESCO, http://www.unesco.org/culture/ich/, accessed on 20/01/2016, for more details regarding the aims and methodologies that are advocated by this organisation.
[99] 'What is Intangible Cultural Heritage', UNESCO, http://www.unesco.org/culture/ich/en/what-is-intangible-heritage-00003, accessed on 20/01/2016.
[100] 'Text of the Convention for the Safeguarding of the Intangible Cultural Heritage' UNESCO, http://www.unesco.org/culture/ich/en/convention, accessed on 31/01/2016.
[101] For details of this organisation see 'The Oral History Society', http://www.ohs.org.uk/, accessed on 29/01/2016.
[102] The Heritage Lottery Fund, https://www.hlf.org.uk/our-projects, accessed on

(HLF). With its own journal,[103] the OHS (formed in 1970 thus predating the UNESCO convention[104]) is the arbiter of good practice in the UK and provides those wishing to engage in recording oral histories with a 'one stop shop' in terms of advice and training. Photography (whether still images or video recordings) is another significant method of preservation by recording. A combination of these techniques, as well as the reading aloud of letters and diaries, was used extensively to record and share the experiences and memories of those involved in World War I, resulting in a rich archive of television and radio programmes,[105] as well as adding to the National Archives where many of these recollections will be kept for posterity. More typically, this type of safeguarding is practiced on a much smaller scale, in the context of minority communities, and has its own peculiar challenges. As discussed by Cosson, the question of ownership sometimes creates an unwillingness to share community or cultural memories with 'outsiders'[106] due to the element of self-identification that is inherent within the elements of ICH and which open ICH up to subjective evaluation.[107]

Subjective evaluation of ICH can be seen in many contexts and where a society as a whole (perhaps national) does not deem a practice suitable for safeguarding it may be legislated against or supressed in other ways. Fox hunting has been legislated against in England and Wales;[108] bullfighting is the subject of ongoing debates and campaigns aimed at outlawing and discontinuing the practice;[109] wearing certain clothes may be discouraged (as illustrated by the BBC

---

29/01/2016.
[103] The Oral History Society Journal.
[104] UNESCO Convention for Safeguarding Intangible Cultural Heritage.
[105] An example of this is the 'Soldiers' Stories Audio Gallery', BBC History, http://www.bbc.co.uk/history/worldwars/wwone/soldiers_stories_gallery.shtml, accessed on 29/01/2016.
[106] Fiona Cosson, 'Voice of the Community? Reflections on accessing, working with and representing Communities', Oral History, Vol. 38, No. 2, Autumn 2010, p. 98.
[107] Federico Lenzerini, 'Intangible Cultural Heritage: The Living Culture of Peoples', The European Journal of International Law, 22, 1, 2011, p.108, accessed online via Primo on 21/01/2016.
[108] 'The Hunting Act 2004', http://www.legislation.gov.uk/ukpga/2004/37/contents, accessed on 29/01/2016.
[109] 'Stop Bullfighting', http://www.stopbullfighting.org.uk/index.htm, accessed on 29/01/2016.

news report of 26th January 2016 that 'Ofsted chief Sir Michael Wilshaw has told inspectors in England they can fail schools for allowing face veils');[110] and at the extreme end of the spectrum, there is the tireless fight by human rights groups to ban arranged marriages as well as the practice of female genital mutilation.[111] From these examples, it is easy to draw the conclusion that practices which do not fit our national or international political agenda or moral view will meet with active opposition despite the ICH having a legitimate (?) place in the 'owning' culture. By contrast, where ICH is valued, funding is available to assist in the safeguarding.

The HLF provides many ICH projects with funding to assist in their aims of preservation. In Somerset, the Carnivals in Somerset Promotion Project (CISPP) received funding from the HLF in 2010.[112] The aims of the CISPP include 'promote the historical and contemporary importance of the unique West Country illuminated carnivals' and 'develop partnerships with interested groups to ensure the future of West Country illuminated carnivals'[113] which are both in keeping with the broad aims inherent in the UNESCO Convention. However, and perhaps problematically, 'stimulate tourism through West Country illuminated carnivals' is also listed.

Heritage tourism and the associated selling of the heritage 'product' has become big business the world over[114] and the safeguarding of ICH in festival form can be particularly problematic when the festival is designated a tourist attraction. When we examine the CISPP

---

[110] 'Ofsted can downgrade schools for Islamic veils', BBC News, http://www.bbc.co.uk/news/education-35411518, accessed on 29/01/2016.
[111] Some of the organisations are Equality Now, http://www.equalitynow.org, Forward UK, http://forwarduk.org.uk and Plan UK, http://www.plan-uk.org/because-i-am-a-girl/female-genital-mutilation-fgm/, all accessed on 29/01/2016.
[112] 'Heritage Lottery Fund bid success for CISPP', Heritage Lottery Fund, https://www.hlf.org.uk/about-us/media-centre/press-releases/heritage-lottery-fund-bid-success-cispp, accessed on 31/01/2016.
[113] For the complete list of aims see Carnivals in Somerset Promotion Project, 'Aims', http://cispp.org.uk/cisppaims.html, accessed on 29/01/2016.
[114] Richard Prentice, 'Heritage: A key sector in the 'new' tourism', in *Heritage, Museums and Galleries,* ed. by Gerard Cozane, (Routledge; 2005), p.247. For more discussions on heritage tourism see Brian Graham, G.J. Ashworth, J.E. Tunbridge, *A Geography of Heritage: Power, Culture & Economy,* (Arnold, 2000); Dallen J. Timothy, *Cultural Heritage and Tourism: An Introduction,* (Channel View Publications; 2011).

example this is not particularly apparent but we must ask, if the carnivals have evolved to their current incarnation over a period of 400 years[115] will they continue to evolve or has the act of safeguarding through this project resulted in a tradition that will now remain static for the sake of onlookers and no longer represent the evolving ICH? This negative transformational potential can also be seen in the 'Up-Helly-Aa' festivals in Shetland.[116] The largest of these, held in Lerwick, is rooted in the cultural heritage of the island but is now as much an 'outward-facing tourist event' as it is a local one. While exact visitor numbers are not available, the permanent 'Up-Helly-Aa' exhibition attracted 12,000 visitors in 2005 which is hugely significant for an island whose population is approximately 22,000.[117] The obvious economic impact of these numbers may result in freezing the festival in its current form rather than enabling the continual evolution of the tradition due to the consumer value system superseding those of the community, thus changing the ICH from the representative living tradition of the community to an historical curiosity performed for the benefit of the on-lookers.[118] Daher points out that tourism is known to have caused the breakdown of social and economic structures as well as social disintegration of family values, particularly in third world countries.[119]

---

[115] 'Failed gunpowder plot sparks carnival history', BBC, http://www.bbc.co.uk/somerset/content/articles/2007/11/08/carnival_history_feature.shtml, accessed on 31/01/2016.
[116] Alison McCleery, Alistair McCleery, Linda Gunn & David Hill, 'Scoping and Mapping Intangible Cultural Heritage in Scotland, Final Report', (Napier University Centre for Cultural and Creative Studies in association with Museums and Galleries Scotland; 2008), pp.17-19, http://www.museumsgalleriesscotland.org.uk/research-and-resources/resources/publications/publication/71/scoping-and-mapping-intangible-cultural-heritage-in-scotland-final-report, accessed on 21/01/2016.
[117] Shetland.org, http://www.shetland.org/plan/areas/lerwick, accessed on 31/01/2016.
[118] Nuzi Izzati Mohd Rodzi, Saniah Ahmad Zaki & Syed Mohd Hassan Syed Subli, 'Between Tourism and Intangible Cultural Heritage', *Social and Behavioural Sciences*, 85, 2013, pp.411-420, accessed on 21/01/2016.
[119] Rami Farouk Daher, 'Dismantling a community's heritage: 'heritage tourism: Conflict, inequality, and a search for social justice in the age of globalisation'', in *Reflections on International Tourism: Tourism and Heritage Relationships: Global, National and Local Perspectives*, ed. by Mike Robinson, Nigel Evans, Philip Long, Richard Sharpley & John Swarbrooke, (University of Northumbria at Newcastle & Sheffield Hallam University; 2000), pp.105-128.

Of course consumers in the guise of heritage tourists and their ability to spend money should not be viewed in an entirely negative light. In Lancashire, the legacy of the Pendle Witches has been actively promoted and commodified by the tourist board. This has made a significant contribution to the social and economic regeneration of the region with the notorious 17<sup>th</sup> century witch trials being exploited in the marketing of attractions including 'bewitching short breaks', 'witch trails' and the Pendle Visitor centre.[120]

When tourism is removed from the equation and community values remain the focus the results may be quite different. One doesn't have to look very far to discover annual traditions such as May Day celebrations, folk music clubs or traditional dancing classes and groups. There are also many examples of traditional manufacturing methods still in use such as those used to produce Harris Tweed. Although the UK government has not ratified the Convention this has not thwarted the collective will to safeguard ICH with some arguing that there is no need to adopt the Convention as 'it duplicated efforts that the UK was already undertaking ... '.[121] When one considers that funding is available through initiatives such as the HLF and that many traditions and traditional practices are encouraged throughout the country, it seems that there is validity in this viewpoint. Counter to the English and official British approach, Scotland has adopted many of the recommendations of the Convention.

ICH is actively promoted by the Scottish government with initiatives such as the Gaelic Language Plan[122] which has resulted in bilingual road signs[123] and Gaelic being taught in schools where the language is viewed as both an integral part of the community heritage and where it is deemed to be under threat. The education system in Scotland has been noted as a 'potential and actual mechanism for transmitting

---

[120] Visit Lancashire, http://www.visitlancashire.com/inspire-me/pendle-witches, accessed on 05/02/2016.
[121] Attributed to English Heritage in McCleery et al, 'Scoping and Mapping Intangible Cultural Heritage in Scotland, Final Report', p.46.
[122] 'Gaelic Language Plan, 2010', The Scottish Government, http://www.gov.scot/Publications/2010/07/06161418/0, accessed on 30/01/2016.
[123] 'Road Signage in Scotland', Transport Scotland, http://www.transportscotland.gov.uk/research/road-signage-scotland-5542, accessed on 30/01/2016.

knowledge about many aspects of intangible Scottish culture"[124] and the efficacy of this approach is demonstrated by examples such as the Highland Council's Travellers' Tales project[125] as well as the teaching of Scottish dancing in schools which contributes to the ongoing popularity of Ceilidhs.[126] Scotland's government backed approach to safeguarding ICH can be viewed as exemplary and it seems to be their aim to become a true leader in the field, with an extensive catalogue of ICH in Scotland held on the ICH 'Wiki'.[127] However if one looks a little closer, other factors present themselves which must be considered.

As we have already seen in the example presented by Cosson,[128] there is an element of self-identification inherent in ICH and it is the presence of self-identification which makes ICH valuable. The subjective view of the practitioners who recognise the ICH as an integral and essential part of their identity ensures the ongoing efforts to safeguard the ICH even if it is viewed as unimportant or worthless by external observers.[129] But it is also this element of self-identification that facilitates the distortion of ICH for political ends. Scotland provides a clear illustration of how ICH can be leveraged to support the political agenda. Following the Scottish National Party (SNP) gaining a majority in the Scottish Parliament in 2007,[130] the Museums and Galleries report[131] was promptly commissioned and

---

[124] McCleery et al, 'Scoping and Mapping Intangible Cultural Heritage in Scotland, Final Report', pp.35-36.
[125] McCleery et al, 'Scoping and Mapping Intangible Cultural Heritage in Scotland, Final Report', p.36.
[126] There are many Ceilidh events held throughout Scotland on a weekly basis. A quick internet search reveals hundreds of clubs and bands throughout the country. Visit Scotland also features ceilidhs throughout Scotland, http://www.visitscotland.com/about/arts-culture/uniquely-scottish/ceilidhs, accessed on 06/02/2016.
[127] ICH Scotland Wiki, http://ichscotland.org/, accessed on 04/02/2016.
[128] Cosson, 'Voice of the Community? Reflections on accessing, working with and representing Communities', pp.95-101.
[129] Federico Lenzerini, 'Intangible Cultural Heritage: The Living Culture of Peoples', The European Journal of International Law, 22, 1, 2011, pp.101-120, accessed online via Primo on 21/01/2016.
[130] Scottish National Party, http://www.snp.org/our_party, accessed on 04/02/2016.
[131] McCleery et al, 'Scoping and Mapping Intangible Cultural Heritage in

published in 2008. Although one cannot say definitively that the Scottish Parliamentary motivation for safeguarding ICH is political, the nationalist agenda can only be well served by fostering a sense of common identity. As demonstrated by the 2015 referendum on Scottish independence, there can be no doubt that a large number of Scots regard themselves as apart from the English in terms of culture but it is unclear whether so many would have considered themselves as 'other' if the government weren't actively promoting the message. There is perhaps a correlation between the SNP's use of ICH to support the nationalist agenda and the separatist politics of Catalonia which, in 2009, held the largest number of cultural festivals in Spain, accounting for the highest proportion of festivals at 18.2%.[132] The corollary of safeguarding ICH to support and foster national identity is arguably the loss of national or community identity and an increase in globalisation.

The conclusions that can be drawn from this discussion, based on the case studies presented, highlight that

*The paradigm of intangible cultural heritage is not the result of scientific research and debate; rather, it emerges from a complex process of political negotiations in which issues of development and globalization play out against normative and often contradictory notions of culture, diversity, human rights, and equality of nations.*[133]

Politically, ICH is susceptible to both suppression and distortion while economic factors open the door to commodification and the potential to transform ICH from community expression of cultural identity to performance staged for the benefit of the tourist

---

Scotland, Final Report'.
[132] Maria José Del Barrio, Maria Devesa & Luis César Herrero, 'Evaluating intangible cultural heritage: The case of cultural festivals', *City, Culture and Society*, 3, 2012, p.238, accessed online via Primo on 21/01/2016. The possible correlation with Scotland is based on my own knowledge of Catalonia's separatist politics.
[133] Walter Leimgruber, 'Switzerland and the UNESCO Convention on Intangible Cultural Heritage', *Journal of Folklore Research*, 47, 1/2, 2010, pp.164-165, accessed online via Primo on 21/01/2016.

audience. However, these challenges have not diminished the desire to safeguard ICH. Certainly in the modern British context our appetite and enthusiasm for the preservation of traditions and traditional values continues to encourage and promote many practices that may otherwise fade away. ICH has been (and will continue to be) preserved and safeguarded in modern contexts to a great extent where it can be accommodated within the parameters of our national morality and value system. The success of this preservation is less clear cut as the impact of commodification and political factors will only become apparent over time but if we measure success as the continued involvement of the community and the transmission of the heritage from generation to generation it is apparent that, in the examples of preservation by recording and the ongoing enjoyment of community activities such as the Scottish Ceilidh, preservation has been achieved with a large degree of success.

**Bibliography**

Cosson, Fiona, 'Voice of the Community? Reflections on accessing, working with and representing Communities', *Oral History*, Vol. 38, No. 2, Autumn 2010, pp.95-101.
Daher, Rami Farouk, 'Dismantling a community's heritage: 'heritage tourism: Conflict, inequality, and a search for social justice in the age of globalisation'', in *Reflections on International Tourism: Tourism and Heritage Relationships: Global, National and Local Perspectives*, ed. by Mike Robinson, Nigel Evans, Philip Long, Richard Sharpley & John Swarbrooke, (University of Northumbria at Newcastle & Sheffield Hallam University; 2000), pp.105-128.
Del Barrio, Maria José, Devesa, Maria & Herrero, Luis César, 'Evaluating intangible cultural heritage: The case of cultural festivals', *City, Culture and Society*, 3, 2012, pp.235-244, accessed online via Primo on 21/01/2016.
Graham, Brian, Ashworth, G.J., Tunbridge, J.E., *A Geography of Heritage: Power, Culture & Economy*, (Arnold, 2000).
Leimgruber, Walter, 'Switzerland and the UNESCO Convention on Intangible Cultural Heritage', *Journal of Folklore Research*, 47, 1/2, 2010, pp.161-196, accessed online via Primo on 21/01/2016.
Lenzerini, Federico, 'Intangible Cultural Heritage: The Living Culture of Peoples', *The European Journal of International Law*, 22, 1, 2011, pp.101-120, accessed online via Primo on 21/01/2016.
McCleery, Alison, McCleery, Alistair, Gunn, Linda & Hill, David, 'Scoping and Mapping Intangible Cultural Heritage in Scotland, Final Report', (Napier University Centre for Cultural and Creative Studies in association with

Museums Galleries Scotland; 2008), http://www.museumsgalleriesscotland.org.uk/research-and-resources/resources/publications/publication/71/scoping-and-mapping-intangible-cultural-heritage-in-scotland-final-report, accessed on 21/01/2016.
Prentice, Richard, 'Heritage: A key sector in the 'new' tourism', in *Heritage, Museums and Galleries*, ed. by Gerard Cozane, (Routledge; 2005), pp.243-256.
Rodzi, Nuzi Izzati Mohd, Zaki, Saniah Ahmad & Subli, Syed Mohd Hassan Syed, 'Between Tourism and Intangible Cultural Heritage', *Social and Behavioural Sciences*, 85, 2013, pp.411-420, accessed online via Primo on 21/01/2016.
Timothy, Dallen. J., *Cultural Heritage and Tourism: An Introduction*, (Channel View Publications; 2011).
'Failed gunpowder plot sparks carnival history', BBC, http://www.bbc.co.uk/somerset/content/articles/2007/11/08/carnival_history_feature.shtml, accessed on 31/01/2016.
'Soldiers' Stories Audio Gallery', BBC History, http://www.bbc.co.uk/history/worldwars/wwone/soldiers_stories_gallery.shtml, accessed on 29/01/2016.
'Ofsted can downgrade schools for Islamic veils', BBC News, http://www.bbc.co.uk/news/education-35411518, accessed on 29/01/2016.
Carnivals in Somerset Promotion Project, 'Aims', http://cispp.org.uk/cisppaims.html, accessed on 29/01/2016.
'Heritage Lottery Fund bid success for CISPP', Heritage Lottery Fund, https://www.hlf.org.uk/about-us/media-centre/press-releases/heritage-lottery-fund-bid-success-cispp, accessed on 31/01/2016.
'Gaelic Language Plan, 2010', The Scottish Government, http://www.gov.scot/Publications/2010/07/06161418/0, accessed on 30/01/2016.
'The Hunting Act 2004', http://www.legislation.gov.uk/ukpga/2004/37/contents, accessed on 29/01/2016.
'Stop Bullfighting', http://www.stopbullfighting.org.uk/index.htm, accessed on 29/01/2016.
'Road Signage in Scotland', Transport Scotland, http://www.transportscotland.gov.uk/research/road-signage-scotland-5542, accessed on 30/01/2016.
'Intangible Cultural Heritage' UNESCO, http://www.unesco.org/culture/ich/, accessed on 20/01/2016.
'Text of the Convention for the Safeguarding of the Intangible Cultural Heritage' UNESCO, http://www.unesco.org/culture/ich/en/convention, accessed on 31/01/2016.
'What is Intangible Cultural Heritage', UNESCO, http://www.unesco.org/culture/ich/en/what-is-intangible-heritage-00003, accessed on 20/01/2016.

Equality Now, http://www.equalitynow.org, accessed on 29/01/2016.
Forward UK, http://forwarduk.org.uk, accessed on 29/01/2016.
The Heritage Lottery Fund, https://www.hlf.org.uk/our-projects, accessed on 29/01/2016.
ICH Scotland Wiki, http://ichscotland.org/ , accessed on 04/02/2016.
The Oral History Society, http://www.ohs.org.uk/, accessed on 29/01/2016.
Plan UK, http://www.plan-uk.org/because-i-am-a-girl/female-genital-mutilation-fgm/, accessed on 29/01/2016.
Shetland.org, http://www.shetland.org/plan/areas/lerwick, accessed on 31/01/2016.
Scottish National Party, http://www.snp.org/our_party, accessed on 04/02/2016.
Visit Lancashire, http://www.visitlancashire.com/inspire-me/pendle-witches, accessed on 05/02/2016.
Visit Scotland, http://www.visitscotland.com/about/arts-culture/uniquely-scottish/ceilidhs, accessed on 06/02/2016.

# 4 Heritage and its interpretation

## Museology

Museology – the study of museums – is derived from the Classical World's goddesses of the arts: the three Muses. 'Museum' means literally 'shrine of the Muses'.

In 1889 the world's first museum association, Britain's Museums Association (MA), was established. Today it represents a membership of 5,200 museum professionals, 250 corporate members, and 600 institutional members. Its mission is:

*'To enhance the value of museums to society by sharing knowledge, developing skills, inspiring innovation, and providing leadership.'*[134]

To these ends it provides training programmes and professional development opportunities and puts on Europe's largest annual conference for people working in the heritage industry. It offers advice on work placements and career opportunities and also serves as a pressure group in engaging with government strategies regarding heritage issues.

In a recent survey the Museums Association concluded there were around 2,500 'museums' in the United Kingdom, visited by something in the region of 100 million people each year. In 1998 the MA provided a definition for what constituted the purpose of a museum:

*'Museums enable people to explore collections for inspiration, learning and enjoyment. They are institutions that collect, safeguard and make accessible artefacts and specimens, which they hold in trust for society.'*[135]

Thus private collections, of paintings for example, that are not shared with the general public are not included. The definition provides an

---

134  http://www.museumsassociation.org Accessed January 2013
135  http://www.museumsassociation.org Accessed January 2013

excellent starting place in any evaluation of a museum – an essential skill for those involved in the curation and interpretation of collections.

The range of museums in the UK is vast. The MA identifies eight distinct types of museum, defined by their ownership, management and funding:

- **National museums** are established and funded by central government through the Department of Culture, Media and Sport (DCMS). They are generally larger institutions that hold collections considered to be of national importance. There are currently 54 national museums in the UK
- **Local authority museums** are owned and run by town, parish, borough, city, or county councils and other local authority bodies. They generally house collections that reflect local history and heritage
- **University museums** are owned and managed by universities and their collections often relate to specific areas of academic interest
- **English Heritage properties** are buildings and monuments of historic interest, many of which also hold collections inside. They are managed by English Heritage, a non-departmental public body of the UK government
- **Independent museums** are owned by registered charities and other independent bodies or trusts. They are not funded directly by the state but may receive support through government programmes such as Renaissance in the Regions
- **National Trust properties** are similar to English Heritage sites, but are owned and run by the National Trust (or the National Trust for Scotland), an independent charity. The National Trust remit extends to historic houses and gardens, castles, industrial monuments and social history sites, as well as areas of natural beauty
- **Regimental museums and armouries** collate and preserve Britain's military heritage and are often managed by the armed services
- Britain's **unoccupied royal palaces** are run by Historic Royal Palaces, an independent charity[136]

Not all museums define themselves as museums; in recent years a plethora of 'heritage centres' has emerged. However, in essence, these function in the same way as traditional museums and fulfill the

---

136  http://www.museumsassociation.org Accessed January 2013

same roles. Ambrose and Paine have classified museums according to a wider range of criteria than the MA, including the way in which they function:

Classified by collections:

- general museums
- archaeology museums
- art museums
- history museums
- ethnography museums
- natural history museums
- science museums
- geology museums
- industrial museums
- military museums

Classified by who runs them:

- government museums
- municipal museums
- university museums
- independent (charitable trust) museums
- army museums
- commercial company museums
- private museums

Classified by the area they serve:

- national museums
- regional museums
- city museums
- local museums

Classified by the audience they serve:

- general public museums
- educational museums
- specialist museums

*Classified by the way they exhibit their collections:*

- *traditional museums*
- *historic house museums*
- *open-air museums*
- *interactive museums*[137]

The effectiveness of a museum can be measured against its own 'mission' as well as that of bodies like the MA and the International Council of Museums. Such issues as access (in cultural as well as physical respects), its engagement (both in and out of the museum) with the communities it serves, its profession of expert advice, its economic performance, its 'sustainability', its representation of gender, and its representation of minority groups, are all factors in any effective museum analysis and evaluation. The issue of access includes consideration of how 'inviting' the museum is, its 'ambience', its interactive provision, the readability of its display boards (a large proportion of the UK's annual museum visitors are children), and the impact of different modes of interpretation such as reconstructions and re-enactments. With the advent of new communications technologies museum outreach initiatives should also be taken into consideration through the analysis of the traditional souvenir guidebook to the evaluation of websites and 'virtual' museums.

**Interpretation**

Techniques of interpretation can be divided into two basic types: static and dynamic. Static modes include:

Objects
Texts and labels
Models
Drawings
Photographs
Dioramas
Tableaux
Information sheets
Guidebooks

---

137   Ambrose and Paine (2006), p. 7

Worksheets

Dynamic modes of interpretation include:

Live interpretation
Sound-guides
Guided talks and walks
Lectures
Film / video / slides
Working models and animatronics
Computer-based activities
Mechanical interactives
Objects for handling
Drama
Interactive web sites[138]

As a general rule the wider the range of interpretative techniques used the broader will be its appeal to potential visitors.

In 2011 the Museum of Somerset, formerly the Somerset County Museum, was opened in Taunton Castle – the outcome of a £6.6 million two year project funded by the Heritage Lottery Fund and Somerset County Council. The new museum, in its own words, 'tells the county's story from prehistoric times to the present day using real objects combined with evocative films, sounds and images, and the voices and words of Somerset people past and present'.[139] Of paramount importance in the design of a modern museum are its modes of interpretation. The following guidance document was compiled by Helen Mansfield, Somerset's Heritage and Libraries Service Learning Manager at the start of the project. It provides an excellent starting place for the analysis and evaluation of interpretation at any museum or heritage centre.

The starting place for the interpretation of a collection and its effective communication is a careful consideration of the target audience:

---

[138] After Ambrose and Paine (2006), p.80
139 http://www.somerset.gov.uk/irj/public/services/directory Accessed February 2013

'Who are we writing for?

Many of our visitors will be:

- on the move
- tired of standing
- distracted
- suffering from information overload
- may scan a label quickly, even when it appears that they don't read them
- may know very little about the subject, or be an expert
- unlikely to have read every label, in the right order.

Things to consider:

- Most visitors spend less than 30 seconds looking at an object.
- The average reading age of visitors in the UK is 12-13 years. 1 in 4 adults in the UK have reading or writing difficulties (also, most do not make this known).
- The most common progressive sight degeneration is long sight. There are more partially sighted people than ever before. Over 19,000 people read Braille in the UK.
- 1 in 12 men have some degree of colour blindness (predominantly red/green).
- 8 million people have arthritis.
- Hearing loss affects over 14% of the population.'[140]

The content of any statement of interpretation is immaterial if it is inaccessible. The following statement summarises the general principles regarding readability:

**'Museum Interpretation: accessing the text**

Location

---

[140] Helen Mansfield, Museum of Somerset Text Guidelines, c.2010

- Eye level of adult standing up – 1400 to 1600mm
- Eye level of wheelchair user and children – 900 to 1200mm
- Labels – point size 18 to 36. (Size 18 at maximum viewing distance of 700mm, and size 36 at maximum of 1400mm).
- Main text – around 48 point.
- Wall labels should be placed around 140cm from the floor.
- Case labels should be placed at a height of 91 to 122cm (at an angle of between 30 and 45 degrees). Labels laid flat can be difficult or impossible for children and people in wheelchairs to read.
- Avoid glossy finishes as they can result in glare or reflection.
- Check the position of panels and labels in relation to gallery lighting to ensure that:

    o lighting levels will be sufficient for text to be read easily.
    o visitors will not cast shadows over the panels and labels by standing between displays and light sources.
    o visibility will not be affected by glare from surfaces.

Contrast and Colour

- Good contrast is required both on the panel and against the surroundings.
- Text should be black or as dark as possible, on a light background.
- Avoid words overlaid on graphics unless the contrast between the text and background is 70%.
- Avoid colours that can be confused by people with colour blindness - principally red, brown, orange, yellow and green.
- Use bold carefully as it reduces the distance between letters

Font Style

- Avoid changing font style within a label / panel.
- Avoid fancy typefaces.
- Make numerals as clear as possible.
- Avoid italics unless quoting the title of a book, film etc. – it reduces the impact of text for many readers.
- Avoid continuous use of capital letters.

Spacing

- Stick to even word spacing.
- Leave reasonable space between lines (same font size as your text).
- Leave double point size spaces between sections.
- Justify text to the left to keep even spacing.
- Avoid splitting words across lines.
- Avoid splitting sections across columns/pages.
- Avoid fitting text around unusual shapes such as diagrams.

Use of pictures / graphics

- Text should not be run over photographs, graphics or illustrations.
- Picture captions should help tell the story.'[141]

When it comes to content the same general principles apply as those that underpin any effective mode of communication including academic report and essay writing. The target audience however is not the same, as detailed below:

'Text Strategy Guidance Document'[142]

Planning what to write

**Write for your audience**

Aim for a reading age of 12 years. Write for a range of learning styles. Variety is the key to interpretation.

When deciding what to write for the text panel / label, consider what your learning outcomes are: what will people know from reading your panel?

**Let the objects 'speak'**

---

[141] Helen Mansfield, Museum of Somerset Text Guidelines, c.2010
[142] Helen Mansfield, Museum of Somerset Text Guidelines, c.2010

Text should refer as much as possible to what can be seen in the displays. Don't say what you see – let the interesting thing about the object speak. Look at the object with 'new' eyes – what's fascinating about it?

Don't talk about objects beyond the display. Instead link unfamiliar facts to everyday experiences / subjects.

**Know what your key points are**

Use the storyline. Show how the objects you're looking at relate to the story and its key messages.

We need to decide what we want to say, and make that point quickly. We have to know what visitors will want to discover. Clear writing depends on clear thinking.

One point is usually enough for object labels. Introductory panels will have more, and should introduce any sub-sections. This will reduce the need for lengthy explanation in other labels.

**Put the most important information first**

Visitors will probably scan text, so put the most important information first. It's contrary to writing essays. Titles and headings should grab visitors' attention.

Avoid referring to other text panels or labels – visitors may not have read them. Always write text panels so they can be understood on their own.

**Bring in the human element**

We need to connect the objects with the theme of the display and with the visitor's experience. People connect with people – human interest.

Write exhibition text as if you were walking someone round the displays, not writing a book. Consider visitors will find interesting, and what they might already know. Anticipate and answer questions, and deal with common misconceptions.

If don't know about something, admit it. Let visitors make their own guess.

Ask questions of visitors to draw them into the displays. But avoid 'yes / no' approaches. Encourage people to reflect on their experience of the display/objects. This can be done by self or sharing in groups e.g. 'Are you a King's man, or a rebel?' in relation to the Monmouth Rebellion.

**Background context can be useful**

Historical context is another area where visitors need support and where text can be vital. Audience research at the V&A has shown that visitors are particularly interested in knowing where artists and designers get their ideas and how objects are made.
Don't use too many dates and figures, but do explain historical context with a well-known date.

**What can be better shown visually?**

Sometimes images are more efficient ways of conveying your message. For example, rather than describing a part of an object that can't be seen, such as inside fittings, it may be simpler to include a photograph.

**Write as you would speak**

Adopt a chatty, conversational tone. It's about simple language, not simple ideas.

Use the 'active' voice, not 'passive'. It's not like writing an official report, policy document, or essay. So try 'Romans used these pots to cook food in', rather than 'These pots were used by Romans to cook their food in'.

Adopt a conversational, chatty tone. We want to be able to read text to people visiting the museum without having to reword it. Address the audience directly – 'If you look closely at the fossil, you can see...'

Avoid superlatives – 'beautiful' – let visitors make their own minds up. Well-chosen quotes can break up the pace well. Insert short quotations if they add interest to main text. [Show them in a speech bubble?]'

These general strategies are combined with specific directives with regard to grammar, vocabulary, numbers and syntax:

**'General guidelines**[143]

**Grammar**

Ensure that you:

- Write one theme per paragraph.
- Include one point per sentence. No more than 17 words.
- Choose short words over long ones.
- Avoid vague sentences. Be clear.
- Avoid double negatives – be positive.
- Avoid exclamation marks, semi-colons, colons, and brackets. Use dashes to break up text.
- Don't use italics as many visually impaired people can't read them.
- Use 'it's' rather than 'it is', and 'they're' rather than 'they are' as much as possible.
- Avoid too many proper nouns – especially names of people without saying who they are e.g. 'the curator, William Bidgood' (as not everyone knows).

Remember:

- It's okay to start sentences with 'And' and 'But' where appropriate.
- Keep words as short and simple as possible without affecting

---

[143] Helen Mansfield, Museum of Somerset Text Guidelines, c.2010

meaning e.g. "moved" instead of "manoeuvred".

**Vocabulary**

- Avoid technical terms, or explain them. Put them in a context in which they can make sense.
- Avoid too many proper nouns and specialist vocabulary. If a popular term doesn't exist, explain it.

**Dates and numbers**

Consistency is needed with dates and numbers:

- Write dates out in full. 10 April 2008, not 10$^{th}$ April 2008 or the tenth of April 2006.
- When referring to centuries, write '1800s' rather than '19th Century'. If you do have to refer to a whole century, use numerals (e.g. 19th) rather than writing out the number in words.
- Write the full decade out, as in 1950s. Don't write '50s.

Many people with low vision can easily misread 3, 5, 6, 8, 9, 0. Take care when using them.

**Tone and Authorship**

Try to avoid:

- Gender bias or stereotyping. Instead of "before the evolution of Man" try 'human evolution'. Be as precise as possible.
- Religious or racial stereotyping. Instead of the 'Indian Mutiny', refer to the 'War of Indian Independence'. Check correct spellings of any religious and cultural terms.
- Alienating people with learning or physical disabilities. Use words that refer to the senses. For example, describing texture helps people connect with certain objects.'

Various strategies can be adopted to test the readability of completed text. In addition to 'cloze' tests (numerous examples of which can easily be found on-line) these include:

Reading it out loud. If it sounds patronising, stilted or gushy, re-write it. If it reads like a textbook rewrite it.

Check readability. To use the Microsoft Word test, do the following:

1. Go to **Tools** then select **Options**
2. Go to **Spelling and Grammar** tab
3. Click **'Check grammar with spelling'** (if it's not been ticked already)
4. Click in the box for **'Show readability statistics'** (you must do this after turning on the grammar option). Once you have turned it on, statistics will come up at the end of any spell check.

There are two readability scores:

Flesch reading ease and Flesch-Kincaid grade level.

Aim for reading ease of above 50 and a grade level of below 9 (this corresponds with ages 14-15). The test also shows the percentage of passive sentences – which we should try to avoid.

SMOG Readability Formula – matches the reading level of written information to the 'reading with understanding' level of the reader. It's supported by the Basic Skills Agency. (For further details of the test and levels and for access to a free 'SMOG readability calculator' go to the 'ed:it lab' hosted by the University of Nottingham at www.niace.org.uk/misc/SMOG-calculator/smogcalc.php)

FOG Index – rough guide for general audiences:
1) Count 100 words, stopping at the nearest whole sentence.
2) Count the number of whole sentences making up the 100 words.
3) Divide the number of words by the number of sentences to find the average number of words per sentence.

| Average words per sentence | Rating | Readers reached % |
|---|---|---|
| 1 to 8 | Very easy | 90 |

| 9 to 11 | Fairly easy | 86 |
| 12 to 17 | Standard | 75 |
| 18 to 21 | Fairly difficult | 40 |
| 22 to 25 | Difficult | 24 |
| 26 or more | Very difficult | 5 |

Using these techniques, try evaluating this piece of text for an object on display:

**The Alfred Jewel**

Dating from the second half of the eighth century AD (750-800) this beautiful object was probably a gift from the Saxon King of Wessex, Alfred the Great, to one of his bishops. It was discovered in North Petherton in Somerset in 1693, just eight miles (thirteen kilometres) away from the monastery Alfred founded at Athelney. Around its side are the Old English words, 'Aelfred Mec Heht Gewyrcan' which mean 'Alfred had me made'. It was probably the handle for a bone pointer – a gift from Alfred to his bishop to use when reading sacred texts. It is made of filigreed gold surrounding a rock crystal laid over the image of a figure which probably represents Christ. Six similar objects, all of which are smaller and less elaborate, have since been found in Wessex region.

**Display**

Curators look after collections but also make key decisions on what to put out on show and how to display this material. The display needs to be fit for purpose of course but, as with modes of interpretation, a range of display types is likely to enhance the appeal of a museum collection. Ambrose and Paine (2006) have identified six main types of display in museums:

'Contemplative display. Here beautiful or inspiring things are put on display for the visitor to contemplate. This is the theme adopted by most art galleries, though even they often try to tell a story as well, if only by grouping paintings or statues by similar artists together.

Didactic display. Here the display tries to tell a story, to teach something. *The story may, for example, be the prehistory of the country, or the biology of lizards, or the folk art of the region; objects help to tell the story.*

Reconstruction display. *In this case a genuine or imaginary scene is reconstructed. Open-air museums like Skansen in Sweden, where whole streets of historic buildings are rebuilt and refurbished, fall into this type, as do small tableaux in museum galleries.*

Grouped display. *Here groups of objects are displayed together, often with very little interpretation. Archaeological museums, for example, often have a room labelled 'Bronze Age', with many objects but very little to tell the visitor why they are important or what happened in the Bronze Age. This type of display is probably the most common type of all, and is found in museums all over the world because it is so easy to do: it requires very little thought. But it is also the least useful or interesting to visitors, except to specialists.*

Visible storage. *Early museums used to put everything they owned on display. Then curators learned that people could enjoy a few objects well displayed and interpreted, more than hundreds of objects crowded together. Many museums put only their best things on display, and assigned the rest to storage. But now visitors are asking 'why can't we see the thousands of things you've got hidden in your stores?'. One answer is to keep the fine displays, but to open the stores to interested visitors, making only those improvements needed to protect the collections.*

Discovery displays. *This is almost the opposite of the didactic display. There are organising principles, but collections are displayed in a non-conventional way, for example not in chronological or thematic order and without labels or texts. Instead, visitors are encouraged to explore the displayed objects and make their own connections and discoveries. The museum can of course help visitors to follow their particular interests and make their own discoveries through providing different forms of interpretation, for example, booklets and sound guides.'*[144]

---

[144] Ambrose and Paine (2006), p.97

## Visitor experiences in museums

Recent research work at the great American museum collective, the Smithsonian Institute, further clarified for its staff the nature of its visitors' expectations and experiences. Data was collated from a range of sources including in-depth interviews and visitor comments. This data was gathered under four categories of experience: object experience, cognitive experience, introspective experience and social experience. From this a 14 point (see below) questionnaire was created in order to establish which of one of these experiences was most valued by the visitor. Studies in nine Smithsonian museums 'support the four experience types as distinct' and led to the following conclusion:

*'Visitors are diverse in their interests and are looking for these different types of experiences in museums. If museums want to be accountable to their visitors, they should at least respect and consider as valid each of these four types of museum experiences. Museums should contain different kinds of spaces explicitly designed to enhance these experiences – places that foster the direct experience of objects; those that present learning as a first-rate experience; those that encourage private imagination; and those that enhance interactions among visitors.'*[145]

### Four types of satisfying experiences

*Object experiences*

    Being moved by beauty
    Seeing rare / uncommon / valuable things
    Seeing 'the real thing'
    Thinking what it would be like to own such things
    Continuing my professional development

*Cognitive experiences*

    Enriching my understanding

---

[145] Zahava D. Doering, 'Visitor experiences in museums' in Sandell and James (2007), p.339

Gaining information or knowledge

*Introspective experiences*

Reflecting on the meaning of what I was looking at
Imagining other times or places
Recalling my travels / childhood experiences / other memories
Feeling a spiritual connection
Feeling a sense of belonging or connectedness

*Social experiences*

Spending time with friends / family / other people
Seeing my children learn new things[146]

## Research surveys

Carrying out research surveys is recognised as a tool that is invaluable in museum management and the evaluation of present practices. Surveys most obviously address those that visit the museum but it is equally appropriate for those assessing a museum's performance to profile those in the community who do not use the facility. Samples of between 200 and 300 are usually considered the minimum for the generation of useful data.

Appropriate survey questions can be based upon a wide range of factors, some of the most obvious being:

- *age range – up to 12, 12-18, 18-25, 26-35, 36-45, 46-55, 56-65, 66-75, 75 and over;*
- *gender – male / female;*
- *group numbers – adults / children;*
- *occupation / occupation of head of household;*
- *type of transport to museum – foot, bicycle, bus / coach, train, car, other;*
- *distance travelled from home or holiday residence;*

---

[146] Zahava D. Doering, 'Visitor experiences in museums' in Sandell and James (2007), p.340

- *reason(s) for visit;*
- *length of visit;*
- *frequency of visits;*
- *enjoyment of visit;*
- *suggestions for improvements.*[147]

Data collated from surveys can prompt managers into addressing such matters as entry pricing policy, image and branding, exhibition and events policies. Incentives such as free cups of tea in the museum's café have helped market researchers achieve their minimum sample target!

## Evaluating displays and exhibitions

The preliminary evaluation of displays and exhibitions, essential to the success of a project, are carried out by museum staff and others involved in the set-up such as graphic designers. This process is summed up by the terms beginning or 'front end' evaluation, and middle or 'formative' evaluation. The final stage in the assessment is end or 'summative' evaluation. This involves three key techniques: watching / tracking visitors and monitoring their behaviour to see how the exhibition or display 'works'; interviewing a sample of visitors to assess what they have learned, what they found most interesting, and to receive their suggestions for improvements; bringing in an expert from outside the organisation / institution to provide a critical appraisal of the exhibition / display.[148]

Visitor interviews can highlight the perceived 'ambience' of the museum or heritage centre: clean, cared-for, welcoming environments are likely to create a positive impression. Carpeted floors, log fires, flowers, gentle music, trickling water, and scented air can all help 'sell' a museum and its collection in the same way that they can help sell a home or win over a hotel guest. In a larger museum an effective approach to display is one that provides a range of experiences with each room / display area having its own distinctive character and atmosphere. Careful use of colour, sound, and other elements can heighten the drama of the visit by both exciting the emotions and

---

[147] Ambrose and Paine (2006), p.25
[148] Ambrose and Paine (2006), pp.112-115

engendering moments of calm reflection.

## Access

Disability issues are central in any discussion of access in relation to museums and heritage centres. Access audits need to consider how far the institution promotes access to the institution from the outside:

'Orientation for disabled visitors. *Are there appropriate signs/landmarks for blind/ partially sighted visitors? Are marketing materials available in large text size?*

Access routes/paths. *Are access routes clearly marked and free of obstructions? Are kerbs and edges defined and surfaces slip-free? Are signs, gratings, litter bins a hazard? Do windows/doors open outwards or inwards?*

Ramps and steps. *Are entrances well signposted and accessible for people in wheelchairs? Are ramps for wheelchair users at the correct gradient? Are there handrails alongside ramps and steps? Is there adequate lighting?*

Entrance doors and halls. *Are doors wide enough for wheelchair users? Is the door too heavy to open? Are there steps associated with the door? Can people see through the doors? Are glazed doors clearly marked? Can automatic doors be used instead of swing doors? Do halls and lobbies allow for wheelchair manoeuvre?*'[149]

Inside the museum an access audit needs to consider the following:

'Orientation. *Is there sufficient, legible signing for partially sighted visitors? Are there aural or tactile landmarks to assist blind / partially sighted visitors? Do the surface colours of walls/floors aid or impede orientation?*

Levels. *Are there warnings about changes in floor levels? Are stairs well lit and signposted? Are information desks / hooks / washbasins / shop displays / telephones at a suitable level for wheelchair users?*

---

[149] Ambrose and Paine (2006), p.40

Lifts. Are control buttons easily seen and located? Is there a handrail inside the lift? Are signs and directions clearly marked and lighted?

Seating. Is there sufficient seating available for visitors? Is it stable and at varied heights?

Materials and surface finishes. Are surface finishes chosen with a view to avoiding discomfort or injury? Are there sharp angles on walls or junctions? Is sound or light reflection an aid or a hindrance? Can colours be used to provide guidance? Are displays presented without distracting surfaces behind them so that objects stand out effectively?

Lighting. Are windows designed to minimise glare? Can they be opened and locked easily? Is display lighting effective for partially sighted visitors?

Heating. Are heating systems such as radiators dangerous to touch?
Disaster management. Will disabled people be able to get out of a museum building easily in the case of fire or other disaster? Are there procedures laid down for staff to follow? Do staff know what to do in case of emergencies?

Induction loops. Is the museum/gallery/lecture room/education centre fitted with an induction loop to help people who use hearing aids?

Signs. Are signs legible and consistent? Are they positioned well? Are Braille letters within hand reach and at an appropriate level and angle?

Touch exhibitions / displays / tours / workshops. Does the museum provide touch exhibits/ handling opportunities for blind or partially sighted visitors?

Café / restaurant. Are serving arrangements accessible and appropriate for visitors in wheelchairs?

Toilets. Are there specially designed toilets for disabled visitors?

Guided tours. Does the museum organise guided tours and events *specifically for people with disabilities?"*[150]

## Open Air Museums

**Butser Ancient Farm**

In 1969 Peter Reynolds, a Classics teacher at Prince Henry's Grammar School in Evesham, acquired land on Bredon Hill in Gloucestershire on the edge of the Cotwolds, and established the first open air centre for archaeological experimentation. It was constructed next to the Bredon Hill hillfort and his work focused on the technologies of the Iron Age. Thus began a career that would have a huge impact upon approaches to the past in Britain:

> *Almost single-handedly, he put the British Iron Age on the map of contemporary study, to the extent that national curriculum history no longer begins with what he called the "rotten Romans", but encompasses the diverse riches of the Celts in the centuries immediately preceding the Roman Conquest. Perhaps more importantly, he introduced the concept of what is now known as experimental archaeology to the mainstream of archaeological thought.*[151]

The three year Bredon Hill project led to the establishment a couple of years later of an 'Iron Age' farm at Butser Hill near Waterlooville in Hampshire, backed by funding from the Council for British Archaeology (CBA) and Hampshire County Council. Of this initiative Reynolds wrote: *It was in response to the need for scientific experiment - prehistoric archaeology that the Butser Ancient Farm research Project was set up in 1972. Its object is to reconstruct a farm dating to about 300 BC, in the mainstream of the Iron Age period. In reality it is an open-air scientific research laboratory, unique in world archaeology. The purpose is to explore all the aspects of such a farm, the structures and processes, the plant cultivation and animal husbandry, and to consider not only how each particular aspect itself may operate but also how all the aspects integrate together. It is a massive, and most exciting undertaking. The concept of setting up such a research project goes far beyond a simple*

---

[150] Ambrose and Paine (2006), p.40-1
[151] Mick Aston (05/10/2001), Peter Reynolds' obituary in *The Guardian*

reconstruction. It sets out to define the basic evidence, to evaluate and test ideas and theories, and to focus attention upon the essential details. In effect, it adds a new dimension to prehistoric archaeology.'[152]

It consisted of 23 hectares of land on a chalk ridge. Reynolds gained his doctorate (University of Leicester) in 1978 for the work he conducted there on the potential of deep pits as long term stores for seed grain: the use to which he suspected many of the pits found on hillfort sites had been put in antiquity. He also pioneered the construction of full-scale roundhouses, based on archaeological evidence, with his building of the 'Pimperne House'. Its construction involved 0.5 ha of hazel coppice, the use of over 200 trees, and around 12 tonnes of thatching straw[153]. Among other things his thatched roundhouses proved that they functioned perfectly well without a hole cut in the roof to let out smoke from the central fireplace, and that a hole in the roof would create a draught that would soon cause the roof to ignite. Reynolds' roundhouses were based on the archaeology of those excavated at Maiden Castle (Dorset) and Balksbury (Hampshire) however, since these amounted to little more than sets of post holes and ditches he was keen to stress that they were 'not necessarily at all like the buildings of Iron Age. [...] Each reconstruction is but a physical realisation of one possible interpretation, and for each set of archaeological data there are many possible interpretations.'[154] These 'reconstructions' he subsequently defined as 'constructions' since 'Strictly a reconstruction is the rebuilding of a structure either on its original location or elsewhere, which has fallen down or deteriorated and would otherwise be lost.' The Butser roundhouses were based on much flimsier evidence than the known building that has collapsed presents and hence 'all the purported reconstructions of Neolithic, Bronze Age and Iron Age buildings are really constructs.'[155] Hence, in a paper published in 1995, he was adamant that 'In no sense should the resultant structure be regarded as a reconstruction. It was, in fact, a three dimensional projection of the data built at a 1:1 scale.'[156]

The roundhouse construction experiments and associated farming

---

[152] Reynolds (1979), p.17
[153] Reynolds (1995), p.2
[154] Reynolds (1979), pp.29-30
[155] Reynolds (1989), p.35
[156] Reynolds (1995), p.1

practices amply demonstrated the need for careful woodland management in the Iron Age. In addition to the felling of the dozens of trees a substantial building demanded, hazel coppicing was also an integral process for the provision of wattle and fencing.

The employment of highly skilled modern professional thatchers led to the conclusion that, for them, the roof of the Pimperne House represented six weeks work. This in turn convinced Reynolds that specialists / professionals were almost certainly involved in the Iron Age building business, just as they are now.

Many years later, the demolition of the Pimperne House, brought about 'by the stupidity and fickleness of local government officials who determined that a research zone of 15 years standing had to be converted into a barbecue area'[157], provided further opportunities for scientific analysis of the structure. A shallow gully frequently found as a ring feature around the foundations of excavated roundhouses had long been interpreted as a drip gully created naturally by the displacement of water from the roof of the house. When the Pimperne House was dismantled it transpired that 'all the stakes which formed the uprights in the wall had rotted away below a depth of 100mm from the old ground surface'. The activities of rodents had subsequently disturbed the spaces between the postholes thus forming the gully feature. For Reynolds this suggested a new solution to the 'drip gully' riddle:

> *In all the research devoted to roundhouse constructs conducted by the writer over some 25 years the phenomenon of the drip gully has signally failed to occur. The reverse, a humic lump, is the normal result, being the product of protected vegetative habitat.*[158]

He concluded that either the activities of rodents in association with rotted postholes, or human construction were the most viable explanations for the presence of these gully features.

In 1979 he published the record of his endeavours in *Iron Age Farm: the Butser experiment*, a book that inspired numerous experiments

---

[157] Reynolds (1995), p.1
[158] Reynolds (1995), p.4

thereafter. The farm was relocated to a new site at nearby Bascomb Copse in 1991.

Adopting a rigorous scientific approach in his inquiries Reynolds distanced the work at Butser from that of earlier attempts in explaining archaeology by experiment:

> Experiments in archaeology have been carried out from the very beginning of man's interest in his own past. Scientific experiment, on the other hand, is relatively recent and represents the most progressive element in archaeology today. The subject is multi-disciplinary and ranges from thermodynamics through to mycology, the study of fungi and bacteria. Throughout, the standards of each individual science involved are to be adopted. There is a clearly defined gulf between real experiment and demonstration. Both have their place in archaeology, the latter most importantly in explaining comprehensibly to as large an audience as possible the findings of excavation.[159]

By creating a whole farm context Reynolds and his successors made available insights that the isolated archaeological experiment could not. He was concerned not just with the viability of particular activities but that of the farm as a whole, how, for example the training of livestock interacted with the growing of crops. As well as the construction and analysis of buildings and grain stores, he experimented with crops known to have been available and planted in the Iron Age. Using Ion Age tools and techniques he monitored their yield and quality. Dexter cattle, the closest match to extinct Iron Age breeds, were harnessed to pull ards, sledges and carts. Modern Soay sheep, again, similar to the livestock of the Iron Age, were monitored for yield (milk, meat, wool) and an Iron Age style loom was set up to weave their wool into cloth. Reynolds however had no interest in attempting to *live* the Iron Age – such exercises were bound to fail:

> There is here no thought of playing at being Iron-Age people. Any attempt to relive the remote past is destined to failure, because the knowledge 'and experience of previous generations are denied us. To place modern man into a prehistoric context, given the

---

[159] Reynolds (1979), p.16

*limitations of our knowledge, is only to observe how modern people may react both to the conditions and to each other.*[160]

Within a few years of its opening Reynolds felt enough had been achieved to declare that 'By observation of the various processes and structures it has already been proved possible not only to isolate previously unrecognised significant features, but also to reverse generally accepted but unproven theories.' Furthermore he found it to be a highly cost-effective way of advancing archaeological understanding when compared with more conventional approaches: 'the total expenditure incurred by the project throughout its six-year life has been less than the cost of a small six- week excavation.' In addition, 'Educationally, the benefits of the project are enormous', since the centre, open to the public, provided opportunities for visitors to engage with, on a participatory as well as an observational level, 'a real working interpretation of the past'.[161] In more recent times the project's essential commitment to organic farming methods for the purpose of historical accuracy, has resonated with modern concerns regarding the use of chemical fertilisers, herbicides, pesticides and genetically modified crops.

The experience of farming in the style of the Iron Age has helped fill in the gaps that the incomplete evidence of the excavated past does not fill. For example Reynolds soon discovered how completely he and his small team relied on fencing in the maintenance of livestock, an essential technology that is rarely evident in the archaeological record. One assumption he challenged through experiment was the effectiveness of Iron Age 'sickles' to do the job for which they were named:

> *In classical literature we read that the Celts only reaped the ear of the cereal. The problem is that, unlike modern varieties which have been selectively bred to a standard height [...] It is no easy matter to grasp a handful of ears [of emmer and spelt] and deliver a neat cut with a sickle. On several tests with groups of volunteers, reconstructed sickles were tried and quickly discarded in favour of fingers. (This is a practice I recently observed in Spain where a family*

---

[160] Reynolds (1979), p.14
[161] Reynolds (1979), p.23

reaped a field, first picking off all the heads and putting them in baskets, and afterwards cutting the straw and tying it into bundles, or yealms.) The head breaks off easily enough at the rachis and the speed differential is remarkable. Also, the process does not disagree with the classical reference. However, it does leave a remarkable number of cutting objects at present called sickles. Although they are not particularly suited for the job, it does not necessarily mean they were not used for it. From their relative abundance at archaeological sites they must represent a common tool and, if not a sickle, a plausible and very practical alternative is the spar-hook. This is a small, often crescent-shaped blade used for splitting hazel rods, willow withes and brambles. That this task was an extremely common one is supported not only by archaeological evidence, but also by our hard-earned experience from the research programme as a whole.[162]

One of Reynolds' most important sets of experiments were those concerning the possible uses of the numerous pits, some over three metres deep, found on hillfort sites all over southern England. Once erroneously identified as the subterranean dwellings, they were still frequently dismissed as mere rubbish pits. Reynolds recognized that for a society creating mostly organic waste, much that would soon rot down and produce valuable manure (not 'rubbish'), this was an inadequate explanation. Although they could certainly serve the role of modern rubbish and compost bins, Reynolds was drawn more to the possibility that they were purpose-built underground grain silos, a practice well known among social historians and anthropologists. The first experiment to test the explanation, which 'marked the beginning of agricultural experiment'[163], was carried out in the early 1960s by H. C. Bowen and P. D. Wood, and swiftly followed by Peter Reynolds' own experiments. That at least some of the Iron Age pits were used for this purpose is fairly certain but the effectiveness of this system of storage is not evident in the excavated archaeological record. Therefore Reynolds set up an experimental programme 'to examine exactly what happens inside a storage pit and to compare the effects on storage of different pit shapes and types of lining material'[164], these being linings

---

[162] Reynolds (1979), pp.64-65
[163] Reynolds (1988), p.24
[164] Reynolds (1979), p.74

of clay and linings of basketwork, both of which are suggested by excavated archaeological evidence. His initial findings were 'dramatic' in revealing a technology that was rather more efficient than the experimenters had expected:

> *The implications, even at this stage, are critically important. Contrary to accepted theories, it is not necessary to parch the grain before storage. Not only is there a distinct lack of archaeological evidence for parching the grain, but also it is counterproductive to do so, because the stored mass would be likely to attract moisture. More important, grain stored in this way has a high germination quality and could well be thought of as seed grain and not consumption grain. The argument for population estimations based upon pit capacity and per capita consumption cannot now be logically applied. In addition, there is no evidence forthcoming from some consecutive years of pit usage to support the principle that a pit becomes musty or contaminated in some way to prohibit its further use. Pits can be used again and again without any apparent reason for their abandonment. Should a pit go wrong, the reasons for storage failure cannot be attributed to the pit itself. The only reason for pit failure other than bad sealing or rodent infestation is excessive rainfall, which causes lateral flow instead of vertical flow, thus allowing water penetration at underground levels.*[165]

If indeed these pits were designed to store seed grain and not grain for daily consumption, which, presumably, was stored in raised granaries above ground (also constructed and scientifically tested at Butser), it now seemed possible that Iron Age farming methods might have supported significantly larger populations than those suggested by other interpretations of the evidence:

> *On a large number of sites there are literally hundreds of pits of suitable shape and size to qualify as grain storage pits, and even with only a very small percentage in contemporary use, a great area of land must have been in cultivation. [...] the major implication is that in the Iron Age there was virtually total domination of the landscape and a proportionately large population.*[166]

---

[165] Reynolds (1979), p.76
[166] Reynolds (1979), p.77

Not only did Reynolds' pit experiments suggest important implications concerning Iron Age demography but they also pointed to a sophisticated economic base, and one reflecting the engagement of the southern tribes in cross-Channel trade on the eve of the Roman invasion:

> It is extremely attractive to consider these pits, if indeed they were used for the bulk storage of grain, as indicators of the successful nature of agricultural economy of the Iron Age when surplus rather than sufficiency was the norm. Similarly there is the implication that such bulk grain storage may have had something to do with export as stated by the classical writers.[167]

Always conscious of the diversity of human activity and the multiple purposes to which any one structure might be put, Reynolds also considered the capacity of pits for the salting of meat, silage-making, the storing vegetables and nuts, for storing water, for tanning leather and dyeing woollen cloth. All of which were potential candidates for archaeological experiments.

In addition to demonstrating what was possible, Reynolds' experiments with pits and structures endeavoured to support interpretations of excavated evidence by carefully recording the taphonomic processes that could be observed after pits were abandoned and as structures began to decay.

A later roundhouse, the Longbridge Deverill Cowdown roundhouse, built on the new site, began to collapse after just 14 years and was dismantled 2006. Its relatively short life was likely to have been because its main timbers were made of ash not oak. The careful analysis of its remains by a University of Reading team led by Martin Bell demonstrated how slight the archaeological record for such a building might be:

> A central hearth created on the roundhouse's ground surface had been in very regular use over the 14 year life of the building, and when sectioned it showed remarkably superficial sub-surface traces

---

[167] Reynolds (1988), p.26

*of heat reddening. Charcoal was sparse and the maximum depth visibly affected by heat was 130mm. The trampled floor only retained its distinctive form where protected from the elements; where wetting and drying occurred subsequent to the removal of the roof, earth- worms had begun to appear and trampled floor layers were indistinct after just a few weeks exposure. [...] many traces of the building such as the floor, hearth, wattlework, and drip feature from the roof produced only superficial traces which might not survive over archaeological timescales, especially if the site was subsequently cultivated.*[168]

In carrying out a wide range of experiments in house construction, pottery firing, testing of storage techniques and the like, Reynolds considered how the expertise and experience of the craftsman / technologist could affect the results, particularly regarding the time taken in the process. This poses problems but does not negate the validity of the approach:

*As far as is possible, the individual element of skill is removed from any experiment. This does not detract from the experimental process at all, but it does emphasise the danger of assuming that because an experiment has a valid result it is therefore right. It also removes the equal danger of assessing the time taken to achieve an end product. An experimenter may take ten hours to accomplish a valid end product which an expert could have achieved in one hour. The transfer of the former result could err by a factor of ten. On the other hand, the modern expert may well be more or even less accomplished than his prehistoric counterpart, and further error may be compounded. Besides, the time element is of less importance initially. First we need to know how and why.*[169]

A further limitation that all experimenters have to recognize is that 'more than one valid hypothesis can be raised on exactly the same basic data. Therefore, when using hypotheses to explain an excavation, it is necessary to select the one most likely to relate to the whole of the material.'[170]

---

[168] Bell (2008), p.8
[169] Reynolds (1979), pp. 15-16
[170] Reynolds (1979), p.16

Peter Reynolds died suddenly at the age of 61 in 2001 but his farm, visited by scores of school parties and hundreds of heritage tourists each year, lives on as 'not just a great Hampshire day out' but 'also one of the most interesting archaeological sites in the UK, a real working farm that we use as an open-air research laboratory to explore the ancient world.'[171]

**West Stow**

The site of the Anglo-Saxon village at West Stow near Bury St Edmunds in Suffolk was excavated between 1965 and 1972. Although little evidence of the timber of the buildings above ground had survived, the archaeology was rich enough to enable reasonable presumptions regarding their construction and use. Evidence for over 70 buildings was discovered and two main types of building were identified.

Type A are known as 'sunken featured buildings' (SFBs), formerly known as *Grubenhauser* ('sunken houses' in German), because of the distinctive pit that was dug before the rest of the structure was built. The larger of these pits were around 5m long, 3m wide, and 1m deep and had sloping sides and a flat base. The old assumption regarding this curious feature was that the pit provided the 'living floor' for the people using the building, but at the West Stow Anglo Saxon Centre the assumption is that the pit would have been sealed beneath floorboards. Following this assumption, and building structures that appear to work very well as potential homes and workshops, the Centre has suggested an alternative interpretation to that originally invoked by the discovery of *Grubenhauser:* 'The bulk of the people, we can now be assured, were content with something that hardly deserves a better title than a hovel.'[172] Instead 'We do not have to accept the concept of Anglo-Saxons as unkempt barbarians [...] who lived in utter squalor in dark holes in the ground.'[173]

Type B are buildings without pits. Defined as 'halls', these are larger than the SFBs, being between 8 and 10m long and over 4m wide. The

---

[171] www.butserancientfarm.co.uk, accessed 12/10/13
[172] Leeds (1926) in Coles (1979), p.146
[173] West, Stanley, *et al* (2000), *Understanding West Stow*, Jarrold Publishing, p.6

SFBs at West Stow were grouped around the halls.

The West Stow settlement has been dated to the 200 years between 450AD and 650AD. The site interpretation suggests it was occupied at any one time by three or four extended 'family units', each with its hall as a focal point and a cluster of SFB houses and ancillary buildings. On the site archaeologists have attempted to reconstruct just one of these 'family units', comprising a single hall and five SFBs. The first reconstruction, in the style of and on the site of SFB 21, was completed in 1974.

In 1976 another SFB was constructed to test the traditional *Grubenhaus* interpretation that the pit's base was the living floor. The roof therefore was constructed at ground level as a lid over the sunken house. By constructing such a building the practicality of it being a viable home could be tested and the findings were predictably gloomy: 'The dwelling had little floor space, was damp and dark, and to some at least it seemed wholly unsatisfactory as a permanent house.'[174] A similar building had been constructed at the West Dean (Singleton) open air museum of buildings in 1970.

The main hall was completed in 1980 on the site of Hall 2, but based upon the smaller Hall 1. In 1987 a planked floor was introduced to reduce the amount of dust in the building.

The main woodworking tool for the first house reconstruction was the adze. For the building of this one, the 'weaving house', the axe was the tool of choice. This structure was based on the evidence of three excavated SFBs on the site – 15, 19 and 49 – and it was completed in 1984.

The next to be built (1987) was, like the first, built on the site of the SFB (5) it was designed to replicate. A different technique was tried out for the fitting together of the planks that constituted the walls. Initially radial split planks of oaks were used in its construction but these were abandoned in favour of tangential split planks that proved to be more fit for purpose.

---

[174] Coles (1979), p.146

In 1991 a large new Hall went up, based upon finds from another site in Suffolk, and used as a workshop and store for the Centre, and in 1997 another SFB was built on the site of, and modelled upon, SFB 12.

In 1979 John Coles summed up the importance of the West Stow project: 'the West Stow project has already demonstrated that a careful association between excavation evidence and experimental testing theories can yield information essential to any understanding of the original site.'[175] In addition to testing theories regarding the construction of houses, workshops and stores, the Centre, like Butser, was designed to explore old methods for working the land and its related technologies. Visitors to the Centre are likely to witness, and perhaps have opportunities to engage in, a variety of 'Anglo-Saxon' activities including woodworking with a pole lathe, pottery making, leather working, basketry, metalworking, bone and antler-working, spinning and weaving.

**The Lunt**

At around the time of the Boudican Revolt of A.D. 60-61, near to the point where two major Roman roads, the Fosse and Watling Street, meet, a small fort was built near to Coventry on a highpoint overlooking a fording place on the River Sowe. It consisted of a turf rampart and a wooden palisade, enclosing a granary and other buildings, and a gateway surmounted by a wooden tower. It seems to have been abandoned within about 20 years, at the time when Agricola, the new governor of Britain, decided to extend the frontier to the north. Using posthole and foundation ditch evidence, the granary was reconstructed together with the gatehouse and parts of the rampart and palisade. Of course, strictly speaking, these are constructions, not reconstructions, since the height and other details of the original buildings above ground is unknown. Pieces of oak and elm recovered from the Roman well on the site prompted the architects to use the same in the reconstructions. The new structures were erected by a team of Royal Engineers. John Coles summarised their approach to the construction of the granary in 1973:

'The building was raised almost 1·0 m above the ground, just as

---

[175] Coles (1979), p.148

surviving granaries are. No archaeological evidence existed for construction beyond floor level, and so multiples of Roman units were chosen. The walls were made about 3 m high, and loading bays for carts were put at the ends of the building. The walls were built up with overlapping plank tiles nailed on to the framework, and the roof had elm shingles. Although the materials were prepared by modern methods, the actual building operation was conducted in appropriate "Roman" fashion so far as could be deduced. The officer in charge of the Engineers arranged for a crane to assist, but the men preferred to haul the timber by ropes and the crane soon became redundant. Simple wooden joints were employed, such as were found at a waterlogged Roman site in Holland. The whole operation took about two weeks.'[176]

The main thrust of the build as an archaeological experiment was the consideration of the amount of work in man-hours, using the same tools and techniques as the Romans, such structures represent. It took a little over 1000 man-hours in 1966 for a group of volunteers for H.M. Prison, Leicester, to construct 11m of rampart. This was 5.4m wide at the base, and 3.6m high. It constituted about 5500 turves, cut at a rate of, on average, 5.5 turves per hour. The fort is thought to have been designed to house a garrison of about 420 foot-soldiers and 120 cavalry, and it was estimated that the whole 'the whole fort could have been put up in 9-12 days by 200-300 men'.[177] Coles summarized the value of the experiment, and its limitations, as follows:

'Estimates such as this are valuable, not because they pretend to be precise and wholly accurate, but because they provide a guide to the archaeologist in his attempt to postulate the rates of movement of, in this case, Roman armies, and the length of undefended time in a newly occupied territory. They are less accurate if extrapolated to much larger monuments such as Hadrian's Wall where the manpower could have wildly fluctuated.'[178]

In 1970 the gatehouse was put up by the Royal Engineers using a design based on trajan's Column in Rome and other archaeological evidence for double-gated structures without guardhouses. It demonstrated

---

[176] Coles (1979), p. 136
[177] Coles (1979), p. 136
[178] Coles (1979), pp. 136-7

that, ten men working with a single pole and pulleys, could be erected a structure like this, prefabricated and made of pine, in just three days. In 1977, the gyrus, a 34 diameter palisade enclosed ring for, it is presumed, cavalry training was reconstructed. It was levelled and covered in sand and took the 18 men from 31 Base Squadron, working 6 hours a day, ten days to create.[179]

## Industrial Archaeology (Claire Gore)

*In the following article[180] a Level 6 History, Heritage and Archaeology student, Claire Gore, considers contemporary interest, both popular and academic, in industrial archaeology. Her research for this essay was extensive; note in particular her use of a wide range of academic journals.*

"Everywhere I was reminded of the fierce activity of former days, and every stick and stone of the place seemed to have absorbed something of its white hot violence".[181]

Rolt's description of Ironbridge goes to the heart of industrial archaeology: that now we are left only with the physical remains of something that was primarily about "doing" and "making". The idea of "doing" in the past has had a unique and lasting interest for the public. However, industrial archaeology's place academically has been less certain, even though the broader field of social and economic history has become a large, well-regarded part of the discipline of history.[182]

Industrial archaeology isn't even described easily: its popular manifestation in places such as Ironbridge, the restored Avon and Kennet Canal and the Didcot Railway Centre is more usually termed industrial heritage; academics themselves nowadays exclude all industrial archaeology from before the Industrial Revolution and the

---

[179] ExArc, Open Archaeology, http://openarchaeology.info/venues/lunt-roman-fort-en accessed December 2013
[180] Claire Gore, submission for *History, Heritage and Archaeology* Module SHHA 302, Strode College in partnership with Plymouth University, 2015-2016.
[181] L. T. C. Rolt, *Landscape with Canals* (Allen Lane, London, 1977), p. 55.
[182] R. A. Buchanan, *Industrial Archaeology in Britain* (Allen Lane, London, 1980), pp. 374-375.

academic field of industrial archaeology is synonymous with the academic field known as "history of technology".[183] For the purposes of this essay, these various manifestations will all be considered as industrial archaeology.

In the eighteenth and nineteenth centuries, Britain founded an industrial revolution that is still pounding away today around the world. However, Britain's position as leading industrial manufacturer ground to a halt in the first half of the twentieth century as its own raw materials became scarce or obsolete and as domestic labour costs and availability declined in relation to other countries. After the Second World War and over the next twenty or so years, the physical legacy of Britain's manufacturing heyday merged with the ruins and artefacts thrown up by the Second World War and was perceived as so much rubble and waste; there was a great desire amongst British policy-makers to look forward, to clear up and to start again. However, the demolition of icons such as the Euston Arch and steam railway locomotives in the late 1950s and early 1960s led to popular outcry: various groups were formed to preserve the heritage of "Britain's glory era" and government and academe followed public opinion in belatedly paying attention to Britain's industrial archaeology.

Even if consideration of Britain's industrial archaeology is limited to a starting point at the beginning of the Industrial Revolution, there is an enormous volume of physical evidence. Raw materials were dug up and processed in mines and steelworks, manufacturing works produced machinery and goods, canals and railways were constructed on an enormous scale to move the raw materials and end products around the country and ships were constructed and used to import and export. One area of industrial archaeology at the very heart of the Industrial Revolution was the steam railway. Buchanan describes the steam engine as the "greatest single invention of the Industrial Revolution period" and its adaptation as a locomotive allowed the creation of the "arteries of the national economic system".[184] It was the premature demolition of some of the railway's

---

[183] H. Orange, 'Industrial Archaeology: Its Place Within the Academic Discipline, the Public Realm and the Heritage Industry', 85-95, *Industrial Archaeology Review* (30, 2, 2008), p. 85.
[184] R. A. Buchanan, *Industrial Archaeology in Britain*, pp. 262 & 320.

most significant heritage by an unthinking British Rail that kick-started much of the groundswell of support for industrial archaeology that still exists in Britain today.

This essay will identify and attempt to understand the reasons for the continuing interest in industrial archaeology, considering the public, academe and also government policy. As the subject matter is so vast, the essay will limit its scope to Britain, with a particular focus on the industrial archaeology of railways.

Britain's physical industrial heritage has gained in popularity as the passing of time since it was used has grown. Orange asserts that this physical heritage was unpopular with the public straight after the Second World War, as the British public were coming to terms with the loss of empire and the nation's change of fortune.[185] Time has also enabled the archaeology to become visible: whilst and just after use it was too familiar to be seen, both its aesthetic and memory values were invisible.[186] This may be part of the reason for public ambiguity about Grimsby's ice factory. On the one hand, the Council for British Archaeology nominated it to join the World Monuments Fund Watch, seeing it as crucial evidence of Grimsby's fishing history, the oldest and largest factory of its kind in Europe.[187] On the other hand, many Grimsby residents want it pulled down or covered up.[188]

There is an inherent tension in the desire to keep the aesthetic parts of the industrial landscape but not the ugly, messy parts.[189] Coupled with this is the new aesthetic role of industrial spaces: artefacts and edifices such as Tate Modern can be sculptures reclaimed from capitalist production, with their original use re-imagined.[190] The huge volumes within industrial spaces form part of this new aesthetic.[191]

---

[185] Orange, 'Industrial Archaeology', p. 85.
[186] Orange, 'Industrial Archaeology', p. 87.
[187] M. Heyworth, 'Correspondent', *British Archaeology* (No. 134, January February 2014), p. 62; Anon., 'Factfile: Grimsby Ice Factory and Kasbah', ITV news website (8 October 2013).
[188] 'Grimsby Ice Factory: Bulldoze it or call in Banksy!', *Grimsby Telegraph* (21 March 2015).
[189] Orange, 'Industrial Archaeology', p. 90.
[190] Jones, R. A., 'Industrial Ruins: Space, Aesthetics and Materiality', 821-822, review, *Technology and Culture* (47.4, 2006), p. 822.
[191] Jones, 'Industrial Ruins', p. 822.

This, of course, is visible in the contemporary popularity of industrial spaces for domestic "loft living".

Inevitably, these archaeological sites have become a major part of tourism; for example many cruise ship on-shore itineraries include heritage train rides.[192] Within the railway industry alignment with tourism has existed since the railways' foundation. The Great Western Railway Company deliberately manipulated marketing and public relations to create an image of itself as the "holiday line".[193] Even the post-war schoolboy addiction to trainspotting was created as a public relations exercise, with one million ABC locomotive guides sold annually in the 1950s.[194] As those schoolboys are now at retirement age, this passion for trains, engendered in them by the railway industry, is still apparent in the popularity of railway heritage.

Brunel's personal appeal due to his legendary status in the history of the British Industrial Revolution has also added to the popularity of industrial archaeology. Although Brunel was arguably Rolt's "last great figure of the European Renaissance", he too benefited from hardworking publicists.[195] Not many people in Britain have a university named after them.

Furthermore, Brunel's importance to the nation, exemplified when he came a close second to Churchill in the BBC's 100 greatest Britons survey in 2002, demonstrates the "immense importance of Britain's role as the first industrial nation" in the formation of its national identity.[196]

---

[192] Upadhya, A., 'Railway heritage and tourism: global perspectives', review, *Journal of Heritage Tourism,* review (June 2015), p. 1.
[193] Burdett, W. R., *Go Great Western: A History of GWR Publicity* (David & Charles, Newton Abbot, 1970), pp. 24-27.
[194] Anon., 'Ian Allan, trainspotter – obituary', *The Telegraph* (30 June 2015).
[195] L. T. C. Rolt, *Isambard Kingdom Brunel* (Penguin, London, 1970); L. T. C. Rolt, *Isambard Kingdom Brunel* (Penguin, London, 1970); I. Fillis and R. Herman, 'A Biographical Study of Isambard Kingdom Brunel as insight into entrepreneurial marketing endeavour', *Journal of Enterprising Culture* (Vol. 13, No. 3, September 2005), p. 1.
[196] Anon., 'Churchill voted greatest Briton', *BBC website* at http://news.bbc.co.uk/1/hi/entertainment/2509465.stm (accessed 26 January 2016); Orange, 'Industrial Archaeology, p. 85; Stewart, P. J., and Strathern, A., 'Introduction', *Landscape, Memory and History. Anthropological Perspectives* (Pluto Press, London, 2003), p. 2.

In 2011, English Heritage commissioned a survey to explore the public's motivation for visiting sites of industrial archaeological importance.[197] English Heritage's survey of reasons for popular interest is important as Orange asserts that there is a real dearth of such research.[198] The key reasons identified were national and regional identity and pride (as explored above); preservation of memories; acknowledgment of family employment connections (particularly in the Midlands and north); and education, especially of visitors' children. These elements clearly all link into ideas of identity and the passing on of that cultural inheritance.

One manifestation of the popularity of education is the success of industrial history museums in Britain. The National Railway Museum in York has seen visitor numbers increase annually, with 926,000 in 2013/14.[199] The museum breaks down the motivation for visiting to family learning, rail enthusiasm and general York tourism. Ironbridge has similarly high numbers, with 525,000 in 2013 (most recent figures available).[200]

Hems and Blockley assert that much of the success of industrial archaeology heritage is the opportunity provided for learning through experiencing the industrial process.[201] At the site of the Crofton beam engine on the Kennet and Avon Canal, volunteers who are involved in making the engine work are mostly retired, providing 15,600 man hours for the Kennet and Avon Canal Trust in Wiltshire in 2015.[202] The government's 2014 cross-party review of railway heritage recorded 18,000 volunteers working on preserved heritage railways alone.[203] One reason for the increased popularity of volunteering was

---

[197] English Heritage, *Industrial Heritage at Risk Public Attitudes Survey* (bdrc continental, February 2011).
[198] Orange, 'Industrial Archaeology', p. 93.
[199] Science Museum *Annual Report 2013-14*, p. 19.
[200] Ironbridge Gorge Museum Trust Limited, *Annual Review 2013*, p. 4; Ironbridge Gorge Museum Trust Limited, *Annual Review 2014*, p. 4.
[201] Blockley, M., and Hems, A., *Heritage Interpretation* (Routledge, London, 2006), p. 117.
[202] G. Wallis, 'Working Historic Machinery – can it be safe?', 108-123, Buchanan, R. A. (Ed.), *Landscape with Technology. Essays in Honour of L. T. C. Rolt* (Millstream Books, Bath, 2011), p.115; Kennet and Avon Canal Trust, *Annual Accounts 2015*, p. 7.
[203] Anon., 'Report on the Value of Heritage Railways', *All Party Parliamentary*

the change in legislation that limited working hours and facilitated increased leisure opportunities.[204]

One further impetus for support for railway heritage is the continued popularity of model railways. Model railways have been given a new lease of life by computer-aided design and computer-aided manufacturing (CAD/CAM) and 3D printing and this is raising interest amongst a younger generation.[205] The popularity of railway industrial archaeology and model railways keeps seven specialist railway bookshops open in Britain. In addition, the publisher David and Charles has been a significant supporter of railway industrial heritage, keeping popular interest in it alive.[206] The circulation figures of railway magazines are a further testament to the huge enthusiasm for this aspect of Britain's heritage. Steam Railway magazine produces 13 issues a year with a steady circulation of over 32,000 (figures from 2008 to 2012).[207]

Divall argues that eight million visitors ride on trains each year and that ten per cent of British museums are transport linked but that the popularity of "doing" industrial archaeology is such that industrial archaeology attractions don't work hard enough to provide context and background learning, often merely providing a train ride.[208] Divall criticizes the transport museum sector for not conducting the sort of research that has enabled other museum sectors to improve their visitor education.

The 2014 cross-party government railway heritage review confirms heritage railway popularity, with evidence that the sector brings in

---

Group on Heritage Rail, (July 2014), p. 5.
[204] Stevenson, J. British Society 1914-45 (Penguin, Harmondsworth, 1984), p. 400.
[205] Personal communication with Castens, S., owner, Titfield Thunderbolt bookshop, Bath (24 January 2016).
[206] Buchanan, Industrial Archaeology in Britain, p. 368; J. R. Harris, Business History, 129-134 (volume 12, 2, July 1970), p. 132.
[207] Ponsford, D., 'Mag ABCs: Breakdown of circulation for all 500 titles', Press Gazette (16 February 2012); The Fact Compiler, 'Latest ABC figures show circulation remains steady', Railway Eye – the railway blog (12 February 2010) at http://railwayeye.blogspot.co.uk/2010/02/latest-abc-figures-show-circulation.html (accessed 26 January 2016).
[208] Divall, C., 'Going places? Visitors, enthusiasts and the public history of transport', Institute of Railway Studies (12 March 1999).

£250 million per annum.[209] Indeed the one might suggest that the mere existence of such a government review demonstrates its importance to the British economy. The sector is so large that it is supported by its own umbrella trade association, the Heritage Railway Association.[210]

Although railway industrial heritage has maintained its popularity, industrial archaeology transformed for public visits has not been universally successful. Although on the one hand, venues such as Ironbridge show the potential for public interest, other major museums such as the Royal Armouries in Leeds and the National Glass Centre in Sunderland have struggled to survive.[211]

The second important element in considering the popularity of industrial archaeology is government involvement. Public action, such as the outcry over the demolition of the Euston Arch in 1962, has had the power to shape government policy to preserve industrial heritage.[212] In a country with as little spare land as Britain, it is difficult to decide which of Britain's historically important industrial buildings must be saved and which demolished. Regenerating industrial heritage can also help to regenerate a whole community and add to the value of the real estate.[213] Beginning with the 1963 Industrial Monuments Survey, government policy, carried out by local Councils through the *Planning Policy Statement 5: Planning for the historic environment*, has been the arbiter of which industrial archaeology can be saved.[214]

In addition, government bodies such as Historic England have worked to preserve industrial archaeology, for example carrying out its *Industrial Heritage at Risk: Public Attitudes Survey* in 2011.[215] This

---

[209] Anon. 'Report on the Value of Heritage Railways", p. 5.
[210] Heritage Railway Association, Annual Report 2014.
[211] Ward, D., and Denny, C., 'Crisis talks aim to save armouries museum', *The Guardian* (31 July 1999); Stratton, M., and Trinder, B., *Twentieth Century Industrial Archaeology* (Taylor and Francis, London, 2014), p. 197.
[212] Orange, 'Industrial Archaeology', p. 85.
[213] Orange, 'Industrial Archaeology', p. 89.
[214] Orange, 'Industrial Archaeology', p. 84; Wallis, 'Working Historic Machinery', p. 110.
[215] Bdrc continental, *Industrial Heritage at Risk, Public Attitudes Survey*, for Historic England (February 2011).

research was able to prove that eight out of ten people think it is important to preserve Britain's industrial heritage. Similar work is undertaken at a global level by the United Nations Educational, Scientific and Cultural Organization (UNESCO), which protects important world heritage sites. After the 1997 UNESCO conference in London flagged up the underrepresentation of industrial heritage, eleven of the twenty-one sites put forward to UNESCO were industrial.[216]

One further statutory body helping to preserve Britain's railway industrial archaeology is the Railway Heritage Trust. Formed in 1985, in 2014 it administered £48million of Network Rail money and £63million of other funding in 1,500 grants.[217]

The third aspect of the popularity of industrial archaeology that needs to be considered is academic enthusiasm.

Buchanan asserts that the setting up by the Council for British Archaeology of an industrial Research Committee in the early 1960s followed by the founding of the Association for Industrial Archaeology (AIA) in 1973 gave academic backing to statutory support.[218] The AIA now has over fifty affiliated regional subdivisions, champions industrial archaeology within the Victorian Society and the Institute of Town Planning, endorses the company Heritage of Industry's website, *ourindustrialpast.org*, and produces the journal *Industrial Archaeology Review* three times a year.

This academic involvement in industrial archaeology was a natural development as post-Second World War universities started to embrace social and economic history and also began to set up archaeology departments. Bath University developed a Centre for the History of Technology and carried out the Industrial Monuments Survey completely after 1977.[219] In 1979, Harris achieved a

---

[216] K. Falconer, 'Industrial World Heritage Sites: from icons to landscapes', 10-21, Buchanan, R. A. (Ed.), *Landscape with Technology. Essays in Honour of L. T. C. Rolt* (Millstream Books, Bath, 2011), p. 13.
[217] Railway Heritage Trust annual report 2014/2015, pp. 3 & 32.
[218] Buchanan, *Industrial Archaeology in Britain*, pp. 356-357; Orange, 'Industrial Archaeology', p. 84.
[219] Buchanan, *Industrial Archaeology in Britain*, pp. 358-359.

longstanding ambition, linking the University of Birmingham, with a strong tradition of economic and social history, to the Ironbridge Institute at the Ironbridge Gorge Museum to create a post-graduate degree. The University of York runs a post-graduate diploma in conjunction with the Institute of Railway Studies, based at the National Railway Museum in York.[220]

Harris, writing in 1970, was hopeful that the interest in industrial archaeology, which he considered partly born of economic historians' new interest in periods of growth, had finally come of age.[221] However, Buchanan, writing in 1980, was beginning to anticipate problems besetting the academic position of industrial archaeology .[222] Divall and Orange, writing in 2000 and 2008 respectively, confirm that problems have arisen since the 1970s.[223] Both Buchanan and Orange start by identifying inherent problems in defining and positioning industrial archaeology.[224] For example, Bath University's industrial archaeology element was termed the "History of Technology Unit", formerly the "History of Technology". The hundred-year old Newcomen Society also positions itself as concerned with the history of technology and is based at the Science Museum rather than a more historical or archaeological institution. Buchanan considers that industrial archaeology can only be a field of study within the (itself new) discipline of archaeology and yet it must suffer from its lack of "disciplinary core".[225] Although, its study remit of the Industrial Revolution onwards would render beneficial a cross-discipline approach with social and economic history, the natural division between these departments in universities has limited the possibility of this in reality.[226] One further problem, identified by Harris, is that only someone with engineering knowledge can

---

[220] Buchanan, *Industrial Archaeology in Britain*, pp. 387-388, B. Trinder, 'A new course in Industrial Archaeology', *World Archaeology*, 218-223 (volume 15, no. 2, October 1983), pp. 218-219.
[221] Harris, 'Industrial Archaeology and its Future', p.129.
[222] Buchanan, *Industrial Archaeology in Britain*, pp. 372-373 & 386-387.
[223] Divall, 'Perspectives on Industrial Archaeology', p. 456; Orange, 'Industrial Archaeology', p. 84.
[224] Buchanan, *Industrial Archaeology in Britain*, pp. 374-375; Orange, 'Industrial Archaeology', p. 84.
[225] R. A. Buchanan, 'The Industrial Archaeology of Shropshire', review, *Technology and Culture,* 319-321 (39.2, April 1998), p.319.; Buchanan, *Industrial Archaeology in Britain*, p. 373.
[226] Harris, 'Industrial Archaeology and its Future', p. 129.

properly make sense of industrial archaeology, which limits the field for other archaeologists.[227]

Divall asserts that industrial archaeologists have continued to approach study in their field narrowly and have failed to absorb the current academic post-processual approach with its social context.[228] Industrial archaeology may be less popular because it does not often involve excavation, nor is it as essential in understanding human history as pre-historic archaeology, where there are no written or pictorial records to bear witness to past activity; furthermore, academics have tended snobbily to link industrial archaeologists with the "hobbyist" world of industrial heritage.[229] It may also be the case that post-modern archaeologists, conscious of conceptual ideas of jingoism or intra-national competitiveness, are uneasy at the potential for British Empire glorification, which is a tendency of Britain's post-Industrial Revolution heritage.[230] Conversely, Cossons sees Britain's history as the originator of modern industrialization and thus as important in understanding the trajectory of growth of industrialization across the world.[231]

A final example of the problems of current industrial archaeology in academia is the recent demise of the Rolt Fellowship at Bath University in 2012, with the History of Technology Research Unit putting the last of its funding into a centenary publication before permanently disbanding.[232]

Although academic interest in industrial archaeology is nowadays diminished somewhat from its 1970s heyday, it still forms a seemingly permanent module element of several archaeology degrees.[233]

---

[227] Harris, 'Industrial Archaeology and its Future', pp. 130-131.
[228] C. Divall, 'Perspectives on Industrial Archaeology', review, *The British Journal for the History of Science,* 456-457 (volume 34, issue 04, December 2001), pp. 456-457.
[229] Orange, 'Industrial Archaeology', p. 84.
[230] Stewart and Strathern, 'Landscape, Memory and History', p. 2.
[231] N. Cossons, 'Industrial Archaeology: the Challenge of the Evidence', *The Antiquaries Journal,* 1-52 (volume 87, September 2007), p.1.
[232] History of Technology Research Unit Annual Report 2010-2011, p. 3; History of Technology Research Unit Annual Report 2011-12, pp. 2-3.
[233] For example: University of Leicester, University of Birmingham, University of Salford, Bristol University, Manchester University

In conclusion, there is plenty of evidence for widespread interest in industrial archaeology. Whatever the current state of play in academe, academic work over many years by a preceding generation of academics, along with campaigning by statutory bodies and a highly vocal public has been effective in raising awareness of the importance of Britain's industrial archaeology. This high profile has ensured the consideration of the cultural value of individual sites when development is mooted and safeguarded the evidence of Britain's Industrial Revolution for future generations. This interest is evidenced in the large number of managed industrial heritage sites and preserved industrial buildings and the increasing listing of industrial archaeology sites.

This interest in Britain's industrial archaeology is inseparable from wider interest in Britain's economic and social history. The desire to preserve material remains has emerged in direct relation to the decline of Britain's manufacturing industry, as a nation seeks to ensure the preservation of the memory of an aspect of Britain because it is an important part of its national identity.

It might be argued that focusing on the industrial archaeology of steam railways provides a misleadingly positive account of the popularity of industrial archaeology today because it is only one aspect of Britain's industrial archaeological heritage. However, to quote from Samuel:

"It was not the economic historian but the steam fanatics – and after them the industrial archaeologists – who resuscitated the crumbling walls and rusting ironwork of eighteenth century furnaces and kilns; who kept alive, or revivified a sense of wonder at the miracles of invention which made mid-Victorian Britain the 'workshop of the world'."[234]

**Bibliography**

**Books**

---

[234] Orange, 'Industrial Archaeology', quoting Samuel, R., *Theatres of Memory. Volume 1 Past and Present in Contemporary Culture* (Verso, 1994), p. 276.

Blockley, M., and Hems, A., *Heritage Interpretation* (Routledge, London, 2006).
Buchanan, R. A., *Industrial Archaeology in Britain* (Allen Lane, London, 1980).
Burdett, W. R., *Go Great Western: A History of GWR Publicity* (David & Charles, Newton Abbot, 1970).
Rolt, L. T. C., *Isambard Kingdom Brunel* (Penguin, London, 1970).
Rolt, L. T. C., *Landscape with Canals* (Allen Lane, London, 1977).
Stevenson, J. *British Society 1914-45* (Penguin, Harmondsworth, 1984).
Wilson, R. B., *Go Great Western: A History of GWR Publicity*. (David & Charles, Newton Abbot, 1970).

**Articles**
Anon., 'Factfile: Grimsby Ice Factory and Kasbah', ITV news website (8 October 2013).
Anon., 'Grimsby Ice Factory: Bulldoze it or call in Banksy!', *Grimsby Telegraph* (21 March 2015).
Anon., 'Ian Allan, trainspotter – obituary', *The Telegraph* (30 June 2015).
Anon., 'Report on the Value of Heritage Railways', *All Party Parliamentary Group on Heritage Rail*, (July 2014).
Bdrc continental, *Industrial Heritage at Risk, Public Attitudes Survey*, for Historic England (February 2011).
Buchanan, R. A., 'Introduction', 7-9, Buchanan, R. A. (Ed.), *Landscape with Technology. Essays in Honour of L. T. C. Rolt* (Millstream Books, Bath, 2011).
Buchanan, R. A., 'The Industrial Archaeology of Shropshire', review, *Technology and Culture*, 319-321 (39.2, Apr 1998).
Cossons, N., 'Industrial Archaeology: the Challenge of the Evidence', *The Antiquaries Journal*, 1-52 (volume 87, September 2007)
Divall, C., 'Going places? Visitors, enthusiasts and the public history of transport', *Institute of Railway Studies* (12 March 1999).
Divall, C., 'Perspectives on Industrial Archaeology', review, 453-481, *The British Journal for the History of Science* (volume 34, issue 04, December 2001).
Falconer, K., 'Industrial World Heritage Sites: from icons to landscapes', 10-21, Buchanan, R. A. (Ed.), *Landscape with Technology. Essays in Honour of L. T. C. Rolt* (Millstream Books, Bath, 2011),
Fillis. I., and Herman, I., 'A Biographical Study of Isambard Kingdom Brunel as insight into entrepreneurial marketing endeavour', *Journal of Enterprising Culture* (Vol. 13, No. 3, September 2005).
Harris, J. R., Industrial Archaeology and its Future, 129-134, *Business History* (07/1970, vol. 12).
Heritage Railway Association, *Annual Report 2014*.
History of Technology Research Unit Annual Report 2010-2011.History of Technology Research Unit Annual Report 2011-2012.
Ironbridge Gorge Museum Trust Limited, *Annual Review 2013*.
Ironbridge Gorge Museum Trust Limited, *Annual Review 2014*.
Jones, R. A., 'Industrial Ruins: Space, Aesthetics and Materiality', 821-822,

review, *Technology and Culture* (47.4, 2006).
Kennet and Avon Canal Trust, *Annual Accounts 2015*.
Medcalf, A., "We are always learning: Marketing the Great Western Railway, 1921-39', *The Journal of Transport History* (33.2, December 2012).
Orange, H., 'Industrial Archaeology: Its Place Within the Academic Discipline, the Public Realm and the Heritage Industry', 85-95, *Industrial Archaeology Review* (XXX, 2, 2008).
Ponsford, D., 'Mag ABCs: Breakdown of circulation for all 500 titles', *Press Gazette* (16 February 2012).
Science Museum, *Annual Report 2013-14*.
Stewart, P. J., and Strathern, A., 'Introduction', *Landscape, Memory and History. Anthropological Perspectives* (Pluto Press, London, 2003).
Stratton, M., and Trinder, B., *Twentieth Century Industrial Archaeology* (Taylor and Francis, London, 2014).
Trinder, B., 'A new course in Industrial Archaeology', *World Archaeology*, 218-223 (volume 15, no. 2, October 1983).
Upadhya, A., 'Railway heritage and tourism: global perspectives', review, *Journal of Heritage Tourism* (June 2015).
Wallis, G., 'Working Historic Machinery – can it be safe? The Case of Crofton Pumping Station', 108-123, Buchanan, R. A. (Ed.), *Landscape with Technology. Essays in Honour of L. T. C. Rolt* (Millstream Books, Bath, 2011.
Ward, D., and Denny, C., 'Crisis talks aim to save armouries museum', *The Guardian* (31 July 1999).

**Websites**
Anon., 'Churchill voted greatest Briton', *BBC website* at http://news.bbc.co.uk/1/hi/entertainment/2509465.stmhttp://news.bbc.co.uk/1/hi/entertainment/tv_and_radio/2341661.stm (accessed 26 January 2016).
Railway Heritage Trust website, at http://railwayheritagetrust.co.uk/ (accessed 25 January 2016).
The Fact Compiler, 'Latest ABC figures show circulation remains steady', *Railway Eye – the railway blog* (12 February 2010) at http://railwayeye.blogspot.co.uk/2010/02/latest-abc-figures-show-circulation.html (accessed 26 January 2016)

## Museum Education

Most museum managers consider education a core function of the museum. Larger museums have education officers who aim to deliver high quality and dynamic programmes of learning and participation. They ensure that a museum's collections act as a learning resource for all ages. They work both within the galleries or museums and also in a community context.

Museum education officers develop, deliver and evaluate programmes and events for classes, groups or individuals, often designed to engage those who may not normally use the museum or gallery, such as hard to reach young people, young children, older people and families. Their responsibilities might include:

- creating a learning strategy to engage the public in line with the ethos of the museum;
- developing programmes of talks, activities and workshops around particular exhibitions or in response to particular themes or annual festivals;
- liaising with schools, colleges and teachers to promote the use of the collections and activities of the museum in line with the national curriculum;
- creating and developing educational resources for visitors, schools, families and special interest groups;
- delivering talks, workshops and activities in partnership with storytellers, craftspeople and artists;
- managing programmes, budgets and teams of volunteers;
- facilitating history-inspired activities in the local community in response to requests from schools and community groups or to promote particular exhibitions;
- collating, analysing and applying feedback on the educational activities provided;
- working with other museum staff to develop and market the museum and the events programme;
- representing and promoting the museum on external educational bodies in order to establish a network of useful and productive partnerships.[235]

GEM, 'the voice for heritage learning', produces a variety of publications for those interested in and engaged in Museum education. These include:

- JEM - the annual Journal of Education in Museums
- Case Studies - a twice yearly publication in magazine format

---

[235] prospects.ac.uk

- GEM e-News - a monthly email newsletter sent to members
- Museum Education Bibliography

## The abuse of cultural heritage

'Western' archaeology in the second half of the twentieth century became preoccupied with the pursuit of an objective account of the past. Internationalist perspectives, as opposed to individualist and nationalist, became the norm. Some exponents of 'The New Archaeology' in the middle of that period even began to distance the archaeologist from the difficult process of analysing past lives by focusing on evolving technologies. Earlier approaches to archaeology were sometimes revealed as debased, the legacy of nineteenth century imperialism, nationalism and social-Darwinism. In post-war Germany in particular the abuse of the past, especially during the 1930s, left a kind of intellectual vacuum in which archaeology, together with other forms of *völkisch* studies, was regarded with suspicion by the war-damaged inheritors of the Third Reich.

If an archaeological *zeitgeist* could be identified for Germany as she entered the third millennium, it was perhaps best exemplified by the remarkable museum of cultural evolution opened in October 1996 in the Neander Valley. Here 'Neanderthal Man' is no longer the primitive ape as conceived by an earlier, perhaps more self-confident, generation which believed wholeheartedly in its own cultural and biological supremacy. Here the origins of that modern culture are depicted as the inheritance of all - a prehistory that does not respect national boundaries. The museum shatters both of those comfortable assumptions by which the past is either viewed as the narrative of progress or as a halcyon era of lost innocence and simplicity. Quite probably it tells us more about the present than the past it seeks to depict in much the same way, though more honourably, than the writings of Nazi-influenced archaeologists in the 1930s.[236]

From the earliest times archaeology and politics have been intertwined. When John Leland, royal chaplain and librarian, prepared in 1533 to undertake his itinerary through Henrician England for his

---

236 With thanks to Richard Nate for his guidance at the Neanderthal Museum, the *Hermannsdenkmal*, and the *Externsteine*.

royal master, he seems to have had a double agenda: first he was to help initiate the Dissolution process by identifying and securing for the king valuable manuscripts in ecclesiastical libraries throughout the land; second he would record the other antiquities which, collectively, defined the essence of England and her history, to which Henry now laid claim as both spiritual and temporal head. In a remarkable cultural revolution the symbols of 'un-Englishness' - the buildings that shouted loyalty to Rome - were pulled down stone by stone. As John Leland made his way through the abbeys and cathedrals of Somerset - Bath to Wells, to Glastonbury, to Bruton - he took a curious detour to the monumental remains of the hillfort at South Cadbury. In his most quoted passage he called it "Camelot"[237]; at Glastonbury he had seen the bridge from which King Arthur hurled his sword into the lake formed of the flood waters of the River Brue. Such observations were bound to please his benefactor for the Tudor dynasty claimed direct descent from Arthur, the name Henry VII had bestowed on his first born son. In the 1530s Henry VIII needed to exploit every means available to him to prove his legitimacy as he began to wrench Catholic England from her papal traditions.

This desire to reassert identity has been a theme that has always run through antiquarianism and archaeology. In an increasingly cosmopolitan world England's unique heritage would continue to serve the needs of both conservatives and reformists. In the eighteenth century John Wood, the architect of Bath's Royal Crescent and the Circus, was inspired as much by indigenous "druidic" architecture as he was by that of classical Greece and Rome.

The detail adhered to neo-classical conventions and tastes but the concept paid homage to the henge monuments of Somerset and the Salisbury Plain. The enigmatic ruins of Stanton Drew, Stonehenge and Avebury, with which he was so familiar, provided Wood with the mystique and majesty that causes his buildings to be recognised as the definitive English urban domestic structures of his age. In their rebellion against the modern industrial and commercial age, the Pre-Raphaelite Brotherhood in the 1840s sought solace in the architecture

---

237 "Right at the south end of South Cadbury church stands Camelot. This was once a noted town or castle, set on a real peak of a hill, and with marvellously strong natural defences. [...] The only information local people can offer is that they have heard that Arthur frequently came to Camelot."

and aspirations of pre-industrial England. Meanwhile, in a wave of Anglo-centricity, underpinned by unmatched commercial prosperity, the Establishment Gothicised its churches, factories and prisons. While Queen Victoria's Houses of Parliament were redesigned along pseudo-Gothic lines, William Morris invoked the medieval in his communistic tirade against the modern age.

In this period many Germans felt an even greater need to reassert their national identity. The economic community of German states, the Zollverein, anticipated their political unification by Bismarck in the 1860s. With all German states except Austria under the Prussian king by 1871, Bismarck's next great task was that of convincing the subject population, which included Catholic Bavarian nationalists as well as Lutheran Prussian junkers, that theirs was a shared national history and a common destiny. From its birth the new Germany, the Second Reich, stood for the myth of Teutonic heroism, defiant in the face of cultural assault from without. No gesture in this period was quite as dramatic as the building of a colossus: the *Hermannsdenkmal* or Arminius Monument, a huge hollow bronze built in 1875 depicting the warrior-leader who defeated the Roman legions in 9 AD having united the tribal peoples of modem Westphalia and Hessen. Where some of the overtly Nazi monumental building of the 1930s has been razed to the ground, this icon of the Kaiser-Reich has survived the post-war reconstruction of two twentieth century conflicts, and remains a popular tourist attraction to this day.

By the time the Arminius Monument was being constructed the self-appointed cultural supremacy of northern Europe's imperialist powers was beginning to find 'justification' in science. As Darwin's theories pervaded western thinking attempts to explain human activity along genetic lines became a commonplace. Even before Emile Durkheim published his classic study *Suicide* in 1897, early statisticians and sociologists across Europe were exploring the degenerative effects of uncontrolled breeding upon society as a whole. By the turn of the century the cultural chauvinism of upper class northern European imperialists was transforming into full-blown racialism. Perhaps because of its shorter history and an insecurity bred of encirclement by potentially hostile powers, this was nowhere more evident than in newly unified Germany. Kaiser Wilhelm II, and his *Weltpolitik* epitomised the national paranoia and the obsessive pursuit of the nation's restoration to greatness on the world stage. In this context Gustaf Kossinna (1858-1931) began to develop his theory that European culture was founded in the Schleswig-Holstein region of north Germany, and that it owed nothing to a diffusion of ideas and a migration of people emanating from the Near East. With his book *Die deutsche Vorgeschichte: Eine hervorragend nationale Wissenschaft* (1912) he confirmed the emerging Aryan myth.[238]

Defeat in World War One and political revolution destroyed monarchy and autocracy in Germany but, even in the decade of its greatest experiment in democracy, German nationalism remained a potent concept in the Weimar Republic. Post-war recrimination, the fear of Bolshevism, the burden of reparations, and the legend that Germany had been "stabbed in the back" by leftists in 1918, all contributed to a society in which, if anything, xenophobia and racialism were increasing.

This was a period of cultural as well as political polarisation: while Weimar Germany spawned the dynamism of the Bauhaus, the theatre of Bertolt Brecht, anti-war films like *Im Westen nichts Neues* ('All Quiet on the Western Front'[239]), and the novels of Hermann Hesse and Thomas Mann, it is also associated with the emergence of *völkisch* organisations, set up in direct opposition to the intellectual culture of the Left and a popular culture founded on 'decadent' American values as well as American dollars.[240] In so doing tradition and nineteenth century values were deployed in the wider political struggle.

The place of history and archaeology in the Third Reich is hard to locate with precision. Nazi Germany has often been depicted as a morass of conflicting opinions and ideologies, and the contradictions inherent in a regime that could be both politically revolutionary and culturally conservative are especially apparent in its manipulation of the past. If it can be said that Weimar culture sought a break with the past, Nazi culture embraced it. Social realism and shock tactics in the arts were

---

238 Kossinna (1912)
239 Based on the novel by Erich Maria Remarque (1929)
240 In his *Betrachtungen eines Unpolitischen* ('Observations of an Unpolitical Man'), written during World War I and published in 1918, Thomas Mann had expressed similar conservative / rightist views. After the war, however, he became a supporter of the Weimar Republic.

replaced by romantic, idealised and, above all, nostalgic rural idylls, designed to comfort and reassure rather than provoke. The realities of modern industrial life were effectively denied as Nazi propagandists urged the people to struggle to the defence of an imaginary landscape peopled by hardy peasants and their well-fed, decent families. The confusion of the past with the idealism of the present caused Hitler to be portrayed in some paintings as a Teutonic knight- hero, resplendent in shining armour and mounted on a white charger. While Walther Darré, the minister for agriculture, spoke of restoring Germany to a communal, co-operative society of small-scale organic farmers[241], Alfred Rosenberg invented a Nordic 'religion', supposedly based on ancient beliefs, which did not really represent anything other than 'Aryan' isolationism and the rejection of Judaeo-Christian traditions.[242]

Hitler's own sense of history was restricted to little more than a diatribe against the Jews, scapegoats for the disasters that had beset Germany during his lifetime. He plundered history and prehistory where it suited his purpose, probably admired Napoleon, and was impressed by Roman civilisation. The full exploitation of the past was left to his lackeys: men like Heinrich Himmler and Alfred Rosenberg, and those shaping education policies for the schools and universities. Hitler's own interests extended little beyond the Munich Putsch of 1923: the history he chose to invoke in his speeches and writings was his own and that of the Party.

For Rosenberg however "an individual to whom the tradition of his people (*Volkstum*) and the honour of his people (*Volksehre*) is not a supreme value, has forfeited the right to be protected by that people".[243] His interest lay primarily in a prehistoric Germany and its echoes which he believed could be heard in Nordic folklore. Prehistorians, previously overshadowed by the Romanists, were elevated under the Nazis: eight new chairs were created in German Prehistory and unprecedented funding for their work was made available."[244] The profile of history was raised in German museums, films dealing with prehistory were produced, and Neolithic and Iron

---

241 Darré (1929)
242 Rosenberg (1930)
243 in Arnold (1996), p.550
244 Arnold (1996), p.554

Age lake settlements were reconstructed on Lake Constanza.[245] Archaeologists working in non-Germanic fields were likely to arouse suspicion. Hitler however was not greatly impressed by the endeavours of Rosenberg and other 'Germanomaniacs'; Germany's prehistory if anything was a cause for national embarrassment, as noted by Albert Speer:

> *Why do we call the whole world's attention to the fact that we have no past? It's bad enough that the Romans were erecting great buildings when our forefathers were still living in mud huts: now Himmler is starting to dig up these villages of mud huts and enthusing over every potsherd and stone axe he finds. All we prove by that is that we were still throwing stone hatchets and crouching around open fires when Greece and Rome had already reached the highest stage of culture. We really should do our best to keep quiet about this past. Instead Himmler makes a great fuss about it all. The present-day Romans must be having a laugh at these revelations"*[246]

Hitler perhaps felt happier about the nine week expedition to Greece in support of the notion that Greek culture was the result of Germanic / Aryan migration into southern Europe. The most absurd theorising based on archaeological evidence was Himmler's suggestion that Germany's 'Venus' figurines were characteristically 'Hottentot' and thus the product of a once indigenous but now extinct northern European race. For Himmler they were evidence of an ancient struggle between the Nordic peoples and, what he considered, racially inferior *Untermenschen* which, presumably, the Aryans had won.[247] Thus Himmler contrived to demonstrate the eternal nature of the Darwinian struggle - the Third Reich's inheritance and destiny.

Although archaeological works of lasting value were carried out by German archaeologists during this period, some excavations, particularly those supervised by the SS, were a travesty of academic principles - activities that "can only be described as looting".[248] Drawing on Kossinna's 'evidence' and the findings of their own excavations, archaeology was manipulated to help justify modern

---

245 Arnold (1996), p.555
246 Arnold (1996), p. 556
247 McCann (1990), p.85
248 McCann (1990), p.3

German expansion into supposed former German territories.[249]

The ambiguity of archaeological evidence makes it susceptible to abuse. In the case outlined above it was hijacked by racialists and employed in the cynical pursuit of Lebensraum. In a dictatorship such things are possible, in a democracy the freedom of discourse permits alternative interpretations, and education systems in democracies should provide individuals with the skills to draw their own conclusions. However, even under these conditions, the way in which societies handle their 'national' heritage is biased by the moral mores of the age, their self-image and how they would choose to be seen by others. In countries like the UK, where heritage is the mainstay of the tourist industry, the national image is partially shaped by market forces.

The past continues to serve the social and political needs of the present. It is salutary to observe that over half a century since the demise of the Third Reich its then most celebrated ancient monument, the *Externsteine*, a dramatic outcrop of rocks near Detmold carved as a Christian place of worship in the eleventh and twelfth centuries, now regularly provides the backdrop for the contradictory ritual activities of both neo-Nazis and twenty-first century hippy-druids.

## CASE STUDY: heritage and hidden history

### Bristol and Transatlantic Slavery

In the late 1990s Madge Dresser made the following observations:

*'In the last few years there has been a shift in attitude towards Bristol's slave trade. Many Bristolians still appear loath to discuss certain aspects of the past and all too ready to let sleeping dogs lie. There is a reluctance to feel guilty for something that happened ages ago and a tremendous defensiveness as if to talk about the subject is tantamount to besmirching the name of Bristol and its inhabitants.'*[250]

---

249 McCann (1990), p.84
250 Martin (1999), p.159

'Hidden from history' until recent times, the city of Bristol has made a considerable effort over the last couple of decades to highlight this aspect of its heritage. The *Cabot 500* celebrations of 1996 prompted interest in illuminating this other aspect of Bristol's maritime history. The Bristol City Council's Leisure Department set up the Bristol Slave Trade Action Group (BSTAG) which was active until May 2000. Paul Smith, Chair of the Leisure Services Committee at the time explained its role:

*'Slavery and the plantations it supported funded 120 years of immense growth in Bristol and it is therefore considered essential that it is given a high profile in telling the story of the City. The effects of eighteenth century slavery are evident in both modern Bristol and Africa and it is as relevant today as it has ever been.'*[251]

The BSTAG was wrapped up, claiming to have met this objective. It was responsible for the display illustrating the connections of the Pinney family with the slave trade at the Georgian House – a well-preserved, dignified, Georgian mansion, restored to its former glory, furniture and all, and open to the public. The Slave Heritage Trail created shortly afterwards was a further initiative. In March 1999, in conjunction with the City Council and local community groups, the BSTAG launched a temporary exhibition at the City Museum and Art Gallery, *A Respectable Trade? Bristol and the Atlantic Slave Trade*. Associated community events included an evening of multicultural entertainments at the Bristol Old Vic entitled *A Respectable Trade - the Legacy*. One of the museum's most popular exhibitions ever, it attracted over 160,000 visitors in the six months of its run. Subsequently it was relocated to the Bristol Industrial Museum.

Where the motivation came from it is hard to say but the slave trade at the end of the 20th century had a higher public profile in this country than at any other time since the televising of *Roots* in the late 1970s. It is possible that some of this new interest stemmed from the making of Spielberg's slave epic *Amistad* (1997), itself the successor to his *Schindler's List* (1994), the story of other race related atrocities in danger of being neglected as the world entered a new millennium.

---

[251] (http://www.bristol-city.gov.uk) Accessed in 1999

The Bristol trade specifically provided the background for a popular BBC TV series *A Respectable Trade* (1998), a documentary history of the trade was screened by the Channel 4 (*The English Slave Trade* 1999), the BBC covered the subject in 1998 in a *Timewatch* documentary, Channel 4's *Time Team* excavated the Pinney's slave-run sugar plantation on Nevis (broadcast March 1999), and, in 1998, Hugh Thomas published a major new history of the European trade. This turn of the century flurry of interest in past persecution speaks volumes of the confidence of the present age as society bravely faces the iniquities of the past and attempts to set an agenda for the future.

Meanwhile the slavery legacy remains a burning issue in race relations and, at least in contemporary black propaganda, it is one which is anything but 'history'. Bristol faces a dilemma which it has not yet resolved: does exposure of its slaving past promote racial harmony or heighten racial tensions? Black activists in America have demanded compensation from the once slave-owning state in much the same way as post-imperial aboriginal communities and post-Holocaust Jews. Official recognition of the place of the slave trade in English history very likely has opened, not closed, the book.

The slave trade exhibition at Bristol City Museum was officially opened by Paul Boateng MP on March 16, 1999. He was joined by Channel 4's *Timeteam* whose excavations at Nevis were broadcast five days later. During the opening ceremony finds from the Bristol owned Pinney plantation on Nevis were loaned to the museum for the new exhibition. It was rehoused at Bristol's Industrial Museum in April 2000. It sought to address 'some of the issues raised by Bristol's involvement in the slave trade' and to provide 'a context for looking at Black cultural identity, together with aspects of the city's history from the 18th-20th centuries'.[252]

The exhibition was chronological in design and delivered information through a combination of artefactual evidence, audio-visual resources and the written word. Artefacts on display included, among others: brassware, manillas, trade beads, items crafted by African peoples in Africa, and various artefacts related to tobacco, rum, sugar and tea.

---

[252] Bristol Museums and Art Gallery (2000), p.2

Some ecofactual material was also displayed such as herbs and calabash. Both historic and contemporary images were displayed, and listening posts included readings from the writings of slaves, abolitionists and twentieth century commentators. A video showed scenes from the film *Amistad*. The accompanying interpretative text was clear and coherent, combining historic and contemporary comment, all of which was richly illustrated with facsimiles of eighteenth and nineteenth century images, and modem maps and other graphics. In the heart of the gallery a full size eighteenth century room interior had been created, replete with waxwork figures: white gentleman, white lady and black 'servant'.

An open forum at the Malcom X Centre, St Paul's, was held in August 1999 to air the views of me public regarding the success, or otherwise, of the exhibition and to discuss its future.

Perhaps the greatest problem the managers of this exhibition faced was that the trade in slaves was dehumanising and it is hard to convey through either artefacts or historical records the fact that these displaced people were not one homogenous mass of characterless drones. This of course is how they were perceived by the civilisations that exploited them and the lie of their inferiority 'justified' their bestial treatment. When ex-slave Olaudah Equiano wrote his astonishing autobiography in the 1780s[253] he prefaced the tale of his enslavement with a detailed account of the near idyllic life he was tom from at the age often. He describes the beauty and bounty of the country in which he was born and the comparatively simple but eminently sensible mode of living his people enjoyed. Bristol's slavery exhibition began to convey a similar message with a small display of artefacts celebrating Africa's cultural heritage prior to describing the horrors of the slave trade and its effects upon a plethora of mother countries.

At much the same time the Bristol Slave Trail was devised as a laudable attempt to reveal standing buildings and other structures in the middle of Bristol in their association with the African trade for, as Philippa Gregory pointed out in a 1998 BBC TV programme (*Travels with Pevsner*) 'The slave trade is hardly spoken of today but the

---

[253] Carretta (1995)

extent of it can be seen in many of the buildings of Bristol.'

No plaques were placed on buildings but a 26 page booklet, published in 1998, comprising a map of central Bristol, forty-two location points, and accompanying descriptions and illustrative material, provided a guided tour for interested parties. Taking a day to do properly, the trail included three museums, several houses owned by slavers, planters and suchlike, pubs where the great abolitionist Thomas Clarkson gathered damning evidence and slavers recruited crews, churches, theatres and halls endowed by Bristol merchants, finance houses and commercial centres, and structures such as the Wills Memorial Tower which recalled Bristol's past reliance on colonial imports such as tobacco and sugar. A Quaker burial ground along the way and the site of Hannah More's schoolhouse illuminated Bristolians' contributions to ending the trade in slaves in 1807.

For the first time tourists visiting Bristol were encouraged by the city's tourist board to view such splendid monuments as Queen's Square and the Cathedral with something other than undiluted admiration. Even the city fathers of yesteryear were brought to book: Edward Colston, the well-known philanthropist, whose statue enjoys a central place in the heart of Bristol, was described in the guidebook as 'a prominent sugar merchant with interests in the Caribbean island of St Kitts'.[254] The plaque on his commemorative statue erected in the mid-1890s makes no mention of his membership of the Court of Assistants to the Royal African Company, which enjoyed a monopoly on the African slave trade until 1698, but, instead, speaks of his endowments to the people of Bristol. In 1998 the reggae-rock band Massive Attack refused to perform at Bristol's Colston Hall because of Colston's slave trade connections. Many would like to see the statue removed altogether, like a post-*Perestroika* Lenin or Stalin.

The current vogue for the unmolested preservation of historic monuments, from prehistoric henges to pre-fabs, is at odds with the 'clean up' mentality that demolishes Victorian slums and the homes of mass-murderers. The legacy of the eighteenth century slave trade is a contemporary political issue and civil rights activists demand gestures bolder than town trails and museum exhibitions. Doubtless it is

---

[254] Slave Trade Trail (1998), p.32

argued in some quarters that Bristol's *fin de siecle* endeavour to come to terms with the darker aspects of its past has fanned the flames of present confrontation. If the guardians of our heritage think they can steer an objective path through the tangle of it all they are well-intentioned but misguided.

Madge Dresser observed that:

*'It was never really publicly acknowledged in any ceremonies or plaques or what have you. There was a silence about slavery in some quarters and I think this was because there were still families who felt they had made their wealth from activities allied with the slave trade.'*[255]

This was something the Bristol Slave Trail, in particular, addressed. 'Colston' was not the only famous name linked by the trail to the trade in slaves: Tyndall, Farr, Miles, Goldney, Elton and Hobhouse all received mention in the accompanying booklet. However some effort was made to highlight the place of some old slaver planter families, such as the Hobhouses, in the abolition movement. Of the Wills dynasty it remarks 'By the late 18th century the family were actively involved in a number of philanthropic activities in Bristol and subscribed to the 1793 edition of Olaudah Equiano's classic *Autobiography of a Slave*. Just as, no doubt, those that carry the name of their illustrious forbears would choose to be remembered for the family's' good works' so too would the inheritors of the mantle of eighteenth century Bristol commerce: the trail and its accompanying publication was produced by Bristol City Council with sponsorship from the Society of Merchant Venturers. Others thanked for their contribution to the project include English Heritage and 'all those members of the public who attended the public consultation meeting at the Malcolm X Centre and so thoughtfully commented on the various drafts of the slave trail'.

Slave Trade Trail site number 40 is the former home of John Pinney (1740-1818), a sugar plantation owner, and now The Georgian House Museum. The Pinney family has a particularly fascinating 'slave trade' history. Azariah Pinney was transported to the Caribbean by Judge Jeffries and his cronies for supporting the Duke of Monmouth and his

---

[255] in Martin (1999), p.159

ill-fated rebellion which ended on the field of Sedgemoor in 1685. Having worked the plantations himself, back in the days when white convicts and indentured servants provided the labour, Azariah's freedom was purchased by his sister and he established a thriving business of his own on the island of Nevis, subsequently inherited by his grandson John.

John Pinney's Nevis mansion became familiar to millions of Sunday teatime armchair archaeologists as Channel 4's 'Time Team' roamed its grounds in 1999, and No 7 Great George Street opens its doors each year to the visitors who pay to have a look at the inside of his townhouse in Bristol and enjoy the symmetrical charm and Chippendale elegance of eighteenth century architecture and Georgian fittings. In 1998, with the Slave Trade Trail guide in hand, some came to find out more about the trade that enabled him to leave his heirs a fortune of £340,000. They left, at best, a little disappointed and, at worst, angry. Although sugar loaf and tongs, globes and paintings of Pinney's ships in the Caribbean adorned the rooms below, it was not until the visitor arrived at a small room way up on the top floor that slavery got a look-in. Here a small display (text and illustration) gave an account of Pinney's reliance on slaves. Possibly this room was inhabited by his favourite 'servant', Pero, who he brought with him on his return to England in 1783.

Just as Edward Colston has fallen from grace, Pero has become a new hero for a new Bristol. In April 1999 a footbridge in Bristol's docks, the 'Pero Bridge', was opened by civic dignitaries with a small attendant audience of both black and white Bristolians. Pero, at first sight, is an unlikely hero - towards the end of his life his master complained he might have to get rid of him because of his frequent drunkenness. He died in his forties without having done anything very remarkable unlike other 'Afro-Britons' of the eighteenth century such as Olaudah Equiano. However he represents for some the hero-victim, driven to drink and an early grave by the iniquities of those who displaced him and condemned him to a life of physical and psychological enslavement. He embodies, despite the tragedy of his own life, the foundation of Black consciousness and the identity of disparate peoples united by the common heritage of slavery and the colour of their skin.

The Georgian House Museum raises important questions regarding how we should interpret and manage historic buildings. The endeavour here has been to recreate the house as it appeared when first built. Only in the 'Pero room' did the curators, perhaps under pressure from the BSTAG, deviated from this principle. On October 1998, when the museum had a 'living history' day with costumed guides describing domestic life in well-heeled Georgian society, an improvised play about the horrors of the slave trade was performed in this room by a group of Black American actors. This unsolicited 'guerrilla theatre' was designed to highlight the inadequacy of the gesture; to playwright Lee Simon, the declaration in this display that there is no room in the house for a full testimony to slavery is, in itself, a racist statement:

*'John Pinney and others like him were racist, evil men, simple as that. Why does the city of Bristol in the year 1998 celebrate this monster [...] Is Bristol a racist city? There is only room for indictment of a mentality which allowed human beings to be treated as animals.'*[256]

Within five minutes of opening they had been evicted from the building and the play continued on its steps to an audience of journalists and curious passers-by.

In the same way as synagogues in German cities such as Essen have been turned into Holocaust memorial-museums, perhaps this very significant site should be reinterpreted in terms of its wider associations as opposed to architecture, design and domestic life. Arguably the natural home of the Transatlantic Slavery Exhibition was neither the City Museum nor the Industrial Museum but this, the home of the man who built it through the sweat and blood of African slaves, and also that of his manservant - poor broken-hearted Pero.

In the 1990s the Africa reparations movement emerged, demanding compensation for the suffering and diaspora of African peoples due to the slave trade. Whether or not a financial settlement can ever be reached, the more immediate and attainable demand is for official apologies by governments or, in the case of Bristol, city councils. Such demands were met by Australian Aboriginees in 2008 when Kevin

---

[256] (http://www.hotwells.freeserve.co.uk) Accessed 1998

Rudd in Canberra read a lengthy carefully worded formal statement presented as a national apology particularly to the 'Stolen Generation' of aboriginal children forcefully removed from their parents and communities. His critics argued that such a gesture would open the door to those demanding reparations. In 2006, on eve the $200^{th}$ anniversary of the abolition of Britain's slave trade, demands for an apology, from all quarters including the Archbishop of York, became particularly vociferous. Prime Minister Tony Blair went as far as expressing 'deep sorrow' on a personal, informal level, but went no further. Some commentators at the time suggested the bicentenary should be greeted with celebration, not sorrow, since it marked Britain's lead in challenging the age-old acceptance of the slavery principle shared by most civilisations up to that point in time.

As mentioned above demands have been made for the removal of Colston's statue; less controversially requests are also made for the further recognition of Bristol's Black history in the form of a slave trade memorial site and new pieces of public art identifying and celebrating Bristol's African heritage. Meanwhile the 1998 Bristol Slave Trail has survived to the present day, enhanced by further publications and new web-based technology including a downloadable audio-guide. Although no formal apology was offered to those with a Bristol slavery heritage, in 2007 a major new £1 million exhibition on the subject ran for two years at Bristol's British Empire and Commonwealth Museum. A permanent display of artefacts and commentary can also be found in The M Shed, Bristol's excellent modern museum of social, cultural and economic history.

# Part 3 ARCHAEOLOGY

## 5 Archaeological methods and practices

### What is Archaeology?

Archaeology is the study of the past through the close examination of material evidence. It is not 'prehistory' although, since prehistory is the term used to describe the human past from which no written records exist, it is the essential approach in prehistoric studies. Nevertheless archaeology is as relevant to 'history' as it is to prehistory; archaeology is as relevant to the study of our recent industrial past as it is to the technologies of palaeolithic Europe.

Just as the archaeologist has a great deal in common with the historian, and archaeologists, particular those focusing on the material evidence of the last two thousand years or so, are likely to be capable historians (and, sometimes, *vice versa*), so too does archaeology share a platform with geographers in its approach to places and landscapes ('geoarchaeology' / landscape archaeology), with sociologists in its attempt to identify and explain social organisation, and with social anthropologists in its analysis of human behaviour.

This richest of multi-disciplinary subjects also draws on the skills of natural scientists, linguists, theologians, geophysicists, geologists and many other experts. Consequently there has long been a debate regarding whether academic archaeology should be defined as an arts subject or a science. In the UK some universities award FdAs, BAs and MAs (Foundation, Bachelor and Master of Arts degrees), while others award FdAs, BScs and MScs (Foundation, Bachelor and Master of Science degrees). There are many specialisms within archaeology, some having a more obviously scientific bent, for example forensic archaeology, others leaning more towards the 'arts' (history, philosophy, theology etc.) such as classical archaeology. As in history and several of the other academic disciplines closely associated with archaeology, its practitioners are sometimes defined by their approach. As defined in the opening section of this book, there are, for example, 'feminist', 'Marxist' and 'postmodern' archaeologists.

## Archaeology and Planning Guidance

Since November 1990, with the introduction of Planning Policy Guidance statement 16 (PPG 16), the archaeology of sites identified for proposed development has been a major consideration in development proposals. Not only did it raise awareness among planners of the importance of preserving or carefully recording both the visible and hidden archaeological heritage of sites but it also introduced the principle that where archaeological work was deemed necessary (e.g. surveying, excavating) the developer should pay. Its introduction vastly increased the amount of archaeological work undertaken in the UK and thus created numerous new job opportunities for graduate archaeologists.

In 2010 PPG 16 and PPG 15, dealing with historic buildings and environments, were replaced by Planning Policy Statement 5 (PPS5). This document advises local authorities to collect and collate evidence regarding the heritage of places under their jurisdiction. Central to this is the relevant Historic Environment Record (HER):

'All local authorities have access to a Historic Environment Record (HER). HERs will usually provide the core of information needed for plan-making and individual planning decisions. HERs are information services that aim to provide comprehensive access and regularly updated resources relating to the historic environment of a defined geographical area for public benefit and use. They consist of databases linked to a Geographic Information System (GIS), together with associated reference collections and are managed by dedicated staff. HERs are unique repositories of, and signposts to, information relating to landscapes, buildings, sites and artefacts spanning from the Palaeolithic period to modern times. Their content complements and enriches the collections of museums, archives and libraries, and underpins the work of historic environment services in local authorities to identify, record, protect, conserve and interpret the historic environment designation and planning decisions. DCMS intends to publish guidance for local authorities on the maintenance

Archaeological methods and practices

of HERs.

Although it is not a replacement for direct consultation with HERs and other evidence sources, the Heritage Gateway is a portal that provides cross-searchable online access to records of designated heritage assets, local HERs and many other sources of historic information (www.heritagegateway.org.uk).'[257]

PPS5 recommends a 'desk-top survey' prior to an on-site examination of the site identified for development:

'In accordance with HE6.1, an applicant will need to undertake an assessment of significance to an extent necessary to understand the potential impact (positive or negative) of the proposal and to a level of thoroughness proportionate to the relative importance of the asset whose fabric or setting is affected. Given the obvious burden of the process, local planning authorities will need to be careful to only ask the applicant for what is genuinely needed to satisfy the policy requirement. Although there is no limit on the sources of information that might be consulted or the exercises that might be carried out to fulfil that requirement, the most common steps an applicant might take are as follows. The first three steps will be undertaken in almost every case.

- Check the development plan, main local and national records including the relevant Historic Environment Record, statutory and local lists, the Heritage Gateway, the NMR, and other relevant sources of information that would provide an understanding of the history of the place and the value the asset holds for society.
- Examine the asset and its setting.
- Consider whether the nature of the affected significance requires an expert assessment to gain the necessary level of understanding.
- Consider whether there are any special techniques that need to be employed because of the type of asset.

---

257 English Heritage (2012) PPS5: Planning for the Historic Environment Practice Guide, p.13

- Seek advice on the best means of assessing the nature and extent of any archaeological interest e.g. geophysical survey, physical appraisal of visible structures and/or trial trenching for buried remains.
- Consider, in the case of certain buildings whether physical intervention, such as the removal of plaster, may be needed to reveal important details hidden behind later additions and alterations.
- Carry out additional assessment where the initial research has established an architectural, historic, artistic and/or archaeological interest but the extent, nature or importance of which needs to be established more clearly before safe decisions can be made about change to the site. This may require a desk-based assessment and/or on-site evaluation. Such may be necessary for all types of asset, including buildings, areas and wreck sites, where understanding of the asset's history and significance is incomplete. Where applicants are to commission assessment or evaluation they are advised to discuss the scope of the work with the local planning authority in advance and to agree a written scheme of investigation, if necessary, before commencement.
- Consider, and if necessary confirm, whether any investigative work may itself require planning permission or other consent.'[258]

In the same document desk-based assessment is defined as

'an assessment only of existing information, such as that contained in the main national and local records; topographic, cartographic, and other historical sources; site-specific information e.g. existing soil engineers' reports of ground conditions and contamination reports; geophysical and geotechnical surveys; and existing and proposed site plans. Further guidance is available, for example, the Landscape Design Trust's Parks and Gardens: a Researcher's Guide to Documentary Sources for Designed Landscapes, (2006). The aim is to assemble the available information about the architectural, historic, artistic and/or archaeological interest of the site and to assess what, if

---

258  English Heritage (2012) PPS5: Planning for the Historic Environment Practice Guide, pp.20-21

any, further expert investigation and on-site evaluation may be needed.'²⁵⁹

A desk-based assessment may not provide sufficient evidence for an appropriate planning decision to be made, in which case additional strategies may need to be employed:

'Where a desk-based assessment does not provide sufficient evidence for confident prediction of the impact of the proposal, it may be necessary to establish the extent, nature and importance of the asset's significance through on-site evaluation. This may be achieved through a number of techniques, some of which may potentially be harmful to the asset and will need careful consideration. These include ground-penetrating radar, trial-trenching, test-pitting, field-walking, x-ray and other forms of remote-sensing, geo-archaeological borehole investigation, opening-up and building analysis and recording.'²⁶⁰

Any archaeological works to be undertaken are expected to conform to the principles outlined by English Heritage:

'Where a written scheme of investigation is to be provided, it may include the following. Advice on what is proportionate and appropriate in any given case can be sought from the local planning authority's historic environment advisers.

Background information and context

This information could be extracted from the application documents.

1) A summary of the planning background and the reason for the project, including any relevant planning conditions or obligations.
2) A summary of information from existing sources and of the results of any pre-decision-making research and investigations.

---

259 English Heritage (2012) PPS5: Planning for the Historic Environment Practice Guide, p.21
260 English Heritage (2012) PPS5: Planning for the Historic Environment Practice Guide, pp.21-22

3) A description of the asset or assets in question (focusing especially on those parts that will be altered, damaged or destroyed by the proposed change).
4) An assessment of the significance of the asset in its wider historical and geographical context (focusing especially on those parts of the asset that will be altered, damaged or destroyed by the proposed change).
5) A summary of how any loss of significance will be mitigated/provided for by the project.

Proposals for the investigation and publication of the results

1) A statement of the research questions which will guide the investigation and their relation to regional and national research frameworks.
2) Where appropriate, a statement of how the local community and other interested parties will be informed about and engage with the investigation.
3) Proposals for site investigation prior to works commencing (particularly for excavation) and/or investigation in co-ordination with site works, such as analysis of building fabric revealed as stripping-out or demolition is underway.
4) Proposals for assessment and analysis of the results, with proposals from the investigating expert for an appropriate level of publication and dissemination of the results dependent on what is found.
5) Proposals for the preparation and publication of a suitable report on the investigation, its results and the advancement in understanding that those results bring.
6) A statement of the methods to be adopted and an explanation of how these link to, and seek to fulfil, the research aims of the investigation.
7) Provision for the submission of a report to the HER summarising the investigation and how its results have been disseminated.
8) Provision for the deposition of the records of the investigation, including drawings, photographs, surveys, artefacts and samples, in an appropriate archive, museum or other depository. The Institute for Archaeologists publishes standards and guidance for the creation, compilation, transfer

and deposition of archaeological archives. Advice is also available from the Museums, Libraries and Archives Council, the Museums Association and individual museums and archives.

Operational matters

1) The proposed resourcing of the investigation, excluding commercially sensitive information.
2) An indicative timetable for the completion of each of the stages of the investigation.
3) A statement of the experience and expertise of the investigating body and of the key members of staff who will be responsible for the investigation.
4) A commitment to complying with relevant professional standards, for example those set by the Institute of Archaeologists or the Institute of Historic Building Conservation, to ensure the quality and consistency of the results.
5) Consideration of any wildlife issues that may have implications for the investigation, such as the presence of protected species.'[261]

The statement further declares that all findings of archaeological investigations undertaken must be published.

## Some important developments

Arguably the single most important part of the archaeological process is securing a date for an artefact or an archaeological context. Where calendar dates are unavailable a wide range of relative and absolute dating techniques is now available to the archaeologist. The principal relative dating techniques are stratigraphic dating (the analysis of the context in which material is found), and typological dating (dating something according to its attributes such as its style). The principal absolute ('scientific') dating methods are dendrochronological dating (using tree rings), radio-carbon dating (for organic material) and

---

261 English Heritage (2012) PPS5: Planning for the Historic Environment Practice Guide, pp.37-39

thermoluminescence dating (for inorganic material that has been heated such as pottery). Chemical dating, based on the known rates of decline of nitrogen and the absorption of fluorine and uranium, can be used on bone. Typological dating involves the examination of an object's 'attributes' (shape, design, construction etc.). We are all experts in this: for example, we can identify by type the approximate age of a car, a mobile phone, a TV set, the decor of a living room. We can order such things in sequential terms, for example, development by decade – clothing fashions of the 1960s, 1970s, 1980s etc. Stratigraphic dating involves dating an object according to where it was found in an excavation, the premise being that, usually (but not always!) the deeper we dig the further back in time we go, and objects found in the same layer of soil are likely to date from the same period. Objects that have a relationship with each other, such as coming from the same archaeological layer or 'context', are defined as an assemblage. Archaeologists who are experienced diggers (and many archaeologists are not!) become expert in the skills of relative dating but the scientific dating methods are the business of laboratory technicians. What matters to the archaeologist most is not how the science works but how it can be applied to the interpretation of the material they or their colleagues dig up.

When asked 'What was the most important development or event in British archaeology this century?' these were the responses of a range of academics working in archaeology in Britain at the end of the twentieth century:

**David Miles** Chief Archaeologist, English Heritage
PPG16
Why? Because it fundamentally changed the position of archaeology in British society. It also led to the appreciation that the whole landscape is full of archaeology.

**Mark Redknap** Medievalist, National Museum of Wales
Radio-carbon dating
Why? It provides an independent eye on the past. Without it, it would be far harder to date things as we do today.

**Warwick Rodwell** Church archaeologist

Dendrochronology
Why? It's far more important than radiocarbon because it's so precise. It gives you 6,500 years of continuous chronology, and benefits everyone from early prehistorians to people working on 18th century houses.

**George Lambrick** CBA Director
New appreciation of the historic environment as a whole
Why? It made us realise that it's not just individual sites and monuments that are of historic interest in the landscape.

**David Longley** Director, Gwynedd Archaeological Trust
Growth of public awareness of the historic environment
Why? Archaeology now has its rightful place as an environmental issue - alongside furry creatures.

**Francis Pryor** CBA President, and Director of Flag Fen
PPG16
Why? Developers now spend £50 million a year on archaeology in Britain. Before PPG 16 came along, English Heritage's budget for archaeology (in England) was zilch.

**Gordon Maxwell** Former head of archaeology, Scottish Royal Commission
Aerial photography of JKS St Joseph
Why? His pioneering work revolutionised the quantity of archaeological data, and inspired those with eyes to see and brains to think.

**Mick Sharp** Photographer
Discovery of astronomical alignments at prehistoric monuments
Why? People used to think Neolithic and Bronze Age people were just a superior form of cavemen. We now know they were highly skilled.

**John Barrett** Philosopher of archaeology, Sheffield University
Handing back the Elgin Marbles to Greece
(Huh? That hasn't taken place - ed.) I know. It's my wished-for event.

It would recognise at last that Britain doesn't have a cultural hegemony over the rest of the world.

**Charlotte Roberts** Palaeopathologist, Bradford University
Biomolecular techniques like DNA analysis
Why? Health is of such major importance in all societies, past and present. You can't get evidence for most diseases from skeletons alone.

**Hedley Swain Head of Early Department, Museum of London**
Time Team [Hugely popular Channel 4 TV series that ran from 1994 to 2013]
Why? Because Time Team is the thing that's done best what archaeology is supposed to do - engage with ordinary people.[262]

## Non-intrusive Archaeology

Archaeologists investigate 'sites' by which we mean any place, big or small, that reveals archaeological evidence of past human activity. The identification of archaeological sites and the interpretation of visible features relies on a range of approaches. These include the use of historical sources, the study of maps and place names, the analysis of site reports and the Historic Environments Record (HER), local knowledge, 'lumps and bumps' and other standing remains, field walking, aerial photographs, and geophysical prospection.

## Field-walking

Any account and interpretation of plough soil evidence must take into account the likelihood of post-depositional disturbance[263]. The dispersal of pottery at least as early as the first century AD on a site is very likely to be the product of manuring or 'middening' activity[264]. The effects of cultivation upon the spread and preservation of finds is also

---

262 Interviews by Simon Denison in *British Archaeology* magazine, December 1999
263 Schofield (1991), p.27
264 Hayes (1991), p.82

an issue[265]. Areas with a history of permanent pasture are much less likely to have received quantities of transported manure[266]. In fields with a long history of ploughing it is likely that topsoil finds have been displaced some distance from the place of their primary deposition. It has been calculated that in the space of two or three decades of ploughing artefacts can be displaced anywhere between 20cm and 10m[267]. A tile however, it has been demonstrated, is less subject to displacement[268] and furthermore it is less likely to be removed from its original location in a primary manuring related deposition than smaller and lighter 'rubbish'.

Some finds, such as those of lithic material, are a good deal more resilient in a ploughed soil context than others, for example early Anglo-Saxon pottery. The history of cultivation of a field therefore is likely to shape, quite profoundly, the subsequent field-walking record. Any analysis of the quantity of finds types must take into consideration the durability of each. In the opinion of Hayes[269]:

*'It is self-evident that no interpretation or analysis of real survey data can afford to ignore the question of bias caused by differential recovery of material due to different rates of post-depositional loss in different parts of the survey area.'*

It is well known that some artefacts are more readily identifiable by field walkers as artefacts than others; to even the trained eye a piece of Roman samian ware is less likely to miss collection than a fragment of black burnished ware. Quantities of finds reveal only a part of the picture of past activity: total weights of material are of great importance as is identification of a material type. This is especially true of data listed as 'flint' which could, conceivably, span hundreds of thousands of years of human activity in the area. Climatic conditions and related conditions, such as brightness and soil moisture, can have a significant impact on field-walking data[270]. When the total finds of a particular type for a whole period are slight this becomes a very

---

265 Allen (1991), p.39
266 Hayes (1991), p.82
267 Clark and Schofield (1991), p.93
268 Clark and Schofield (1991), p.93
269 Hayes (1991), p.81
270 Hayes (1991), p.81

important consideration indeed.

The topography of a site is also of critical importance; topography and geology, for example, influence the nature and rapidity of soil erosion[271]. The rate of soil erosion furthermore is influenced by exposure to modern ploughing methods. Allen's observations regarding the frequency of artefact finds in soils of different depths, as defined by the process of erosion, highlights the issue. Slopes and subsequent soil-creep are likely to accelerate the process of artefact displacement[272]. On the other hand it has been suggested, following experiment, that on flat surfaces lateral displacement is usually slight, even over long periods of time[273].

The comparative abundance of material in a particular location might imply a density of settlement activity in that place. This could be very misleading since it has been recorded as the inclination of 'primitive' peoples in modern times to dispose of their rubbish at some distance from their dwelling places[274]. On the other hand it is the opinion of some that:

> 'Until the development of communal refuse collection for disposal in large rubbish dumps, most domestic refuse, including broken pottery, seems to have been discarded close to where it was made or used, resulting in high concentrations of artefacts and bones in the immediate vicinity of permanent or long-term occupation.'[275]

As the findings of Simms and Cribb have demonstrated[276] the rubbish deposition habits of one people might be the antithesis of another. 'Clusters' of material might be identified, but the host of factors which can produce the clustering effect make interpretation difficult.

Although firm conclusions can rarely be drawn on the evidence of the field-walking data alone, enough evidence can be gathered to enable archaeologists to develop hypotheses. Trial excavations may well

---

271   Allen (1991), p.41
272   Haselgrove (1985), p.8
273   Gingell (1980), cited in Haselgrove (1985), p.8
274   Schofield (1991), p.6
275   Hayes (1991), p.82
276   Simms (1988), Cribb (1983), cited in Schofield (1991), p.117

demonstrate their validity and, in so doing, further the understanding of field-walking data and the place of field survey in the reconstruction of ancient landscapes.

## Geophysics

The application of geophysical surveying techniques to the study of landscapes has vastly extended our knowledge and understanding of sites and wrought a revolution in landscape archaeology. Since the 1940s geo-prospection has provided information on numerous known sites and revealed many features previously unknown. Originally employed at sites such as South Cadbury[277] to complement archaeological excavation projects, geophysical surveying is now seen as an end in itself. In the 1990s geo-prospection became almost as routine as other non-intrusive exploratory activities such as field-walking. Since the mid-1980s private companies such as Stratascan and GSB have set up to provide geophysical services for archaeologists and it is now possible to gain higher degrees in archaeological prospection.

Typically, geophysical prospection is employed in the further investigation of sites evident perhaps as 'lumps and bumps' in the landscape, or those revealed by aerial photography and field walking. In some rare instances geophysics has located sites previously unknown. Geophysical techniques are invaluable as a means of uncovering information which would otherwise elude the archaeological record except, perhaps, after excavation. No one geophysical method can be regarded as superior to the rest: all are affected in different ways by the particular conditions of the land surveyed and each has both its strengths and limitations. In an ideal world, and occasionally in the real, all of the principal techniques would be used simultaneously on the same site.

Barry Cunliffe in a major survey of 18 Wessex hillforts in 1996 and 1997 revealed the value of the magnetometer. 'It's a brilliant tool' was his verdict as he assessed the project.[278] Magnetometry confirmed for him the fact that no two hillforts are entirely alike: the one thing hillforts

---

[277] Excavations directed by Leslie Alcock, 1966-70
278 N. Hawkes, 'The Folk who lived on the Hill' in *Heritage Today* (December 1998)

have in common is that they are all atypical! In some instances magnetometers revealed a great deal of sub-surface archaeological evidence whereas in others there was very little at all. (This of course may be explained by factors such as soil composition affecting readings as opposed to an absence of human activity.) The project provided data concerning thousands of buried pits. Geophysics appears to confirm the conclusion drawn after excavation (Cunliffe revealed four and a half thousand pits at Danebury alone) that some hillforts served a function as granaries for surrounded communities. Magnetometry also indicated the density of settlement by indicating supposed post-holes thought to represent the former presence of buildings. Defensive structures, such as those at Oldbury Castle, were revealed and contributed to an archaeological record which, previously, had excluded them. In the case of Norsebury Ring one huge circular structure, 30m across, was discovered - a tantalising revelation which prompted thoughts of chieftains' huts, communal halls, and shrines. Such sites can be surveyed with a handheld fluxgate gradiometer at the rate of around two hectares a day. At a cost of £30,000 eighteen hillforts were investigated - a fraction of the price of conventional excavation. It has been estimated that all 400 of Wessex' hillforts could be analysed for the cost of excavation of just one. Furthermore, geophysics left no mark on the landscape and the archaeology is preserved intact.

One of the most spectacular discoveries associated with magnetometers is the 'woodhenge' at Stanton Drew in Somerset. Here the surviving megaliths, it was revealed[279], are part of a much more elaborate site than was previously supposed. Nine concentric rings comprising great pits a meter apart, and a meter or more in diameter, were identified within the largest existing ring of stones. Working on the assumption that these once housed great poles, Stanton Drew was identified as the site of the largest wooden henge yet recorded. Furthermore a great buried enclosure ditch around the Great Circle came to light, 135m in outer diameter and 7m wide, confirming Stanton Drew as genuine henge monument, and one equally worthy of World Heritage Site status as Stonehenge and Avebury. Stanton Drew presented a perfect environment for

---

279  English Heritage (1998) Stanton Drew Stone Circles leaflet

magnetometry: a quiet, rural, unploughed (at least, in recent times) location, cleared of shrubs and trees, and with few of the problems attendant in urban surveying projects posed by elements such as overhead power cables, traffic, and the fabric of modern buildings.

Resistance surveys for archaeological purposes predate magnetometry and were pioneered by Richard Atkinson in 1946. Resistivity meters now are far less cumbersome and dangerous than his 'Meggar Earth Tester'. Substantial structures have been revealed using resistivity such as the Turkdean Roman villa in Gloucestershire and King Alfred's abbey at Athelney in Somerset. Although the magnetometer is often the preferred tool of archaeologists for its speed and higher resolution, a survey using a resistivity meter, conducted by Stratascan at Chester[280], revealed much more of a Roman marching camp than the magnetometer also used on the same site. The sandy soil at the Sutton Hoo ship burial site proved more receptive to resistivity meters than both proton magnetometers and fluxgate gradiometers.

Ground penetrating radar has also been used to good effect in producing a picture of what lies buried beneath our feet. 'Britain's Pompeii', Wroxeter, has been examined by radar. By penetrating the ground to different depths, the evolution of a major settlement has been revealed, in part, without needing to lift a sod. Simon Buteaux of Birmingham University, directing the dig, has echoed Cunliffe's thoughts on the application of geophysics in modern archaeology in commenting: 'With a place like Wroxeter you can't realistically dig the whole city, so you've got to use these techniques to combine with the archaeology.'

Ground probing radar and other geophysics tools have a place in providing information about ritual landscapes. At Sutton Hoo the radar technique was pioneered in the mid-80s.[281] Radar is able to penetrate further than magnetometry which is useful only to the depth of a couple of meters. Deep under Mound 12 a further burial chamber was detected, and a robber trench was discovered running through Mound 2. Remote sensing thus guided the hand of the excavator and also

---

280  P. Barker, *Stratascan News* (October 1994)
281  Carver (1998), p.62

added to the overall picture by enhancing the mapping of a whole site. The absence of particular features was as valuable a discovery as those found; for example geophysics did not reveal ring-ditches such as might have been expected in conjunction with ancient burial mounds.

In underwater archaeology sonar has been used to good effect and provided information that was not detected by other sub-surface surveying techniques. The initial excavation work on the *Mary Rose* site, for example, followed the successful application of sonar techniques in identifying the location of the ship, in a context where underwater magnetometers and resistivity meters had failed to provide useful results.

Unfortunately geophysical surveys are unable to provide the detailed information gleaned from excavation. Although typology / analogy can help archaeologists date structures using geophysical surveys alone, the capacity of geophysics to provide a chronology for a site is extremely limited. Modern earthworks are at least as likely to appear as anomalies in a geophysical survey as features of archaeological interest; GSB working on Channel 4's *Time Team* programme caused brief excitement when a modern water pipe was taken for a continuation of the magnificent Cornish **fogou** known as the Boleigh fogou, a few hundred yards away from the Merry Maidens stone circle at Lands End. However the whole site had been surveyed within an hour of their arrival so the results were disappointing but not hugely time consuming.[282] Recent developments have made more possible vertical and three dimensional profiles of sites and geo-prospection as a reliable tool for stratigraphic data collection is an exciting prospect.

In the wrong hands geophysical equipment can lead to extensive destruction. It is often said, perhaps erroneously, that the simplest form of magnetometer is the metal detector.[283] Archaeologists,

---

282 May (1996), pp.117-8
283 This is disputed by some archaeologists who find themselves bound by law in *The National Heritage Act* (1983) designed to protect scheduled ancient monuments from detectorists. Gaffney, Gater and Ovenden lamented: 'As far as the magnetometer is concerned, the instrument is not a metal detector, since technically, it operates on different scientific principles. Similarly, a resistivity meter cannot be called a metal detector. Despite this, the use of any geophysical technique on a protected site has been interpreted by English Heritage as requiring permission under Section 42 of the Act.'

traditionally, are wary of detectorists although they have been employed to good effect at sites such as Sutton Hoo. Detectorists and archaeologists share a 'treasure seeking' passion but, unfortunately, the typical detectorist's 'treasure' is that which glitters. Detectorists use the technology of geophysics in a similar way to its earliest exponents in the archaeological fraternity: as a guide to digging. Few metal detectorists have shown regard for context and, while detectorists seek fortunes, fortunes need to be spent in protecting sites.

Geophysical surveying, particularly resistivity, is highly susceptible to autonomous factors. Heavy rain for example can affect readings. When English Heritage surveyed the abbey site at Athelney in the mid 1980s nothing significant was found. A few years later a springtime survey, when moisture contrast was reduced, provided the evidence that the earlier survey had neglected. As in aerial photography, sites with a potential for results are worth revisiting.

Urban sites are far more problematic than rural locations for the geophysicist. Existing buildings lend to the inaccessibility of the archaeology and modern rubble and rubbish, electricity cables and water pipes, frustrate surveyors using magnetic and electrical resistivity techniques. Radar, as appreciated by the Lincoln Archaeology Unit in a recent survey of their city, is a more viable technique in such 'cluttered' locations. The archaeology of London has had to rely to a very considerable extent on excavation and soil analysis. Even in rural locations results from magnetic surveys are likely to be improved if the plough soil is removed.

The composition of the plough soil itself however is now recognised as having some value for understanding sub-surface archaeology. The science of geochemical analysis is likely to play an increasingly important role in archaeology and one that complements the remote sensing techniques described above. The potential of phosphate analysis was first recognised back in the 1920s and its place in the evaluation of settlement has been demonstrated at such sites as the excavated Romano-British farmstead at Cefn Graenog in North Wales. Geophysical surveying is a science still in its infancy and enormous progress has been made in the last half century. Advances in techniques of data collection have also been accompanied by advances in forms of communication, not least three dimensional imaging by combining survey data with topographic sections.

The West Heslerton project in Yorkshire[284], funded by English Heritage, has helped confirm the importance of geoprospection in contemporary archaeology and pointed to an exciting future as the technology and methodology become more sophisticated. More time consuming high resolution surveys at this site have provided exceptionally high quality results and demonstrated the potential of geophysics in detecting stratified sequences. Later earthworks, cutting across earlier, (e.g. middle Saxon trench cut across a Roman enclosure) had a different and distinct magnetic susceptibility, thus providing evidence for the stratigraphic relationship of the features indicated. Although, as a general rule, excavation is still irreplaceable as the best means of identifying and recording the detail of any archaeological site, the West Heslerton surveys revealed the presence of post holes which, after excavation, were not at first visible to the naked eye. Only after rain and subsequent drying did they emerge to confirm the findings of geophysics! On the other hand some post holes revealed through excavation were not picked up at all, even using high resolution, by fluxgate gradiometers.

Geophysical prospection has played a very important role in contemporary archaeology, particularly since the introduction of PPG 16 in 1990. The relatively new technology measuring magnetic susceptibility has proved particularly useful for quickly assessing the archaeological significance of large areas subject to large-scale developments such as the Daventry International Rail freight Terminal in 1994, and the widening of the M1 in Bedfordshire, also in the mid-90s. It is possible of course that important features may not be revealed by geo-prospection in such a situation but geophysics offers a cheaper and less destructive alternative to trial excavations, and may reduce the necessity for the hazardous application of a watching brief.

As well as reinforcing our understanding of known features visible on the ground or as soil / crop marks in aerial photographs, geophysics has revealed many features undetectable by other non-intrusive means.

---

284  Lyall J. and Powlesland D. October 1997 West Heslerton Parish Project report in *Internet Archaeology*

Broad interval magnetic susceptibility surveys are now providing evidence for 'the bigger picture' and they help archaeologists reconstruct whole landscapes. Different geophysical surveying techniques complement each other just as geophysics at large complements APs, field-walking, traditional surveying, augering, and excavation. Sub-surface surveys provide information of the context in which trial trenches are placed: an invaluable tool in helping archaeologists make sense of what has been excavated and in directing them in their decision on where to dig in the first place. Furthermore geophysics helps redress the balance in material culture-biased archaeology by elevating the value of evidence other than the artefacts gathered by field-walkers and the structures exposed through excavation. As Renfrew and Bahn[285] have noted, geophysical survey can now be seen 'not simply as prospection' prior to excavation but a science that can both complement excavation and exist as an end in itself.

The most important geophysical survey development in recent times is the application in archaeology of Airborne **lidar** (an abbreviation of 'light detection and ranging'). It makes possible the mapping of features in a landscape surface at metre and sub-metre resolution. It is in fact a comparatively old technology dating back to the 1960s but its potential for archaeology was not fully realised until the early 2000s. The initial breakthrough was summarised by English Heritage:

'The possibilities of lidar for archaeological recording in the UK were first recognised at a NATO sponsored workshop to discuss future practices in aerial archaeology, held in Leszno, Poland in November 2000, where a survey covering the River Wharfe in Yorkshire revealed evidence for the earthwork survival of a Roman fort that had previously been thought to have been completely levelled by ploughing.

Following on from this and recognising the potential for lidar to record very slight earthwork remains English Heritage contracted the Environment Agency Geomatics Group to fly a survey of the Stonehenge World Heritage Site and has since worked with both the Environment Agency Geomatics Group and the Unit for Landscape

---

285  Renfrew and Bahn (1996), p.99

Modelling (ULM) looking at different areas of the country with varying levels of monument survival.'

Of particular value is lidar's ability to penetrate dense vegetation and to provide images of what lies beneath. The survey of Savernake Forest in Wiltshire by the Cambridge University Unit for Landscape Modelling, for example, revealed a previously unknown earthworks such as Iron Age enclosures.

For further information on this project and others like it refer to the relevant pages at the English Heritage website.[286] English Heritage has published an interesting on-line booklet, *The Light Fantastic: using airborne lidar in archaeological survey*. This can be downloaded at www.english-heritage.org.uk/publications/light-fantastic

## Excavation

Since excavation is destruction and archaeological levels cannot be replaced once they have been dug, archaeologists need to consider carefully the implications of a planned excavation and to provide a rationale that justifies any decision to go ahead. In the case of a **research dig** this will include the identification of a series of questions about the site that the excavation is designed to answer. In the case of a **rescue dig** in the United Kingdom where the excavation is a planning condition, the proposal will need to conform to the requirements of the National Planning Policy Framework, and, specifically, Planning Policy Statement 5 (PPS5), introduced in 2012. Archaeologists in the UK are represented by their professional body, the Institute for Archaeology (IfA) which provides a code of conduct to guide its members even when their work is not constrained by planning permissions. Its rules are detailed under the heading of five key principles:

> Principle 1
> A member shall adhere to high standards of ethical and responsible behaviour in the conduct of archaeological affairs.

---

[286] http://www.english-heritage.org.uk/professional/research/landscapes-and-areas/aerial-survey/archaeology/lidar/

*Principle 2*
*The member has a responsibility for the conservation of the historic environment.*

*Principle 3*
*The member shall conduct his/her work in such a way that reliable information about the past may be acquired, and shall ensure that the results be properly recorded.*

*Principle 4*
*The member has responsibility for making available the results of archaeological work with reasonable dispatch.*

*Principle 5*
*The member shall recognise the aspirations of employees, colleagues and helpers with regard to all matters relating to employment, including career development, health and safety, terms and conditions of employment and equality of opportunity.*[287]

Various approaches to excavation are taken including the digging of narrow trenches and the complete excavation of open areas. Whatever the strategy, the most important part of the excavation process is the recording of finds and their contexts with photographs, context sheets, and section drawings. The stratigraphic record this provides enables the archaeologist to construct a matrix that reveals the relationship between strata in terms of their deposition. The matrix plan itself reduces the appearance of strata as recorded in sketches and photographs to a series of numbers and symbols that define each context.

## Tools and technology: attributes

The visual analysis of artefacts focuses on four characteristics: form, style, material, and manufacture. The science of **typology** (the defining of artefacts according to their distinctive attributes) is of vital importance for many reasons including the relative dating of objects,

---

287 By-laws of the Institute for Archaeologists, *Code of conduct*, revised edition, October 2012, IfA, University of Reading

identifying status, and revealing contact between cultures.

The visual analysis of artefacts is supported by the scientific. The microscopic analysis of material can reveal its origins, for example, in terms of its **petrology**, as can its 'chemical fingerprints' through the identification of trace elements. Such approaches have revealed a great deal about the early trade in Irish and Welsh copper, and the presence of Mendip lead at Pompeii. The term **'archaeometry'** has been coined to define the scientific methods employed in the analysis of archaeological material.

## CASE STUDY: 'Otzi' the Iceman

The remains of 'Otzi the Iceman', as he came to known, were discovered by two hikers in the Otzal Alps, in South Tyrol in northern Italy, in September 1991. He lay in a gully 3210 m above sea level so close to the border that, at first the find spot was presumed to be Austrian. Initially the corpse, exposed by the temporary summertime melting of the ice in which he was frozen, was presumed to be that of another hiker who had perished in the mountains in relatively recent times. Various objects, including an axe, pieces of leather, lengths of sting, and bundles of hay, were found strewn around the body. Everything the team from the University of Innsbruck Institute of Forensic Medicine had found was sent to the university for further analysis.

At this point archaeologists became involved and the first archaeological survey of the site was carried out in October 1991. The typology of the axe indicated the great age of the remains – initially identified as being in the region of 4000 years B.P. Several C-14 dating experiments, undertaken in four separate institutions, provided a date range for the remains of between 3350 and 3100 B.C., thus predating the stone monuments at Stonehenge by hundreds of years. A second archaeological investigation in the summer of 1992, involving the use of hot air blowers to melt ice, resulted in many more finds including the individual's bearskin cap and part of a broken longbow.

As a 'wet' mummy, a body that had not been dried out as part of the mummification process, the Iceman is an exceptional find. The remarkable survival of the organic materials from which most of his clothing and equipment was made provides unique insights into prehistory. The science of forensics and D.N.A. testing has enabled a series of reconstructions of his body and appearance. Remarkable details include the evidence that he wavy, dark coloured hair, and brown eyes. The arsenic content of strands of his hair strongly implies he was sometimes engaged in copper smelting. Evidence of fractured and healed ribs indicated past accidents, and the analysis of striations on the one fingernail that was recovered suggested episodes of ill health 8, 13 1nd 16 weeks before he died. His stomach contents revealed a last meal of vegetables, meat and grain (einkorn – very likely prepared as bread). Various marks, tattooed in charcoal in incisions in his skin, have been interpreted as evidence of a healing practices and rituals associated with acupuncture. A flint arrowhead embedded in his shoulder, discovered in 2001, indicates a violent death. A skull fracture, probably sustained at the time of death, either by a blow from an assailant or in falling to the ground, was also identified.

Jacqui Wood was invited by the South Tyrol Archaeological Museum at Bolzano to reconstruct items of the Iceman's clothing. Sections of matting had been found. What they signified were uncertain. Suggestions included a mat for sitting or lying upon, a cape for warmth and protection from the wind and rain, or the rest of the backpack, the U shaped hazel frame of which had been found. Wood demonstrated that this material and technology could produce a viable cloak:

*It consists of panels of long honey-golden grasses, 90cm long tapering to 1mm points, tied together with seven bands of lime bast string. One suitable grass is the upright brome grass (Gramineae zerna erecta).*

*I found the remains of a shoulder strap at the neck of the Iceman's cloak, indicating that the completed cloak was worn slightly off the shoulder. At the front was a line of looped bast cord on both sides, with long cords attached at the neck, which suggests that the cloak was laced up the front. When I first laced the cloak together, however, it was like a strait-jacket. In my opinion the cloak must have had arm slits, otherwise it would have been impossible for the Iceman to move his* arms when the cloak was laced up. The original cloak is too fragmentary to prove the point.[288]

The cloak took ten hours to make and it was 'lightweight, hard-wearing, and extremely warm to wear'. The Iceman's shoes comprised a netting frame with uppers made of deerskin and a sole of bearskin. When Jacqui Wood constructed a replica pair she found they were very comfortable and also waterproof. Their considerable width suggested to her that they were specifically designed for walking in snow. With plenty of practice she was able to make a pair in a day. Nevertheless the design was highly sophisticated:

*The bear skin soles are first cut into an oval shape 17cm wide by 29cm long. In length, this is about a size 6 (UK shoe-size) - which is a child's or smallish woman's size today. Next, 34 small slits are cut around the edge, to accommodate a leather strap which allows the lime bast net to be joined to the sole.*

*The lime net is of very intricate design. A single long piece of bast is used. A quarter of its length is looped around the ankle, while the remainder is twisted and threaded repeatedly between the leather straps in the sole and the ankle loop. The bast fibres cannot be made into twine beforehand, but have to be twisted extremely tightly as the shoe is in the process of being made. The loop around the ankle acts as a draw string, allowing the shoe to be tightened once it has been put on.*

*Next, slightly twisted bast strings are knotted horizontally across the vertical cords in order to complete the net. A short cord is then attached near the ankle to form - together with the end of the main ankle loop - the two laces used for tying up the shoe. The shoe can now be stuffed with grasses to fill out the net while the deer skin panels are attached.*

*Slits are cut in the panels, and strips of deer skin are threaded through the slits in both the panels and the soles to form a tight seam, and to enclose the front of the foot and toes. Before the foot is placed into the shoe, however, it should be wrapped in bundles of soft grass for warmth and to make the shoe more comfortable to wear.*

---

[288] Jacqui Wood in *British Archaeology*, 49, November 1999

*In summer, the deer skin panels can be removed and the shoe worn as a comfortable and light sandal.*[289]

Remains of a hide coat, stitched together with animal sinews, were discovered. A prehistoric concern for aesthetics was evident in the care taken to stitch alternate sections of dark and light coloured hide. It was worn with the fur on the outside. No evidence of sleeves was found. He wore a loin cloth and leggings of goatskin. The leggings were tied with deer hide to his shoes to prevent them from riding up when walking. They were held up with laces tied to his two metre long calfskin belt. A leather belt pouch contained a toolkit including, among other items, a bone awl and a flint scraper. It also contained a wad of fungus to serve as tinder and iron pyrite to make the spark to ignite it.

The yew haft of the axe, almost pure copper, axe had survived, together with the leather straps and birch bark securing the axehead. Experiments have demonstrated that it could have felled a yew tree, without sharpening, in just 35 minutes. This precious object therefore was a very viable tool. Alternatively it might have been, primarily, a weapon, or a status symbol. His flint dagger with its ash handle, binding and belt-sheath of sewn grass was also recovered. A 'retoucheur' for fine flint working was found. This composite tool was a shaft of lime wood with a central canal into which a point of fire-hardened antler had been driven at one end. It resembles a fat pencil and, like a pencil, the antler point could be sharpened.

The bow was made of wood and was clearly unfinished. This hypothesis has been proven, not through experiments testing an actual reconstruction of the bow but by a virtual reconstruction of the bow using computer modeling – a much easier approach. The conclusion is that

*In its original state, the bow was extremely powerful and would have broken on the first shot because the compressive strain in the limbs (1.5%) was so great. The bast fiber bowstring was probably much too thin to support a bow of this weight. The simplest way to transform this*

---

[289] Jacqui Wood in *British Archaeology*, 49, November 1999

stave into a weapon pulling 50 pounds at 26 inches would be to reduce the thickness along the limbs to 69 % of its present value (the cube root of 50/150.9), leaving the width unmodified. This would reduce the maximum strain to 0.97 %, a very safe conservative value for a yew bow."[290]

No evidence of a bowstring was found. It had been coated in blood to repel water. Replica bows of this kind have demonstrated that they have an effective range of between 30 and 50 metres.

A full chamois leather quiver of arrows was also found. Most of the arrows were also unfinished; the bark had been removed but the shafts were not yet smoothed. The quiver contained just two finished arrows. Birch bark tar and thread had been used to attach the flint arrowheads. Birch tar was also used for the fletching. These are the most complete arrows surviving from prehistory and the only ones where the fletching is preserved. The expertise of ancient technologist Harm Paulsen, revealed that, almost certainly, one of the arrows was fletched by a left-handed person, and the other by someone who was right-handed.

A string net, made of twisted tree-bast, has been interpreted as a device for catching small animals such as rabbits and birds. A pair of birch bark beakers were clearly used as containers and one contained maples leaves thought to have been intended as further kindling for fire making. The Iceman also carried with him, fastened with two strips of hide, two lumps of birch polypore fungus. This has been interpreted as a basic 'first aid kit' since this is known to have styptic and antibiotic qualities and could also have been effective in countering the intestinal parasites (whipworm) with which he was infected.

Reconstructions have included the Iceman's clothing, equipment, physique and appearance. Shawn Woods, a member of the Puget Sound Knappers in America, a 20 year-old 400 strong association of flint tool enthusiasts and knappers, has reconstructed and tested the Iceman's arrows and his backpack. These reconstructions were filmed

---

[290] Baugh, Brizzi and Baker (2006), 'Otzi's Bow' in *The Bulletin of Primitive Technology*, Spring 2006, issue 31

and are readily available to view on-line.[291] In 2012 'Otzi' had a 'makeover' based on the application of cutting-edge 3-D scan technology to produce the most accurate replication of his appearance to date. In his latest reincarnation, created by Dutch artists Alfons and Adrie Kennis and on show in the Iceman's dedicated museum in South Tyrol, he appears, not as a healthy adventurer in his prime and at the peak of physical fitness as in former reconstructions, but as a weather-beaten, rugged mountain-man, physically ravaged by his tough and dangerous existence in a hostile environment.

## The investigation of domestic buildings

The investigation of domestic buildings is concerned with both what can be seen on the ground and the evidence for what can no longer be seen. Enquiries into the origins and evolution of standing buildings combine archaeological and historical approaches. Until recently the study of 'polite' architecture has been dominated by historical approaches whereas that of **'vernacular'** has been more associated with the archaeologist's preoccupation with material culture. In recent years however historical sources have been more thoroughly trawled in the reconstruction of vernacular building history, and grander buildings, with a rich historical record, have been subjected to more rigorous fabric analysis. Although there are no hard and fast rules regarding the starting place for assessing the age and history of a domestic building, it is logical, at least in the case of one with a slight historical record, to begin with a detailed survey of what is standing before moving on to the examination of other types of evidence. This could result in a more objective survey since the archaeologist will approach the material with fewer preconceptions which might prove to be misconceptions.

## Structure and fittings.

Few domestic buildings survive materially unaltered, even across comparatively short periods of time. Changing needs, aesthetics and cultural attributes of the generations succeeding that which first

---

[291] http://pugetsoundknappers.com

occupied the building will impact upon its form. For example much has been written about the desire for greater privacy, a cultural shift reflected in the enclosure of communal land, and made more possible by the technology of the chimney (e.g. Hoskins 1953). Consequently many buildings, particularly those in towns where building space carries a premium, have been altered beyond recognition and their antiquity becomes a source of debate among owners and vernacular architecture enthusiasts.

Some buildings however retain, more or less, their original form, readily identified by the tutored eye. A good example is the highland zone, rural 'longhouse', particularly common in north-east England and the south-west. The form is distinctive: long but just one room deep, with off-centre entrances and an axial chimney stack to one side[292]. It derives from a medieval design for rural living in which one end of the structure would provide unheated accommodation for livestock. However the definition 'longhouse' does not necessarily signify 'medieval' since, as a form of building, it continued long after people in these areas commonly shared their living space with their animals: the unheated barn annex (typically) was transformed into a workshop or storage space in altered and later examples. While it might be possible to arrive at fairly accurate dates for the age of such a structure in the context of an excavation, such as that of the celebrated Wharram Percy **DMV** (deserted medieval village) project, it might well be harder to demonstrate the antiquity of a standing longhouse that has been subjected to numerous changes since it was first erected. Clues as to its original function however might be recognised in, say, the discovery of an open drain at one end of the house.

Standing buildings built before the sixteenth century, other than those of high status, of course are very rare[293]. In most parts of Britain perishable materials like wood, mud, wattle and daub, prevailed over more permanent building materials. Stone and brick tended to be reserved for defensive structures such as castles, high status communal buildings like churches and guild halls, and buildings of considerable economic importance like the great 'tithe barns'. The

---

292  Hey (1996), p.293
293  'it is argued that no truly vernacular buildings survive before the mid-sixteenth century' Pearson (1997), p.34

great bulk of buildings so far surveyed by the Vernacular Architecture Group (established 1954) and its affiliates date from the era of the so-called **'Great Rebuilding'**[294] when more permanent building techniques were commonly adopted for 'ordinary' dwellings.

Hoskins' Great Rebuilding thesis is intimately associated with the hall house and its evolution from open fire and open hall to the hooded fireplace and chambers with ceilings. Some spectacular examples of medieval halls have survived and can be viewed in a restored condition at such places as the Avoncroft Museum near Bromsgrove in Worcestershire or the Open Air Museum at Singleton in Sussex. Such examples provide architectural templates for studies of more altered buildings that might share some of the classic characteristics of hall houses. Fabric analysis combined with measurement might for example reveal evidence for a cross passage, smoke blackened timbers, inserted ceilings, and a former jetty.

The most telling feature of a timbered building in terms of determining its age is the timber structure itself. Chimneys, windows, roofing materials, portals and so on might be added, changed or removed but the skeleton, in part, remains. Many buildings prove to be much older than they appear at first sight. In Ludlow for example there are whole streets of medieval houses sporting a Georgian facade. Wall frames, jetties and, especially, roof structure can all reveal something of the antiquity of the building. The jetty where the broadest side of the timber lies flat, for example, is almost certainly older than one which sits on its narrow edge.[295] Cruck framed houses have been identified as early as 1275.[296] Late medieval structures are likely to have a roof raised on king-posts.[297]

The fabric of a building will reveal something of its age: steel girders are likely to post-date oak beams, wooden pegs probably pre-date iron nails; machine made bricks are later than handmade, and early bricks (c.1600) are typically an inch thinner than their late eighteenth century, post-brick tax, 3" counterparts,[298] design and decoration, the

---

294 Hoskins (1953)
295 Dowdy, Miller, Austin (1997), p.95
296 Iredale & Barrett (1991), p.24
297 Harris (1993), p.42
298 Iredale and Barrett (1991), p.21

chamfering of beams, paintwork, plaster and so on, can all provide evidence for the dating of a building. Even fittings thought to post-date the original buildings can at least provide a **terminus ante quem**. Everything, pretty much, from windows and doors, to infill and plaster, can be dated according to the principle of typology. Stratigraphy also has a place in the study of buildings: in Bruton in Somerset for example stone-lined late medieval cellars are overlaid by the bricks of subsequent Edwardian townhouses. The context in which the building is located in horizontal terms is also important: dateable structures such as a new eighteenth century road or an adjacent house, each of which might abut and overlay earlier features of the house studied, will contribute to establishing its antiquity.

In addition to relative dating techniques the architectural historian can also employ the absolute dating technique of dendrochronology. Tree-ring dating has its limitations, notably because of the reuse of old timbers or the decision of a carpenter to strip away the outer layers of the timber being used[299], but it does offer the potential, many times proven, for providing an accurate date for the construction of a building or, at least, the date at which a timber was felled.

Where possible a number of cores will be extracted for dendrochronological dating in order to accommodate the possibility that a supposed original timber is a later insertion or that a particular timber has a tree-ring record that cannot be measured due to a 'freak' ecological environment in which the tree grew. Many timbers may not be of sufficient ring depth for a core to be successfully read: a building with a high timber content will not necessarily provide a dendro-date. Some areas have a more complete master chronology than others and thus dendrochronology is a more effective approach in some areas than others. In some places in certain periods trees grew so fast that they could be felled for building purposes far sooner than was 'typical'; a dendrochronologist is unlikely to be able to provide a date for a timber that has much less than eighty rings and so this presents further difficulties. At present a core sample has to be obtained but, soon it is to be hoped, photographic evidence of the exposed cut of a timber will

---

299   Daniel Miles (1997) has highlighted problems associated with builder stockpiles of recently cut and previously used timbers, as well as the difficulties posed by estimating sapwood rings.

be sufficiently diagnostic for the dendrochronologist to match it with a master sequence. Most tree-ring dating in Britain is associated with oak: the elm, widely used by medieval builders in, say, Somerset, is far less amenable to the establishment of a dendrochronology.[300]

Despite the difficulties associated with dendrochronology some spectacular results have been achieved and with each new test the record is expanded and the reliability of the method increased. Sarah Pearson has identified a number of instances where the dendro-date has replicated a date provided by documentary evidence: for example 'the Abbot's House, Shrewsbury, where precise felling dates of 1457 and 1458 were obtained, and in 1459 a building ceremony was recorded, attended by the Abbot of Lilleshall, his carpenter and borough officials.[301]

Tree-ring dates provide information on the development of construction and techniques. While on the one hand a dendro-date provides an absolute date for a single timber and, perhaps, the building with which it is associated, it also develops our typological awareness regarding building methods employed in a given place at a given time. For example, Cecil Hewett has used dendrochronology as an approach to establishing a typological sequence for timber jointing techniques.[302]

In some rare situations a date might be acquired by radio carbon-14 dating, by which other organic matter, such as horsehair in plaster, might be dated, as well as wood incapable of providing a tree-ring date. However the relative inaccuracy of the technique makes it inappropriate for all but very ancient structures. It would not, for example, resolve an argument concerned with whether a particular building should be defined as 'late medieval' or 'early modern'.

## Documentary sources

The most accessible documents containing evidence of buildings are maps. Although **cartography** is, like archaeology, an infant science, and

---

300 Pearson (1997), p.26
301 Pearson (1997), p.29
302 Pearson (1997), p.32

detailed map making for most areas is less than two hundred years old, older maps do exist, and a great deal from the distant past is revealed even by the most recent maps. John Speed, in the early sixteenth century, helped pioneer the detailed mapping of towns, most of which had at least one map by the end of the eighteenth century. The one inch to one mile maps of the Ordnance Survey represented a revolution in cartography, and one which was completed for most areas by the middle of the nineteenth century. Their regular upkeep provides accurate information on changes of appearance and function of existing buildings and the emergence of new ones. All maps, particularly the earlier ones, provide a geographical 'fix'[303] and opportunities for back projection and the recreation of older landscapes. A wealth of other related sources also exist including estate maps, tithe maps, and early photographs.

Title deeds are of huge importance in the study of buildings, many of which were deposited in county records offices after the Law of Property Act in 1925. The descriptions and plans they contain reveal architectural clues which could help determine a date for the original structure. Medieval documents concerned with exchange and ownership have also survived such as *feet of fines* and bills of *bargain and sale*[304]. In the modern period estate agents notices in newspapers are often a valuable resource.

Other documentary sources worth mentioning in this context are tax returns (e.g. hearth tax, land tax), census records, ecclesiastical surveys such as *glebe terriers*, and business registers such as *Kelley's Directory*. The fascinating records of individuals, such as *inquisitions post mortem*, wills and probate inventories, have also sometimes shed light on the houses they lived in.

Some buildings proudly display the date of their construction but most do not. Virtually all houses have a documentary record but for most houses built before the middle of the nineteenth century this record, in the form of deeds and maps and suchlike, does not extend as far back as the date of construction. Beyond this period **morphology** and

---

303   Henstock (1988), p.69
304   Numerous examples of such documents have been assembled by Salzman (1952)

typology are the most rewarding approaches to establishing a building's history and hence survey is often the favoured starting place. Allied to this is the remarkable science of dendrochronology which, for timber framed structures at least, has wrought a revolution in the dating of domestic buildings.

## Experimental archaeology

The great exponent of experimental archaeology in the UK, John Coles, once defined the approach as 'a convenient way of describing the collection of facts, theories and fictions that has been assembled through a century of interest in the reconstruction and function of ancient remains.'[305] Francis Pryor, the well-known 'TV archaeologist' and expert on the prehistory of the Fens, defines experimental archaeology as 'the attempt to recreate life in the past by practical means'.[306] Paul Bahn's *Dictionary of Archaeology* defines it as:

> The controlled replication of ancient technologies and behaviour, in order to provide hypotheses that can be tested by actual archaeological data. Experiments can range in size from the reproduction of ancient tools in order to learn about their processes of manufacture and use, to the construction of whole villages and ancient subsistence practices in long-term experiments.[307]

Experimental archaeology aims to interpret archaeological evidence by testing hypotheses using a rigorous scientific methodology. Much of the focus of archaeology is on the material evidence for past technologies and experimental archaeology is largely to do with the business of shedding light on these technologies.

The study of evidence for tool use, 'micro-wear' analysis, enhanced by the modern electron microscopes, has benefitted from archaeological reconstructions, pioneered by A. A. Rhode in 1720, a German who experimented with the replication of stone tools. The numerous experiments in relation to tool manufacture and use have added a great deal to understanding these fundamental, culture-defining

---

[305] Coles (1967), p.1
[306] Pryor (2011), p. 23
[307] Bahn (1992), p. 165

aspects of the past. It took an experiment to demonstrate the availability of spear technology to the earliest hominids found in the UK; until a round hole in the scapula of a horse butchered at Boxgrove in Sussex 500,000 years ago could be shown to match exactly the impact a fire hardened spear hurled at such material, there was much debate regarding whether 'Boxgrove Man' was a hunter or a mere scavenger.

Experimental archaeology is sometimes confused with *experiential* approaches to the past. Dressing up in ancient style costumes and attempting to live the lives of people in the past in imagined contexts cannot hope to enhance the archaeological record in any significant way, interesting though such projects might be as sociological experiments. True experimental archaeology focuses on any one or more of the following:

- Construction: testing hypothetical designs (e.g. for the structure of a building) based on the surviving archaeological evidence.
- Function: testing how the effectiveness of tools and other technologies, such as forms of storage.
- Simulation: testing archaeological processes ('taphonomy') such as rates of decay or the build-up of archaeological processes.
- Eventuality trialling: testing how specific events in the course of time, such as extreme weather episodes might affect archaeological features, artefacts or systems (such as agricultural methods).
- Modern technology: testing modern technologies such as geophysics in relation to their application in archaeology.

The man traditionally regarded as the founding father of modern archaeology, Augustus Fox (General Pitt-Rivers), was a pioneer in experimental archaeology as well as excavation. Working in the closing decades of the nineteenth century at his country-seat at Cranborne Chase in Dorset, he became interested in the possibility of testing the functions attributed to certain tool types. John Coles has summarised his findings regarding antler picks and ox shoulder blade shovels and other tools recovered at Cissbury Rings, an Iron Age hillfort and

Neolithic flint mine site on the Sussex Downs:

*In his experiments, Fox produced a set of tools from one pair of antlers; this yielded two picks, 1 mandril, 2 wedges and 5 tine punches. The tools were cut from the antler with flints, and the wedges were ground smooth on wet sandstone. They were then employed to cut into a smooth chalk face, which represented a situation encountered by prehistoric man in either digging a ditch around the camp, or quarrying into the chalk in search of flint nodules. With the antler tools, one man could excavate almost one cubic metre in 1.5 hours, and Fox suggested therefore that the longest side gallery in the prehistoric mine, 9 metres long and of a diameter suitable for only one man, could have been cut in twelve hours.*

*Experiments were also carried out using antler picks to prise out lumps of chalk from the sides of the mine shaft leading down to the galleries. The wedges and punches were hammered into cracks in the chalk, and the picks and mandril used to detach the lumps. Fox observed that the marks left by his tools in the chalk matched those observed in the sides of the prehistoric shaft and galleries. The removal of the chalk blocks and rubble from the galleries and shafts would have been a major task. Fox considered that the ox-shoulder blades might have served as shovels in this work, and he attempted to test this idea. He cut off the sharp spines of three modern ox bones, and experimented with the resulting shovel-like blades. He found it easier to move chalk rubble by filling his wheelbarrow by hand rather than by using the blade which was sharp and difficult to manipulate. By attaching a wooden handle he produced a very efficient tool, which was twice as effective as bare hands for lifting the rubble as well as being easier on the skin. Fox concluded that the excavation of the flint mines at Cissbury was well within the capabilities of a small group of men, and required relatively simple tools easily made from local materials.*[308]

Working half a century before the radiocarbon dating revolution Pitt-Rivers exposed the original cut of ditches around the Wor Barrow, a late Neolithic tomb on Cranborne Chase, and began recording the rate

---

[308] Coles (1979), p.18

at which the ditch silted up in order to help him estimate how much time had passed since the structure was built. After four years 70 cm of chalk and soil had accumulated at the bottom of the ditch. The evidence was insufficient in helping him to reach any firm conclusions regarding its antiquity but the principle has been imitated by more recent experimental archaeologists, notably those engaged in the Overton Down ditch and bank project.

John Evans, the father of Sir Arthur Evans, celebrated for his excavation of Knossos on Crete and discovery of the 'Minoan' culture, was a highly regarded archaeologist in his own right. His books on stone and bronze technology remain classics and an important resource, superbly illustrated with remarkable impressions of axes and other objects. One issue that puzzled Evans was the means by which people had produced the perforations in certain types of stone tool and he conducted experiments, informed by anthropological observation of indigenous South Americans, to demonstrate that the combination of a soft drill, made of such material as bone or wood, was effective in drilling stone when fed with sand or grit containing corundum, which is harder than any material other than diamond, and can be derived from igneous rock, shale or limestone.

The polishing of stone axes was equally intriguing and this too was explicable in part through anthropological observation. In America in 1878 J. D. McGuire set out to test the validity of an eighteenth century account in Lafitau's *Moeurs des Sauvages Ameriquains*:

*Hatchets have been used over the whole of America from time to time immemorial. They are made of a pebble hard and difficult to break. They require a great deal of time to make them serviceable. The method of preparing them is to sharpen them by rubbing them on a sandstone, and to give them, by means of time and work, very much the appearance of our hatchets, or of a wedge. Often the life of a savage was not sufficient for this purpose from which it comes that such an article, though rough and imperfect, is a precious heritage to their children.*[309]

Coles has summed up McGuire's findings, published in 1892:

---

[309] Cited in Coles (1979), p. 22

*A hammer of black porphyry was pecked out and grooved in about 5 hours, using diorite and quartzite stones. Other rocks were also pecked and ground, and quartzite was considered to be a suitable hammerstone for most of these. A long experiment on nephrite, however, was more arduous. Nephrite is a variety of jade and is hard and tough. McGuire began work on a nephrite chunk knocked from a boulder and pecked away at this with quartzite hammers; most of these lasted for under 10 minutes before shattering and about 40 were ruined before a close-grained specimen was found that survived for about 8 hours. Other hammers, of gneiss and granite, were useless on the nephrite. Eventually a yellow jasper hammer was employed and this completed the pecking operation after another 40 hours of work. Both nephrite and jasper had lost the same weight of stone dust through this pounding. The roughed-out axe was then ground with granite for 5 hours, polished with a quartzite pebble for 6 hours and then rubbed with a piece of wood and animal skin. The result was an incomplete but recognizable grooved axehead, representing 55 hours of pecking and pounding with stone hammers, during which time over 460,000 blows were delivered upon it. Certainly not a lifetime, but nonetheless hard work.[310]*

McGuire, along with W. Gowland, was among the first archaeologists to explore by experiment the creation of Stonehenge. Together, working independently on blocks of equivalent stone, they were able to demonstrate the likely process by which the sarsens were dressed. Hezzledine Warren undertook a series of experiments to explore the evidence for human activity, as opposed to geological, in the shaping of stone objects. His methodology and findings were published in 1904 in *On the origin of Eoliths*. After this period there appears to have been little experimental archaeology of significance until a new wave of interest in the approach in the 1940s and 50s.

The most impressive of the nineteenth century archaeological experiments was the construction and sailing of a longship based on the Viking era boat excavated at Lover Gokstad, near Oslo in 1880. Thought to have been used in the burial of an eminent Viking dignitary, the remains were a thousand years old but sufficiently complete to

---

[310] Coles (1979), pp. 22-23

enable a Norwegian sailor and editor, Captain Magnus Andersen, to construct a full-scale [CHECK] replica. Its capacity as an ocean-going vessel was demonstrated by its voyage from Norway to Chicago in 1893. Here a World Fair was being held, in part to celebrate the anniversary of Christopher Columbus' 'discovery' of America 400 years earlier. The Gokstad replica made the crossing from Bergen to Newfoundland in just 27 days and thus demonstrated the possibility that European sea-farers might have got their long before – a Scandinavian tradition now proven by the discovery of Viking age artefacts excavated in American soil.

Deeply impressed by the effectiveness of his ship's design Andersen commented:

> The bottom of the ship was an object of primary interest. As will be remembered, it was fastened to the ribs with withy, below the crossbeams. The bottom, as well as the keel, could therefore yield to the movement of the ship, and in a heavy head sea it would rise and fall as much as three-quarters of an inch. But strangely enough the ship was watertight all the same. Its elasticity was apparent also in other ways. In a heavy sea the gunwhale would twist up to six inches out of line. All this elasticity, combined with the fine lines, naturally made for speed, and we often had the pleasure of darting through the water at speeds of ten, and sometimes even eleven knots.[311]

## CASE STUDY: The Kon Tiki Expedition

*No tempest at sea is harder on a man than to stand alone encircled by a firing squad of international authorities.*
(Thor Heyerdahl[312])

Among the most famous archaeological experiments was Thor Heyerdahl's pioneering 'Kon Tiki expedition' of 1947. This employed ancient technologies to demonstrate the possibility of direct contact by boat between the Polynesian islands and South America in antiquity.

---

[311] Andersen in Coles (1979), p. 78
[312] Hyerdahl (1984), p.xiv

Paul Theroux, a highly regarded travel writer and novelist, but not an archaeologist, made some pretty scathing remarks concerning Thor Heyerdahl, adventurer and anthropologist, in his book on contemporary culture in the Pacific, *The Happy Isles of Oceania* (1992). On Easter Island Theroux met an archaeologist, Dave Steadman, at work, excavating among the famous *moai*, the Easter Island statues.

*Inevitably, our discussion turned to Thor Heyerdahl. Dave, who as an archeologist was the straightest talker I had met, as well as the most down-to-earth, said, "Thor Heyerdahl is perhaps the most fanciful adventurer to hit the Pacific. [...] He dreams something one night, makes a connection, and the next day he puts it into his book. See, he already has his theory. He just looks for ways of proving it. That's not scientific. And he commits the worst sin of an archeologist - he has been known to buy artifacts from the locals as well as carrying out digs. If you dig them up you get provenential information. But when you buy them you know nothing."*[313]

Theroux joined the ranks Heyerdahl's many detractors with his own cutting observations:

*Thor Heyerdahl is shrill but mistaken in many of his assumptions. [...] He is an amateur, a popularizer, an impresario, with a zoology degree from the University of Oslo. And his efforts in the Pacific greatly resemble the muddling attentions of, say, the hack writer of detective stories when faced with an actual crime scene - someone who ignores the minutiae of evidence, hair analysis, or electrophoresis (for typing bloodstains) and in blundering around a crime scene, muttering "The butler did it!", makes a complete hash of it for the forensic scientists. The mention of Heyerdahl's name in academic circles frequently produces embarrassment or anger...*[314]

Heyerdahl, writing a few years earlier in 1984, justified himself by the many rewards he had received over the years, notably the Royal Gold Medal of the Royal Geographic Society in 1964, that had been heaped upon him in recognition of his undeniably remarkable achievements.

---

[313] Theroux (1992), pp.620-1
[314] Theroux (1992), pp.626-7

So what was the fuss all about?

Thor Heyerdahl first entered the cross-continent archaeological and anthropological academic battleground when, in 1947, he undertook the most famous of all archaeological experiments: the *Kon Tiki* expedition. A visit to Polynesia on a zoological quest gave rise to his interest in how the islands of the Pacific were peopled and he was soon questioning the assumptions of academia:

*Scholars had invariably assumed that all early voyagers into the Pacific had sailed and paddled straight from Southeast Asia. I disagreed. Prevailing winds and currents would prevent their traveling directly eastward from Asia. Yet there were two feasible sea routes to Polynesia: One was a circuitous route from Southeast Asia by way of Northwest America to Hawaii, and the other from South America directly to eastern Polynesia.*[315]

When publishers refused to print his thesis that Peruvians could have peopled Polynesia in antiquity, and that this could account for the curious similarities between aspects of Polynesian and South American material culture, he set out to prove that such a navigation would have been possible by constructing and sailing a balsa raft across the Pacific. It was named *Kon Tiki* after Tiki, a legendary figure in Polynesian folklore who was said to have brought his people to the islands from a place far to the east. An Inca tale spoke of another hero, Con-Tici, who, according to tradition, had fled across the ocean in about 500 BC.

*Kon Tiki*, a 60 foot long raft was modelled on images of ancient Indian ships. It was sailed by Heyerdahl and five of his friends and, 'contrary to the predictions of scientists and sailors, the South American balsa raft, which scholars had claimed would sink if it were not regularly dried out ashore. stayed buoyant as a cork. And Polynesia, held to be inaccessible for a watercraft from ancient America, proved to be well within the range of aboriginal voyagers from Peru.'[316]

In three months, with currents and trade winds in their favour, the

---

[315] Heyerdahl (1984), p.xii
[316] Heyerdahl (1984), p.xii

crew sailed and drifted 4,300 nautical miles across the Pacific from Peru Tuamoto Island, an equivalent distance to that between Chicago and Moscow. Paul Theroux, himself an educated adventurer and explorer with a nautical bent, was unimpressed: 'In a lifetime of nutty theorizing, Heyerdahl's single success was his proof, in Kon- Tiki, that six middle-class Scandinavians could successfully crash-land their raft on a coral atoll in the middle of nowhere.'[317] Modern DNA studies have concluded that 'In spite of Thor Heyerdahl's crossing of the Pacific on a raft, there is no evidence of any genetic connection between Pacific Islanders and Peru. Population genetics has sunk the Kon- Tiki.'[318]

However the expedition had a huge impact, not least in spawning many other daredevil navigations, including a further three launched by Heyerdahl himself. John Coles expressed a certain amount of respect for this pioneer nautical experimental archaeologist when he declared in 1979: 'Without doubt, pride of place in any list of boat experiments must go the *Kon-Tiki* expedition. This was not the first experiment dealing with boats, it was not the first long-distance voyage, and its results have not led to a major revision of views; but as a dramatic yet academically sound event, it has not really been surpassed by anything before or since.'[319] Having taken care to film the expedition from the building of the raft to the end of the trip, Heyerdahl's subsequent cinema documentary won an Oscar in 1951. An effective self-publicist, Heyerdahl founded a *Kon Tiki* museum where, centre-stage, the raft remains. The book had sold over 30 million copies in sixty-seven languages by the time of his death in 2002,[320] and a new movie, *Kon Tiki* (2012), has prompted a revival of interest in his exploits.

In an attempt to face-down his critics in the aftermath of the *Kon Tiki* expedition, Heyerdahl spent several years seeking archaeological evidence on Polynesian islands, notably in excavations on Easter Island, to prove his theory of their South American colonization. He first found what he was looking for in the Galapagos Islands: *Having discovered that Inca balsa rafts were entirely capable of*

---

[317] Theroux (1992), p.629
[318] Dr Steve Jones of University College, London, BBC Reith Lectures,1991
[319] Coles (1979), p.57
[320] *Daily Telegraph* obituary, 2002

*reaching the Galapagos. I brought the first two archaeologists to investigate the islands in 1953. We searched in the few level places where early rafts could have landed between the rugged lava cliffs and rocks. Four prehistoric campsites were located on three of these arid islands. From the barren soil, the trowels of the scientists scraped up large quantities of potsherds and other artefacts, many of them identified as pre-Inca by the U.S. National Museum. This proved that numerous voyagers from Peru and Ecuador had visited the island group in pre-Columbian times. Permanent settlement had been prevented by only seasonal access to drinking water.*[321]

His critics however turned this evidence against him by pointing out that if the Galapagos Islands, close to South America, were not colonized by South Americans, then what reason was there to suppose they settled on islands thousands of nautical miles further west? His subsequent excavations of the statues and associated stone house remains on Easter Island convince, for a time, many experts that there apparent similarity to pre-Inca structures could well be explained by ancient voyages from South America after all. For some years, until the science of DNA revealed the Asian and Australasian aboriginal ancestry of the Polynesian peoples, 'The fierce fighting on all fronts now petered out to occasional sniping. [...] invitations from universities and scientific academies allowed me to present and defend my case widely. Honorary professorates and doctor's degrees, scientific medals, and fellowship in academies of science from New York to Moscow reflected that the tide had turned.'[322]

With the knowledge that Heyerdahl's theory had been shattered by DNA, his theories were ridiculed once more and Theroux saved his most cutting invective for Heyerdahl's interpretation of his 1956 Easter Island excavations:

*Far from solving the Easter Island mystery, he has succeeded in making the solution more difficult for qualified scientists and made something of a fool of himself in the process. [...] the view [that the Polynesians are of American Indian ancestry] is supported by almost everyone*

---

[321] Heyerdahl (1984), p.xiii
[322] Heyerdahl (1984), p.xiv

*except Heyerdahl himself, who clings to his absurd theory that Peruvian voyagers carried their culture - their stonework, their gods, their sweet potato - into the Pacific. Polynesians came later, he says, and brought these thriving cultures to an abrupt halt.*

What Theroux found particularly offensive was Heyerdahl's propensity for rejecting the possibility that the ancestors of modern Polynesians could have accomplished the significant achievements of the great Polynesian monument builders:

*[...] Probably the most obnoxious aspect of Heyerdahl is that he appears to display a contemptuous bias against Polynesians. [...] he maintains that the Marquesans are too lazy to have created the ambitious stonework and carvings on Hiva Oa. [...] reflecting on the stonework of Easter Island, he writes, 'One thing is certain. This was not the work of a canoeload of Polynesian wood carvers...' [...] he rubbishes the Rapa Nui people even more: 'No Polynesian fisherman would have been capable of conceiving, much less building, such a wall.' Too lazy, too uncreative, too stupid.*

*This extraordinary prejudice is not only without foundation, but is the opposite of the truth. A review of his last book in the magazine Archeology called it 'a litany of hypocrisy, superciliousness, and prejudice against Polynesians in general and the inhabitants of Easter Island, the Rapa Nui, in particular.' One of Heyerdahl's most offensive theories is that the Rapa Nui were brought to Easter Island, from another island, possibly as slaves, by ancient Peruvian navigators who were cruising and being artistic elsewhere in Oceania.*[323]

Nevertheless Heyerdahl remains a figure of heroic stature, at least for many Scandinavians; in 1999 he was voted 'Norwegian of the Century'.

While some of his theories have been successfully challenged his contribution remains significant. One biographer has gone as far as stating 'Like [Pasteur, Freud and Darwin] he has permanently changed our perception of the planet on which we all live. Never again will it be possible to think of the oceans as barriers to early man

---

[323] Theroux (1992), p.628-9

in his search for enlightenment.'[324] Now, what might Paul Theroux have had to say about that?

## CASE STUDY: The Brendan Voyage

Thor Heyerdahl's *Kon Tiki* expedition had been inspired by archaeological remains, albeit ones misinterpreted as having a connection with those of South America. He had at least demonstrated that settlement of Polynesian islands by people sailing from the Americas was, theoretically, possible and thus successfully challenged 'blind dogma and popular ideas'.[325] Many more vessels were constructed in the years that followed and used to test hypotheses regarding the seafaring capabilities of societies in the past. One such was the 'Brendan voyage', prompted not by archaeological evidence but a curious historical record: the *Navigatio Sancti Brendani Abbatis*. This document, written in the eighth or ninth centuries, tells the tale of Saint Brendan, a daring sailor who, it was said, lived a long life circa 488 to 577 A.D. In a leather boat this early explorer and his crew sailed to various places, the descriptions of which have been interpreted as marking out a route from Ireland to Newfoundland via the Hebrides, the Faroe Islands, Iceland and Greenland.

Sailing in 1976, the *Brendan* voyage was Tim Severin's first major project: 'The purpose was simply to show that the technology of the Irish monks was capable of reaching North America'.[326] His vessel was modeled on that described in the *Navigatio*:

*St Brendan and his companions, using iron implements, prepared a light vessel, with wicker sides and ribs, such as is usually made in that country, and covered it with cow-hide, tanned in oak-bark, tarring the joints thereof, and put on board provisions for forty days, with butter enough to dress hides for covering the boat and all utensils needed for the use of the crew. He then ordered the monks to embark, in the name of the Father, and of the Son, and of the Holy Ghost.*

---

[324] Ralling (1990), p.282
[325] Coles (1979), p.62
[326] Tim Severin (3 October, 2005), *Atlantic Navigators: the Brendan Voyage*, Gresham College lecture

Severin combined combined ethnographic evidence with the historical legend in his construction of the kind of boat in which Brendan might have set sail. Ancient boat-building techniques were still employed in Ireland in the 1970s in the fashioning of traditional currachs. The one Severin constructed was 36' (11 m) long and two-masted. Its ash frame was bound together with two miles length of leather straps and 1600 knots. It was covered by the hides of 49 cattle, carefully selected to acknowledge the smaller breeds available to boat builders in the sixth century. The hides, as described in the *Navigatio* manuscript, were tanned in oak bark. Medieval Bible satchels were examined closely to shed light on medieval stitching (flax), and tannage. Tests demonstrated how leather soaked in wool grease would prove hardier than many alternative modern treatments. Taking some huge risks that almost proved fatal when the vessel sprang a leak in Arctic waters, Severin's principal experiment was focused on this material as a viable option in sea-faring boat manufacture:

*Watching the waves, I recalled the bleak warning of one of the world's leading authorities on leather science before we started our voyage:*

*"Oxhide," he had explained in his precise, university tone, "is very high in protein. It resembles a piece of steak, if you like. It will decompose in the same way, either quickly or slowly, depending on various factors such as the temperature, how well it has been tanned to turn it into leather, and the amount of stress imposed upon it."*

*"What happens when the leather is soaking wet in sea water?" I had asked.*

*"Ah, well. That I'm not sure," he replied. "We've never been asked to test it. But leather will usually break down more quickly if it is wet, though perhaps the salt in sea water may have a pickling effect. I really don't know...."*

*"And what happens in the end?"*

*"Just the same as if you left a piece of steak out in the air on a saucer, In time it will turn into a nasty, evil-smelling blob of jelly. Just like a rotting*

*piece of oxhide."*[327]

Severin's aim throughout was to be exact in the replication of early medieval technology. Testing the vessel was the objective of the trip and, although they chose to wear mostly woollen clothing and ate freshly caught fish and seabirds along the way, at no point were they trying to replicate the lives of medieval monks. However they were undertaking a unique experiment and one that differed from that of Heyerdahl's and other recent nautical experiments in two fundamental ways:

*We were attempting a voyage which differed in two important respects from many previous voyages in reconstructed historic vessels. First, we were embarking in a true boat not a raft. Brendan was not simply a platform on which the winds and currents might carry us to our destination if we were lucky. She would have to be sailed properly if she were to survive, and there was little margin for error. A single mistake - a rope jammed around a cleat in a squall, or a sail suddenly blown hard against the mast - could capsize her with disastrous results. Second, and more important, we were about to venture into cold waters where few modern yachts cared to go. This was not to be a sun-drenched cruise in bathing suits. We were about to take a very small, open boat into sub-Arctic conditions, where we would have to be muffled in heavy clothing for weeks on end, frequently soaked by rain and spray, and according to the Royal Navy survival experts who had drilled us in safety procedures, if anyone fell overboard incorrectly dressed, he would be dead within five minutes.*[328]

After about four years of preparation, including four to five months of boat building, the Brendan was ready to sail. After testing on the river Shannon, she was launched at Crosshaven by the Bishop of Kerry in May, 1976. From here Severin sailed from the coast of Kerry to Brendan's Creek from where Saint Brendan allegedly set sail. On the very first night they struck a severe gale:

*No one could tell us how to steer our boat through the gale. No boat quite like her had been afloat for the past thousand years or so. To a*

---

[327] Severin (1978), p.2
[328] Severin (1978), p.130

*casual observer our craft looked like a floating banana: long and slim, with her tapering bow and stern curved gently upward in an odd fashion. Yet her most extraordinary feature was only apparent if one examined her closely: the boat was made of leather. Her hull was nothing more than forty-nine oxhides stitched together to form a patchwork quilt and stretched over a wooden frame. It was this thin skin, only a quarter of an inch thick, flexing and shifting as the boat moved - just like the skin over a man's ribcage - that now stood between us and the fury of the Atlantic.*[329]

This initial frightening experience would prove useful in building their confidence when they encountered even more challenging later in the voyage.

Achieving a speed of up to nine knots the *Brendan* compared well with modern sailing yachts. Reaching the Faroe islands they stepped ashore at another 'Brendan's Creek' and, perhaps like Brendan before them, 'In the island they found many flocks of sheep, all pure white, so numerous as to hide the face of the land.'

Sailing further north Severin and his crew were constantly attended by whales of various kinds. They seemed to regard the boat as another whale, and certainly something worth taking a close look at. For Severin this intimacy on the voyage with the ocean's greatest inhabitants helped him to identify with the fantastic story in the *Navigatio* concerning the time Brendan mistook some gigantic denizen of the sea, a whale one can presume, for an island.

For a time the *Brendan* was covering approximately 120 mile in just 24 hours. By the middle of July, 1976, they had reached Iceland, a place the Vikings had settled and recorded as having been formerly inhabited by Christian monks. Here they took the boat out of the water, cleared it of barnacles, checked it over, and found it to be in excellent condition.

Iceland is well known for its volcanic eruptions and these, like the Faeroes sheep and the whales of the North Atlantic, have been identified in Brendan's itinerary:

---

[329] Severin (1978), pp.1-2

*On another day there came into view a large and high mountain in the ocean, not far off, towards the north, with misty clouds about it, and a great smoke issuing from its summit, when suddenly the wind drove the boat rapidly towards the island until it almost touched the shore. The cliffs were so high they could scarce see the top, were black as coal, and upright like a wall. [...] Afterwards a favourable breeze caught the boat, and drove them southwards; and as they looked back, they saw the peak of the mountain unclouded, and shooting up flames into the sky, which it drew back again to itself, so that the mountain seemed a burning pyre.*

Setting sail for Greenland in the spring of 1977, the Brendan, after about ten days, they encountered the notoriously bad weather of the Denmark Strait. In a force nine gale they greatly feared being capsized or swamped. However, the boat rode the waves without harm, terrifying though the experience was for its sailors.

Beyond Greenland they encountered a dense fog, a particular phenomenon of the Grand Banks off Newfoundland, that also was reminiscent of the experiences of Brendan:

*At the end of forty days, towards evening, a dense cloud overshadowed them, so dark that they could scarce see one another. Then the procurator said to St Brendan: 'Do you know, father, what darkness is this?' And the saint replied that he knew not. 'This darkness,' said he, 'surrounds the island you have sought for seven years; you will soon see that it is the entrance to it' and after an hour had elapsed a great light shone around them, and the boat stood by the shore.*

Disaster hit the Brendan off Labrador when, one night, she crashed into pack-ice and suffered a puncture. Fortunately the crew located the hole and managed to patch it with spare oxhide, sewing it in place with flaxen thread, working in freezing cold water. Just two days before the same pack-ice had sunk a steel-hull ice-breaker vessel. If they had embarked in a wooden boat they would certainly have been crushed in navigating a passage through the ice.

The Navigatio, at the appropriate point if indeed it does describe a navigation from Ireland to America, contains some glorious descriptions of the icebergs Saint Brendan also had to pass between:

*One day, on which three Masses had been said, they saw a column in the sea, which seemed not far off, yet they could not reach it for three days. When they drew near it St Brendan looked towards its summit, but could not see it, because of its great height which seemed to pierce the skies. It was covered over with rare canopy, the material of which they knew not; but it had the colour of silver and was hard as marble, while the column itself was of the clearest crystal St Brendan ordered the brethren to take in their oars, and to lower the sails and mast, and directed some of them to hold onto the fringes of the canopy which extended about a mile from the column, and about the same depth into the sea. When this had been done. St Brendan said: 'Run in the boat now through an opening, that we may get a closer view of the wonderful works of God'. And when they had passed through the opening, and looked around them, the sea seemed to transparent like glass, so that they could plainly see everything beneath them, even the base of the column, and the skirts of the canopy lying on the ground, for the sun shone as brightly within as without.*

Severin and his team finally arrived at Newfoundland towards the end of June 1977. The *Brendan*, despite its puncture, was still in excellent condition. Not only had the voyage demonstrated the extraordinary sea-worthiness of this primitive yet highly sophisticated style of boat-building, it had also shed light on certain details of early technology and other aspects of medieval navigation:

*Brendan had also shown us that the quality of medieval boat equipment was easily equal to the task of promoting the oceangoing ambitions of the sailor-monks. Indeed, it was an interesting fact that the medieval equipment on Brendan was often a match for its modern equivalent, and occasionally superior to it when used in the grindingly harsh conditions of an open boat in the North Atlantic. Timber, leather, and flax proved to be more durable in many instances than metal, plastic, and nylon; and certainly the former were much easier to work with and could be adapted for day-to-day requirements. This was vitally important when, aboard our small craft, we were only able to carry a few hand tools and a very limited stock of spares. The modern equipment worked better, until it broke, but then the traditional gear, clumsy and inefficient though it was, managed to survive the adverse* conditions - and this is what mattered. Perhaps historians do not realise just how well the medieval seafarers were equipped for their endeavours with bronze fittings, handpicked timbers, leather, and flax cordage; and the modern seafarer forgets the tremendous advantages of flexibility and durability in the traditional materials which are all-important when the crises occur, as they always do at sea.

Similarly, there is little that the medieval sailor would want to borrow from the modern sailor to improve his personal comfort and sustenance. Apart from modern waterproof outer clothing, the medieval sailor was better clad in his woollen trousers, shirt, and cloak than in garments of synthetic fibres. And when he embarked on a cold, wet voyage in an open boat, his diet of dried meats and fish, oats, fruit, and nuts was unsurpassed. It was more nutritious and palatable, and lasted better, than the dehydrated packaged foods of today. His supply of drinking water could be carried in leather flasks, and replenished in emergency by the ample rainfall of northern waters collected in upturned sheets of leather, or topped up by landings on the islands of the Stepping Stone Route. For extra food the medieval sailor could fish or take seabirds from the wealth of the sea around him. Saint Brendan and his monks were lucky to salvage a dead whale, which gave them enough meat for three months, but it is equally clear that they were accustomed to picking up fresh provisions at every inhabited island they visited, and they were using what amounted to a chain of supply places along the Stepping Stone Route to ease their logistical problems.

The experiment was not quite over, as John Coles recorded shortly after its triumphant voyage:

*The performance of this remarkable boat was not measured with great precision during its ocean voyages, partly because it was grossly undermanned. However, after arrival in America, rowing trials were held in Boston. These trials showed that a crew of ten could make headway in most conditions, and that even six men could edge upwind. But essentially the curragh was a sailing vessel. Under sail the vessel averaged c. 65 km a day during her voyages across the Atlantic, and a cruising speed of 2-3 knots was judged satisfactory in a force 3-4 wind; a following wind or force 5-6 allowed speeds of up to 7 knots, and occasionally 12 knots was recorded. Adverse winds actually drove the boat backwards as she sat up in the water and her stretched sides* caught the wind. Against a headwind Brendan could point 50°- 60° off the wind, but she could not sail closer. Her most impressive quality was her safety even in rough weather; the stability of the craft was in part due to 0.8 tonne of fresh water ballast, which helped prevent any tendency to capsize.[330]

The Brendan now resides in a museum in County Mayo back in Ireland, and footage of the voyage, taken by Severin using a clockwork camera, preserves the voyage for posterity. Like Heyerdahl and the Kon Tiki before him, Severin had proved, by experiment, what was possible. Other archaeological methods must be employed to prove what actually happened.

## CASE STUDY: The Overton Down earthwork

It is now more than half a century since a 21 metre long, two metre high, seven metre wide bank and accompanying ditch was constructed at Overton Down, near to Marlborough in Wiltshire, for experimental purposes. It took 1150 person hours to build and cost £323, including the cost of photography.[331]

The project was an outcome of a meeting of the British Association for the Advancement of Science in 1958. A research committee was formed 'to investigate by experiment the denudation and burial of archaeological structures.'[332] The longevity of the experiment makes it exceptional and it was, from the start, designed to continue for at least 128 years. A second earthwork, as exact a replica as its builders could achieve, but a very different geological context, was constructed in 1963 on Morden Bog, near Wareham in Dorset. Markers were set in the banks to support attempts to measure the rate of movement through erosion and compaction. The committee, from the start, seem to have anticipated the limitations of their ambitious experiment:

---

[330] Coles (1979), p.82
[331] The 1992 excavation cost £5000 and a further £21000 was spent post-excavation.
[332] In Bell, M., Fowler, P. J., Hillson, S. W. (1996), *The Experimental Earthwork Project, 1962-1992*, Council for British Archaeology

'At no point do the experiment's publications specify that the definition of laws was an objective. Perhaps that reflects a recognition by the originators of the problematic nature of law definition in the historical sciences, archaeology and ecology. In any case the recognition of pattern and regularity does not necessarily presuppose the existence of underlying laws.'[333]

The construction of the earthworks became important evidence for archaeologists interested in work rates. It was estimated that ten people could construct a small barrow in the space of a week and the colossal Dorset Cursus on Cranborne Chase would have taken 100 people approximately 740 days to build.[334]

Buried within both banks are pieces of leather, pottery, textiles, bone, wood, flint and other materials. The object of the exercise is to enable archaeologists to observe the way in which these objects are affected over time and how the bank and ditch alter. Thus the project comprises two principal experimental strands.

Sections have already been cut to measure these developments, five to date: 1962, 1964, 1968, 1976 and 1992. At intervals of 2, 4, 8, 16, 32, 64 and 128 years, the next section is due to be cut in 2024. The Morden Bog structure has been sectioned in 1965, 1967, 1972, 1980 and 1996. These timings reflected the assumption, and a correct one on the basis of the evidence of the first few excavations, that changes in the earthworks would occur 'more or less at an exponentially decreasing rate.'[335]

The bad winter of 1962-3 hastened the process of slope recession as a number of turfs became dislodged and fell into the ditch, but less new material was deposited in the ditch than in mild winters. In the first few years the changes were relatively dramatic but by the mid-1970s the structure had stabilized and changes were slight.

---

[333] Bell, M., Fowler, P. J., Hillson, S. W. (1996), *The Experimental Earthwork Project, 1962-1992*, Council for British Archaeology, p.229
[334] Bell, M., Fowler, P. J., Hillson, S. W. (1996), *The Experimental Earthwork Project, 1962-1992*, Council for British Archaeology, p.244
[335] Bell, M., Fowler, P. J., Hillson, S. W. (1996), *The Experimental Earthwork Project, 1962-1992*, Council for British Archaeology, p.230

Following the 1968 sectioning by the University of Bristol's Extra-Mural Studies department, and its analysis, the findings reaffirmed the complexity of stratigraphic interpretation:

'The Overton Down ditch [...] probably poses more doubts and questions than it answers on the interpretation of sections in geomorphology and archaeology. The complexity of the stratigraphy after only eight years suggests the need for extensive excavations of archaeological sites if stratigraphy is to play a major part[336] in interpretation.'[337]

In addition to the movement of the bank and the infill of the ditch, faunal activity, including that of worms and moles was recorded ('One worm was found in the top of the bank'[338]) as was the flora on site and its colonization by vegetation during the first few years of its existence.

In 1979, after careful consideration, a new experiment was conceived: 'This was contrary to [the Committee's] general earthwork management policy but it could not see that any interference with the existing experiments would be incurred. Furthermore, as was the case in allowing glass to be inserted into the Wareham Earthwork, it appreciated that an opportunity had arisen to generate more data without disturbing existing arrangements.

The form of the experiment, proposed by Professor Richard Atkinson, was that mint-condition coins should be inserted into the bank and along the outer edge of the ditch to monitor soil movement. They were to be placed vertically on edge parallel to the long axis of the monument at a depth of about 50mm (2in), at which level they would be most sensitive to soil movement. Any evidence of wear patterns on the coin surfaces would be a bonus to the primary objective. The proposals were subsequently modified slightly by a decision to position the ditch coins on the inner rather than outer side. Coins

---

[336] 'plan' in the original text – presumably a typing error.
[337] Crabtree, K. (1971), 'Overton Experimental Earthwork, Wiltshire, 1968' in *Proceedings of the University of Bristol Spelaeological Society*, 1971, 12 (3), p.244
[338] Peter Fowler, 'The 1968 Overton excavation' in Bell, M., Fowler, P. J., Hillson, S. W. (1996), *The Experimental Earthwork Project, 1962-1992*, Council for British Archaeology, p.30

were to be placed in both excavated and unexcavated zones.'[339]

A range of pottery items were included, each type being the focus of a specific experiment. These were summarised as:

Sherd type 1: Hodges-sherds

Experiment –
W: to study physical change in the sherds themselves
X: chemical change in the sherds themselves
Sherd type 2: flower-pot sherds

Experiment –
Y: to mimic pre-earthwork conditions
Sherd type 3: baked clay roundels

Experiment –
Z: to indicate morphological changes in the earthwork a: numbered b: unnumbered
Sherd type 4: baked clay triangles

Experiment -
Z: to indicate morphological changes in the earthwork[340]

In a review of these individual experiments in 1996 the following conclusions were reached:

'Only the 'Hodges-sherds' (type 1) are, strictly speaking, 'buried materials' in the sense that the intended experiment concerned changes in the sherds themselves; but the two experiments (W, X) they were meant to carry have so far proved abortive.

The other three ceramic types (2, 3, 4), in contrast, have proved an extremely valuable mechanism in indicating morphological change (experiments Y and Z), the main thrust of the experiment in its

---

[339] Bell, M., Fowler, P. J., Hillson, S. W. (1996), *The Experimental Earthwork Project, 1962-1992*, Council for British Archaeology, p.12
[340] Bell, M., Fowler, P. J., Hillson, S. W. (1996), *The Experimental Earthwork Project, 1962-1992*, Council for British Archaeology, p.45

founders' minds. Some concern was expressed at an early stage about the amount of disruption being caused to this aspect of the experiment by casual visitors picking up and throwing potsherds around. Clearly this happened, and undoubtedly some sherds did disappear or have been found in potentially misleading situations; but, over the three decades, the threat has reduced to minimal significance. Presumably fewer sherds have been visible on the surface to the casual visitor as the earthwork has settled down after the flurry of activity in its early years; but, more significantly, the sheer number of sherds found in 'correct' or 'theoretically acceptable' positions over five excavations has more than offset the interpretative liabilities of 'lost' i.e. unrecovered, sherds and a relatively few 'rogue' sherds.'[341]

A set of ceramic discs was also buried 'as a key mechanism in achieving one of the primary objectives of the Project, that is to study morphological change'[342] When the 1968 section was cut across the structure the rate of recovery of these discs was surprising:

'38 out of 56 discs were retrieved, a recovery rate of 68%. Expressed the other way round, however, the implications could be a little alarming from an archaeological point of view: a reasonably competent, very simple excavation to find a known type of virtually indestructible artefact placed in known numbers in known positions failed, only eight years after their burial, to find 32% of them. A one-third 'cultural loss' within a decade might well give food for thought.'[343]

Animal activity, particularly that of moles, was identified as a principal cause of dispersion and loss. The analysis of the 1976 data regarding the movement of discs suggested that, short of a major disturbance such as an earthquake, after just a few years 'for some sherds at least [...] the great journey of their life-time was already over.'[344]

---

[341] Bell, M., Fowler, P. J., Hillson, S. W. (1996), *The Experimental Earthwork Project, 1962-1992*, Council for British Archaeology, p.46
[342] Bell, M., Fowler, P. J., Hillson, S. W. (1996), *The Experimental Earthwork Project, 1962-1992*, Council for British Archaeology, p.46
[343] Bell, M., Fowler, P. J., Hillson, S. W. (1996), *The Experimental Earthwork Project, 1962-1992*, Council for British Archaeology, p.47
[344] Bell, M., Fowler, P. J., Hillson, S. W. (1996), *The Experimental Earthwork Project, 1962-1992*, Council for British Archaeology, p.49

As might be expected, a scatter of flower pot sherds 'strewn on the surface before work began on site in 1960, which was meant to represent contemporary occupation', [345] ended up in the ditch within 16 years of the start of the project.

At various stages the different inorganic objects and organic materials buried were the subject of extensive reports when recovered in subsequent excavations. As time went on new techniques of analysis, such as scanning electron microscopy, were employed. By 1992 the imperial measurement system of the original project had given way to the metric system of modern archaeology.

Following the 1992 section of the Overton Down structure the CBA published a monograph (1996) that summarized the value of the experiment and its most recent analysis by section:

'In particular, it records the more detailed programme of analytical work which it was possible to implement at Overton in 1992. This concentrated on the preservation of biological and environmental evidence in the 32 year old buried soil as analogues for archaeological buried soils, and on the analysis of a range of organic and inorganic materials which had been buried in 1960. Included here is work on vegetation history, a linked study of soil micromorphology and chemistry, seeds and pollen, Scanning Electron Microscope studies of bone, wood and textiles, and a microbiological study.'[346] At the start of the project time and motion studies were its originators primary concern. As time has passed the scientific studies of these buried materials, together with the micro-morphological and chemical analysis of the buried soils, has become particularly significant.

The extensive 1996 interim report closed with a final evaluation as a summary of the experiment's strengths and weaknesses. These included the following:

Problems with the experiment

---

[345] Bell, M., Fowler, P. J., Hillson, S. W. (1996), *The Experimental Earthwork Project, 1962-1992*, Council for British Archaeology, p.50
[346] Bell, M., Fowler, P. J., Hillson, S. W. (1996), *The Experimental Earthwork Project, 1962-1992*, Council for British Archaeology, p.xix

- It is difficult to take account of the role of chance and chaos in interpreting the results of such an experiment.
- The lack of replication of samples within an individual section was a basic methodological flaw [...] the earthwork as a whole is unique and without replicates which can be used to test hypotheses. It should be noted, however, that chance variations in a whole range of environmental conditions such as faunal activity mean that the concept of a replicate in this context is somewhat problematic.
- The buried materials were said to be similar to those used in prehistoric times. That applies to most inorganic materials (with the exception of the choice of metal alloys used at Wareham), but not the organic materials, many of which had been treated in ways which differ significantly from prehistoric practice.
- Each section cannot be seen as a perfect replica in a time series. Each will have its own unique properties of, for example, chemistry or post-burial faunal history which may, or may not, have a significant influence on the outcome of the experiment. Similarly, each of the buried material samples and the contexts in which they are placed will not be perfect replicates.
- Grazing animals are excluded from Overton but not Wareham, where deer activity is quite frequent on the bank.
- The experiments are limited to chalk and sand geologies where most excavation was taking place in the 1950s and 1960s. Since then excavation has expanded on to a much wider range of other geologies.

Merits of the experiment

1) From the beginning the project had clearly stated aims and method.
2) The project helped to make experimental methodology an accepted part of archaeological practice.
3) The interdisciplinary approach is relevant to a range of disciplines concerned with change over time.
4) The project helped the development of a team approach to the application of science in archaeology. From the beginning specialists worked on the site providing the opportunity to appreciate the contexts from which samples were derived. The experiment is a welcome attempt to address issues of medium-term change.

5) The care with which the experiment was set up makes it possible to use the site for a range of studies which were not originally foreseen.[347]

The detailed analysis of silt formation in the ditch was particularly interesting:
'During the period when Overton was eroding, annual winter/summer banding was recorded in the silts washed into the ditch. This was an entirely new discovery, and may establish whether prehistoric ritual activity was seasonal. Ritual deposits are often found in ditches, and analysis of silt banding may provide clues as to the time of year they were buried.'[348]

After 33 years some of the textiles buried at the sites proved to be in a better state of preservation than had been expected. These findings could be useful to forensic archaeologists engaged in the analysis of recently buried materials:

'Forensic archaeologists in particular are now looking closely at how the different types of material have decayed over the past three decades, to help them and the police understand what happens to clothing and other items (for instance, leather) associated with present-day buried murder victims.'[349]

The decay of bone at the Wareham site was dramatic – it had all disappeared with the exception of bone that had been cremated. In the chalk soils of Overton Down, as predicted, it was much better preserved but even in this context fungal activity suggested it would not last very much longer.

With its emphasis on formation processes, the project was well ahead of its time when it was initiated with the building of the Overton earthwork in 1960. It has provided some excellent data for developing the debate regarding the value of experimental

---

[347] Bell, M., Fowler, P. J., Hillson, S. W. (1996), *The Experimental Earthwork Project, 1962-1992*, Council for British Archaeology, p.244
[348] Bell, M (1996), 'Understanding how earthworks change', *British Archaeology*, 17, September 1996.
[349] Bell, M (1996), 'Understanding how earthworks change', *British Archaeology*, 17, September 1996.

archaeology, its strengths and its limitations. Even after 32 years the verdict was that 'It is still a little too soon to judge whether the Experimental Earthworks Project is worthwhile.'[350] Perhaps when the Overton Down earthwork project arrives at its intended conclusion in 2088, and the Wareham project in 2091, something of great importance will have been discovered. Quite possibly its main significance will reveal itself as a record of climate change and its impact at a time of fast developing environmental awareness and concern. At the very least it provides, and will continue to do so, an interesting focus for the study of the evolution of archaeological approaches, techniques, and interpretations: 'a sort of open air laboratory in which successive generations of archaeologists can think through issues of formation processes and the timescales of change and help to build a bridge between individual short-term observations and archaeological time.'[351]

## Experiential approaches to the past

'If I've learned one thing on this project it is an enormous respect for Iron Age man. I hadn't realised when I started just how clever and ingenious and knowledgeable they were.'[352]

Many archaeological experiments have an *experiential* dimension that, informative as it may seem to the participants, does not equate to the empirical evidence that experimental archaeology is designed to generate. Consequently experimental archaeology and attempts to 'experience' archaeology are related, but they not always comfortable bed-fellows. At the same time that Peter Reynolds was establishing his 'Iron Age' farmstead at Butser on the Hampshire-Sussex border, the BBC created its own 'Iron Age' farm near the village of Gussage All Saints in Dorset with a view to filming people *living* on site as opposed to merely using the farm as an outdoor experimental laboratory, as at Butser. Peter Reynolds' involvement in the project was somewhat ambivalent: on the one hand he dismissed out of hand the possibility

---

[350] Bell, M., Fowler, P. J., Hillson, S. W. (1996), *The Experimental Earthwork Project, 1962-1992*, Council for British Archaeology, p.xiv

[351] Bell, M., Fowler, P. J., Hillson, S. W. (1996), *The Experimental Earthwork Project, 1962-1992*, Council for British Archaeology, p.246

[352] Pete Little, Iron Age re-enactor, quoted in Percival (1980), p.157

that twentieth-century people could come anywhere close to recreating a truly Iron age lifestyle and yet, at the same time, he was much involved in the project as a technical consultant: 'It was they [Reynolds and his partner at Butser, Jack Langley] and the team of expert of expert advisers on the Committee for Ancient Agriculture, who suggested the most suitable livestock, who provided blueprints for the houses, who advised on all manner of tools and techniques'.[353]

The 'Living in the Past' project was certainly a hugely ambitious one and one that helped pioneer the 'reality shows' of the modern TV era. It aimed to explore if it was possible 'for modern people to readapt [...], to rediscover the ancient skills and learn to prosper within the limits of a simple technology'.[354] Butser in fact was not the original model for the project, but instead a 'reconstructed' Iron Age village in Denmark run by an archaeologist - Hans Olle Hansen. Free of the health and safety controls that would make such a programme that much harder to make today, its plan involved the creation and working of a prehistoric type of farm by six couples and three children. They were destined to stay on site, 'living' the Iron Age, for a whole year. It was screened between February and May, 1978, in a dozen 50 minute episodes. As at Butser, the structures were modeled on the evidence of excavation, and the tools and other technology, once the farm was built, replicated artefacts and other evidence of Iron Age antiquity. After a few weeks the food the community consumed was derived from the livestock they were provided with by the producer, John Percival, the fish they trapped in a nearby stream, and the wheat and corn they sowed and harvested. Controversially, Percival was convinced that 'to get a group of volunteers actually living in the houses, depending on the crops and the livestock for their subsistence, relying on the tools for their livelihood would bring a new dimension to our understanding of prehistory'.[355] He challenged those detractors who would argue that experiential approach lacked the validity of the experimental, and went even further, arguing that:

> It is not enough to know how a job may have been done; it is not enough even to do the job oneself and repeat the demonstration,

---

[353] Percival (1980), p.9
[354] Percival (1980), p.7
[355] Percival (1980), p.9

*with all the monitoring devices, the weighing and measuring and timing that scientific experimental archaeology demands. It is necessary to do the job day after day, to depend upon its being done satisfactorily to fulfil your everyday needs. It is necessary to live an experience in order fully to comprehend it.*[356]

However, Percival was well aware of the obvious limitations of his approach, recognizing that 'It was clearly impossible to recapture the beliefs and superstitions, the skills and experience, the basic social attitudes of prehistoric people and this was never our intention.'[357]

The experience of trying to make a viable living out of farming the site spawned a number of trial and error, if not strictly 'scientific', experiments along with Reynolds' own observations regarding the efficacy of replica 'sickles' for the job after which they are named. In the same vein the inhabitants of BBC's farm when, for example devising housing for goats and chickens, soon discovered that 'The only test that could be applied to any theory derived from archaeological evidence was whether it worked.'[358] Rectilinear structures proved a good more difficult to build than equivalent sized roundhouses:

*the square and rectangular structures which had to be reinforced with diagonal struts with all the joints mortised in, because although the group were using some basic modern tools - saws, axes and a few chisels - they had to manage without nails, which would have been an expensive luxury in the Iron Age. A small round house on the other hand can be put up with a single ring of fairly light posts hammered into the ground. The rafters are then tied with cord to the tops of the posts and drawn upwards to form a conical roof which is lashed together at the top, rather like a Red Indian tepee. In fact the volunteers chose to mortise some of the rafters to the tops of the posts, just to be on the safe side, but the little hut went up with surprising speed.*[359]

Despite having a textbook knowledge of ancient technologies, such

---

[356] Percival (1980), pp.9-10
[357] Percival (1980), p.15
[358] Percival (1980), p.19
[359] Percival (1980), p.21

activities as creating fire and making cooking pots that did not explode when filled with a stew and heated, at least at first, defied their students. It took the potters seven months of experimenting with clays, grogs and kilns before they produced earthenware pots that were suitable for cooking.

The experience of attempting to live an 'Iron Age' life demonstrated how inappropriate the very term is since many of the community's tools, and certainly the bulk of their materials, were organic – wood, straw, skin, antler and bone. Nevertheless, the project provided ample opportunities to put to the test the various metal tools the BBC had provided, all close replicas of artefacts in museum collections:

> 'The axe isn't very good,' he [John Rockliff] explained, 'It's badly balanced and I think I've only used it once or twice, to cut a mortise in a big log of wood.' He took up another axe-like tool, but this time with the blade set at right angles to the plane of the handle: 'The adzes on the other hand are excellent, really useful. I've had hardly any experience using an adze before and I'm amazed how good a tool it is. I can't think why they're not used more today.'
>
> He also had a little collection of billhooks. These were very carefully copied from Iron Age models, which may have been worn or rusted away long before they were abandoned for the archaeologists to find, and I had been worried that they were too light to be really effective.
>
> 'Yes they are light,' agreed John. 'They're more like spar hooks, the ones thatchers use, than a modern hedging billhook, but that's what makes me think that the Iron Age people used hazel a great deal. You see,' he lifted a little hook in his hand, 'this tool is absolutely ideal for hazel. You can use it to cut the stems from the coppice – provided they're not too thick - you can split hazel with it and you can use it very lightly, to get a fine point or whatever you want. As soon as you start using it you realise that it's tailor-made for the job.'[360]

Without scythes, let-alone mowing machines, harvesting proved to be

---

[360] Percival (1980), pp.65-7

very labour intensive, hard, back-breaking work.

The community was provided with one pair of shears. At the time the only shears that had been found and dated were of Romano-British antiquity but the supposition was (correctly) that they were in use well before the Conquest. As with Reynolds' sickle, they were ineffective, at least for the job, sheep-shearing, it was usually presumed they were designed:

> 'They're very slow,' explained Kate, as she tugged away at a prostrate sheep and they tend to chew at the fleece. We find the best way is simply to pull the top layer of wool free by pulling at it gently with our fingers, but around the flanks it doesn't come off at all well, so now we use a sharp flake of flint and this works a lot quicker than shears. In fact we now think those shears are for cutting hair, because they're quite good for that.'[361]

The construction of an effective bread oven led to further trial-and-error experiments. Initially the bakers sealed the opening of the clay dome structure with turfs but these dried out and were burned away before the bread was baked; thereafter they sealed the oven with stones. Cloth was woven on a reconstructed loom, and dyed using plants and berries available in the vicinity, furrows were scored for planting with their self-built ard, and a small amount of honey and plenty of beeswax were successfully harvested from their hives without any of the protective clothing worn by modern beekeepers. Some activities, especially in inexperienced hands, were immensely time-consuming. The weaving a piece of cloth is a good example: it took most of two days to arrange the warp threads on the loom before any weaving could begin. The production of a simple woollen skirt – spinning, weaving and sewing - represented about a month's work for a twentieth century re-enactor; even a skilled worker, it can be presumed, must have spent 20 days or so doing the same.

As at Butser, the absence of evidence regarding the exact techniques employed by Iron Age farmers in the harvesting, threshing and storing grain, provided ample opportunity for experimentation:

---

[361] Percival (1980), p.69

There were nearly two acres of wheat to bring in and this of course was the most important crop of all. The barley and oats, already cut and stacked, was mainly for animal feed. So the wheat harvest was crucial. Once again, as they planned how to go about bringing in the grain, the vexed question of storage came up. In addition to the pits that are found on almost all Iron Age sites, there is a very common arrangement of post holes set in squares about four feet apart, which are usually interpreted as granaries. Working on this theory John Rossetti and John Rockliff built two square structures with platforms set on top of four posts about four feet above the ground. On top of the platforms they constructed woven baskets of hazel, topping them off with little conical roofs of thatch. The idea was to fill these granaries with ears of wheat, cutting them high on the stalk and leaving the straw standing in the field in the manner so often depicted in medieval manuscripts. Unfortunately, whereas medieval farmers possessed both threshing floors and flails with which to beat out the grain from the ear, neither flails nor smooth floors for threshing are found on Iron Age sites. This meant that they would have to devise an alternative method for extracting the grain. It seemed more sensible to start off with the ears on long straw rather than short, so that they could keep their options open on how they threshed the wheat and also make more use of the straw for thatching, basket making and animal bedding.

Accordingly they cut the wheat close to the ground, just as they had cut the barley and oats. But the stiffer wheat straw allowed them to stook the sheaves in the field before they brought them in. For a blessed few days the weather stayed fine. The reapers worked their way slowly and rhythmically across the field followed by another line of workers binding the cut wheat into sheaves and standing the sheaves to dry. From time to time they would change places in the reaping line, the women taking their turn with the men in the long, hard, back, breaking toil. Once the harvest was in full swing a third group of workers made great bundles of wheat sheaves, hoisted them on to their backs and carried them back to the round house until they had accumulated enough for another stack.[362]

The community's solution to the threshing was particularly interesting

---

[362] Percival (1980), pp.108-9

and, once again, challenged old assumptions:

> *[...] the villagers were both resourceful and ingenious. They set up a beam of split ash on twin posts about three feet above the ground. They spread hides underneath and then, holding a sheaf of wheat with one hand and a baton of wood in the other, beat out the grain over the beam. Eventually there were three of these threshing rails, one under cover in the small store house and two in the open compound. The interesting thing about these from the archaeologists' point of view is that the pairs of post holes dug into the chalk for each threshing beam closely match similar pairs of post holes found on many Iron Age sites. These have usually been interpreted as drying racks for hay or cereals, but the villagers ridiculed this suggestion as hopelessly impractical.*
>
> *'We've got six tons of hay in those stacks,' Pete Ainsworth pointed out. 'Now imagine how many racks you would need for that lot ... fifty? A hundred? Anyway, you don't need a pair of bloody great posts for a drying rack ... and exactly the same goes for drying the grain. You'd need hundreds of racks for a decent harvest; anyway it dries in stooks in the field and keeps perfectly well in a stack.'*[363]

Furthermore Iron Age farmers would have had no need to protect their harvest from rats by raising it on racks since the rat is not an indigenous species and was not introduced into Britain until the Middle Ages. The less destructive vermin – mice, voles and birds – were all that they had to contend with.

To dry the threshed grain ready for grinding into flour the villagers set a fire in a pit dug in the store-house floor and covered it with blue lias slabs on which the grain could be dried out as the fire burned. However, what they ended up with was less than ideal:

> *If the stones were too hot the grain got burnt.*
>
> *'Sometimes the flour is like cocoa,' complained Sarah with a laugh, 'all black and gritty.'*

---

[363] Percival (1980), p.115

*'But the main trouble,' Sharon pointed out, 'is that you can't knead it properly. I suppose it destroys the gluten or something, because the flour won't stick together and the loaves won't rise at all.'*

*'I think our dirt intake has gone up somewhat since we started threshing our own grain,' observed Jill drily. 'Talk about wholemeal bread! Ours is whole chaff, whole sticks and whole stones.'*[364]

This inspired the villagers to seek an alternative solution and soon found one without any assistance from the archaeological record:

*Before long they had devised an alternative to the parcher, so simple and yet so effective that they could not imagine why they had not thought of it before. I came into the round house one morning and as my eyes grew accustomed to the usual smoky darkness I noticed a new rack placed on top of the beam from which the cauldron was suspended. On top of this rack was a shapeless bag, no doubt made out of surplus underwear.*

*'What's that?' I asked Sharon, who was sitting by the fire.*

*'Oh that's our new grain parcher,' she explained. 'We just stick the wheat in a bag and leave it over the fire and it dries out beautifully. No burning, no over parching, and it querns perfectly.'*

*So the parcher was abandoned and the querns spun freely, bearings permitting, for the remainder of the project.*[365]

Another question the archaeology does not clearly answer is that concerned with the issue of footwear. Did Iron Age people, as a general rule, wear shoes? The experience of living in the village was inconclusive. The leather sandals they constructed wore out very quickly and a good number of the people involved chose to work bare-footed, at least during the summer. Others though, particularly one who sustained a nasty gash on a piece of flint on the ball one foot and impaled the heel of the other on a thorn, insisted on staying shod most of the time. Most of the group, bare-footed or otherwise, were inclined

---

[364] Percival (1980), p.116-7
[365] Percival (1980), p.117

to the belief that Iron Age people, because of the wear-and-tear issue, would have stayed barefooted until it was too cold to do so without great discomfort. Of course, feet that were used to the practice were likely to have tougher skins than those of 1970s' re-enactors. When the winter did arrive they found their homemade leather sandals were scarcely fit for purpose and his prompted further experimentation:

> *Sarah had discarded her shoes, not out of masochism, but because they were soaked through and it was generally agreed that wet shoes were even more miserable than bare feet, because they took longer to warm up again. The solution was pattens, separate soles of wood, platforms for the feet, fixed by a variety of methods to the underside of the leather shoes. All the villagers developed a slow, trudging, flat-footed walk to cope with the unyielding pattens and the slippery mire.*[366]

When the villagers decided to celebrate Solstice they decorated their roundhouse with simple clay lamps containing wicks floating in precious lard. This was a luxury and, in any case, an ineffectual way of lighting the building – the lamps around wall produced much less light than the fire in the centre – but they did create 'a delightful festive atmosphere'. John Percival concluded one need 'Look no further for the significance of Christmas candles and fairy lights. Poor people can afford lights only for festivals.'[367]

A very specific experiment was carried out by one of the women in the group, producing results that again challenged existing assumptions:

> *Sharon, who did not rate her own skill with her hands very highly, had turned out a very creditable copy of a hairnet found in a peat bog at Forarden in Denmark. This net was found, still loosely attached to the coiled blond hair of the girl who had worn it in life over two thousand years before. It has been acclaimed by archaeologists as an example of the skilled craftsmanship of prehistoric people. 'It's quite interesting because most people who've studied it don't seem to be sure how it was worn,' said Sharon. 'But when we made it we found it was quite obvious.'*

---

[366] Percival (1980), p.146
[367] Percival (1980), p.140

*She bullied Sarah into putting the thing on for the sake of the film camera. 'I think it's a bonnet rather than a hairnet. It's the right size and there are drawstrings on three sides so it all gathers together very easily. The archaeologists said it was a luxury article, but it only took me three days, working with very fine wool. I don't see that it's a luxury item at all.'*[368]

When the year was at an end, several archaeologists were invited on site. Peter Reynolds had become increasingly sceptical regarding the value of the project, particularly since the farm had no chief – it was an egalitarian set-up, 'rule by committee, and I think in any kind of agricultural society this is so rare as to be almost non-existent. We must have a hierarchy and this we haven't got.'[369] Within a year of the broadcasting of the TV series he published his book on the Butser project in which, doubtless reflecting on this project, he sourly declared that:

*Any attempt to relive the remote past is destined to failure, because the knowledge and experience of previous generations are denied us. To place modern man into a prehistoric context, given the limitations of our knowledge, is only to observe how modern people may react both to the conditions and to each other.*[370]

Others were more sympathetic – Professor Dimbleby from the Institute of Archaeology in London regretted the project had to come to an end so soon, convinced it had more to reveal regarding the approaches management and use of natural resources, and Geoffrey Wainwright, who had excavated an Iron Age settlement nearby concluded 'it gave one a very clear feeling of what it must have been like.'[371] The esteemed Iron Age expert, Barry Cunliffe, also seemed to find aspects the experiment enlightening. Cunliffe identified several 'small things' of particular interest which together added up to 'something considerable':

*[He] explained how he had taken an interest in the little hollows in*

---

[368] Percival (1980), p.162
[369] Peter Reynolds quoted in Percival (1980), p.168
[370] Reynolds (1979), p.14
[371] Geoffrey Wainwright quoted in Percival (1980), p.169

*the earth, just inside the round house doors. These were made by chickens which came into the house, especially on wet days, and made use of the dry earth as a dust bath. 'Well, I can't now say that every scoop I find in an Iron Age house is a dust bath for chickens, but it makes me understand just that little bit more the conditions under which people lived, and the range of explanations that are possible.'*[372]

Peter Reynolds found the solution to the cold, wet feet problem 'particularly interesting'[373] given the lack of evidence for prehistoric footwear.

Shortly afterwards the site was burned to the ground to prevent it from attracting unwanted visitors. The social experiment was over, but for Peter Reynolds this marked the beginning, not the end, of a long-term project with real potential for the scientific study of taphonomic and excavation processes:

*The site itself is of 'archaeological interest'. It has been extensively photographed, accurately measured and recorded. In years to come it will be gradually excavated, the activity areas examined for remnant traces, decomposition of materials monitored and the distribution of artefacts plotted. Because we have a good record of what actually happened on the site, evidence recovered by excavation can be analysed accordingly. Not only will it allow us to evaluate the various techniques of excavation in terms of their recovery levels but also it may well engender new and improved techniques.*[374]

In 2000 the BBC revisited the 'Living in the Past' and launched a second 'living history' series: 'Surviving the Iron Age'. This time a group of 17 volunteers aimed to spend just seven weeks living in a mock-up 'Iron Age' farmstead. The site chosen was Castell Henllys, a Welsh promontory hillfort in North Pembrokeshire. This time the roundhouses were already standing when the film crew arrived. The site was excavated by students, led by Harold Mytum, in association

---

[372] Percival (1980), p.171
[373] Reynolds (1979) 'Living in the Past' exhibition notes, p.2
[374] Reynolds (1979) 'Living in the Past' exhibition notes, p.4

with the universities of York and Liverpool, over 27 seasons between 1981 and 2008. Its four roundhouses and related structures were constructed with painstaking attention to the detail of the postholes of the original Iron Age buildings uncovered on the hilltop. Three of the four stand on the very site of the excavated remains on which they are based. Guided by the principles of Peter Reynolds and the Butser project, the custodians of Castell Henllys, Pembrokeshire Coast National Park, maintain the site as a centre for heritage education, where visitors, including dozens of school parties each year, can have a go at trying out various Iron age activities such as using a quern, and as a centre for experimental archaeology:

> Through the reconstruction at Castell Henllys we are able to learn about sustainability and land management from the way people lived their lives in the Iron Age.'[375] However, as is the case with sites of this kind, which have proliferated remarkably over the past few decades, its primary business is experience more than experiment. As well as attracting parties of schoolchildren it is an important player in the local tourist industry in a part of Wales famous for its stunning landscapes.

Castell Henllys must be ranked alongside the likes of Danebury (Hants) and Maiden Castle (Dorset) as one of the most thoroughly excavated hillfort sites in the UK. It is multivallated and excavation revealed evidence of numerous roundhouses covering the period 500-100 BC. Compared to Maiden Castle it is tiny – half a hectare to the Dorset hillfort's nineteen. As at Danebury and Maiden Castle, a slingshot ammunition dump seemed to confirm the defensive nature of the site – a true 'fort' – as did the exceptionally unusual 'cheveaux-de-frise' feature: multiple lines of upright stones on the outside of the ditch and bank system presumed to hinder advance on the fort by chariots. Similar structures have been found at hillfort sites in Spain.

From the start the series' producer, Peter Firstbrook, recognized that this 'ambitious experiment' had the same limitations as that carried out twenty years before:

> there was never any intention to try to understand how people lived

---

[375] www.pembrokeshirecoast.org.uk, accessed 26/10/13

*during the Iron Age. Our volunteers were from the twenty-first century and nothing could eradicate their accumulated knowledge of past history and present experience. It was not for them to try to second-guess how the Iron Age people lived; those prehistoric people were influenced by pagan beliefs and a profound suspicion of the outside world which we could never hope to fully understand, let alone replicate.*[376]

Instead it was to be another social experiment 'to see if a group of people from the modern world could organize themselves in an alien, prehistoric environment'[377]. In this alien environment they would have to learn to feed themselves, to cope with the shelter of roundhouses through cold nights, and, dressed in rough woolen Iron Age style clothing, to learn to exist without any of the modern amenities central to survival in the twenty-first century.

In the spirit of the 'reality' TV shows of the period, the volunteers were given a series of 'time challenges', printed on paper scrolls and given to the group at regular intervals.

A criticism of the 'Living in the Past' project had been the anachronistic egalitarian, democratic, non-hierarchical organisation of the community. To address this the 'Surviving the Iron Age' group was instructed to elect a chieftain with absolute authority.

Early on in the experiment it became apparent that the laborious and exhausting business of bringing firewood and water some considerable distance, uphill, each day might jeopardise the 'time challenges'. Consequently a crew of BBC bearers and carriers took on the role of the slaves it was conveniently presumed the community would have relied on in the past, thus releasing the volunteers for tasks that would make better television. Ample supplies of wood and charcoal were provided and the water tap was moved close to the settlement.

Health and safety concerns, legislation and the BBC's duty of care to its employees further undermined attempts to 'experience' life in the Iron

---

[376] Firstbrook (2000), p.10
[377] Firstbrook (2000), p.10

Age. A potential outbreak of bacterial infection when one of the children fell ill necessitated some twenty-first century interventions in the form of washing powder, disinfectant, anti-bacterial handwash, and a hot shower for each of the volunteers. Everyone was given a roll of toilet paper. As in the 'Living in the Past' project the footwear dilemma soon emerged. As before, one member of the group gashed his foot but, whereas in 1978 the community was left to its own devices to resolve the issue, in 2000 the BBC responded by providing wellington boots for all!

One of the 'time challenges' facing the Castell Henllys group was the making and firing of Iron Age style pottery. Although numerous people had done this numerous times before and hence it was highly unlikely that their attempts would add anything to our understanding of the processes involved, it could still be argued that their activities were a form of experimental archaeology since, as John Coles stated, 'Series of experiments, building on the results of previous work, can lead to greater understanding as well as exposing new problems.'[378]

> Mark and Tom first tried to fire their pots using a pit clamp, which was similar in principle to the charcoal clamp. They lined the base of a pit with hot embers, followed by two or three layers of green wood, then they placed their pots on top. Next, they piled dry wood over the pots to make a mound, which was then covered with damp bracken and soil. They then left the clamp to burn out over a couple of days. This technique is notorious for its low success rate, but Mark and Tom were delighted to find that about 20 per cent of their pots were intact - about average for a pottery clamp.

> For their second batch, they used an up-draught kiln which had been built on the site during the summer, ready for use during their stay at the hillfort. The up-draught kiln is made from a framework of hazel branches covered with daub and is a much more sophisticated way of firing pottery that was used during the late Iron Age. It can achieve temperatures of over 900°C, but it requires careful firing. The pots are placed at the far end of the kiln on earthen shelves situated below the chimney. Then a fire is lit at the mouth of the kiln

---

[378] Coles (1979), pp. 47-8

*and gently brought up to temperature. In order to stop the pots from cracking, the temperature has to be raised very slowly, although of course they had no method of recording it. The process took Tom and Mark long into the evening and then they had to leave the kiln for a further two days to cool down. However, their patience was rewarded with an almost 100 per cent success rate. Mark found the process very rewarding. 'To start from the beginning, to make your pots from clay and then fire them in the way the Iron Age people did, was really satisfying. But it did take a really long time, because you had to leave the pots for two weeks to dry out before putting them in the kiln.'*[379]

The task of ploughing with an ard confirmed the method of ploughing in the Iron Age as indicated by other forms of evidence:

*Because the ard only breaks up the soil and does not turn it over like a plough, Iron Age fields were often ploughed twice in opposite directions. Chris found this a very effective technique. 'The first time we ploughed, the field was really difficult - the soil was packed hard. But then we ploughed it a second time at right angles and it really worked well. Now we've planted winter wheat and I want to come back in the spring to see how it's grown!' The criss-cross pattern made by double ploughing with an ard during the Iron Age can still occasionally be identified in aerial photographs.*[380]

Two members of the team, a blacksmith and his wife, were given various metal-working tasks. They succeeded in making an iron sword, a bronze chalice, and, using the 'lost wax' method, a small bronze boar figurine. Their most challenging task however was not creating artefacts but smelting iron. This was the most ambitious and most important archaeological experiment carried out by the community. Since the evidence for the design of Iron Age furnaces is so slight, the furnace built for the TV series was not destroyed after the show but left to deteriorate gradually to enable the careful recording of its deterioration and, ultimately, its archaeological footprint.

As was the case with the *Living in the Past* series, Iron Age expert Barry

---

[379] Firstbrook (2000), p.148
[380] Firstbrook (2000), p.148

Cunliffe was invited to comment on the experiment. The amount of labour involved in maintaining life in the farmstead, as demonstrated by its 21$^{st}$ century inhabitants before the BBC 'slaves' came to their rescue and the community's water tap was moved closer to the site, struck him most forcefully:

> There's no doubt that the amount of physical work needed at certain times of the year just to stay alive was far, far more than we can anticipate. Just going down to get the water from the nearby spring would have been perfectly normal for most Iron Age societies. Here it's not terribly far away, but at one of the sites I excavated in Hampshire at Danebury hillfort, water was about a kilometre or a kilometre and a half away, and every day people would have had to go down and bring water up. The maintenance of the fields with primitive tools, looking after the flocks, bringing in the hay - all of these things would have been colossally labour-intensive.[381]

Most usefully, in Barry Cunliffe's opinion, *experiential* archaeology of this kind 'opens up the mind' and helps the archaeologist to understand, at least in some small way, the mentalities of people in the past.

> The sort of thing that I am learning is people's different concept of time. Yesterday I was watching people moving about the place. They were moving slowly and fairly purposefully, but not in a busy way. All of their sense of time was different...

> I was talking to the blacksmith in the house that was used as his forge. There was a girl there working the bellows and it was the most beautiful, quite relaxing time. This must have affected the minds of the people and the way they responded to nature, the way they responded to each other, the way they responded to their own creative abilities.

> Now, none of this you can get by being an archaeologist, no matter how good you are. You've got to experience all these intangible things, and that opens up the mind. It makes you think very

---

[381] Barry Cunliffe in Firstbrook (2000), pp.179-80

*differently [...] That's the sort of thing I get out of an experience like this.*³⁸²

---

³⁸² Barry Cunliffe in Firstbrook (2000), p.180

# 6 Archaeological theories and interpretations

## Prehistory

In 1819 Christian Thomsen, the curator of the Danish National Museum, reordered its exhibits according to the distinctive materials underpinning the defining tool technology of different periods of the past – stone, bronze and iron. From this emerged the 'three age system' of classification for prehistory that divides the past into the Stone Age, the Bronze Age and the Iron Age. Of course, these are simplistic constructs designed to help prehistorians navigate the past. Modern archaeologists subdivide the big three ages into many shorter periods. Some are troubled by these definitions for the great epochs of prehistory. They complain that Thomsen seems to have neglected the fact that Stone Age people were at least as reliant on wood and other materials as they were on stone, and that wood, stone and many other materials were of huge importance in the ages after people started using metal. In any case, the three age system was named after the tools made of the most durable material and hence those that had the best chance of survival in the archaeological record – the 'palaeolithic' is at best a misnomer for a period in which wood and other organic material must have played a bigger role in the technology of the time. Perhaps, as Paul Bahn has suggested, 'palaeoxylic' ('old wood age') would be a more accurate definition.

By naming his 'ages' after the material that survived, and ignoring that which did not, Thomsen had created a misleading impression of the past that survives to the present day. As the old adage goes: 'Absence of evidence is not evidence of absence'. Prehistorians need to consider both archaeological 'tangibles' and 'intangibles' in any attempt to reconstruct the past. Some have attempted to move beyond the confines of these terms entirely, arguing, for instance, that changing belief systems and forms of social organization define culture more completely than changing technologies. Hence the later 'Stone Age' has been defined as the 'Age of Ancestors' and the 'Age of Astronomy', while the middle Bronze Age 'Age of Land Divisions' preceded the Iron

Age 'Age of Water Cults'.[383]

## The Palaeolithic period (c. 500,000 BP, in the UK, to c. 8000 BC)

The Old Stone Age or 'Palaeolithic' period defines the hundreds of thousands of years over which modern humans – Homo Sapiens – evolved. For Britain it begins around 500,000 years ago – the estimated age of the earliest hominid remains (belonging to Homo Hiedelbergensis) found at Boxgrove, a gravel quarry in Sussex. The early Palaeolithic is defined as the Lower Palaeolithic, the later periods, identified by advances in flint tool technology, being the Middle and Upper Palaeolithic periods. Ice Age conditions made Britain uninhabitable for long periods of time, tens of thousands of years, during the time after 'Boxgrove Man' was at large.

## The Mesolithic period (c. 8000 BC to c. 4000 BC)

The end of the last Ice Age greatly changed the topography, flora and fauna of what would eventually become the British Isles (still connected to continental Europe at the start of this period). The need to adapt to new conditions and the evolution of a host of new tools, particularly composites deploying flint 'microliths' such as the teeth of harpoons and the heads of arrows, caused prehistorians to distinguish the hunter-gathers of the post 10,000 BC period with those that came after. This Middle Stone Age, 'Mesolithic' period ended with the rise of agriculture and the beginnings of settled society in the New Stone Age, the Neolithic period.

## The Neolithic Period (c. 4000 BC – c. 1800 BC)

The earliest monumental structures were constructed by the people of the New Stone Age, the Neolithic age, when settled farming communities first emerged. Pottery, heavy and fragile and hence inappropriate for nomadic peoples, began to be made, animals and plants began to be domesticated. Such colossal changes, combined with the evidence of sophisticated religious beliefs and rituals, and a highly sophisticated social organisation, have earned the period the title 'Neolithic revolution'. This was the age in which the great henge

---

[383] Souden (1997), pp.14-15

monuments, long barrows, causewayed enclosures, and cursuses appeared.

### The Bronze Age (c. 1800 BC – c. 800 BC)

Defined by the first use of metals, the Bronze Age is sometimes subdivided into and Early Bronze Age (c. 2300 – 1200 BC) and a Late Bronze Age (c. 1200 – 700 BC). Britain is not recognised as having a Copper Age; the technology that produced the alloy bronze (c. 10% tin to 90% copper) appears to have been developed elsewhere and introduced fully-fledged by the first British metallurgists. The tin however, unavailable from sources in most of Europe, was acquired from tin-rich Cornwall and combined with copper mined in Ireland and Wales. Control over the acquisition and trade of such precious resources played a part in the rise of 'chiefdoms' – sophisticated hierarchical tribal societies with a rapidly developing concept of territorial rights and ownership.

### The Iron Age (c. 800 BC – 43 AD)

The development of iron founding technology further revolutionised life in prehistoric Britain, not least in the spread of iron edged plough shares that greatly enhanced agricultural production. Britain's Late Iron Age includes the history of how the British Isles fell within the orbit of the expanding Roman Empire – a development at least as significant as the introduction of iron. Barry Cunliffe has further divided this late Iron Age period into two phases: 'contact' (c. 100 BC – c. 50 BC) and 'impact' (c. 50 BC – 43 AD). In 43 AD Britannia was incorporated into the Roman empire and would remain a part of it until the early fifth century AD. This era is usually referred to as the 'Romano-British' (43 AD – c. 410 AD).

## Hawkes' 'ladder of inference'

The past can be explored in many ways. Most obviously it can be considered both chronologically and thematically. For archaeologists, working with material evidence, analysing and interpreting this as evidence for past tools and technology is usually the most accessible thematic approach. Economic systems are less easily explained, modes of social organisation such as family structures and gender roles are often even harder to identify, and, most inscrutable of all are the beliefs and rituals of ancient non-literate societies. In 1954 Christopher Hawkes established this five level hierarchy as a general truth in archaeological enquiry; it is now known as Hawkes' 'ladder of inference' – each rung up the four steps represents one of the major themes and their relative accessibility.

| Beliefs, religion and ritual - ideology |
|---|
| Social organisation – social and political systems and behaviour |
| Economic systems - modes of production and subsistence |
| Tools and technology - processes that create sites and materials |

## Social organisation

An American anthropologist, Elman Rogers Service (1915 -1996), has played an important part in developing theories for the evolution of human societies. His studies of the history of the social organisation of Central and South American cultures inspired his influential model that identifies four phases through which society passes in the evolution of its political organisation and accompanying social and economic characteristics.

*PHASE 1: Band*

*Total numbers: less than 100*
*Social organisation: egalitarian; informal leadership*
*Economic organisation: mobile hunter-gatherers*
*Settlement pattern: temporary camps*
*Religious organisation: shamans*
*Architecture: temporary shelters*
*Archaeological examples: all Palaeolithic societies, including Palaeo-Indians*
*Modern examples: Eskimo; Kalahari Bushmen; Australian Aborigines*

*PHASE 2: Segmentary society*

*Total numbers: up to a few 1000*
*Social organisation: segmentary society; pan-tribal associations; raids by*

*small groups*
*Economic organisation: settled farmers; pastoralist herders*
*Settlement pattern: permanent villages*
*Religious organisation: religious elders; calendrical rites*
*Architecture: permanent huts; burial mounds; shrines*
*Archaeological examples: all early farmers*
*Modern examples: Pueblos, Southwest USA; New Guinea Highlanders; Nuer and Dinka in East Africa*

*PHASE 3: Chiefdom*

*Total numbers: 5,000-20,000 +*
*Social organisation: kinship-based ranking under hereditary leader; high-ranking warriors*
*Economic organisation: central accumulation and redistribution; some craft specialisation*
*Settlement pattern: fortified centres; ritual centres*
*Religious organisation: hereditary chief with religious duties*
*Architecture: large-scale monuments*
*Archaeological examples: many early metal-working societies; smaller African kingdoms*
*Modern examples: Northwest Coast Indians, USA; 18$^{th}$ century Polynesian chiefdoms in Tonga, Tahiti, Hawaii*

*PHASE 4: State*

*Total numbers: generally 20,000 +*
*Social organisation: class-based hierarchy under king or emperor; armies*
*Economic organisation: centralised bureaucracy; tribute-based; taxation; laws*
*Settlement pattern: urban: cities, towns; frontier defences, roads*
*Religious organisation: priestly class; pantheistic or monotheistic religion*
*Architecture: palaces, temples and other public buildings*
*Archaeological examples: all ancient civilisations e.g. in Mesoamerica, Peru, Near East, India, China, Greece, Rome*
*Modern examples: all modern states*[384]

This model has proved to be a useful starting place for attempts to

---

384 Renfrew and Bahn (2000), p.167

define societies on the basis of the available archaeological evidence.

## CASE STUDY: The socio-economic organisation of Britain in the Late Iron Age - evidence for warriors and warfare

'the whole race is madly fond of war, high-spirited, and quick to battle, but otherwise straightforward and not of evil character.'
(Strabo on the 'Celtic' peoples of north-west Europe quoted in Cunliffe (1994), p.362)

'the material culture [from c 150 BC], the apparent social structure and the development of hillforts all point to the increasing commonness of warfare.'
(Cunliffe (1978 b), p.70)

In the opinion of some commentators, notably Barry Cunliffe, the economic and commercial revolution in southern Britain in the first half of the second century BC was paralleled by equally dramatic changes in technology and socio-political organisation. Such developments in the pre-Conquest period include wine drinking, cremations, and the use of the potter's wheel.[385]

There is also extensive evidence for expanding warfare and the restructuring, along overtly military lines, of settlement activity. Traditionally[386] such 'cultural transformation' was attributed to 'invasions' - the migration of Armorican tribes people, for example, escaping the wrath of Caesar in the middle of the second century. Although the invasion hypothesis is not entirely moribund[387], processual explanations are more fashionable, and the developing continental trade described above, 'after several hundred years of relative isolation', is now more usually identified as the principal factor.[388]

Although political events on the continent after the middle of the

---

385 Cunliffe (1984), p.13
386 e.g. Hawkes and Dunning (1931)
387 Cunliffe (1984)
388 Cunliffe (1978), pp.64-5

second century BC very likely did lead to the arrival of newcomers, perhaps even a 'warrior elite', in southern Britain, and doubtless some 'merchants' settled in the vicinity of the ports of those with whom they traded, Mortimer Wheeler's hypothesis that the appearance of the great developed hillforts was simply a 'response to the stimulus of invasion' is now untenable.[389] What they may well represent however is a response to heightened insecurity and a growth of indigenous, even 'civil', warfare. It certainly seems likely that the creation of hillforts and their development were symptomatic of more violent times and 'a heavy lacing of new chieftains'[390] directing their construction.

The creation of hillforts has often been linked to the appearance of iron: the new technology freed communities from the constraints of reliance upon the ancient trade networks that provided them with the rare and crucial commodities of tin and copper and the related bronze product. Settlements amalgamated into large self-reliant, largely self-sufficient, and assertive communities.[391] The picture most commonly painted is one of a broadly co-operative economic structure in Bronze Age southern Britain giving way to a competitive and aggressive tribal economy in the Iron Age. Although this is over-simplistic and recent work has highlighted evidence for pre-Iron Age violence [392] while firm evidence for post-Bronze Age violence is slight in the archaeological record[393], there can be little doubt that the propensity for large-scale conflict was greater in the Iron Age than the Bronze.

The function of the original hillforts has long been a subject of debate. Clearly not all served the same purpose and their role, just as their shape, very likely changed significantly as time passed. The connections between the Iron Age structures and Bronze Age and Neolithic ritual activities at places like Westbury (Wilts: long barrow), Maiden Castle (Dorset: causewayed enclosure), and Smalldown Camp (Somerset: round barrows) cannot be ignored. The rectangular

---

389 Cunliffe (1978, 1991), pp.345-6
390 Stanford (1971), p.48
391 Sharples (1991), p.82
392 e.g. Bridgford (1997)
393 Sharples (1991), p.82

'shrines' found at Danebury and South Cadbury support the notion that some hillforts at least started life as religious centres[394]. Cunliffe and others have depicted hillforts as 'central places' in the political and economic life of large agrarian communities.[395] Stanford envisaged them as 'tribal centres with buildings for retainers and open spaces for the gathering of the clans when military, social or religious needs dictated'.[396] Among a range of functions they provided *protection* for product and people[397]. This product certainly included grain as revealed by the storage pits excavated by Alcock at Cadbury and Cunliffe at Danebury, as well as the geophysics data generated by the latter's extensive survey of the Wessex hillforts. In addition it is reasonable to presume they provided safe houses for goods *en route* to markets as well as being themselves centres of trading activity. While the commercial activity of the Bronze Age thrived on harmonious relations between diverse mutually dependent communities, that of the Iron Age appears to have been tainted by aggression and insecurity. Whatever else they might signify, the great developed hillforts of the late Iron Age indicate the coercion of people into vast workforces, quite possibly they are even indicative of slave using societies.

While the massive development of some hillforts in the Middle and Late Iron Age doubtless conferred status on tribal leaders, and may have been as much to do with status as defence[398], it would be perverse to argue that the massive defences which defined these structures did not have a defensive role. Although Haselgrove thinks status may have been the bigger factor, Cunliffe firmly equates re-enforcement with military considerations: 'An even greater emphasis on defence is indicative of escalating aggression.'[399] Ever since Wheeler's discovery of the huge cache of 22,000 sling stones at Maiden Castle, gathered from nearby Chesil Beach, it has been argued that the multiple ramparts of the developed forts were built as a direct response to the introduction of the sling: the use of which the Veneti, the dominant tribe in the Cross-Channel trade according to

---

394  Sharples (1991), p.113
395  Cunliffe (1978, 1991), p.273
396  Stanford (1971), p.48
397  Cunliffe (1978), p.63
398  Haselgrove (1999), p.130
399  Cunliffe (1994), p.368

proto-history, was particularly adept.[400] However clay sling shot have been discovered at Kimmeridge (Dorset) and Swallowcliffe Down (Wilts) which are two or three centuries older than the multivallation of the developed hillforts.[401]

The greater incidence of warfare, more than the spread of new military technologies, would seem to account for the new fortifications. In Cunliffe's opinion: 'territories were being more closely defined and warfare was increasing'.[402] Human remains at the early first century BC Danebury 'massacre' site testify to violence in the Wessex hillfort record long before the Conquest and suppression of the southern hillforts by Vespasian. The 'war cemeteries' of Worlebury and Bredon, dated by their association to saucepan pot finds to the first half of the first century BC, also indicate 'inter-tribal warfare or raiding': the product perhaps of local rivalries together with the threat posed by establishment of the new Belgic dynasties in the south-east in the period c. 150-80 BC.[403] Certainly, for whatever reason, even by the Middle Iron Age, the evidence, according to Cunliffe, points to endemic warfare in the centre south of Britain, while, elsewhere, greater stability prevailed.[404] Haselgrove, on the other hand, has recently claimed that 'The view of the period as dominated by endemic warfare is being overturned'. He has remarked on the rarity of evidence for war inflicted injuries and violent death in Iron Age burials and maintains that 'warfare need not have been any more frequent than in other prehistoric societies'.[405] Still, this southern hillfort dominated zone may well have furnished indigenous and continental markets with supplies of slaves.[406] Trading interests, such as the acquisition of booty and tribute and the extension of trading routes, could well account for sporadic warfare during the period and, in turn, it is likely to have been a major influence on the development of defended *oppida* in western Europe.[407] Where there was likely to have been a significant slave-

---

400 Peddie (1987), p.5
401 Cunliffe (1978, 1991), p.278
402 Cunliffe (1978, 1991), p.278
403 Cunliffe (1978, 1991), p.72
404 Cunliffe (1995), p.97
405 Haselgrove (1999), p.132
406 Cunliffe (1997), p.220
407 Collis (1984), p.157

acquiring interest, added to other contributory factors such as population growth and climatic deterioration, as in the west Hallstatt zone and the Marne-Moselle region, the situation could have been greatly exacerbated.[408]

The Belgic *emigres* from the Seine basin and Picardy had evolved their warrior societies through years of providing slaves for the Italian markets, occupying a geographical environment which promoted 'purely military sources of revenue'.[409] In Nash's opinion it was likely that any slaves passing through the port of Hengistbury Head in the period were acquired from these warrior communities of the south-east.[410] The western zone in this period, which she defines as 'purely agrarian societies', she thinks was militarily active but not equipped for 'wars of extensive foreign conquest or for systematic plundering raids', unlike the 'warrior agrarian societies' of the south-east.[411] Certainly, in the second half of the first century BC the south-east was in the ascendant while the fortunes of the south-west appear to have been in decline. The socio-economic order was, according to Cunliffe, 'suddenly disrupted',[412] the old hillforts of Sussex, Hampshire and much of Wiltshire being abandoned as new enclosed settlements, typically placed at major river crossings, appeared.[413] Most likely this was the direct consequence of political events: Caesar's smashing of the Veneti and the sinking of their fleet in Morbihan Bay, the ensuing demise of the Armorican-Hengistbury Head trade, and the growth of Roman contact with the south-east.

By the beginning of the first century BC society in the centre-south appears to have been organised in accordance with the needs of trade, including the lucrative continental trade passing through one or more south coast ports-of-trade. Fall-off analysis of pot finds and, particularly, coin evidence reveals vast territories associated with single tribes. The work of Cunliffe and others for example has shown that the homeland of the Durotriges extended at least as far as the River Char in the west, the southern Avon in the East, and the River

---

408 Cunliffe (1994), p.352
409 Nash (1984), p.103
410 Nash (1984), p.102
411 Nash (1984), p.98
412 Cunliffe (1978), p.64
413 Cunliffe (1978), p.64

Brue, dissecting the Somerset Moors, in the north. This apparently sophisticated, centralised society, it has been suggested (e.g. Castledon), was subdivided into at least three great territories focused on the developed hillforts of South Cadbury in the north-west, Hod Hill in the centre-east, and Maiden Castle in the south-west. Near to the middle of the three forts stands the curious Cerne Abbas Giant. Rodney Castledon (1996) has made a powerful case for this being an Iron Age deity marking the spiritual centre of the Durotriges; a meeting place perhaps for the leaders of this widespread 'tribe' to gather on occasions in order to reassert their relationship with each other. At what point, if at all, the Durotriges became a political entity, as well as a cultural entity, is open to question[414], but it is reasonable to suppose that, by the middle of the first century BC the Durotrigian 'tribal zone' had developed the fundamental characteristics of a state or 'single polity' as Cunliffe has described it.[415]

All three of the hillforts mentioned above were sited adjacent to important river systems. South Cadbury is near to the source of the River Cam which feeds into the Parrett, flowing into the Bristol Channel and thus providing a trade link that connects with the Midlands and Wales via the Severn estuary. Slightly to the East of the source of the Cam is that of River Stour, which flows directly beneath Hod Hill to its mouth at Hengistbury Head. Maiden Castle sits at the source of the River Frome, less than 30 km from its mouth in Poole Harbour.

The excavations at Maiden Castle, Hod Hill and South Cadbury, allied with similar sites in other tribal zones, notably Danebury, have revealed a great deal regarding the function of the developed hillforts of the Durotriges, although some, particularly Ham Hill, remain enigmatic. It is the evidence for exchange and violence which is of particular interest.

In all three cases there is ample evidence for these locations serving as centres where goods were stored, sometimes manufactured, and exchanged. The abundance of grain pits, supposed raised granaries, and animal bones at all three sites highlights the place of these

---

414  Barret, Freeman and Woodward (2000), p.248
415  Cunliffe (1993), p.176

embryonic towns in extensive agrarian landscapes. Just as it is impossible to determine exactly what the relationship was between these hillforts and their environs, so too is it impossible to fully account for the storage of floral and faunal product at these sites. It is tempting to find here evidence for something more than the need to feed and clothe a local community: possibly some of this material from the later period represents the residue of a trade in agricultural product - Strabo's 'corn, cattle [...] hides [...] and clever hunting dogs' destined maybe for Hengistbury Head and mainland Europe! Whatever else can be said, it is clear that these places housed far more product than the hilltop communities required for their own consumption.[416]

Evidence for exchange at these sites appears in the form of coinage, currency bars and what appears to be weighing equipment. South Cadbury produced thirteen Iron Age coins, twelve of which were of local issue - the second largest concentration, after Maiden Castle, of excavated finds from an Iron Age hillfort in the south-west.[417] These coins date from the very late Iron Age and, given their density of silver, they may well represent ritual offerings as opposed to coins lost in routine commercial transactions. At Maiden Castle and Hod Hill, however, it is apparent that coins were in regular use in the first half of the first century BC.[418] Although the excavations at Hod Hill between 1951 and 1958 turned up just one 'Celtic' coin, at least twenty five others had been recorded as found on the site in preceding years.[419] The same excavations also turned up a number of currency bars, several in excellent condition.[420] Another splendid example of a currency bar, linked to the first century BC by its excavator[421] was discovered in a hoard of iron objects attributed to the recycling activities of a blacksmith. South Cadbury produced a variety of both perforated and non-perforated stone and clay 'weights', all from undated contexts. A cast copper alloy balance weight appeared at Cadbury and also 'a possible weighing balance with a broken loop'.[422]

---

416   Sharples (1991), pp.96-7
417   Barrett, Freeman and Woodward (2000), p.248
418   Barrett, Freeman and Woodward (2000), p.252
419   Richmond (1968), p.43
420   Brailsford (1962), p.15
421   Alcock (1972), p.154
422   Barrett, Freeman and Woodward (2000), p.248

A 'beam from a balance' also appears in a photograph of 'miscellaneous objects of bronze' in the 1962 Hod Hill excavations report.[423]

John Collis made some interesting observations regarding the relationship between the hillforts of south Dorset and Hengistbury Head.[424] By tracing the limited spread of pre-Caesarian bronze coinage, as opposed to the more dispersed gold and silver, he pictured Maiden Castle, Hod Hill and Badbury Rings, where bronze coins have turned up, as satellites centred upon the Hengistbury Head *oppidum*. This bronze coin-using nucleus, he argued, had a peripheral zone extending into the south-west, Somerset, Hampshire and Normandy.

It is likely that whatever was being exchanged at these sites, in addition to animal products, was mostly imported to the sites. Some metalworking doubtless did take place on site but probably on a small scale and largely merely to provide tools and the like for the uses of the hilltop communities.[425] The only other manufacturing process definitely undertaken at Maiden Castle was textile production. The abundance of bone tools, identified as bobbins, needles and (probably erroneously) weaving combs, together with chalk loom weights and spindle whorls, testifies to quite large scale production, and one which may well have been designed to satisfy more than a local demand.[426] The South Cadbury evidence produces a similar picture of small-scale metal-working, probably mostly the reworking of scrap metal.[427] Parts of 42 'weaving combs' were found at South Cadbury, as well as bone and stone spindle whorls.[428]

Pottery manufacture certainly did not take place to any great extent at any of the three sites, not least because of the problem of adequate water supplies on hilltop sites. Instead quality wares, such as Glastonbury ware, were imported from manufacturers in the

---

423 Brailsford (1962), pl. XI and p.17
424 Collis (1971), p.100
425 Sharples (1991), p.113
426 Sharples (1991), p.111-3
427 Barrett, Freeman and Woodward (2000), p.291-301
428 Barrett, Freeman and Woodward (2000), p.179-183

peripheral zone.[429] It is tempting to see Iron Age hillforts as embryonic towns but, in fact, they are quite distinct settlement types that did not evolve into true towns. Where towns are service providers and, typically, manufacturing centres, the hillforts appear to have been big consumers but not major producers of manufactured goods.[430] They are associated primarily with trade, redistribution, storage and the control / exploitation of their environs and, presumably, the people who farmed there.

With the opening up of the continental trade in the late second century and first century BC, it is reasonable to suppose that the southern hillforts, particularly those that had river access to coastal ports-of-trade, would serve as depots for all kinds of produce destined for Europe and the Roman Empire. Hod Hill and Badbury Rings for example, both on the Stour, were minor markets with a direct link to the major market at Hengistbury Head.[431] Among other things, they may have served the role of 'holding stations' for consignments of slaves in much the same way as the fortresses built by European slave-purchasers on the West coast of Africa in the eighteenth century. Whatever was contained within the developed hillforts, it would appear that it was of sufficient value to have warranted the building of colossal defences. Lesser earthworks at these hilltop sites, such as Danebury, have sometimes been associated with the corralling of huge herds of cattle, both an economic staple and a status symbol for a warrior aristocracy.[432] Thus they may have served the dual role of keeping attackers out and livestock in. Communities dealing in slaves would have an additional reason to create secure compounds. Rustling of two-legged stock, as well as four-legged, could help account for the aggressive trends of Late Iron Age society.

Both common sense and the historical record link an expanding trade in slaves to heightened levels of violence. Whether or not warfare was being generated in the Late Iron Age in Britain by an external demand for slaves, there is ample evidence to support the notion that the occupants of the developed hillforts of southern Britain were

---

429 Collis (1971), p.10
430 Sharples (1991), p.113
431 Collis (1971), p.99
432 Cunliffe (1971), p.63

living in violent times. The sheer abundance of these fortress settlements appears to confirm the warlike character of British society described in classical texts.[433] For Cunliffe the development of select hillforts after c.350 BC is clearly 'indicative of escalating aggression'.[434] Haselgrove[435] boldly asserts that their defences were 'probably' constructed by 'defeated neighbours'! The Durotriges have been described as 'the major hillfort builders of Britain'[436] because of the abundance of hillforts in Durotrigian territory and the astonishing scale of the bigger works. According to the 'hillfort = violence' equation, this implies centuries of rivalry and internecine warfare. By the Late Iron Age, however, pot and coin evidence, coupled with the appearance of new and vulnerable extra-hillfort communities, and the cessation of massive refortification of the forts themselves, points to less internal stress and a developed sense of tribal identity. Neil Sharples has envisaged a confederation of allied Durotrigan hillfort centred communities capable of competing with other tribal groupings.[437]

The excavations at South Cadbury, Hod Hill and Maiden Castle produced considerable amounts of Late Iron Age weaponry. Cadbury, for example, has produced a variety of daggers, sword hilt fittings, and chapes from the first and second centuries BC.[438] Although a fraction of the number found at Maiden Castle (22000), an impressive total of around 2500 sling stones was also recovered. The vast majority here, as at Maiden Castle, are dated to the Late Iron Age.[439] The Conquest and Boudiccan Revolt era 'massacre' sites at Maiden Castle and Cadbury respectively revealed communities equipped to defend themselves against assault, and the excavated huts of Hod Hill produced evidence for 'cupboards' housing weapons beside the entrance.[440]

The most spectacular pre-Conquest evidence for violent acts at a

---

433  James and Rigby (1997), p.58
434  Cunliffe (1994), p.368
435  Haselgrove (1999), p.121
436  Putnam (1998), p.54
437  Sharples (1991), p.115
438  Barrett, Freeman and Woodward (2000), pp.236-9
439  Barrett, Freeman and Woodward (2000), p.247
440  Williams (1993), p.139

hillfort comes from Danebury near Andover in Hampshire. Around 100 BC its east entrance was redesigned with massive fortifications intended, it seems, to maximise the employment of slings as the principal weapon of defence. Not long afterwards the gate was destroyed by fire. Its excavator, Barry Cunliffe, thinks this could well have been the result of the kind of assault on hillforts described by Julius Caesar:

*'The Gauls and the Belgae use the same method of attack. They surround the whole circuit of the walls with a large number of men and shower it with stones from all sides, so that the defences are denuded of men. Then they form testudo, set fire to the gates and undermine the walls.'*[441]

As at Maiden Castle and South Cadbury, the Danebury excavations produced thousands of sling stones. Human remains recovered from the site produce further evidence of violence: at least ten individuals bore the tell-tale signs of blade cut marks, piercing and other bone damage. In only two cases is their evidence that they, typically young adult males, survived their injuries. Some individuals had been mutilated and dismembered, their bodies flung unceremoniously into a pit.[442]

Violence seems to have precipitated the cessation of activities at Danebury. This hillfort is just one of many that appear to have been quite suddenly abandoned, sometimes even before the completion of their ditch and rampart defences. Of course, disease, famine, and changed economic or political conditions could account for this phenomenon as completely as tribal / internecine warfare.[443]

The picture of endemic warfare in Late Iron Age southern Britain, favoured by some archaeologists, is supported by the mortuary evidence for an emergent military elite. Occasional warrior burials dating from the first century BC and first century AD have been found in Yorkshire, Norfolk, Hampshire and Whitcombe near Dorchester, deep in Durotrigan territory. The male burials, replete with swords

---

441 Cunliffe (1995), p.93
442 Cunliffe (1995), pp.93-5
443 Feachem (1971), p.20

and other 'masculine' artefacts, are paralleled by rich female burials, accompanied, typically, by beautiful mirrors and personal decorative items.[444]

This apparent escalation in aggression, generated, presumably, by a profit motive based upon plunder, booty and tribute, equates with the situation at the close of the Iron Age as described by Tacitus:

*'Once they owed obedience to kings, now they are distracted between the jarring factions of rival chiefs. Indeed nothing has helped us more in war with their strongest nations than this inability to co-operate. It is but seldom that two or three states unite to repel a common danger: fighting in detail they are conquered wholesale.'*[445]

Human remains from the same period in very different contexts further develop the picture of a hierarchical society, ranging, perhaps, as Caesar observed in Gaul, from chieftains to slaves. At a number of settlement sites, including farms and hillforts, whole articulated bodies have been excavated in the rubbish pits into which they were once, unceremoniously dumped.[446]

**Some Conclusions**

The appearance of hillforts in central southern Britain marks the emergence of a new socio-economic order. The decision of communities to construct substantial defences implies competition and conflict, rivalry among near neighbours perhaps or a threat from more distant peoples. Such tension may have been the product of significant late pre-Roman Iron Age population growth[447] and / or economic and technological developments. There is some evidence to suggest that society as a whole was becoming more hierarchical, controlled ultimately, perhaps, by military elites. The substantial expansion and multivallation of some hillforts, coinciding with the apparent decline and abandonment of numerous others, after c 350 BC could indicate aggression on a grander scale and also the establishment of 'tribal' groupings with extensive territories focused

---

444 Cunliffe (1978, 1991), p.317
445 Tacitus, *Agricola* 12, quoted in Cunliffe (1971), p.64
446 Cunliffe (1978), p.316
447 Cunliffe (1971), p.61

on hillfort centres.[448]

The function of hillforts remains unclear but it is evident that the developed hillforts of central-southern Britain were, typically, permanent settlement sites where vast quantities of grain were stored. Spatial analysis of hillforts to date has not shed much light on either the political or economic structure of these sites but there is evidence to suggest that a number of activities were carried out in these settlements, including small scale manufacturing and religious devotions. The positioning of the developed hillforts of the Durotrigian tribal zone would have enabled them to exploit the trade opportunities associated with the rivers Parret, Stour, Avon and Frome. It is likely such places served as redistribution centres and 'storehouses' for goods, which very likely included captive manpower, destined for other markets, particularly the port-of-trade at Hengistbury Head. Coin finds and other first century BC evidence for exchange at these sites supports this hypothesis. It is likely that occupation activity declined at these sites in the later first century BC, possibly linked to the demise of Hengistbury Head as the most significant port following the Caesarean invasions. Possibly *oppida* began to replace the old hillfort centres in the west of the region, as they did in the south-east during this period. Pre-Conquest *oppida* may have existed at Dorchester, below Maiden Castle, and Ilchester, between Ham Hill and South Cadbury.[449]

There is a good deal of evidence to support the idea that the Late Iron Age in central-southern Britain was an era in which warfare was endemic. Typically this would have been small scale localised raiding: the assault of neighbouring settlements in the opportunistic pursuit of booty (Cunliffe 1991: 496; James and Rigby 1997: 58). While people in other areas threw up substantial defences around their settlements, the archaeological evidence indicates that the people of the centre south 'enjoyed it [warfare] to an aggravated degree' (Cunliffe 1991: 497). One hillfort in this area, Danebury, provides tangible evidence of assault and destruction. The defences at Danebury, Maiden Castle and other places were massively developed around the start of the first century (Cunliffe 1991: 118). Their design

---

448 Cunliffe (1991), p.26
449 Cunliffe (1993), p.222

appears to be dictated by the fire power and range of sling users. 'War cemeteries' near to entrances have been excavated at Worlebury in Somerset and Bredon Hill in Worcestershire (Cunliffe 1991: 118, 174). The evident increase in aggression in southern Britain in the first century BC could well have been generated, in part, by a continental demand for slaves centred, until the middle of that century, upon Hengistbury Head. As Hengistbury Head came to be eclipsed by the ports of the south-east the trade in slaves, as in other commodities, presumably was centred upon new ports-of-trade. If anything demand would have increased as contacts with romanised Europe were further developed (Cunliffe 1991: 497) and poorly defended communities to the north and far west, presumably, would have been obvious targets for raiding parties.

## Models for identifying territories

Geographers' models for identifying theoretical territories in the past have been applied by archaeologists. By finding the middle points between clusters of, say, long barrows or hillforts they produce polygons that possibly indicate the area associated with the extended family that placed its dead in the communal barrow or the territory in the orbit of the band that occupied the hillfort. Central place theory works on the principle that markets, schools, courtrooms or whatever have a catchment area that amounts to the 'territory' they serve.

*'Central place theory was developed in 1933 by the German geographer Walter Christaller to describe the central goods and services provided by settlements to serve or be served by regional communities. His basic hierarchy of settlements was defined as hexagonal zones of influence spread out over an ideal level landscape where all other factors, such as soil fertility, water sources and accessibility, were equal. This model enabled simplified understanding of the distribution of levels of settlement function. He then went on to consider traffic optimising, market optimising and administration optimising situations. His ideal hexagonal distribution of places could be arranged to demonstrate:*

- *The hierarchy of roads between ordinary and principal places.*
- *The hierarchy of competition between different villages, towns and cities providing different types of specialised goods and*

services.
- *The hierarchy of administration which can be used to illustrate a network of political and religious power.'[450]*

## Social Organisation: archaeological indicators

When exploring social organization through archaeological evidence a range of attributes need to be considered. These include evidence for:

- Settlement patterning
- Scale
- Specialisation
- Intensification
- Trade
- Communications
- Status
- Artefacts – attributes
- Warfare
- Administration
- Organisation of ritual

Let's take Maiden Castle in Dorset, the greatest hillfort of the late Iron Age tribe of the Durotriges, as an example: [451]

**Settlement patterning:** Maiden Castle seems to have had a special relationship with another hillfort, Poundbury (3km to the north). Maiden Castle became more intensively occupied as other settlements in the region were abandoned. There is likely to have been a relationship between Maiden Castle and the other great 'Durotrigan' developed hillforts: South Cadbury, Ham Hill, Hod Hill.

**Scale:** Maiden Castle became multi-vallated, and acquired exceptionally elaborate hornwork entrances. It was densely occupied (compared to lightly occupied Poundbury). It was the largest hillfort in British Isles (according to Sharples, 1991).

---

[450] Papworth (2011), p.17
[451] Sources: Martin Papworth (2011), *The Search for the Durotriges*, The History Press; Niall Sharples (1991), *Maiden Castle*, Batsford

**Specialisation:** Arable farming (as opposed to pastoral at Poundbury). An ironworking area has been identified near the east entrance. Weaving combs (purpose uncertain – possibly for plucking wool from sheep). Spindle whorls and loom weights. Brooches, pins and toggles (of bone and bronze) imply textile production was important.

**Intensification:** Crop storage (as opposed to corralling of cattle at Poundbury).

**Trade:** Redistribution (grain silos and four-posters thought to represent raised granaries have been found in abundance); it may have served as a market (a hoard of Durotrigan silver coins and one Trinovantian and two Armorican coins have been found at Maiden Castle). Poole Harbour ware is found at the site (the predominant pottery type found at Maiden Castle dating from the late Iron Age). Whetstones and querns from Devon were also found together Kimmeridge shale.

**Communications:** Links to Poole Harbour: River Frome 3 km to the north (at Poundbury); River South Winterbourne immediately south (which flows into Frome).

**Status:** Dominated / replaced other settlement sites in the region. High status burials in the region (e.g. possible chariot burial at Fordington, 2km north; warrior grave at Whitcombe, 3km east).

**Artefacts:** fairly uniform house structures (no clear evidence of hierarchy is found in the architectural evidence).

**Warfare:** fortifications; slingstones; Mortimer Wheeler's 'massacre site' (52 excavated burials, 14 revealing signs of mutilation), reinterpreted as possibly a cemetery for people dying, some in battle, elsewhere.

**Administration:** no evidence for high status private or 'public' buildings.

**Organisation of ritual:** no evidence for this being a major religious centre during the late Iron Age.

CONCLUSIONS:

**ECONOMY:** predominantly agrarian; food production, iron-working, textiles

**SITE TYPE:** not a proto-town, not a town; not a homestead, not a village... 'It is in fact a form of settlement which is unparalleled in the historical records of western society and which therefore has no obvious name – a large settlement dominated by agricultural production and storage.' (Niall Sharples, 1991, p.113)

**CLASSIFICATION (social organisation):** emerging chiefdom

## Trade and Exchange

Modes of exchange can be divided into three types:

- Reciprocity
- Redistribution
- Market exchange

Archaeologists consider a range of evidence in attempting to identify modes of exchange.

In exploring how trade goods get from one place to another there are two main possible explanations:

- Down-the-line – movement of goods through the hands of any number of 'middle men'
- Directional exchange – movement of goods over a distance directly between the giver/seller and the targeted receiver/buyer

Ports of trade, such as the Iron Age community at Hengistbury Head on the Dorset-Hampshire border, have been identified by archaeologists as early centres of exchange.

## CASE STUDY: The expansion of Rome and the resurgence of Britain's continental trade c. 100 – 50 BC

As Rome expanded its demand for raw materials from temperate Europe intensified from c 150 BC.[452] The capture of southern France between 125 and 121 BC opened the floodgates for Mediterranean merchants seeking new markets in the north.[453] From the 'barbarian' periphery slaves and raw materials, particularly metals, were sought in exchange for wine and other Mediterranean luxuries.[454] This demand in Cunliffe's opinion 'cannot have failed to have had a disrupting effect on the traditional embedded economy of the Middle Iron Age'.[455] It could explain the widespread abandonment of many southern hillforts at this time.[456]

Around this time, possibly not before the start of the first century BC, Britain's trade with the continent was renewed.[457] A range of continental influences can be identified in Britain's archaeological record for this period and they include the introduction of the potter's wheel, and continental style cremations. Gallo-Belgic coins appeared in the south-east from the late second century.[458] Meanwhile an aspect of British hillfort design, the glacis rampart, manifested on the continent.[459] The period 100 BC to 43 AD for southern Britain has been described as a 'dramatic cultural and economic revolution'.[460] These changes comprised a sudden rise of marketing centres and their satellite sites, first in the south-west at Hengistbury Head and, later, in the south-east at such places as Colchester and St Albans.[461] Cunliffe's excavations have demonstrated that this revolution was not the result of the 'invasions' once claimed by such luminaries as Sir Mortimer Wheeler, but one shaped by the renewed continental trade.[462] Profound

---

452 Cunliffe (1994), p.420
453 Collis (1984), p.156
454 Cunliffe (1991), p.110
455 Cunliffe (1991), p.110
456 Cunliffe (1991), p.110
457 Collis (1984), p.162
458 Haselgrove (1999), p.12
459 Collis (1984), p.162
460 Cunliffe (1978), p.63
461 John Collis (1971), p.102
462 Cunliffe (1978), p.55

cultural, economic and political changes were the outcome of what Cunliffe has called 'the interchange of peoples' - merchants, mercenaries, ambassadors and invaders.[463]

Prior to the conquest of southern France the principal trade routes seem to have been those that connected Armorica, south-west France and, ultimately, the Mediterranean with south-western Britain.[464] The trade was probably chiefly in metals, particularly copper and Cornish tin. After c 120 BC, in other words after southern France was annexed to the empire, the bulk of Britain's continental trade appears to have shifted eastwards, flowing across the Dorset coast through the port of Hengistbury Head.

The archaeology of Hengistbury Head, 'the first truly urban community in Britain'[465], is central to any endeavour, such as this, to investigate the nature of Britain's continental trade in the first half of the first century BC. In Cunliffe's opinion it emerged 'suddenly' c.100 BC[466] and heralded the 'the end of the old order and the establishment of a settled urban economy' in southern Britain.[467] Its pre-eminence would be short-lived. The virtual absence of Dressel 1b amphorae, appearing in the middle of the first century BC, at Hengistbury Head indicates the dramatic decline, though not complete collapse, of the port in the Caesarian era.[468] From this point ports further to the east mainly handled the continental trade.

Excavations have shed some light on the goods passing through Hengistbury Head. Imports certainly included wine, glass and figs. Iron, copper, silver and gold were brought from the hinterland to the port, presumably for exchange and export.[469] Evidence has been uncovered for iron, silver, lead and copper working as well as the casting of bronze. In addition the port was a centre for the manufacture of armlets of Kimmeridge shale. However, although Rome imported vast quantities of metals from the conquered

---

463 Cunliffe (1991), p.108
464 Cunliffe (1984), p.18
465 Cunliffe (1978), p.14
466 Cunliffe (1978), p.14
467 Cunliffe (1978), p.9
468 Collis (1984), p.163; Peacock (1971), p.173
469 Cunliffe (1994), p.419

territories and beyond, the fact that the principal port-of-trade in southern Britain in this period was located in the central south, rather than further towards the tin and copper rich west, suggests that other trade goods were of greater significance.[470] Cunliffe postulates that of greater importance were 'archaeological intangibles' such as corn, hides and wool derived from the fertile plains of the Wessex region.[471] Two of these and other 'archaeological intangibles' are listed in Strabo's famous description of British exports in the first century BC: 'corn, cattle, gold, silver, hides, slaves and clever hunting-dogs'.[472] Wiedemann provides dates of c. 64/3 BC to after AD 23 for Strabo's commentaries.[473]

Although he cannot verify archaeologically Strabo's identification of a British trade in slaves any more than he can that of hunting-dogs, Cunliffe believes 'there can be little reasonable doubt that one of the main exports passing through Hengistbury would have been captive manpower'.[474] Prior to the reopening of the continental trade there could have been no great demand for British slaves although it is quite likely that domestic slavery was a feature of British social structures. In the contact period however there most certainly was a potential demand for British slaves, and a very considerable one at that. At the time when Hengistbury Head so suddenly emerged as Britain's first urban settlement, it has been estimated that there were 300,000 Gaulish slaves working the *latifundias* and mines of Italy, and that, to maintain numbers, Italy needed to import 15,000 more each year.[475] By the first century AD it has been estimated that in Italy there was a population of 2 million slaves, a third of the total population.[476] Across the empire as a whole in the same period Harris has suggested a total 10 million slaves: one in every five or six people. With a slave life expectancy of twenty years he has calculated an annual imperial demand by this time of 500,000.[477] Madden maintains that the slave population of the Roman Empire was not self-

---

470    Cunliffe (1997), p.22
471    Cunliffe (1984), p.4 –5
472    Strabo iv.5.2 in Cunliffe (1993), p.203
473    Wiedemann (1981), p.270
474    Cunliffe (1993), p.203
475    Cunliffe (1997), p.215
476    Madden (1996), p.1
477    Madden (1996), p.2

propagating, that, as in the Britain's colonies in the eighteenth century, the natural inclination of slave populations was decline, not increase. The new slaves for the most part were acquired through commerce not war. Harris has estimated that in the period 140 – 150 AD only around 2% - 3% of new slaves in an average year were Rome's prisoners of war.[478] Furthermore these were not 'slave wars' - enslavement was a consequence, not a cause of Roman aggression.[479] On the other hand piracy, particularly during the turbulent second century BC, appears to have been an important factor in the provision of slaves.[480] In addition, it has been estimated that Caesar's campaigns in Gaul provided the Roman markets with a million new slaves.[481]

Although the scale of demand may have been exaggerated there is no doubt that by the start of the first century BC slave-dependent Rome needed both regular supplies of slaves and new markets for the surpluses it produced.[482] By the middle of the first century BC possibly more than a million slaves were involved in agriculture in Italy alone. The increased prosperity of the *latifundias* on which they worked spawned new and larger estates and, consequently, an expanding demand for slave labour.[483] The scale of demand probably did not begin to decline until the mid-second century AD.[484] Britain, theoretically, was ideally suited to providing both slaves and markets. Where other raw materials, such as Spanish tin, could be extracted from lands newly embraced by *pax Romana* slaves were more obviously sought *beyond* the frontiers or from the ranks of rebel armies within the Empire itself. After all, enslavement within one of Rome's provinces was illegal.[485] Furthermore the population of Britain on the eve of the Roman Conquest is now thought to have numbered several millions.[486] Judging by the great number of new settlements that appear in the archaeological record for the late Iron Age, it was a

---

478   Madden (1996), p.3
479   Wiedemann (1981), p.7
480   Wiedemann (1981), p.6
481   Cunliffe (1997), p.212
482   Cunliffe (1997), p.216
483   Cunliffe (1994), p.412-
484   Madden (1996), p.2
485   Crawford (1985), p.170
486   James and Rigby (1997), p.76

population which appears to have been rising dramatically.[487]

As in West Africa in the early modern period, many slaves were bought from what were regarded as 'barbarian' tribes at key ports-of-trade.[488] In addition to Britain, Strabo listed the Black Sea as a slave exporting area. The trade he described at the city of Tanais 'where the river Don flows into the Sea of Azov' is likely to have been replicated at southern Britain's port-of-trade, Hengistbury Head:

*'It was the central place of exchange between the nomadic tribes of Asia and Europe and the people who sailed across the Sea of Azov from the Bosporos; the former brought slaves and hides and whatever else nomads have to offer, and in exchange the latter traded them fabrics and wine and all the other things pertaining to civilised living.'*[489]

Strabo's tantalising but brief remarks on how slaves entered the Greek-Romano world from outside during the first century BC represent the best documentary evidence for a theme of huge significance on which surprisingly little comment has survived.[490] The fact that Britain is one of the two slave producing areas mentioned implies that it was a significant player in the human export business.

Cunliffe has remarked:

*'the Roman Mediterranean core came increasingly to rely on the barbarian periphery, and once that periphery had been absorbed there was always another behind it'*[491]

By the start of the second century Britain had become a part of that 'barbarian periphery'. In about 118 BC Narbo, a Mediterranean port on the River Aude was colonised by Rome. Thus the empire was able to exploit, and ultimately dominate, an ancient western route which led to the Atlantic, via the Carcassonne Gap, which had brought Cornish tin into central Europe.[492] Archaeology, in the record for the

---

487  Haselgrove (1999), p.129
488  Wiedemann (1981), p.107
489  Wiedemann (1981), p.107-8
490  Wiedemann (1981), p.6
491  Cunliffe (1994), p.414
492  Cunliffe (1994), p.415

distribution of amphorae, confirms Strabo's declaration that rivers provided the principal trade routes.[493] Hengistbury Head and Poole Harbour were exceptionally well served by the waterways of the Avon and Stour and their tributaries. The river system based on three river Avons provided potential access from Hengistbury Head to the Midlands via the Bristol Channel. How navigable these rivers actually were is uncertain but it is tempting to envisage fully laden boats being hauled up and downstream.[494] Peddie has made some interesting suggestions regarding river borne trade in the Durotrigian tribal zone:

*'The settlement at Combwhich, at the mouth of the Parrett, could be expected to have played a large part in this enterprise, located as it would have been at the end of a trade route extending from the headwaters of that river, along the Hardway to the source of the Stour and thence, passing under the eyes of Hod Hill and Spettisbury to Badbury Rings. From here goods could have been transported either to Poole Harbour or Hengistbury Head. An equally satisfactory and important route could also have been operated from the Parrett to Maiden Castle and thence to join the Stour route to Poole Harbour or Hengistbury: for speedier shipment a port of substantial capacity, from which [...] Maiden Castle [...] possibly derived [its] importance, must have existed somewhere in Weymouth Bay.'*[495]

Interestingly he considers it likely that the community at Hengistbury Head was autonomous: even though it appears to fall within Durotrigian territory (i.e. west of the southern River Avon) he describes the Durotriges as their 'neighbours' and likens the settlement to a twentieth century 'free-port'.[496] Collis also envisaged the possibility of 'foreign traders resident controlling this trade'.[497] Hengistbury certainly stands out from other contemporary settlements as a centre of great wealth, importing luxury items and great quantities of coins.[498] What relationship it had with surrounding communities is debatable, but that it had a relationship, and a very

---

493  Cunliffe (1994), p.41
494  McGrail (1983) in Peddie (1987), p.137
495  Peddie (1987), p.140
496  Peddie (1987), p.144
497  Collis (1971), p.102
498  Cunliffe (1978), p.62

important one at that, is certain. As Martin Papworth (2011) has noted, the very concept of tribalism and the identification of tribal groups, such as the Durotriges, in the period is now open to question. The archaeological record provides more clues as to what was being imported than it does for British exports. Strabo suggested merchants from mainland Europe brought with them ivory necklaces, amber gems, glass vessels and 'other pretty wares of that sort'.[499] Cunliffe's excavations at Hengistbury Head provided firm evidence for the import of Italian wine, raw glass 'and whatever products came in pottery containers made in Armorica'.[500] Of all the archaeological evidence so far uncovered it is the amphora sherds which have played the central role in piecing together the prehistory of trade through Hengistbury Head in the Late Iron Age. Wine amphorae of Dressel's type 1A were clearly being imported into southern Britain via Hengistbury in the first half of the first century BC. The absence of type 1A sherds beyond Hengistbury Head's immediate zone of trade indicates the port's unique role in the importation of this material. By contrast, the virtual absence of the later 1B amphorae at Hengistbury, and clusters of finds in the south-east, demonstrates a dramatic mid-century shift in the focus of the wine trade from Hengistbury Head to one or more ports-of-trade in the south east, probably near to Camulodunum.[501]

The scale on which this import trade was conducted is open to question. As far as Sir Mortimer Wheeler was concerned the few sherds of foreign pottery found so far may have represented nothing more than 'the relics of a few ship-loads of refugees at the time of the Caesarian conquest'.[502] However Peacock's work thirty years ago on Dressel 1A sherds from Hengistbury demonstrated that a minimum of twelve different amphorae were represented and that differences in rim design implied they were acquired from several different shipments.[503] Even so the total number of Dressel 1A finds is small (see Appendix) and in no way proves a thriving continental trade in anything, let alone slaves.

---

499 quoted in Cunliffe 1984: 8
500 Cunliffe (1984), p.4
501 Cunliffe (1978, 1991), p.337
502 Wheeler and Richardson 1957, p.47 in Cunliffe (1978), p.55
503 Cunliffe (1978), pp.55-7

Some writers assume Roman goods in the first century BC were introduced into Britain via Gallic and Breton middlemen.[504] However, the absence of amphora 1A finds in Brittany suggests to others [505] that the wine trade may in fact have been a direct one between Britain and Central France, possibly even Italy. Reinforcing the argument is the evidence of a ship or ships, carrying amphorae 1A, wrecked off Belle Ile, south of the Morbihan.[506] The distribution of Dressel 1 amphorae in France has also led French archaeologists to presume trade ships sailed around western Armorica during the Late Iron Age, following an Atlantic trade route which 'veered northwards as it entered the Channel and headed straight for southern Britain'.[507] The absence of Dressel 1 amphorae from Armorica has led Peacock to conclude that it is 'reasonable to postulate a direct trade link between Italy and Hengistbury, albeit with due tributes paid to the Veneti'.[508] A complete anchor found at Bulberry in Dorset, in conjunction with other material dated to around the first half of the first century BC, and part of an anchor found off the coast of north-west Wales, dated to the first or second centuries BC, are thought to have been of Graeco-Roman origin. In Cunliffe's opinion 'they provide an interesting hint of the type of Mediterranean shipping with which the inhabitants of pre-Roman Britain may have been familiar'.[509]

Although 'the case for Roman merchantmen in British waters cannot be dismissed'[510] the evidence for cross-Channel trade is much stronger. The bulk of that trade seems to have been conducted between Hengistbury Head and Alet, and it was at its height during the era of the conquest of Gaul, c 56 - 50 BC.[511] The flow of that trade is indicated by such evidence as that of Durotrigian coins found on Jersey and plenty of Armorican pottery turning up in Dorset.[512] Coinage from several Armorican tribes has turned up at Hengistbury dating to the first half of the first century BC, including the gold coinage of the Namnetes, Coriosolite silver, and issues of the

---

504 e.g. Haselgrove (1999), pp.131-2
505 e.g. Peacock (1971), p.173
506 Cunliffe (1978), p.67
507 Galliou (1984), pp.27-8
508 Peacock (1971), p.173
509 Cunliffe (1978, 1991), p.158
510 Peacock (1984), p.38
511 Langouet (1984), p.76
512 Langouet (1984), p.73

Baiocasses, Redones, Unelli, Osismii and Veneti.[513] The trade is further supported by the documentary record of Caesar who described the Veneti as a maritime nation 'accustomed to sail to Britain'.[514] The Durotrigian were almost certainly a seafaring people as well - the name is thought to mean 'the water people'.

In Cunliffe's opinion the dramatic rise and fall of Hengistbury as the principal port-of-trade was directly or indirectly determined by Roman intervention. For political rather than economic reasons the trade returned to a localised one when it suited Rome to seek new markets in the south-east of Britain.[515] Most likely, following the annexation of Gaul, new alliances were being forged between Rome and chieftains in the Berkshire and Essex regions that could exploit the potential of the shortest crossing points between Britain and the mainland Europe. Meanwhile the decline of trade in the south west could be indicative of the destruction of the fleet of the Veneti following the suppression of their rebellion in 56 BC and the punishment of those Durotrigian and Armorican refugees in southern Britain who may have supported the rebellion.[516]

Nash is of the opinion that metals from Wales, the Mendips and Cornwall were of central importance in Britain's export trade.[517] Certainly trade before c 120 BC was very much to do with the exploitation of British metals, especially Cornish tin.[518] The coin evidence pre-50 BC does suggest that Hengistbury's British trade links were focused on the metal rich west and south west of England.[519] However the tin trade was established long before the emergence of Hengistbury Head as a major port-of-trade and, given its more easterly location, this would suggest that it was concerned with more than the export of tin, although this may have been of some importance.[520] Local iron is likely to have been exported, and also Kimmeridge shale, but there is good reason to suppose that a

---

513  Cunliffe (1978, 1991), p.157
514  Cunliffe (1978 ), p.7
515  Cunliffe (1984), p.4
516  Galliou (1984), p.30
517  Nash (1984), p.102
518  Cunliffe (1984), p.18
519  Cunliffe (1978), p.67
520  Cunliffe (1978), p.75

significant proportion of the trade was concerned with living, slaughtered and harvested product.

Wool, hides and corn very likely were shipped out from the fertile south of England to Brittany during the period, perhaps to provision garrisons of new troops in an era of imperial expansion. It is equally likely that there was a thriving trade in slaves. Classical accounts testify not just to the 'Celtic' love of wine, but also to the wine in amphora jars being the main bargaining commodity of Roman merchants wishing to purchase slaves. According to Diodorus Siculus:

*'They are exceedingly fond of wine and sate themselves with unmixed wine imported by merchants; their desire makes them drink it greedily and when they become drunk they fall into a stupor or into a maniacal disposition. And therefore many Italian merchants with their usual love of cash look on the Gallic craving for wine as their treasure. They transport the wine by boat on the navigable rivers and by wagon through the plains and receive in return for it an incredibly high price, for one amphora of wine they get in return a slave - a servant in return for a drink.'*[521]

In more recent times alcohol has been a powerful bargaining tool of imperial powers and, as described above, it made an important contribution to the Atlantic slave trade of the eighteenth and nineteenth centuries. It is quite reasonable to suppose therefore that a port on the peripheral zone of a slave demanding empire, which has an archaeological record of its commercial activity largely defined by Italian wine jars, would have imitated its Gallic overseas neighbours and engaged as fully as it could in a lucrative slave trade. Cicero and Didorus both mentioned the Gallic trade in slaves and it is usually assumed that people, as opposed to minerals or agricultural product, were Gaul's principal export.[522] It has been suggested that in the late second and first centuries possibly 15,000 slaves were exchanged by Gallic traders each year in return for wine and other luxury goods.[523] It has been estimated that something in the region of 100,000 hectolitres of north Italian wine changed hands in Gaulish markets

---

521 Cunliffe (1994), p.414
522 Crawford (1985), p.169
523 Bradley (1989), p.2

each year in the early first century BC.[524] Such figures perhaps are more deserving of the epithet 'guess-timates' than estimates but there could be some mileage still in equating amphora finds with the trade in specific goods.

Crawford (1985) has made some very interesting connections between the distribution of denarii and slave-purchasing in Dacia in the Lower Danube basin. He has identified the middle or late 60s onwards as the beginning of the 'massive import' of denarii into the area - 'an anomalous and unique phenomenon'. He can think of no better explanation for this than the amplified demand for slaves following Pompey's suppression of piracy in a series of campaigns in 67 BC. Thus 'a virtual end' was brought to their slave-raiding activities, previously so central to the Roman slave market. The situation was exacerbated in 63 BC when vast new territories were absorbed into the empire, territories that hitherto, outside *pax romana*, had been viable suppliers of slaves. The Spartacus rebellion did not help matters.[525]

Coins dated to the 50s BC are found in less quantity - possibly reflecting a reduced demand at the time of Caesar's slave-producing *razzias* in Gaul. A second massive penetration of coins into Romania occurred during the 40s and 30s BC from which period 25,000 denarii have been retrieved. Crawford suggests that for every one recovered, a couple of thousand more have been lost, perhaps as many as half melted down as soon as they changed hands. Thus, perhaps, a total of 50,000,000 Republican denarii may have been exported to Dacia. Taking at face value Siculus' remark that one slave was worth an amphora of wine, and, estimating the value of an amphora of wine at 50 denarii, he is able to conclude that from c.65 - 30 BC Dacia could have been exporting 30,000 slaves per year to a market which demanded a total of, perhaps, 50,000.[526]

So, in accepting the validity of the commentaries, including Strabo, having identified a dramatic expansion of Roman intervention in an external market, and setting the archaeology firmly in an historical

---

524 Cunliffe (1997), p.212
525 Crawford (1985), pp.232-3
526 Crawford (1985), p.234-5

context, Crawford has been able, tentatively, to place what usually is regarded as an archaeological 'intangible' on a quantifiable, scientific base. Crawford's model can be applied to Dressel 1 (A and B) amphora finds in southern Britain in the Late Iron Age. If, with a great leap of faith, one assumes that Dressel 1 finds, like Crawford's Danubian denarii, represent the purchase of slaves, and one slave was worth one amphora of wine, it is possible to make suggestions regarding the scale of the trade. For example if a generous ratio of, say, one artefact surviving to 500 lost is applied to amphora remains, the fourteen extant rim sherds of Dressel 1A found at Hengistbury Head[527], would represent 7,000 slaves bought and sold!

The coinage record for Britain in the first century BC is interesting too, and certainly indicative of what Cunliffe has described as 'a sudden flowering of international trade'.[528] Coin finds have helped reveal the radical break with the past in the late second century BC and early first. The appearance of Gallo-Belgic coinage in particular indicates the indirect influence of the expanding Roman Empire upon the economy and society.[529] From the same era iron currency bars have turned up, indicating 'the beginnings of commerce',[530] as well as hoards of torcs. Cantian A - E series 'potin' coins, the first coinage minted in Britain, have been found in large numbers in Kent and the Lower Thames valley, dating from around 100 BC.[531] The decade 60 to 50 BC produced 'colossal numbers' of the Gallo-Belgic E gold stater[532], shortly before and during the Gallic Wars. They are thought to have been struck by the Ambiani and conservative estimates imply that over 1,500,000 were put into circulation.[533] A considerable number have been found in Britain, perhaps as payment for mercenaries employed to fight Caesar, or the legacy of Gallic refugees seeking refuge in Britain.[534] Equally, this issue and other continental coinage found in southern Britain in the first half of the century could represent trade in any of the goods listed by Strabo, including slaves.

---

527 Peacock (1971), p.181
528 Cunliffe (1978), p.3
529 Haselgrove (1999), p.13
530 Alcock (1972), p.154
531 Cunliffe (1991), p.113
532 de Jersey (1996), p.17
533 de Jersey (1996), p.18
534 de Jersey (1996), p.18

In fact the reliance on the peripheral zone for both mercenaries *and* slaves is well attested. Both had been sought by the Mediterranean world for centuries and it had long looked to the temperate zone for fresh supplies.[535] It is quite reasonable to assume that any region associated with the supply of the one would be equally capable of providing the other.

The Gallo-Belgic D quarter stater from this period, found mainly in coastal regions around southern Britain, perhaps emphasises the importance of waterborne trade by appearing to depict on one side a stylised image of a boat and three occupants.[536] More diagnostic pictures of shipping on British coins, combined with Caesar's remarks on Breton boats and the archaeology of find sites like Hasholme in Yorkshire, indicate that vessels capable of carrying over five tonnes of cargo were sailing in British coastal and inland waters in the late Iron Age.[537]

Britain's coin record for the second half of the first century indicates the post-Caesarian turbulence and readjustment as the trade with Gaul diminished, and the establishment of closer contacts between south-eastern states and Rome. The coins being struck in the south-east by the end of the century were not only in a Romanised style but derived of alloy almost certainly gleaned from imported denarii.[538] Meanwhile, the comparative absence of Roman influences in the coinage of the Durotriges and Dobunni highlights their isolation from direct contact in this period and, perhaps, an overtly anti-Roman stance.[539]

**Some conclusions**

The economic activity of central southern Britain during the first century BC was greatly influenced by cross-Channel trade. After three hundred years 'of relative isolation'[540] this trade expanded dramatically after c 100 BC and, for the first half of the century, it was

---

535 Nash (1984), p.9
536 de Jersey (1996), p.18
537 Haselgrove (1999), p.131
538 de Jersey (1986), p.29
539 de Jersey (1996), p.39
540 Cunliffe (1978, 1991), p.337

focused on Hengistbury Head, Britain's first major port-of-trade / *oppidum* / town. The take-off, amounting to an economic revolution in the opinion of some commentators, was probably due mainly to the expansion of the Roman Empire in France during this era. Rome however, it has been argued, was the catalyst of change as opposed to being the prime mover.[541] The trade, according to Caesar[542], was handled by the seafaring Veneti of southern Brittany. Some trade was probably conducted with the peoples of Gaul and northern Brittany as well. Trade goods brought from central-southern France appear to have been conveyed directly to Hengistbury Head. These included wine from southern Italy carried in Dressel 1 amphora jars, possibly even at times brought in by long-haul Roman merchant ships. The suppression of the Veneti by Caesar's legions, and the destruction of their fleet in Morbihan Bay in 56 BC, had a direct impact upon this trade which, though it did not suffer a complete collapse, subsequently became focused on the south-east.

It is reasonable to suppose that at least some of this trade would have been in captive manpower. The Roman Empire was slave-dependent during this period and it exerted a constant demand for slaves imported from abroad. These slaves were acquired through war and commerce in the peripheral zones, as indicated by historical sources and supported by artefact evidence such as coin finds and amphora sherds. The continental trade brought with it a new reliance on coinage with the circulation of Gallic and Armorican coins from the late second century in southern Britain and the emergence of indigenous coins modelled on continental issues. The amphora evidence for Britain's continental trade in the hundred and fifty years before the Augustan Conquest attests to the exchange of raw materials for luxury imports. These raw materials almost certainly included slaves, as described by Strabo.

## Religion and ritual

The hardest task for the archaeologist, the highest rung of Hawkes' ladder, is trying to understand ancient belief systems through the evidence of material remains. Colin Renfrew has identified the

---

541   James and Rigby (1997), p.74
542   Chadwick (1971), pp.60-61

following criteria for identifying ritual in archaeology:

*Focusing of attention: ritual may take place in a spot with special, natural associations (cave, grove of trees, spring, mountaintop). Alternatively, ritual may take place in a special building set apart for sacred functions.*

*The structure and equipment used for the ritual may employ attention-focusing devices, reflected in the architecture, special fixtures, and in the movable equipment.*

*The sacred area is likely to be rich in repeated symbols; boundary zone between this world and the next.*

*Ritual may involve both conspicuous public display end expenditure, and hidden exclusive mysteries, whose practice will be reflected in the architecture.*

*Concepts of cleanliness and pollution may be reflected in the facilities and maintenance of the sacred area; presence of the deity.*

*The association with a deity or deities may be reflected in the use of a cult image.*

*The ritualistic symbols will often relate iconographically to the deities worshipped and to their associated myth. Animal symbolism may often be used.*

*The ritualistic symbols may relate to those seen also in rites of passage, participation and offering.*

*Worship will involve prayer and special movements and these may be reflected in the iconography of decorations or images.*

*The ritual may employ various devices for inducing religious experience (e.g., dance, music, drugs, the infliction of pain).*

*The sacrifice of animals or humans may be practiced.*

*Food and drink may be brought and possibly consumed as offerings or burned/poured away.*

*Other material objects may be brought and offered.*

*Great investment of wealth may be reflected both in the equipment used and in the offerings made.*

*Great investment of wealth and resources may be reflected in the structure itself and its facilities.*[543]

Renfrew's criteria provide a useful starting place for the interpretation of enigmatic prehistoric sites such as that of the remarkable Bronze Age wooden platform and causeway at Flag Fen on the outskirts of Peterborough in Cambridgeshire. The massive structure that was constructed in open water and approached by the narrow 'processional' causeway was undoubtedly a device for focusing attention. Its **liminal location** between dryland and wet and evidence for the ritual 'killing' of swords and other objects which appear to have been intentionally broken before being cast from the platform into the water implies this was perceived as a boundary zone between this world and the next. If these objects were deposited in the water as votive gifts it would have been revered as a place where the communicants believed they were in the presence of the deity / deities. The fact that the enormous platform was large enough for many people, used over a long period of time, and a great many objects appear to have been cast from it suggest it was a place of participation and offering.

## Explanations for cultural change

The reasons underpinning cultural changes are complex and likely to have many causes. However a convenient starting place for anyone interested in explaining these in both historic and prehistoric contexts is to consider the possibility that they have either been brought about by contact with outsiders – the diffusion of ideas or the migration of people – or that they are the consequence of internal developments or processes, from which we derive the concept of 'processual archaeology', such as adaptation to a changing natural environment.

---

543 Renfrew and Bahn (2000), pp.405–407

# Ethnoarchaeology

'We are familiar with the cliché that we study the past in order to learn more about the present. We are less comfortable, perhaps, with the idea that we study the present in order to understand the past.'
(Lewis Binford (1983) *In Pursuit of the Past*, Thames and Hudson, p 23)

Ethnoarchaeology combines the disciplines of ethnography / anthropology (the study of humans) and archaeology by observing modern humans and using these observations as a means of interpreting the archaeological record. In the USA archaeology is regarded as a sub-division of anthropology. The best known exponent of the approach is Lewis Binford (1931-2011) who interpreted material evidence of hunter-gatherers in the Palaeolothic period in the light of his observations of hunter-gatherer behaviour and technology, principally that of the Nanamiut, in the modern world.

Anthropological studies are sometimes used as a last resort for archaeologists seeking answers to questions which the material evidence from the past cannot fully answer, for example: who made the pottery, did the hunting, painted the caves - men or women, or both? Anthropological studies of modes of exchange, for example 'reciprocity' (reciprocal exchange / gift-giving) between islanders in the Pacific have suggested an explanation for the distribution of materials across wide areas in prehistoric times among cultures that have left no evidence of currency based trade. Anthropological studies have demonstrated that the typical 'catchment area' or 'home territory' of a hunter-gatherer group is likely to be around about a 6 mile radius from the base camp – about two hours walk from their temporary home.[544] The micro-wear analysis of teeth of known meat-eating cultures and non-meat eating cultures, studied by anthropologists, helps archaeologists to determine the diet of ancient people through the distinctive marks ('striations') on their teeth. Archaeologists interested in exploring ancient mentalities, 'cognitive archaeologists', have been inspired by the mentalities of living people to suggest explanations for evidence of ancient beliefs – the anthropologists' knowledge of contemporary, or at least historic, cave paintings and their painters has been deployed in attempts to explain

---

[544] Henson (2012), p.31

the meanings of those produced by our Palaeolithic ancestors tens of thousands of years ago. Similarly, and less controversially, ethnoarchaeology is an obvious starting place for experimental archaeologists interested in the possibilities it represents regarding the survival of ancient technologies.

## CASE STUDY: Southern Britain's Late Iron Age Slave Trade

*In the following passages anthroplogical and archaeological evidence for the impact of the slave trade upon African society in the eighteenth century is considered in an attempt to explore the place of a trade in slaves in southern Britain towards the end of its Iron Age.*

Occasionally some archaeological evidence allows hypotheses relevant to intangibles, such as social organisation and religious beliefs, to be offered. But these must remain no more than hypotheses.[545]

That a trade in slaves through ports in southern Britain occurred during the couple of centuries before the Claudian conquest is beyond reasonable doubt.[546] What cannot be established with any degree of certainty is the volume of this trade.[547] The direct evidence for slavery in southern Britain during this period is slight and problematic:

*'One slave chain has been found in a bog on Anglesey and another at the hillfort of Bigbury in Kent but two slave chains hardly make an export industry.'*[548]

Barry Cunliffe may reasonably have continued by asking 'when is a slave chain a slave chain?': manacles do not necessarily confine slaves.[549] What has been dubbed 'proto-history' is marginally more reliable and, according to the Greek geographer Strabo, British exports in the periods included 'corn, cattle, gold, silver, hides, slaves

---

545 Corcoran (1971), p.18
546 Cunliffe (1993), p.203
547 Cunliffe (1995), p.97
548 Cunliffe (1995), p.97
549 Laing (1995), p.26

and clever hunting-dogs'.[550]

Although he is the foremost advocate of the possibility of a British Iron Age slave trade, Professor Cunliffe has declared its scale, along with other details of commercial activity in the period, cannot be demonstrated 'archaeologically'.[551] The Atlantic slave trade of the eighteenth century was unique in terms of scale and its social, political and economic impact. While it would be anomalous to compare the detail of modern African history with that of Britain in the first century BC, certain generalisations regarding the likely impact of contact between slave-requiring empires and slave-providing societies upon the latter can be drawn with impunity. Cunliffe clearly feels an affinity with such an approach when he remarks:

*'we have only to look at the situation in west Africa in the seventeenth and eighteenth centuries to see what a devastating social and economic effect on indigenous societies the American consumer market in slaves could have.'*[552]

In attempting to determine issues related to supply in this context it is necessary to consider the more determinable subject of demand. Much has been written on the institution of slavery within the Roman Empire. By the second century BC the demand for slaves was very considerable and one which could not be satisfied by regeneration and conquest alone.[553] Madden assumes that the bulk of slaves was purchased 'from over the boundaries of the empire' and that this happened 'at all major *limites*'.[554] By the middle of the first century BC Britain was very certainly on the boundary of the empire and an obvious source for this precious commodity at the peak of the imperial demand.

The expansion of British trade in the period has been superbly documented by Barry Cunliffe, particularly that associated with the

---

550   Strabo iv. 5. 2. in Cunliffe (1993), p.20
551   Cunliffe (1995: 97), Cunliffe (1978), p.74
552   Cunliffe (1995), p.97
553   Madden (1996), p.3
554   Madden (1995), p.5

principal southern 'port-of-trade', Hengistbury Head.[555] The place of enslavement within this trade has to remain a speculation. It is informed however by Diodorus Siculus' declaration that Gallic slaves were commonly exchanged for amphorae of wine[556]; of all material evidence the amphora sherd distribution for southern Britain in the period could be the most telling in an attempt to establish the case for a trade in slaves.

There is no archaeological evidence to suggest that the trade in slaves had anything like as great an impact on southern British Late Iron Age communities as that of African coastal societies in the eighteenth century. Furthermore there is no firm evidence to demonstrate that slaves were ever anything more than a marginal trade good in this period. After all, slaves and 'clever hunting dogs' are mentioned at the end, not the beginning, of Strabo's famous list. Nevertheless, while heeding Cunliffe's warning that 'We must not allow prehistory to become dominated by pseudo-history again'[557], it still seems reasonable to suppose that, for some Late Iron Age communities, be they predators or victims, the slavery issue could have been of central importance.

The scale of Britain's Late Iron Age trade in slaves cannot be measured. The Roman demand for slaves perhaps can. It has been estimated that Italy needed to import around 15,000 slaves each year[558], and about a third of the population of Italy, and as much as one fifth of the population of the empire as a whole, is thought to have been enslaved.[559] Commerce, not war, was the usual means of provision.[560] The necessary transactions would have originated in zones peripheral to the Roman empires[561], such as first century BC southern Britain and in the vicinity of the Black Sea. Classical sources, notably Strabo, confirm this assumption. In the opinion of Crawford[562] the bulk of the Roman demand for slaves could have

---

555 Christchurch, Dorset; Cunliffe (1978)
556 Cunliffe (1994), p.414
557 Cunliffe (1978, 1991), p.345
558 Cunliffe (1997), p.215
559 Madden (1996), pp.2-3
560 Madden (1996), p.3
561 Cunliffe (1994), p.414
562 Crawford (1985), pp.234-

been met by Dacia in the middle years of the first century BC, a conclusion drawn on the quantifiable evidence of coin finds data. Nevertheless experts in this field believe Rome was supplied with slaves from 'many geographical centers'[563], one of which, it may be presumed, could have been Britain.

The experience of African peoples in the eighteenth century AD provides information on how a prevalent trade in slaves can impact upon predator and victim societies. These can be grouped under the headings *socio-economic effects, effects upon settlement* and *effects upon social organisation*. The general picture that emerges is one that bears striking similarities to that demonstrated archaeologically for the Late Iron Age communities of central southern Britain. However, this may have little to do with the impact of a trade in slaves.

*Socio-economic effects:*

The economic impact of the slave trade upon Africa remains a cause of debate. Classic liberal and Marxist analyses might identify short-term gains but assume that the institution of slavery necessarily becomes moribund and a check on economic, as well as political, progress for slave users and slave providers alike.[564] Some historians perceive general social and economic retardation in eighteenth century Africa, and for decades afterwards, as a result of this trade[565], while other commentators[566] are less convinced. The late prehistory of central southern Britain portrays societies enjoying for the first time imperial luxuries, notably Italian wines, in much the same way as eighteenth century West Africans became importers of rum and *geribata*. The alleged destruction of 'authentic African civilisation'[567], as a result of the Atlantic Slave Trade, is reminiscent of the Romanisation of the economic elite in south-east England in the post-Caesarian period. Fortified trading settlements sprang up on the Gold Coast in eighteenth century Africa in much the same way as the fortified port-of-trade of Hengistbury Head emerged as a major centre due to Rome's imperial expansion. In Africa these fortifications

---

563 Bradley (1989), p.22
564 Davis (1984), p.xiii
565 e.g. Inikori (1982)
566 e.g. Fage (1978)
567 van Dantzig (1982), p.201

were designed to keep people in (i.e. slaves awaiting transportation) as much as they were intended to keep hostile people out.

The demographic impact of the slave trade upon eighteenth century Africa is uncertain. There is no evidence for demographic decline in Late Iron Britain in the first decades of its close contact with the Rome. On the contrary, centres thought to have been heavily engaged in commercial activities in the period, such as the developed hillforts, became more densely populated as the first century BC progressed. As Inkori observed in his studies of African history[568], the places where one might find evidence of population decline / desertion as a result of aggression would be peripheral to those on the coast and along main trade routes. New forms of currency were introduced into Africa as a result of contacts with Europe, notably brass *manillas*, just as closer contact with mainland Europe resulted in the introduction of coinage in Late Iron Age Britain.

*Effects upon settlement:*

It has been observed that during the era of the Atlantic slave trade African communities were likely to select settlement sites that provided better protection, and natural defensive sites, particularly hilltops, were sometimes settled in preference to those that in purely economic terms were more desirable. In some areas settlements were massively fortified with rings of ditches and ramparts[569]. The peoples of central-southern Britain shared the same impulse to occupy multivallated hilltop settlements in the Late Iron Age, though not necessarily for the same reasons. In parts of eighteenth century Africa substantial, formerly prosperous, areas became deserted. While populations were subject to a measure of local relocation in Iron Age Britain, there is no reason to suppose that great tracts of low lying land were abandoned as the developed hillforts expanded and others went out of use altogether.

*Effects upon social organisation:*

The Atlantic slave trade certainly generated warfare in eighteenth

---

568   Inkori (1982), pp.37-8
569   van Dantzig (1982), p.195

century Africa. It has many times been argued that warfare was endemic in Britain in the Late Iron Age. The militarisation of eighteenth century societies in Africa is reminiscent of the apparently heightened preoccupation of Late Iron Age British societies with warfare and its various attributes. In both cases it is appropriate to envisage the establishment of new warrior elites, commanding predatory economies. Their trading interests very likely bound communities together and prompted the evolution of the *civitates* that Caesar recorded in the mid-first century BC. Thus the interests of merchants at Hengistbury Head were bound to those of 'satellite' hillforts. Perhaps their relationship was not so very far removed from that with which Olaudah Equiano was familiar as a child growing up on Africa's eighteenth century Guinea coast:

*'When a trader wants slaves, he applies to a chief for them, and tempts him with wares [...] Accordingly, he falls on his neighbours, and a desperate battle ensues.'*[570]

None of the above proves that a single slave was ever sold to an Armorican merchant (let alone a Roman) on the shores of the England's south coast. What the historical model does confirm, however, is that the demands of vast, alien and technologically advanced empires can irrevocably alter the societies with which it establishes economic and political contact. The history of eighteenth century Africa demonstrates that when a demand for slaves is brought into the equation the most striking consequence of this contact is a heightened level of warfare.

The seemingly unprecedented violence of the Late Iron Age in Britain provides the best chance of demonstrating that slaves could have been a significant commodity in southern British market places. Although it has been suggested that the importance of cattle in 'barbarian' economies of the period 'offered an inducement to raiding and warfare'[571], of all the export goods mentioned by Strabo, the slave is the one and only commodity that, typically, could not be acquired *without* violence. Indeed, as Meillassoux observed when comparing eighteenth century Africa's trade in gold with that of its

---

570   Carretta (1995), p.39
571   Corcoran (1971), p.25

trade in slaves[572], peace is more conducive to trade than war *except when captive manpower is the commodity that is being traded.*

The last hundred years of Britain's Iron Age show every sign of having been a turbulent period. The fact that most of the 'tribes' recorded by Caesar in the 50s BC appear to have disappeared by the time of the Conquest implies an age of dynastic struggles and conflicts[573]. The abundant evidence for a general insecurity in the period has been linked to a variety of factors such as population growth, the Belgic 'invasion', the self-reliance of iron using communities, and the self-aggrandisement of a warrior elite. Very likely all of these contributed.

As an archaeological 'intangible', writers (very sensibly!) have usually steered clear of the trade in slaves as a causal factor, and even its greatest advocate, Barry Cunliffe, who was contemplating back in 1971 the considerable impact the Roman demand for British slaves could have had on 'raiding for the profit motive', has not yet 'found the place to indulge in a detailed consideration of the matter'.[574] In Cunliffe's opinion the Roman demand for slaves was at least as credible an explanation for this heightened tension and insecurity as either the threat of Roman attack or the migration of the Belgae. It is impossible to say whether this trade was ever the mainstay of southern England's trade with Romanised Europe or whether it was of marginal importance. Strabo's commentary on the subject suggests it played a significant role (i.e. worth mentioning) in Britain's mixed economy.

In the later editions of his vast survey of the period, *Iron Age Communities in Britain*, Cunliffe has continued to toy with the place of enslavement in the development of these communities. The discussion, ultimately, comes back to Strabo and his intriguing remark. He records, incidentally, how a surprisingly high number of cows' teeth discovered in Late Iron Age layers at Hengistbury Head 'could hint at the value of hides and salt meat for export'.[575] In so doing he helps confirm the validity of Strabo's account in its reference to 'cattle and hides'. Commentating on the changes after 150 BC

---

572   Inikori (1982), p.80
573   James (1999), p.97
574   Cunliffe (1971), pp.63-4
575   Cunliffe (1991), p.16

Cunliffe remarks: 'All are directly attested in the historical sources and may sometimes, with the eye of faith, be seem dimly reflected in the archaeological evidence.'[576] While no firm conclusions can be drawn, it is certainly possible, with the eye of faith, to paint a credible picture of southern British societies, a hundred years before the Conquest, engaging in a trade in slaves, and launching the necessary raids with which to procure them for insatiable Roman merchants and their Armorican / Gallic middlemen.

---

576   Cunliffe (1991), p.108

# Part 4 PROFESSIONAL PRACTICE

## 7 Practice

**Interpreting and evaluating sources**

**Sources and evidence**

There is a great range of material available to and used by historians. Historians rely on literature of all kinds such as official documents, newspaper articles, personal correspondence, chronicles, works of fiction. In addition, historians frequently work with figures such as statistics, e.g. population growth, economic developments, images such as propaganda posters, cartoons in the press, film, photographs and portraits, tangible evidence of the past in the form of landscapes, structures and other artefacts, the skills of specialists in other fields such as mathematicians, anthropologists, geographers and archaeologists.

The subject the historian studies largely determines the sources the historian is most likely to use. Consider the example of Alfred the Great. Alfred was the king of Wessex, the great Saxon kingdom defining the south and west of Britain in the ninth century CE. The historian is largely restricted to the study of just two major contemporary texts concerning his reign: a biography of the king known as Asser's *Life of Alfred* and the *Anglo-Saxon Chronicle*, a record of English affairs written by monks, probably commissioned by Alfred himself. For Alfred, there are no newspapers, photographs, moving images or propaganda posters to consult and so the historian needs to look elsewhere.

Every historical source has value, but the historian must handle every source with care in order to derive its historical worth. Each source makes a unique contribution to the historical record, but it is also likely to bring with it a particular set of problems in its interpretation. Different types of evidence need to be approached in different ways.

## Official documents

In a world that demands 'accountability', governments and other public institutions in modern democracies are pressured into recording and making available information that can be deemed to be in 'the public interest'. In Britain much of this is available for all to consult in the National Archives. The National Archives, formerly the Public Records Office (PRO), was established in 1838. On its opening, the PRO was declared to be the central depository for 'all rolls, records, writs, books, proceedings, decrees, bills, warrants, accounts, papers, and documents whatsoever of a public nature, belonging to Her Majesty'.

The range of these official British documents is vast and they span well over a thousand years of the country's history, from before the Domesday Book to the Beveridge Report and beyond. Although the National Archives fill around a hundred miles of shelving, the records are neither complete nor automatically reliable. Typically, the further the historian goes back, the sparser becomes the documentary record. Different periods pose particular problems. For example, the Tudor State Papers tend to be confined to incoming correspondence, whereas the Chancery records of earlier times are mainly copies of the government's outgoing letters and decrees and not the responses and requests, and so on, from its subjects. In some instances, for example papers relating to the **Suez Crisis** of 1956, it is evident that embarrassing or incriminating documents have been removed and, presumably, destroyed. The historian handling 'official' documents must always bear in mind the possibility that the official version of events is not necessarily the correct one or the complete one.

Official records are usually associated with political historians. However, the documents relating to the activities of generations of civil servants and other bureaucrats are of equal interest to economic and social historians. Indeed, it is often only through this evidence that we can gain a detailed understanding of the lives of ordinary people. This was amply demonstrated when the French historian, Emmanuel Le Roy Ladurie, in his book *Montaillou* (1978) reconstructed the lives of the illiterate peasants of a village in the French Pyrenees in the early fourteenth century through his analysis of the records of the Inquisition investigating allegations of heresy. A similar approach was taken more recently by Eamon Duffy in *Voices of Morebath* (2001), an investigation of life in a village on the Somerset-Devon border during the Reformation based upon the uniquely detailed parish records kept by its priest, Christopher Trychay. Among other things, it has shed a great deal of light on the nature of popular rebellion in the middle of the sixteenth century.

## Private papers and personal writings

Private papers constitute collections of material both written by and addressed to the individual concerned. Such collections are invaluable to biographers, and it is not unusual for people who have played an important public role to leave this record as a legacy for the benefit of future historians. Equally, such collections reside in any number of attics in the homes of ordinary people, storing for posterity details of the lives of their equally ordinary ancestors. In both cases, historians need to be alert to the likely chance that some form of self-censorship has occurred in the assemblage of such papers as the collator of the collection decides what is worth keeping and what is not.

In a world before emails and telephones, the letter was the principal mode of correspondence. Of course, letters are an invaluable source for understanding social relationships in the past, but they can also greatly enhance the historian's understanding of political history. Just as modern politicians send each other regular emails, the political figures of the not-too-distant past would send each other regular, perhaps daily, letters and memos. As many politicians have found to their cost, such private correspondence is likely to be less circumspect than 'official' communications and, as such, provide wonderful insights into the thoughts of the individuals involved.

Diaries can be even more intimate than letters, particularly if they have been written without the object of anyone other than the author reading them. Plenty of public figures over the last couple of centuries have kept diaries, presumably with a view to recording events as they unfurled, and their involvement in them, for the benefit of future generations. In our own time, some eminent diarists, particularly politicians, have published their diaries within their own lifetimes. Again, the historian needs to consider carefully the diarist's purpose and the prerogative any publishing diarist has regarding the selection of what is permitted to enter the public domain. The publication of the Labour government's press chief Alastair Campbell's diary in 2007 was criticised for drawing a veil across the friction between departing Prime Minister Tony Blair and his successor Gordon Brown, and thus not providing a balanced account of the Blair government.

Arguably, the most reliable diaries are the ones that were never intended for publication. Famous diarists of the last few centuries such as Samuel Pepys (seventeenth century), Parson Woodforde (eighteenth century) and Francis Kilvert (nineteenth century) have provided wonderful insights into the mundane of the periods in which they lived: the food they ate, the clothes they wore, their interests, health, and values. Of course, a diary gives us a very individual perspective on the past which does not necessarily reflect the common experience. Furthermore, historians need to recognise the fact that until modern times such sources were the product of the literate and leisurely upper classes; the voices of the working classes of the past are less often heard, and are almost totally lost before 1800.

## Newspapers

The emergence of newspapers in modern times has made the biggest contribution to providing for some subjects in some places a near-complete historical record. The first newspapers appeared in the seventeenth century. These concentrated on news of national importance, but by the late eighteenth century newspapers dedicated to local ('provincial') matters had also become established. Nowadays, of course there is a plethora of 'dailies' providing information for every group of the reading public.

When evaluating a newspaper source as evidence, the historian is confronted with the tricky issue regarding how far the newspaper reflects history and how far it makes it. The newspaper editorial is a powerful propaganda tool and politicians in particular are aware of the need to have national newspapers on their side in order to succeed. The transfer of support of *The Sun* from the Conservative party to Labour helps explain the triumphs of the latter in the late 1990s. Newspaper articles do not always mirror public opinion and it would be naive to assume that everything stated in a newspaper would meet the approval of its readership.

Read with care and with a keen eye for bias and an understanding of an article's purpose (for example, is it to entertain or inform?) the newspaper is an invaluable source for the historian of more modern times.

## Novels

The novel, like other forms of creative expression such as paintings, poetry, pop-songs and screenplays, is usually the product of a single mind, and offers a personal view. Furthermore, to a greater or lesser degree, the novel is a work of fiction; it tells a story and, ultimately, it is designed to 'entertain', in the broadest sense of the term, in order to sell copies. Often it distorts or oversimplifies the truth to make a point or perhaps simply 'for effect'. As such, it can be a particularly problematic source of evidence for the historian in search of 'facts'.

However, the novel, emerging as an art form in the eighteenth century, is an important and fascinating subject of historical study. It is the product of the times in which it is written and, whatever the subject matter, be it science-fiction or historical, even the most skilful novelist is unable to shed all vestiges of the culture of the age in which the novel is written. The same can be said of historians. Sometimes, issues of great contemporary interest underpin the novel: shortly before Emile Durkheim launched the craft of modern sociology with his classic work *Suicide* (1897) in England, Thomas Hardy's last novel, *Jude the Obscure* (1895), was centred on the same theme - the degeneracy of the modern industrial world as debated by the statisticians, doctors and Social-Darwinians across Europe at that time. In much the same way, George Orwell reflected public concerns in his gloomy 'distopian' vision of the future, *Nineteen Eighty-Four*, at the start of the Cold War.

## Oral accounts and personal histories

Oral history is fallible on two counts: it is determined by what the subject tells the interviewer and what the interviewer asks the subject. Memories are imperfect and people can unintentionally, sometimes intentionally, distort past truths. Interviewers may have an agenda that shapes the interview and they cannot be relied upon to be entirely objective when making the results of the interview available to a wider audience. Recollections, arguably, are less reliable than contemporaneous sources of evidence since people's memories are not infallible. Furthermore, eyewitness accounts of the past are not necessarily any more truthful than the statements of witnesses in courts of law.

However, the oral account is now recognised as a very important historical source. The popularisation of the approach coincided with the widening availability of the technology by which accounts could be recorded and it is now an activity with which anyone interested in the past can easily get involved. Indeed, it must be the simplest and most direct way in which a researcher can acquire a bank of unique and previously unrecorded source material.

The earliest compilations of oral history date to the nineteenth century when Diana Maria Mulock in her *Unsentimental Journey through Cornwall* (1884) recorded the accounts of local people, accounts that up to this point were likely to be lost to the historical record. It can be argued that this kind of record is all the more important than 'elite' oral history since the famous are far more likely to leave their mark for posterity in other places. Not surprisingly, therefore, the technique has proved particularly useful to the writers of the history of women's lives in recent times.

Major projects have been undertaken, including a study in the 1970s by Paul Thompson and Essex University of Edwardian life based upon the systematic interviewing of 500 people from a broad range of backgrounds with memories stretching back at least as far as 1911. Another very important on-going project is the compilation of the Imperial War Museum's Sound Archive. This massive collection of recorded interviews has been compiled over 30 years and contains recollections of all of the major conflicts in which Britain has been involved since the Second Boer War (1899-1902).

Social-Darwinians applied Darwin's laws of evolutionary theory to competition within, and between, human societies. Darwin's theories were used sometimes to justify racist ideologies in the first half of the twentieth century.

The Cold War defines the period of international tension between 1945-46 and 1989. During this time, the dire threat of nuclear weaponry helped prevent the clash between the ideologies of US-style capitalism and the communism of the Soviet Union from erupting into a third world war.

## Maps

Matthew Paris, a thirteenth-century Benedictine monk, is credited with the first English map of the British Isles. By the early fourteenth century, maps accompanied local surveys, and by the end of that century 'town views' were being made for a variety of purposes. Most British towns have at least one map dating from the eighteenth century or earlier. The explosion of commerce in the eighteenth and nineteenth centuries produced detailed road maps and traveller guides. The first Ordnance Survey map appeared in 1801. These detailed, accurate maps started life as maps designed for military purposes during the Napoleonic Wars. Since then, it has become a service for the benefit of the public and the government alike. Modern maps are precision objects of great accuracy. Older maps are not and some are little more than works of geographical fiction! Nevertheless, even these are of value as evidence of the ways in which people in the past have pictured their world.

An extraordinary thirteenth-century map of the world known as the 'Mappa Mundi' can be found in Hereford Cathedral. Although reasonably accurate in some respects, it is wildly fanciful in others, for example its images of mythical creatures associated with various parts of the world. These include one-legged humanoids with a single huge foot to shade them from the sun in far-off hot lands! Following an ancient convention which portrayed the world as a circle with Rome at the centre, at the very centre of this map is the city of Jerusalem. At the top of the map is the image of Christ on the Day of Judgement, turning away sinners but admitting the repentant and righteous into Heaven.

The maps is an essential tool for any historian navigating their way through the past, and both modern and historical maps are excellent sources of evidence in their own right. Old maps provide evidence for detailed developments that are likely to have eluded other documentary records.

Modern maps are also hugely useful in illuminating the past. The shape of field boundaries and roads can indicate the site of structures that no longer exist. Isolated churches may well mark the site of villages deserted perhaps in the aftermath of the Black Death or as a consequence of large-scale enclosures. Street names can reveal the activities formerly associated with specific areas in towns and villages, and the names of whole settlements themselves can reveal the presence of foreign settlers in early times. Some fascinating studies, for example, have been undertaken into the spread of Scandinavian-influenced place names to show the impact of Viking settlement from the ninth century; the suffixes -*thorpe* and -*by* are almost exclusively found to the north of the boundary that separated the areas under the Danelaw from the Anglo-Saxon kingdoms of central and southern Britain.

Historic maps dating from the eighteenth and nineteenth centuries used by historians and archaeologists include estate plans, enclosure maps, Ordnance Survey surveyors' drawings, tithe maps, Ordnance Survey maps, Admiralty charts, and town plans. Modern maps of special value include geological surveys, GIS (Geographical Information Systems) maps, soil surveys, land use and classification maps, street maps, factory plans, vegetation and climatic maps.

## Cartoons and posters

Political cartoons in newspapers, despite being the artist's personal view on a contemporary theme, can usually be relied upon to reflect the attitude of the readership it caters for. Unlike the work of the modern historian, the work of the cartoonist is openly opinionated and designed to provoke an emotional, rather than an intellectual, response. A cartoon that works is one that angers the reader or makes the reader laugh. Cartoons rarely provide a literal truth, but the most useful ones give a direct and succinct insight into the concerns of a time and place regarding some contentious issue. It is their very subjectivity, their bias, that makes them such important sources of evidence. The fact that they tend to use metaphors to make points, that they can grossly exaggerate the truth, and that they sometimes rely on irony, however, can make them problematic sources for historians; without a good knowledge of the historical context in which they appeared, the historian is likely to miss the cartoon's point entirely.

Other visual polemical sources include political posters, advertisements and party political broadcasts on television. All need to be treated with the same care as cartoons since they are essentially propagandist - their object is to provoke the viewer into thinking about a subject and persuading the viewer into a particular line of thinking. As such, it is immensely useful as evidence; even propaganda that lies is of value in illuminating a particular set of values current in a particular place and time.

## Statistics

'There are three kinds of lies: lies, damned lies, and statistics.'
(Mark Twain quoting, he believed, Benjamin Disraeli)

Statistics have a central role in historical enquiries. The political or social historian uses them as much as the economic historian in their investigations of such matters as voting patterns, the growth of literacy and industrial development. They need to be handled with care since the results are only as reliable as the methods by which the statistics were gathered. Enumerators make mistakes and do sometimes lie.

Even when the results can be considered trustworthy, it is easy for historians to misinterpret them. A major debate in British economic history surrounds the impact of the Industrial Revolution upon the standard of living. In 1957, the historian E. J. Hobsbawm in *The British Standard of Living in England, 1800-50* 'proved' that the standard of living for working people in London was falling because meat sales at the Smithfield market fell during the period - meat being the item most indicative of prosperity in any working-class shopping basket in the nineteenth century. R. M. Hartwell (1961) in *The Rising Standard of*

*Living in England, 1800-50* challenged Hobsbawm's conclusion by focusing on the evidence for the increased sale of meat in other markets and also by considering the consumption of fish. As the debate progressed, E. P. Thompson (1967) pointed out that the standard of living cannot be measured in a purely quantitative manner; the quality of life is of equal or even greater importance. It seems that the issue can never be resolved by statistics alone.

B. R. Mitchell (1994) in an interesting article on the subject highlighted the danger of reading too much into percentage increase or decrease when handling statistics: 'A 1000% rise in (say) Bulgarian steel output over five years may seem huge and highly significant - until it is pointed out that the initial output was minute.'

In a similar vein the nineteenth-century English wit and satirist Sydney Smith lampooned the panic that gripped the country when cholera struck again in 1848:

*Cholera made one successful effort at Taunton and not repeated it though a month has elapsed ... The cholera will have killed by the end of the year about one person in every thousand. Therefore it is a thousand to one (supposing the cholera to travel at the same rate) that any person does not die of the cholera in anyone year. This calculation is for the mass, but if you are prudent, temperate and rich your chance is at least five times as good that you do not die of cholera; in other words 5000 to 1. And if it is 5000 to 1 that you do not die of cholera in a year, it is not far from two million to one that you do not die anyone day of cholera.*

In percentage terms the increased incidence of cholera in 1848 was enormous since it had not occurred since 1832, but in terms of the mortality rate, the impact, at least in Taunton, was minimal. Smith's comments also highlight the problem of generalisation: what might be a statistical 'truth' for one group of people is not necessarily true for another.

## Photographs

The photograph is another unique source for the study of recent history. An invention of the first half of the nineteenth century, photography has played a key role in shaping our understanding of the world since the 1850s. As evidence, early photos can be limited since shutter speeds necessitated carefully posed 'unnatural' settings of people and they tended to record the lives and interests of the more privileged. By the end of the nineteenth century, however, the camera was recording most aspects of life, including industrial work and warfare.

As with other sources of evidence, the historian needs to consider the context in which the image was captured. The principle consideration is what motivated the photographer to take that particular photograph in the first place. Political history of the twentieth century is littered with photographs that served a purely propagandist purpose. Of course, this does not make a photograph less valuable, but it does highlight how important it is to avoid falling into the trap of taking a photograph at 'face value'. Furthermore, with digital technology it has become easy to manipulate and falsify images. This has been going on for a long time - 'doctored' photographs from the Edwardian period, for example, survive purporting to show fairies and ghosts. After he achieved full control over the USSR by the late 1920s, Stalin had his arch-rival Trotsky 'airbrushed' from photographs that revealed the latter's central role in the Bolshevik Revolution of 1917.

## Primary and secondary sources

Historians handle both a huge amount and a wide range of evidence. Dealing with evidence effectively necessitates ordering the evidence. As well as dividing evidence by type, historians divide evidence into primary and secondary sources. These terms are determined by the historian's purpose. For example, if a historian is trying to discover what happened in 871 CE, when Alfred the Great was attacked by the Vikings, the contemporary accounts of the events, written down by the people who lived through them are the primary sources, whereas the accounts of these events written by subsequent historians are the secondary sources. Thus Asser's *Life of Alfred* and the *Anglo-Saxon Chronicle*, mentioned earlier, are primary sources for this purpose. However, if the historian decides to explore how the popular image of Alfred the Great has changed over time, the subsequent historical accounts also become primary sources. The focus of the historian's attention is no longer just on the events of the ninth century. It is equally concerned with the events of the Tudor, Stuart, Georgian and Victorian periods that helped shape the interpretation of those who wrote about Alfred in those periods.

## How to read sources

Before reading a source, start by working out what sort of source you are dealing with. When analysing sources, ask yourself the five 'W's: When was the source written? Who created the source? What type of source is it? Where did it come from? Why was the source produced?

## Fines' first five steps to success

A very influential modern teacher of history teachers, John Fines, devised an eight stage approach to the study of any written source. These are the first five and they are as good a place as any to start in the structured analysis of a document.

Step 1 Describe the document - is it a diary extract, an official form, a newspaper article?

Step 2 What information does it contain regarding such things as people, places, time, ideas?

Step 3 What difficult words, phrases and references does it contain? Use a dictionary, encyclopaedia, atlas, etc. to develop your understanding.

Step 4 Read the source again. What words or phrases (if any) help give away the period in which the source was written. This might be reflected in the attitudes of the writer regarding such things as religion and political ideas, or the absence of 'hindsight' (i.e. knowledge of what happened afterwards) as much as it is evident in any archaic language.

Step 5 How reliable is the source? Identify anything that is of dubious reliability because, for example, there is a lack of supporting evidence for a claim, or the source clearly is biased. Look out for any words or phrases which are particularly emotive, subjective, opinionated.[577]

## Context

When an archaeologist is asked to assess a find, the first thing they will want to know about is the context in which it was found - if it has been dug up and there is detailed information of where it lay in the ground, in which layer or 'strata' of the site - it will be of far more value to the archaeologist than if that information has been lost and the object is 'unstratified'. To the archaeologist and the historian alike, context is crucial and evidence cannot be fully understood without it.

Historians use a term that takes centre stage in the world of antique dealers to describe the concept of context: **provenance**. This brings us back to the five Ws – what, who, when, where, why. The provenance of the source is all to do with the time and place in which the document was written, in which the painting was painted, in which the interview was recorded. For historians, it is the metaphorical 'layer' in their excavation of the past.

## Hypotheses

Since the start of the twentieth century, there has been a debate among academics concerning the question, 'Is History a science?' A nineteenth-century German historian, Leopold von Ranke, maintained that it is a science because historians employ, or should employ, a scientific method in the pursuit of historical facts. As in the natural sciences, he maintained, historians' results are the outcome of formulating and testing hypotheses.

Academic history is more than the mere chronicling of events. Historians ask questions in order to understand what happened and why. When they envisage an answer to the question, they form a hypothesis. The hypothesis can then be 'tested' by examining further evidence in order to establish whether or not it is correct, whether it needs modification or whether it should be abandoned.

---

577   adapted from Fines (1988)

Of course, the evidence available is usually incomplete, sometimes hard to make sense of and often contradictory. Historians reach their conclusions about the past on the basis of what seems most likely in the light of their understanding of the available evidence. In so doing they should endeavour to be as objective as possible.

## Counterfactual method

Another approach to trying to understand the past is the 'What if?' approach or counterfactual method. Quite simply, historians can consider how things might have occurred if something had happened differently in the past. It is something we all consider at times in our personal lives, particularly when we draw the conclusion 'If only... !' As often as not we are best advised to forget the 'What ifs' and get on with things as they are. Likewise, some historians consider the counterfactual approach to history counterproductive.

However, serious historical studies of some worth have been based on the counterfactual method. A good example, though now discredited, is Robert Fogel's *The Railroads and American Economic Growth* (1964) in which he endeavoured to quantify the importance of the railway in America's industrial development by considering how things might have turned out without it. He arrived at the conclusion that without the railway, and hence reliance on other means of transport, the net loss to America during the period of its industrial revolution would have been no more than four per cent of its national income.

While a reliance on the counterfactual method to reach specific conclusions might be foolhardy, historians can scarcely avoid the 'What if?' approach entirely. For example, with any study of causation the historian consciously or subconsciously considers whether a series of events might still have occurred as they did if any one possible causal factor were to be removed. This is a particularly valuable technique when trying to understand how one thing led to another and the significance of a particular event or trend.

Consider the case of the outbreak of the Second World War, for example. What if Hitler had been killed in Munich when he attempted to overthrow the government in 1923? Would German democracy still have given way to dictatorship, totalitarianism and war in the 1930s? Such is the reasoning of the historian grappling with the issue of how far any one individual could have provoked such a profound and colossal event as a world war.

## Regressive method

The hypothetical approach detailed above relied upon a considerable number of documentary sources and oral accounts. The regressive method is another approach to understanding the past, typically employed when documentary evidence is lacking. The basic principle works on the assumption that from our knowledge of a particular time and place, we can infer something of what went before. Practitioners of the method, in the words of a great nineteenth-century historian, F. W. Maitland, work 'backwards from the known to the unknown, from the certain to the uncertain'. This approach is of particular relevance to the historians of issues for which few documentary sources have survived. It has been employed, for example, in the reconstruction of population history of England and Wales before the introduction of the Census (1801) or the compulsory recording of baptisms, marriages and funerals in parish registers (1538). The method relies upon the assumption that history is a continuum - that elements of the past can always be found in the present. Landscape historians employ this approach when they consult modern maps and attempt to reveal the geography of the past through the examination of such things as modern field boundaries and place names.

## Essay planning

An essay, by definition, is a short piece of writing – anything between about 500 and 5000 words. It is more discursive than a report, mostly written in complete, grammatically correct prose. It will rarely contain bullet points or subtitles.

The kind of essays you will be expected to write on a Humanities degree programme will be, primarily, evaluative rather than descriptive. They will be structured around key themes that weigh up the two sides of an argument, or the strengths and weaknesses of whatever is being assessed. It is structured around paragraphs; as a general rule each paragraph will make a distinct point.

Essay assignments take many forms – for example, some are direct questions, others are statements that the student is directed to discuss and evaluate. The first thing to do is to analyse the wording of the essay assignment very carefully – the misreading of questions is a common cause of failure. The acronym **'TAP'** is useful as an analytical tool; the **T** stands for topic, the **A** for actions the student is instructed to take, the **P** for parameters of the discussion. Each of these must be identified and addressed to ensure the relevance and completeness of the ensuing essay.

Here is an example: 'To what extent was religion the main cause of rebellion during the era of the 'mid-Tudor crisis'?'

The **T**opic is rebellion (NOT religion or the 'mid-Tudor crisis').

The **A**ction implicit in the phrase 'To what extent' is the consideration of all of the causes of rebellion in the period and the *evaluation* of their relative significance.

The **P**arameters of the discussion are defined by the term 'mid-Tudor crisis' which is usually identified as the period covered by the reigns of Edward VI and Mary I. Hence the Prayer Book Rebellion of 1549 and Wyatt's Rebellion of 1554 will be relevant while the Rebellion of the Northern Earl's in Elizabeth I's reign and the Pilgrimage of Grace in Henry VIII's will not.

The careful planning of an essay is of critical importance. An effective essay will be thematically structured. History essays structured around a narrative of events run the risk of merely 'telling the story' instead of analysing and evaluating key factors.

In the case of the rebellions essay discussed above, a number of factors can be identified: in addition to religion, these include social and economic factors, political factors, and cultural factors (e.g. xenophobia). Each of these provides a focus for each section of the essay.

## Cause and effect

In the following text the impact of the slave trade upon African society is explored using archaeological and historical evidence. It culminates in an attempt to use this evidence to establish a set of likely outcomes for any society, in any place and time, exposed to contact with external slave-reliant economies. These outcomes are broken down into socio=economic effects, effects on settlement, effects on social organisation.

## Towards a model: the impact of the Eighteenth Century Atlantic Slave Trade upon Africa

'The sudden increase in the demand for slaves cannot but have brought about considerable changes in the economic, social and therefore political structures of society.' (van Dantzig (1982), p.190)

Argument has raged over the debate regarding the impact of the Atlantic slave trade upon the indigenous peoples of West Africa. It is currently fashionable, and very likely correct, to assume that it was devastating in terms of the development of indigenous culture and that contemporary problems in parts of Africa can be linked directly to a colonial history spawned from a trade in humanity[578]. Less certain is the economic impact of the trade: some[579] trace the economic and demographic ruin of societies while others dispute such claims:

*'West African communities sold slaves for export with some regard to their capacity to do so without causing serious damage to their populations and economies and their chance of growth.'*[580]

Whether societies prospered or decayed as result of the sudden increased demand for slaves, it certainly brought about major economic and social changes and thus had a considerable impact upon the political structures of societies.[581]

---

578  e.g. Martin (1999)
579  e.g. Inikori (1982)
580  Fage in Inikori (1982), p.38
581  van Dantzig (1982), p.190; Martin (1970), p.217

Estimates for the volume of this traffic are also open to question despite there being a good deal of documentary evidence from ships' logs and the like. Inikori[582] estimates that no less than 15,400,000 slaves were carried across the Atlantic between 1450 and 1850, and almost three million more were exported by Muslim traders across the Sahara in the same period. Without needing to enter the historical debate regarding the accuracy of such figures, the general picture of trade on the grand scale will suffice for our present purposes. The appetite of Europe's colonial powers for slaves was insatiable by the middle of the eighteenth century.

Throughout the period the trade, ultimately, was a coastal one. Here captains of European slavers struck deals with black merchants - private traders and tribal chiefs. They traded their captives for European luxury items, in particular silks, velvets and gold-embroidered cloth.[583] According to Klein[584] *geribata*, an alcoholic drink brewed in Brazil, was highly prized by traders in Angola. Merchants from Luanda relied on imported alcohol and cloth as the means for procuring slaves from the interior, and the demand for gunpowder and firearms increased as the slave raids of the seventeenth century evolved into the wars of the eighteenth and nineteenth.[585] Along the Zambezi imported East Indian cloth and beads were exchanged for ivory and gold.[586] Foreign imports did not necessarily stifle indigenous manufacture: accounts exist which point to its role as a stimulus for the production of coarse cloth on the slave coast.[587]

England's involvement in the slave trade effectively began with the establishment of the Royal African Company in the late seventeenth century, sponsored by Charles II and designed originally to exploit the Guinea gold trade (hence the guinea coin). Fairly rapidly the trade in slaves took over but other goods continued to be exported from Africa to Europe and the colonies. Van Dantzig has identified three

---

582  Inkori (1982), p.20
583  van Dantzig (1982), p.198
584  Klein (1972), p.234
585  Klein (1999), p.114
586  Klein (1999), p.69
587  van Dantzig (1982), p.198

geographical 'belts' of commercial interest parallel to the Guinea Coast in early eighteenth century Africa:

*(1) to the west of Elimina an area where slaves were occasionally sold, but where the mainstay of the trade was in other products, particularly gold;*
*(2) between Elima and the mouth of the Volta an area of a 'mixed economy' in which the slave trade took ever growing importance and sometimes even replaced the gold trade;*
*(3) east of the Volta the real slave coast where slaves constituted the mainstay of the trade with Europeans, but which exported also commodities like palm oil, cotton cloth and ivory.*[588]

Throughout the period, as well as slaves, other goods continued to be traded at the coast. In addition to those listed above these included salt, copper, kola nuts, iron, beeswax, camwood, pepper, dried fish, beads and hides.

Slavery was an established institution in pre-colonial Africa - enslavement often being the penalty for misdemeanours and defeat in war. Indeed, some wars were fought solely with a view to taking captives: the kingdom of Dahomey fought their 'Annual Wars' to fulfil the 'Annual Customs' - the acquisition of sacrificial victims for the sacred rites.[589] What changed, as a result of European involvement, was the scale of such activity. Enslavement became the principal concern of both slave-producing areas and victim areas. In his autobiography, first published in 1789, Olaudah Equiano provided a vivid account of inter-tribal relations in the mid-eighteenth century:

*'when our people go out to till their land, they not only go in a body, but generally take their arms with them, for fear of a surprise; and when they apprehend an invasion they guard the avenues to their dwellings, by driving sticks into the ground, which are so sharp at on end as to pierce the foot, and are generally dipt in poison. From what I can recollect of these battles, they appear to have been irruptions of one little state or district on the other, to obtain prisoners or booty. Perhaps they were incited to this by those traders who brought the European*

---

588 van Dantzig (1982), p.189
589 Inikori (1982), p.48

goods [...] amongst us [...] When a trader wants slaves, he applies to a chief for them, and tempts him with wares [...] Accordingly, he falls on his neighbours, and a desperate battle ensues.'[590]

Equiano proceeds to describe a society preoccupied with, and organised for, warfare:

'We have firearms, bows and arrows, broad two-edged swords and javelins; we have shields also, which cover a man from head to foot. All are taught the use of the weapons. Even our women are warriors, and march boldly out to fight along with the men. Our whole district is a kind of militia [...]'[591]

The scale of warfare as a direct result of Europe's commercial activities was very considerable[592] and certainly greater than before. Regarding the 15.5 million Africans exported across the Atlantic between 1450 and 1850, Inikori estimates that half as many again died in the conflicts that procured these slaves or perished on the way to the coast. In addition, since the wars frequently took place at harvest and sowing times[593], millions more must have died in the famines and epidemics that ensued.[594]

The impact of these supposed slave wars is largely supposition too but one based on documentary and archaeological evidence for changes in social organisation, population growth, patterns of settlement and economic activity. Although Fage maintains the Atlantic trade had no noticeable impact upon African populations, Inikori claims the evidence in fact points to a significant fall in population during the period.[595] In addition to direct losses as a result of kidnapping, slave wars and the famines they engendered, he highlights the demographic impact of consequent economic instability. In particular security, as opposed to economics, became the main consideration of communities in making choices regarding settlement 'thus restricting the opportunities and incentives for

---

590   Carretta (1995), p.38-9
591   Carretta (1995), p.39
592   Inikori (1982), p.27
593   Becker and Martin (1982), p.118
594   Fage (1978), p.260
595   Inikori (1982), p.29

economic growth and development in sub-Saharan Africa'.[596] Such factors resulted in the wholesale desertion of large areas of fertile land in south-eastern Ghana and south-western Tongo, former inhabitants retreating to remote hilltops, comparatively densely populated in this period, and coastal towns.[597] For many displaced communities defence became the main consideration, at the cost of accessibility, communications and suitable building sites.[598] To this day places that once supported substantial populations, such as the northern and western Oyo territory, are virtual wildernesses.[599] Elsewhere, such as Yoruba land, communities stayed put but constructed massive defences around their settlements – multivallate rings of ramparts and ditches.[600] Societies, such as the kingdom of Loango, were fundamentally changed in terms of their political and social structure by their involvement in the slave trade.[601]

Van Dantzig[602] has commented on the political, cultural and economic implications of the trade. Those co-ordinating the trade – chiefs and a merchant elite – became hugely powerful. Success in slave wars relied upon the pooling of resources, and kingdoms like Dahomey came to rely on extreme centralism. African culture, particularly in coastal areas, was mixed with that of South America and Europe, destroying irrevocably what has been described as 'authentic African civilisation'.[603] New plants were imported into Africa from the Americas, including tobacco, peanuts, cacao, coffee, manioc and maize. The new food crops provided the potential for Africa to sustain larger populations. Collectively they represented a revolution in foodstuffs at least as significant as that of the introduction of the potato into Europe and Asia.[604] In addition pigs and some citrus fruits were imported from Europe, and Swedish bar iron was forged by African smiths into efficient agricultural tools.[605] Contact with Europe also introduced new tokens of exchange. In the eighteenth century

---

596 Inikori (1982), p.28
597 van Dantzig (1982), p.195
598 Morton-Williams (1982), p.170
599 Morton-Williams (1982), p.182
600 van Dantzig (1982), p.195
601 Martin (1970), p.217
602 van Dantzig (1982), p.200
603 van Dantzig (1982), p.201
604 Klein (1999), p.62
605 Klein (1999), p.106

beads and bronze bracelets ('manillas') sufficed but in the eighteenth they ceased to be prized by African merchants. Surprisingly Portuguese traders on the Slave Coast in the early eighteenth century purchased slaves with Brazilian gold and, from the seventeenth century on the Upper Guinea Coast, with Spanish American silver minted into 'pieces of eight'. Indigenous currencies, particularly cowry shells, continued to play an important part in transactions.[606]

Herbert Klein has noted that 'enslavement 'facilitated' war and made it economically more viable'.[607] Historians of the African slave trade from the seventeenth to the nineteenth centuries identify an escalation of warfare and new levels of violence and conflict that were mostly the result of that trade and its aftermath.[608] Warfare however was endemic among African societies long before the start of the eighteenth century and wars continued to be fought over issues like succession and territorial claims.[609] Curtin[610] has identified two models for the process of enslavement: an economic model whereby the likely cost of gaining captives is measured against the price they would fetch; and a political model in which the prestige gained by a warrior chief launching a war was of greater importance than economic gain. In fact many captives were taken and sold into slavery as a result of religion – Islamic *jihads* in the region of the Upper Niger.[611] Where simple ambushes may once have been the norm, full-scale slave wars, such as those between Oyo and Dahomey, starting in 1719, began to break out. Meillassoux (1982) has written about the full-scale militarization of societies such as the Mossi kingdoms, permanently geared into war and led by a warrior aristocracy. Furthermore he is convinced that the political structure of such societies was shaped by the trade in slaves and not other commodities such as (and especially) gold:

*'This slaving activity and permanent military deployment that it engendered, explains better than the production and trade in gold, the constitution of aristocrats and warlike states [...] Great war machines*

---

606 Klein (1999), p.107-8
607 Klein (1999), p.117
608 Inikori (1982), p.34
609 Klein (1999), p.72
610 Curtin (1975), p.156
611 Klein (1999), p.59

*were not designed for establishing permanent organized productive activity, nor for its control. The production of gold was mostly the work not of slaves belonging to a ruler, but of independent populations. The peaceful merchants who maintained contact with these gold panners were more suited to preserving the social conditions of production than destructive warriors.'*[612]

The obvious target of such predatory societies was the people of the frontier land and border villages. Such areas became sparsely populated as a result.[613] As victim societies fled to the coast or mountains, societies reliant on taking captives were obliged either to launch raids beyond the frontier zone, or to resort to raiding their neighbours. Alpers (1975) has described the disintegration into civil war of the chiefs of Macuana in the second half of the nineteenth century, frustrated by the desertion of the peripheral areas they had previously depended upon. Many societies played the dual role of victim and predator: the need to fortify villages and to develop other forms of defence, promoted the emergence of a warrior elite which enabled former victim societies to adopt a predatory economy. The escalation of warfare brought with it a rapid evolution of military tactics and weaponry, crucial to those regimes that chose to attack their better defended warlike neighbours than the increasingly remote peasant communities of the hinterland.[614]

New concentrations of population, in the vicinity of the chief slave ports, emerged as other areas became sparsely populated.[615] Only a small proportion of this population however appears to have been directly involved in the slave trade.[616] Although the coastal demand for slaves in West Africa took precedence over other commodities, and doubtless compromised other forms of production[617], the coastal zone was a hive of economic activity. In addition to the textiles and mats produced at the coast, slaves from the interior were bartered for the highly prized sea-salt produced in the vicinity of the ports.[618]

---

612 Meillassoux in Inikori (1982), p.80
613 Becker and Martin (1982), p.122
614 Meillassoux in Inikori (1982), p.78-9
615 van Dantzig (1982), p.201
616 van Dantzig (1982), p.198
617 Meillassoux (1982), p.96
618 Klein (1999), p.59

These ports-of-trade in some instances appear to have been virtual autonomies, dominated economically, and probably politically, by oligarchies of slave-sellers.

## Some conclusions

The Atlantic slave trade of the seventeenth, eighteenth and nineteenth centuries had much in common with that of the trade in slaves associated with the Roman Empire. Territorial expansion, and the new economic demands it created, was, in both cases, the primary factor. The imperial demand for labour necessitated looking beyond the empire in order to recruit a workforce. Most slaves derived from places beyond the imperial periphery were acquired by down-the-line trade arrangements that relied upon the establishment of commercial relations with external suppliers. A slave from such a context, typically, was the victim of violence at the moment of initial captivity.

Taking the Atlantic slave trade as a case study, a number of generalisations can be made regarding the likely impact of a slave-using empire upon slave-supplying and slave-producing states. These can be grouped under the headings of *socio-economic effects*, *effects upon settlement*, and *effects upon social organisation*. It is important to acknowledge however that many of the effects described could be, and in some parts of Africa doubtless were, the consequence of other factors, including commercial activity in which the slave trade was not a dominant feature.

*Socio-economic effects:*

A substantial and enduring demand for slaves has a demographic impact. In some areas there will be shrinkage of population, in others there may be a concentration of population. Population growth generally, due to related factors such as warfare and disease, may well be retarded.

Existing market places may show signs of expansion if they are sited on slave trade routes. If the trade is, ultimately, an overseas trade, expanded and new ports-of-trade are likely to appear on the coasts of slave supplying states.

Luxury imports, such as alcohol and manufactured wares, are introduced in substantial quantity via these markets.

There may well be an increased manufacture of indigenous goods, particularly in coastal regions, to meet both coastal demands and the needs of middlemen purchasing slaves from the hinterland.

The use of existing and new forms of currency, both indigenous forms and those associated with the slave-purchasing empire, will increase during the course of the trade.

*Effects upon settlement:*

Heightened commercial activity, particularly in coastal zones, will stimulate the process of urbanisation.

Settlement sites in slave producing areas will become better defended.

A preference will develop for settlement at places that offer natural defensive advantages, such as hilltop locations.

Some settlements, especially those with few natural defensive advantages, will be abandoned altogether.

*Effects upon social organisation:*

A thriving trade in slaves generates aggression and, sometimes, warfare.

Increased levels of warfare will stimulate, and be produced by, the development of warrior elites and a general militarization of participating societies.

Successful slave-producing states will become stronger in both economic and political respects. They may also become territorially bigger. They will become more centralised with less political autonomy for peripheral communities.

In addition to the emergence / expansion of warrior elites, a powerful merchant interest will develop, particularly at, and in the vicinity of, major ports-of-trade.

## Summary

Slavery was well established in Africa long before the opening up of the Atlantic slave trade. However, the scale of this trade was unparalleled in African history and it had a colossal impact upon African societies, the resonance of which is felt to the present day. In some areas, such as the Guinea Coast, it brought a measured prosperity, in others, such as Kayor and Baol, it wrought a long term socio-economic crisis, characterised by civil war, raids and famine.[619] For many areas, such as Senegal, it paved the way for the imperial annexation of territory.[620] For all concerned, those that gained something and those that lost, it heralded a cultural upheaval.

## Essay writing

Whatever else you decide to do when formatting your manuscript you need to be sure you are **consistent** throughout. You are likely to receive specific guidance for specific assignments but, as a general rule, it is recommended you adhere to the following:

- Submit your essay as a Word document
- Use a standard, unadorned font – Arial or Times New Roman are ideal
- Text should be font size 11 or 12
- Leave a space between lines: 1.5 or double should suffice
- Indent each new paragraph OR indicate a new paragraph by inserting a blank line between it and the one before
- Number the pages
- Follow the guidance below regarding references (footnotes and bibliographies)
- Only use one space after a full-stop

---

619 Becker and Martin (1982), p.118
620 Becker and Martin (1982), p.125

- Use single quotation marks for everything except when you need to indicate a quote within a quote, in which case use double quotation marks
- Italicise names of books, films, paintings, locomotives, boats, newspapers, foreign words
- Spell out numbers up to 100, use numerals thereafter (except when giving measurements e.g. 10 per cent, 25 cm)
- Leave one space between the number and the measurement – 25 cm NOT 25cm
- Use 'per cent' not %
- For numbers over twenty, use hyphens e.g. thirty-six
- When using someone's initials use full stops and spaces – A. J. P. Taylor NOT A J P Taylor, and NOT A.J.P.Taylor
- Do not use full stops after abbreviated titles e.g. Mr, Mrs, Dr
- Dates: Day Month Year (no commas between) e.g. 11 November 1918
- Use British-English, not American-English spellings (analyse, counsellor, organise etc.)
- Note here the formatting for e.g. and etc.
- Make sure all illustrations have a caption

## Report writing

Reports should be concise, clear and objective. Use headings, sub-headings and numbering to identify the main points that are being made and the information that is being presented.

A report usually begins with an **Abstract** or **Summary**. This is an outline of what the report contains, a succinct description that enables the reader to decide whether or not to continue reading.

The **Introduction** comes next – like the introduction to an essay it defines the topic, the problems it poses, and its context.

The **Method** section that follows summarises the plan and procedure of the research that has led to the report. This will include comments on such things as materials used, places visited, sources read, and people interviewed.

The **Results** or **Findings** present the information and data that was gathered. Where appropriate present this in graphic forms such as tables and images. As a general rule of thumb you should include such material only when it advances or further clarifies your main purpose / argument. Avoid using graphics when they serve no purpose beyond a decorative one.

The **Discussion** or **Analysis** is the place where the findings are fully interpreted in relation to the issues and problems identified in the introduction. This is likely to be the longest and certainly, in some ways, the most important section of the whole report.

The **Conclusion and Recommendations** sums up the previous section and makes recommendations regarding, for example, areas that would benefit from further enquiry.

**Checklist for a good report** (adapted by the Plymouth University Learning Development team from Burns and Sinfield, 2008):

1. What is the purpose of this report, and has it fulfilled that clearly?
2. Are your ideas presented logically so that your reader can follow and get sufficient information to make the decisions you hope for? Is there enough accurate, relevant material, or too much?
3. Does it cover the key points? Do you analyse your evidence/data to support your points?
4. Does your conclusion follow logically from your arguments, and do your recommendations follow logically from your conclusions?
5. Are the language, tone, style and pitch clear, direct and formal, suitable for the reader and the subject?
6. Is the grammar, punctuation and spelling correct? Is the report the correct length?
7. Is the layout simple, clear, logical and consistent, with conventional sections, headings, labels and numbers? Is the right material in the right sections?
8. If illustrations such as figures and tables have been included, are they clear and purposeful, usefully integrated and properly referenced?
9. Have you used an appropriate number and range of sources? Have all sources and references been acknowledged, in the main body and at the end in a list of references?
10. Should there be a glossary? If there is one, is it comprehensive?

11. Are the appendices clearly labelled? Is the reader directed to each appendix in the body of the report?
12. Have you left the report on one side for a while before going back to review and edit it?

## Referencing: Harvard and MHRA

Although science students will usually be asked to use Harvard style referencing, historians and many other humanities students in the UK use the MHRA system of referencing. The MHRA style guide can be accessed at:

http://www.mhra.org.uk/Publications/Books/StyleGuide/download.shtml

An electronic MHRA reference generator provided by Queen's University, Belfast, can be found at:

http://www.qub.ac.uk/cite2write/mhra3b.html

The following is based on the MHRA (Modern Humanities Research Association) style guide which can be downloaded for free from:

http://www.mhra.org.uk/Publications/Books/StyleGuide/download.shtml.

## Referencing: bibliographies

A bibliography is an alphabetized list of all books, articles and primary sources consulted that appears at the end of your essay or research project. Each item should be set out as follows:

### Books
- the author's name is inverted, with the surname appearing first, and initials or forename as on title page
- the full title of the book in italics
- the place of publication
- the name of the publisher
- the date of publication

- all entries end in a full-stop

So, for example,
Clark, J. C. D, *Revolution and Rebellion: State and Society in England in the Seventeenth and Eighteenth Centuries* (Cambridge: Cambridge University Press, 1986).

**Edited Books**
Baumann, G., ed., *The Written Word: Literacy in Transition*, Wolfson College Lectures 1985 (Oxford: Clarendon Press, 1986).

**Articles:**
- the author's name is inverted, with surname appearing first, then initials or forename
- the title of the article in single inverted commas
- the name of the journal in italics
- the volume number or numbers of the journal
- the date of publication in brackets
- the page extent numbers of the article (i.e. what page it starts and finishes on).

So, for example,
Clark, J. C. D., 'England's Ancient Regime', *Past and Present*, 117 (1993), 19-37.

**Articles or Essays in Books:**
Anglo, Sydney, 'Image-Making: The Means and the Limitations', in *The Tudor Monarchy*, ed. by John Guy (London: Arnold, 1997), pp. 16-42.

**Article in a Newspaper:**
Schmidt, M., 'Tragedy of Three Star-Crossed Lovers', *The Times*, 1 February 1990, p. 14.

**Reference Works:**
*Dictionary of the Middle Ages*, ed. by Joseph R. Strayer (New York: Scribner, 1982).

**Theses and Dissertations**
Ingram, Robert, 'Historical Drama in Great Britain from 1935 to the Present' (unpublished Ph.D thesis, University of London, 1988).

*Web Pages:*
Increasingly a large amount of very good material is available on the web; but alas there is also a lot of rubbish out there in the ether, so please use caution and only use trusted and reputable historical sites.

When citing electronic sources try to capture as much detail as possible:
- the author of the article
- the title of the article in single quotation marks
- the institution with which the article is associated
- the full web address
- the day on which the article was accessed. This is important since web-based material constantly changes and some sites are inaccessible at future dates.

Smith, Bob, 'Evanston Public Library Strategic Plan, 2000-2010: A Decade of Outreach', Evanston Public Library, http://www.epl.org.library/strategic-plan-00.html (accessed 3 October 2012).

## Referencing: footnotes and endnotes

As well as bringing together all works consulted in a bibliography, you should acknowledge either in footnotes or endnotes your source every time you quote an author or present information which comes entirely from the same source. Footnotes as the name suggests appear at the bottom of the page, endnotes at the end of the essay, before the Bibliography. You may use either system.

- Use a footnote whenever a quotation, a summary of ideas, or paraphrase is used.
- Footnotes must provide complete publication information of the text. (Author, Title, place of publication, publisher, year, page extent - for articles and essays - and page number). Subsequent references can use a shortened form of author and page only (see below). Titles of books and journals must be in italics or underlined, article titles are to be in quotations.
- Notes are single spaced. Numbers should be consecutive.

Short quotations of two lines or less should be enclosed in single inverted commas (') and incorporated in the body of your paragraph. Longer quotations of more than 40 words should start on a new line and be indented so they stand alone in the centre of the page. In all cases the quotation should be followed by footnote in numbered sequence, 1, 2, 3, etc.

*Inserting a footnote in Microsoft Word*

Step 1: click INSERT
Step 2: click REFERENCE, then FOOTNOTE or ENDNOTE
Step 3: click INSERT
Step 4: this opens a box at the bottom of the page for you to write in the reference details.

*Inserting a footnote in the text*

A superscript footnote should appear in the text at the end of a direct quote from a book, article or document, or at the end of a sentence where a work or idea from a work has been referred to. e.g. In the text one might write:

*According to Professor Tom Wilson, 'the idea of the electronic library has emerged as a model for future systems, already implemented in some forms and to some degree in various places'.*
Here is the corresponding note:

1. Tom Wilson, '"In the Beginning Was the Word": Social and Economic Factors in Scholarly Electronic Communication', History Library, 13 (1999), 99-108 (p. 107).

*Subsequent references*

The first time you refer to a work you should set out the details of the book or article in the same way as the bibliography above, except that you now include the page number of the quotation or reference, AND the surname of the author comes AFTER the forename.

So, for example,
1. J. C. D. Clark, *Revolution and Rebellion: State and Society in England in*

*the Seventeenth and Eighteenth Centuries* (Cambridge: Cambridge University Press, 1986), p.142.
2. J. C. D. Clark, 'England's Ancien Regime', *Past and Present*, 117 (1993), 19-37 (p.22).

The second time you refer to a work, and every time thereafter, you should abbreviate the reference to author, short title or identification in the bibliography by date of publication, and page number.

So, for example,
3. Clark, *Revolution and Rebellion*, pp.156-9.
4. Clark, 'Ancient Regime', p.25.
This last aspect of footnoting avoids the need to use terms that do sometimes appear in history books such as *op.cit.* and *ibid.*

## Book reviews

The writing of a book review is commonly set as a task for undergraduate Humanities students and is a skill that any aspiring academic should expect to use at a postgraduate and professional level.

A book review begins with a careful reading of the book! Start by looking carefully at its format and structure; chapter headings will usually be useful in helping you to understand the author's objectives. As you read consider how authoritative the text is in relation to the information upon which the text is based – footnotes, endnotes, appendices and bibliographies will be especially important in determining this. Find out as much as you can about the author to help you to determine his / her validity as an expert in the field. Acquire as much contextual knowledge about the subject as you can – academic texts in the 'real world' are 'peer-reviewed', in other words, experts are reviewed by their fellows. Consider the clarity of the author's argument as well as its strength as an idea. In the process consider the audience at which the book is aimed: is it inscrutable to the lay reader because it is directed at a highly specialised readership or is it just badly written?

The review itself should begin with full bibliographical details of the book, including such things as its ISBN number, number of pages, and number of illustrations (sometimes listed as 'plates'). Your introduction is likely to summarise the content and purpose of the book as well as your main thoughts about its merits and its limitations. The body of the view will expand these, identifying particular areas of interest and particular problems. The conclusion will offer a final assessment and a summative comment on the contribution of this text to the literature of the subject as a whole. Like the book itself, your review should be interesting, informed, well-written; indeed, as a form of journalism it lends itself to the snappy, word-bite, witty strategies of an effective columnist. Even if the book is not a good read try to make certain that your review is!

EXAMPLE:

*Digging for Richard: how archaeology found the king.* By Mike Pitts. Thames and Hudson. 2014. 208 pp. £18.95.

The story of Richard III is as gripping as any in royal biography. From dutiful brother (his motto: 'Loyalty Me Binds'), fighting side-by-side with Edward IV and George, Duke of Clarence, in the field at Tewkesbury 1471, to the tragedies of his short reign, 1483-85, his is as dramatic as it gets. And it is as a *dramatis persona* that, even now, four hundred years since Shakespeare's play was first performed, he is best remembered. Of course, the whole Richard III obsession of modern times, since Horace Walpole expressed his 'historic doubts' in 1768, is entirely to do with unravelling the fact from the fiction. Thus Mike Pitts lays out his account of the discovery and interpretation of Richard's remains in the form of a play – a drama with a prologue in place of a preface, acts in place of chapters, and an epilogue in place of a conclusion. Whether or not Ricardian investigations of this kind are of any great importance in advancing our knowledge and understanding of the past, they are great fun and Pitts' book is certainly entertaining.

In 'Act I' Pitts explores the making of the legend and provides a conventional version of the historical narrative that underpins it. This book however is not a history of a king but a history an archaeological excavation and its aftermath, written by an expert in that field, one more commonly associated with prehistory, notably the remains of early humans (*homo heidelbergensis*), discovered in a quarry at Boxgrove in Sussex, and the Neolithic and Bronze Age archaeology of the Stonehenge-Avebury World Heritage Site complex. For several years he has been the editor of 'British Archaeology', the much admired organ of the Council for British Archaeology. That this particularly excavation should, ultimately, warrant anything much being written about it, let alone this 200 page book, would have seemed most unlikely to Pitts and the rest of the archaeological community, including those who were commissioned by the writer and doyenne of the Richard III Society, Philippa Langley, to undertake it. After all, she believed she had found a lost king's grave in a car park in Leicester beside a lone surviving wall believed to be a remnant of Greyfriars friary, because, when she stood there, 'I had goose bumps so badly I was actually freezing cold to my bones'. The extraordinary thing is she was absolutely right and the bones, subsequently found to be, almost certainly, Richard's, were discovered on the very first day of the excavation.

Of course, Langley had done her historical homework and the archaeologists had searched every record in developing their understanding of the Greyfriars context. Together, with little reward, they had engaged in a geophysical survey of the site. Confident they would gain much from the excavation but pretty convinced the Ricardians would be frustrated in their very particular quest, the archaeologists from the University of Leicester, directed by Matthew Morris, started digging in August 2012. In the event everyone was delighted with the results: Matthew Morris found a church and Philippa Langley had her king. Channel 4, which filmed it all, had a thrilling programme to broadcast. The DNA testing and full autopsy followed, no doubt tempering Ricardian celebrations with the uncomfortable truth that not everything Shakespeare wrote was a pack of lies – whatever else he may have been in life, Richard III had a severely twisted spine that very likely gave him a misshapen appearance, his right shoulder blade rising notably higher than his left, his chest enlarged. He was a man of squat stature who, but for his scoliosis, would have been considerably taller.

Pitts has written a concise record of events that sheds as much light upon ourselves as our ancestors in its commentary on the personalities and motivations of those involved in the project, as well as the broader media and public interest in it all. Beyond this he has succeeded in pulling off that hardest of tricks for the writer of popular histories: even though we already know how the story ends, this remains a gripping account. Francis Pryor's remarks on the back sleeve - 'It's a real page-turner', 'I couldn't put it down' etc. – may have a whiff of hyperbole but, in fact, they come pretty close to the mark. Like Pryor in his *Britain AD: a quest for Arthur, England and the Anglo-Saxons* (2004), Pitts has demonstrated here great skill in weaving together a discussion of our perceptions of heritage and the history and archaeology upon which they are based.

*Digging for Richard* is copiously illustrated with images from medieval manuscripts, portraits, and photographs. The 'Epilogue' includes an interesting, though brief, summary of the equally fascinating advance in recent Ricardian studies – the relocation of the Bosworth battlefield following intensive archaeological survey. It predates, but anticipates, the furore unleashed by the debate regarding the burial of Richard's remains: something that might usefully be added to a second edition.[621]

## Literature review

Some major projects, such as the writing of academic dissertations, necessitate a formal review of the literature (books, articles, reports, websites etc.) on the subject.

*Structure*
Like most academic papers, literature reviews are likely to contain three sections: an **introduction** outlining the subject area; the **body** of the review containing the discussion of the literature; and a **conclusion** at the end.

*Introduction:* This, typically, provides an overview and contextualization of the topic of the literature review. It identifies the aims and objectives of the project.

*Body:* This contains a discussion of sources and is suitably organised (e.g. chronologically, thematically, methodologically). This might be written in a full prose essay format or in bullet-point format in the form of an annotated/expanded bibliography.

---

[621] Andrew Pickering, *Royal Studies Journal*, issue 4, vol. 3, no. 1, 2016

*Conclusions:* This summarises findings that have drawn from reviewing the literature so far. It might identify what areas, if any, are underrepresented in the literature reviewed and how these gaps will be addressed by the research methodology (e.g. site visits, interviews, work placement.)

## The Peasants' Revolt, 1381: literature review (Claire Gore)

*This comprehensive review of the literature on the subject of the Peasants' Revolt was written by a Level 6 History, Heritage and Archaeology student, Claire Gore, in preparation for her dissertation on the subject. The introduction to her work, largely comprising a detailed study of the available medieval sources, is not included here.*

Interest in the Peasants' Rebellion has waxed and waned over the last century and a half. In the nineteenth century it was valuable evidence to Whiggish constitutionalists of Britain's unique history, in comparison with its fellow European states, of shaping a liberal parliamentary democracy: the revolt by the commoners a positive stepping stone nudging democracy along.[622] Stubbs didn't let his liberal views get in the way of a good yarn and in the second volume of his *The Constitutional History of England* he continued to paint a colourful picture of the rebels as stupid rustics. Stow suggests that Stubbs naively took the chroniclers' descriptions at face value and was not skilled at understanding or portraying *mentalités*.[623]

In the same period as Stubbs was writing, Engels and Marx were formulating a more radical idea of political development that would shed national considerations of statehood in favour of a pan-European collective of workers. They believed that developing European polities had facilitated the creation of a rich gentry, the

---

[622] The Whig approach to the revolt is exemplified in Stubbs, *Constitutional History*; S. Berger with M. Donovan and K. Passmore, 'Apologias for the nation-state in Western Europe since 1800', S. Berger, M. Donovan and K. Passmore, *Writing National Histories. Western Europe since 1800* (London: Routledge, 1999), pp. 3-14, p. 5.

[623] G. B. Stow, 'Stubbs, Steel, and Richard II as Insane: The Origin and Evolution of an English Historiographical Myth', *Proceedings of the American Philosophical Society, 143* (1999), 601-638, p. 613, n. 49.

'bourgeoisie', who were continuing deliberately to monopolise wealth and the means of production to the detriment of the lower classes but would inevitably be overturned as the urban lower classes reached critical mass and sufficient political consciousness.[624] The Peasants' Revolt had a part, albeit small, to play in this theory: the rebels attempt to overturn the oppressive state proved the medieval existence of class oppression, although they could not have succeeded in that period due to their pre-capitalist condition and lack of modern ideological consciousness.[625]

This nineteenth-century concern with lower class politics and economics engendered a slight *fin-de-siècle* interest in the revolt, with works by Oman, Réville and Trevelyan, but modern interest in the event really developed in the 1960s, at a time when socialist ideology was becoming culturally mainstream, even academically dominant.[626]

The Marxist historian, Hilton, led this interest, producing seminal works such as *Bond Men Made Free* and *The English Peasantry in the Later Middle Ages).*[627] A group of historians, including Razi, Dyer, Müller and T. Aston, coalesced around Hilton and *Past and Present*, the periodical that he founded, and focused their research on local records, especially manor court records of the English Midlands. These meticulously researched works, albeit with an underlying, but increasingly softening socialist belief in all-pervasive medieval class warfare, have transformed our understanding of the lives of the medieval lower classes.[628] Other economic-historical schools of

---

[624] D. Townson, *The New Penguin Dictionary of Modern History 1789-1945* (London: Penguin, 1995); K. Marx and F. Engels, *The Communist Manifesto*, G. Stedman Jones (ed.), translated by S. Moore (London: Penguin, 2002).
[625] F. Engels, *The Peasant War in Germany*, in *The Peasants' Revolt*, R. B. Dobson (ed.); Faith, 'The 'Great Rumour'', pp. 399-402.
[626] C. Dyer, 'A New Introduction', R. Hilton, *Bond Men Made Free. Medieval Peasant Movements and The English Rising of 1381 (Abingdon: Routledge, 2003),* pp. ix-xv, pp. x-xi.
[627] Hilton, *Bond Men Made Free. Medieval Peasant Movements and The English Rising of 1381* (Abingdon: Routledge, 2003); R. H. Hilton, *The English Peasantry in the Later Middle Ages. The Ford Lectures for 1973 and Related Studies* (Oxford: Clarendon Press 1975).
[628] For example: C. Dyer, *Making a Living in the Middle Ages. The People of Britain 850-1520* (Newhaven, CT: Yale University Press, 2009); C. Dyer, *Everyday Life in Medieval England;* R. Faith, 'The "Great Rumour"'; M. Müller, 'Social control and the hue and cry; J. Birrell, 'Manorial Custumals Reconsidered', pp. 3-37.

thought, such as the neo-Malthusians, led by Postan, and the more neo-classical, Smithian economic-historians from Cambridge, such as Hatcher, Britnell and Campbell, have challenged the economic and social theories of the Marxists.[629] Stone's work, *Decision-Making in Medieval Agriculture*, part of this Cambridge school, is an important work for the Peasants' Revolt as it provides evidence of the economic autonomy and sophistication of the lower classes during the period.[630] Raftis' 'Toronto School' also disagrees with the Marxists but on historical grounds, arguing that 'conciliation was more common than conflict'.[631] Hatcher and Bailey's *Modelling the Middle Ages* clearly lays out the views of these different schools of thought.[632]

Since the flurry of interest in the 1960s and 1970s, remaining disciples of these original schools have continued to bat economic and social arguments back and forth, especially in *Past and Present*, whilst moving towards a more politically centrist, less economically theoretical position.[633]

Also written at the end of the 1960s, Dobson's *The Peasants' Revolt of 1381* was sympathetic to the lower classes but without such an obviously socialist ideology and containing an invaluable set of primary sources.[634] Over the subsequent years, political histories of the revolt have been sporadic and have tended to focus on telling the

---

[629] M. M. Postan, *Essays on Medieval Agriculture and General Problems of the Medieval Economy* (Cambridge: Cambridge University Press, 2008); J. Hatcher, 'English Serfdom and Villeinage: towards a reassessment', *Past and Present*, 90 (1981), 3-39; R. Britnell, *The Commercialisation of English Society, 1000-1500* (Cambridge: Cambridge University Press, 1993); B. M. S. Campbell, *English seigneurial agriculture 1250-1450* (Cambridge: Cambridge University Press, 2006).
[630] D. Stone, *Decision-Making in Medieval Agriculture* (Oxford: Oxford University Press, 2005).
[631] Z. Razi, 'The Toronto School's Reconstitution of Medieval Peasant Society: A Critical View', *Past and Present*, 85 (1979), 141-157, p. 153; J. A. Raftis, *Tenure and Mobility: Studies in the Social History of the Medieval English Village* (Toronto: Pontifical Institute of Mediaeval Studies, 1964).
[632] Hatcher and Bailey, *Modelling the Middle Ages. The History & Theory of England's Economic Development* (Oxford: Oxford University Press, 2001).
[633] C. Dyer, 'The English Medieval Village Community', *Journal of British Studies* volume 33, no. 4 (October 1994), pp. 407-429; C. Dyer, *Everyday Life in Medieval England* (London: Hambledon and London, 2000).
[634] R. B. Dobson, *The Peasants' Revolt* (London: Macmillan, 1970).

exciting story of the revolt. In 1985, Brooks made a brief foray out of Anglo-Saxon England to consider the logistics of the revolt.[635] His fascinating essay, 'The Organisation and Achievements of the Peasants of Kent and Essex in 1381', benefits from his extensive knowledge of Anglo-Saxon military movement in England so that Brooks is able to make intelligent calculations about the level of planning, strategy and logistics involved.

Thirty years after Dobson, Dunn's 2002 *The Peasants' Revolt. England's Failed Revolution of 1381* is a thorough study of the revolt, covering the uprising throughout the country, including the important local politics, factional element in London.[636] Dunn's focus on the actions of individuals in the period naturally leads him to short term political causation and the widespread discontent that the lower classes felt towards the gentry and steers clear of the economists' causation interests. It still forms, with Dobson's, one of the two more politically neutral seminal works on the revolt.

The two very recent popular histories should be mentioned in passing. In 2009 Jones' *Summer of Blood. The Peasants' Revolt of 1381* was published and, in 2014, Barker's *England, arise. The People, The King and The Great Revolt of 1381* was published.[637] Both of these, especially Jones', are lively tales full of the immense drama and historical entertainment of the revolt. Although Jones book is not academically referenced and thus not used in this essay, he provides a very helpful brief overview of sources and historiography. *England, arise* is more difficult to categorise. Barker generally focuses more on the detail than analysis. It is referenced academically but, for example, although Barker stresses the importance of urban uprisings, she does not cite S. Cohn or Lantschner amongst, many other surprising omissions. Barker is also unusual in arguing that Richard II,

---

[635] N. Brooks, 'The Organisation and Achievements of the Peasants of Kent and Essex in 1381', in *Studies in Medieval History Presented to R. H. C. Davis,* Mayr-Harting, H., and Moore, R. I. (eds.) (London: Hambledon Press, 1985), pp. 247-270.
[636] A. Dunn, *The Peasants' Revolt. England's Failed Revolution of 1381* (Stroud: Tempus, 2004)
[637] D. Jones, *Summer of Blood. The Peasants' Revolt of 1381* (London: Harper Collins, 2009); J. Barker, *England, Arise. The People, The King and The Great Revolt of 1381* (London: Little, Brown, 2014).

'the boy-king', supported the rebels.[638]

Of far greater academic value, since the late 1990s Samuel Cohn has extensively studied all the sizeable revolts of England and Europe in the late middle ages.[639] Cohn's main argument is that the post-Black Death period was economically favourable to the newly prosperous rural and urban lower classes and that they seized the opportunity for power and freedom with a 'lust for liberty', an optimism about their potential for agency.[640] Stating that the 1381 revolt has had all the academic attention, he has largely avoided it to focus on all the others.[641] However, his comparative work has inevitably shone fresh light on the 1381 revolt: not least in demonstrating how normal it was within factional, conflictive fourteenth century urban England and Europe and in highlighting particular tension between monastic landlords and their tenants.[642] Cohn is largely supported by Lantschner whose study of late medieval urban conflict leads him to argue that medieval society was inherently far more conflicted than historians have recognised and that revolt should be understood as a normal, expected part of political negotiation.[643]

Several biographies of the period also cover the events of the Peasants' Revolt and are particularly helpful in describing the personal and managerial weaknesses of the seigneurial class and their impact on causation. Ormrod's *Edward III* runs to over 700 pages,

---

[638] J. Barker, *England, arise. The People, The King & The Great Revolt of 1381* (London: Little Brown, 2014), p. 393.
[639] S. K. Cohn, 'After the Black Death: labour legislation and attitudes towards labour in late-medieval western Europe', *Economic History Review*, 60 (2007), pp. 457-485.
; S. K. Cohn, 'Popular Insurrection and the Black Death: A Comparative View', *Past and Present*, 195 (supplement 2) (2007), 188-204; Cohn, *Popular Protest in Late Medieval English Towns Popular Protest in Late Medieval English Towns* (Cambridge: Cambridge University Press, 2013); Cohn, *Popular Protest in Late Medieval Europe* (Manchester: Manchester University Press, 2004); Cohn, *Lust for Liberty: The Politics of Social Revolt in Medieval Europe, 1200-1425; Italy, France and Flanders* (Cambridge, MA: Harvard University Press, 2006).
[640] Cohn, *Lust for Liberty*,
[641] Cohn, *Popular Protest in Late Medieval English Towns*, pp. 3-4.
[642] Cohn, *Popular Protest in Late Medieval English Towns*, pp. 6-7 and 249.
[643] P. Lantschner, *The Logic of Political Conflict in Medieval Cities: Italy and the Southern Low Countries, 1370-1440* (Oxford: Oxford University Press, 2015); P. Lantschner, 'Revolts and the political order of cities in the late Middle Ages', *Past and Present*, 225 (2014), 3-46.

Saul's *Richard II* is similarly comprehensive and Goodman has written a really useful and thorough, if highly favourable, portrait of John of Gaunt.[644]

Another area of historiography relevant to study of the revolt is that of the so-called 'literary turn'. Growth of literacy and changing perception and use of text during the late middle ages is a major area of academic study in itself, drawing together literary scholars and late medieval historians.[645] Scholars of a 'literary turn' have focused on ballads, for example the *Geste of Robin Hood*, (which, although only known to us as a fifteenth-century ballad, had key fourteenth century elements) needs combined literary and historical knowledge to interpret it.[646] Following Stock's illumination of the transformative nature of the growth of literacy in the eleventh and twelfth centuries in *The Implications of Literacy*, Clanchy's *From Memory to Written Record* (second edition) emphasises literacy's reach right down to lower class agricultural management.[647] Justice and Strohm, bringing their literary approach to bear on the middle ages in works such as *Writing and Rebellion* and *Hochon's Arrow* have shown that literacy had an important role in differentiating the lower class in the eyes of the growing gentry class, but that use of legal documents and propaganda allowed the lower class to harness the tools of the seigneurial class: for example, in ideas of 'commonweal', use of handbills and through recourse to law.[648] Literary scholars, along with

---

[644] W. M. Ormrod, *Edward III* (New Haven: Yale University Press, 2013); N. Saul, *Richard II* (London: Yale University Press, 1997); A. Goodman, *John of Gaunt* (Harlow: Longman, 1992).
[645] For the background to this see B. Stock, *The Implications of Literacy. Written Language and Models of Interpretation in the Eleventh and Twelfth Centuries* (Princeton, NJ: Princeton University Press, 1983); M. T. Clanchy, *From Memory to Written Record. England 1066-1307* (Oxford: Blackwell Publishers, 1993); S. Justice, *Writing and Rebellion in England in 1381* (Berkeley: University of California Press, 1996); and P. Strohm, *Hochon's Arrow. The Social Imagination of Fourteenth-Century Texts* (Princeton, NJ: Princeton University Press, 1992).
[646] For a historical approach: J. C. Holt, *Robin Hood* (Thames and Hudson, London, 1989); for a literary approach: S. Knight, *Robin Hood. A Complete Study of the English Outlaw* (Oxford: Blackwell, 1994).
[647] B. Stock, *The Implications of Literacy. Written Language and Models of Interpretation in the Eleventh and Twelfth Centuries* (Princeton, NJ: Princeton University Press, 1983); Clanchy, *From Memory to Written Record*.
[648] Cohn, *Popular Protest in Late Medieval English Towns*, p. 20; S. Justice, 'Religious Dissent, Social Revolt', *Past and Present*, 195 (2007), pp. 205-216; Justice, *Writing and Rebellion*, pp. 142-143; Strohm, *Hochon's Arrow*. p. 36; S.

historiographers such as Kempshall and Gransden, have transformed current understanding about the period, and thus of the revolt, through their intense scrutiny of the cultural norms and deliberate intentions of medieval chroniclers, the narrative sources of the period.

On a broader front, developing political historical theories have had an impact on understanding of the Peasants' Revolt. In the second half of the twentieth century the late medievalist McFarlane dominated thinking about politics in the fourteenth and fifteenth centuries.[649] McFarlane supplanted Stubbs' theories of weak monarchy versus burgeoning parliament with a theory of a more venal nobility, working under a strong monarchy. In the last twenty five years historians, such as Carpenter, Harriss, Ormrod and Musson have continued the debate over the changing strength of monarchy through the fourteenth and fifteenth centuries, considering the effect on it of the growth and characterisation of the gentry as a separate class and of the level of devolution to this class of local military and juridical management.[650] The growing study of the expansion of government fostered increasing study of the role of the gentry and, more recently, acknowledgment of lower class pressure on government in the fifteenth century.[651]

---

Crane, 'The writing lesson of 1381', in *Chaucer's England: literature in historical context,* B. Hanawalt (ed.) (Minneapolis, MN: University of Minnesota Press, 1992), pp. 201-223; E. Steiner, 'Commonalty and Literary Form in the 1370s and 1380s', in *New Medieval Literatures 6,* D. Lawton, W. Scase and R. Copeland (eds.) (Oxford: Oxford University Press, 2003), pp. 199-221.
[649] K. B. McFarlane, *The Nobility of Later Medieval England* (Oxford: Oxford University Press, 1973).
[650] R. W. Kaeuper, *War, Justice and Public Order* (Oxford: Oxford University Press, 1988); Harding, 'The Revolt against the Justices', in *The English Rising of 1381,* Hilton, R. H., (ed.) (Cambridge: Past and Present Society, 1984), pp. 165-193; A. Musson and W. M. Ormrod, *The Evolution of English Justice. Law, Politics and Society in the Fourteenth Century* (Basingstoke: Macmillan, 1999); W. M. Ormrod, *Political Life in Medieval England, 1300-1450* (Basingstoke: Macmillan, 1995); G L. Harriss, 'Political Society and the Growth of Government in Late Medieval England', *Past and Present,* 138 (1993), pp. 28-57.
[651] P. Coss, *The Origins of the English Gentry* (Cambridge: Cambridge University Press, 2003); I. M. W. Harvey, 'Was there popular politics in the fifteenth century?', *The McFarlane Legacy. Studies in Late Medieval Politics and Society,* ed. by R. H. Britnell and A. J. Pollard (Stroud: Alan Sutton Publishing, 1995), pp. 155-174; J. L. Watts, 'The Pressure of the Public on Later Medieval Politics', *Fifteenth Century England IV. Political Culture in Late Medieval Britain* (Woodbridge: Boydell, 2004), pp. 159-180.

This interest in active political engagement throughout English society is now established for the late fourteenth century, in works by Fletcher, Watts, Ormrod and Harriss, although more work specifically on the commoners is needed.[652]

## Presentations

Presentation is an integral aspect of studying for a degree. Most of the time students listen to the presentations of others, principally the Module Leaders, but sometimes they are required to deliver their own presentations. Sometimes these are formally assessed, sometimes they are not. They are likely to have set parameters - for example, there may be a ten-minute presentation time limit, you may be required to use a particular mode of presentation such as a poster, you may be required to use Powerpoint technology. Student involvement in the giving of presentations is an excellent tool for varying the student experience, honing your understanding of specific topics, and developing valuable skills that are likely to be relevant in your future workplace. Indeed presentation is likely to be central in the interview process that might lead to your future employment.

Some students relish the opportunity to stand up in front of their peers and deliver an interesting talk; others do not and find the prospect extremely daunting. Either way, the key to success is preparation – even the most experienced, accomplished and capable public speaker is likely to perform badly in a presentation situation without a good deal of preparation.

Of fundamental importance in preparation for a presentation is the consideration of the target audience. The age range of the audience and the degree of specialist knowledge it is likely to have need to be taken into account as you decide how to 'pitch' your presentation.

---

[652] Ormrod, *Political Life in Medieval England*; V. Challet and I. Forrest, 'The Masses'; Cohn, *Popular Protest in Late Medieval English Towns*; J. Watts, 'The pressure of the public on later medieval politics'; Fletcher, 'Rumour, clamour, murmur and rebellion'; G. L. Harriss, 'The dimensions of politics', in *The McFarlane legacy*, R. H. Britnell and A. J. Pollard, (eds.) (Stroud: Alan Sutton Publishing, 1995), pp. 1-20.

As with any assignment you have been set you need to analyse very carefully the instruction you have been given and, if relevant, the criteria against which you will be assessed. A presentation fulfills much the same role as an essay or a report. Just like these it needs to have an introduction, a 'body' (principal findings, arguments, themes etc.), and a conclusion. As with an essay or report the beginnings and ends are particularly important. You should try to devise a way of 'hooking' your audience at the start of your presentation to capture their attention, and it is especially important to wrap it up with a sound, succinct and, perhaps, entertaining closing remark. Too often speakers run out of things to say without arriving at a well-conceived conclusion, leaving the audience thinking 'Is that it?'.

Unlike a written report or an essay, a public presentation also invites a dialogue between the presenter and the audience, usually in the form of an opportunity for members of the audience to ask questions at the end. An audience expects to be treated with respect and does not enjoy being patronised – it is important to consider this throughout, particularly when attempting to answer questions. It is worth repeating the question to the audience, particularly if the person asking the question has a quiet voice and his/her back to other members of the audience; this will also give you a little more time to reflect on the question before launching into an answer. Whatever you might think of it, the question you have been asked is sufficiently important and meaningful to the person who has asked it to make the effort to do so in the first place. Never humiliate the person who asked the question, however daft it might seem to you, and, if you don't know the answer, say so! Sometimes it is worth inviting other members of the audience to offer their thoughts on a question that you are finding difficult to handle.

Visual aids are an important aspect of presentation. In the case of a poster presentation (see below) they replace oral presentation entirely. Conversely some presentations are exclusively aural – for instance, broadcasts on the radio, and unadorned public talks. When you are given a broad brief and left to your own devices when it comes down to the mode of presentation, it is sensible not just to consider what is most appropriate for your subject matter (an archaeological presentation for example is likely to benefit considerably from the use of site plans, photographs of artefacts etc.), but also what you consider to be your own strengths and limitations as a presenter. To a degree, if public speaking causes you anxiety, you can 'hide' behind a selection of interesting and apposite visual aids (slides, snippets of film, objects, models etc.). However be very careful not to go overboard on visual material – whether you went to school in the 1970s or the 2000s it is likely you were subjected to the tedium of a 'slow death by slides' presentation on more than one occasion!

At some point, whether you like it or not, you will have to address your audience – try to look them in the eye but do not eyeball one member of the audience (e.g. the Module Leader) for the whole of your talk, and try to relax sufficiently to move about a little and make appropriate gestures with your face and hands. If you seem cheerful and relaxed your audience is likely to feel the same. If you are new to public presentation it is sensible to rehearse your talk before delivering so you can sort out timings, check equipment and, if you have one, get some feedback from a 'guinea pig' audience. Do not make your presentation over-complicated – it is much better to make a few strong points than a lot of weak ones. It is especially important to avoid padding out your presentation (e.g. a powerpoint slide) with heaps of extraneous information. As a general rule a read presentation is likely to be a lot less interesting for an audience than one which is more *ad hoc* – a series of remarks based upon a few pointers in your notes. Although the reading of papers is still the norm in certain academic conference situations, comparatively few academics are equipped with the skills to do this in such a way as to maintain the interest of their audience. There is nothing more tedious than listening to a speaker turning page after page of a lengthy paper read in a monotone, and with little or no eye contact with those listening.

Here is a list of questions to ask yourself in preparation for the delivery of a presentation:

1. Do you know who the audience is and have you pitched your presentation accordingly?

2. Have you identified the purpose of the presentation and made the aims and central message clear?

3. Have you gathered the relevant information and identified the key

points?

4. Does the presentation have a clear structure (introduction, main body and conclusion)?

5. Is the introduction engaging and interesting, and does it include an outline of the presentation?

6. Does your conclusion draw together the key points, indicate what might happen next and leave your audience with something to think about?

7. Have you selected an appropriate method of delivery e.g. PowerPoint, and have you checked the technology is working and available on the day e.g. computer and projector?

8. Have you rehearsed the presentation several times, perfecting the timing, fluency (not reading a script), ensuring the flow (like telling a story), and use of body language?

9. Have you considered what questions might be asked and thought about possible answers?[653]

## PowerPoint presentations

PowerPoint technology can be used as a stand-alone presentation resource but, typically, it is used in conjunction with the spoken word and a live presenter. If this is the case the general rule is to keep it simple, clear and concise.

- Use a maximum of two font styles and no smaller than 24pt
- Use plain 'sans-serif' fonts such as Verdana or Arial
- Pale backgrounds with dark texts are easiest to read
- Use **bold** rather than *italics* or underlining
- Do not use all UPPER-CASE
- Don't overload slides: a maximum 6 bullet points per slide[654]

---

[653] 'Presentations', Learning Development, Plymouth University (2010)
[654] 'Presentations', Learning Development, Plymouth University (2010)

## Poster presentations

Where time and space restricts the number of speakers at academic conferences it is now the norm in many disciplines, for example, Archaeology, for researchers to create posters as a means of disseminating information and hypotheses. The same general 'rules' for other forms of public presentation apply to poster presentations. There are also specific principles to which designers of posters are advised to adhere. These include the following:

- Aim for a 50:50 balance between text and graphics/visuals
- It should be readable from 2 - 3 metres away
- There should be a natural flow or storyline through the poster that the eye follows easily
- Keep text brief but informative
- Do not overload it: too much information can reduce the impact of the message[655]

A successful poster presentation will be eye-catching, so consider the careful use of graphics and other aspects of design. The creation of an effective poster is likely to develop your skills in a range of areas such as the use of IT publishing software, photography, and, possibly, drawing.

## Archaeological drawing

The Graphics Archaeology Group (GAG), formally known as the Association of Archaeological Illustrators & Surveyors (AAI&S), is an affiliate of the Institute for Archaeologists (IfA). Its Secretary, Steve Allen, in the introduction to the GAG session at the IfA's 2014 conference, summarised the nature and importance of graphics in archaeology:

*'Archaeological research draws on many different resources during the course of a project and not all of these resources are text-based. Images are used in the course of a project to record data, to try out alternative*

---

[655] 'Presentations', Learning Development, Plymouth University (2010)

*ideas and to analyse the information we collect. Similarly, the output, the end result of the research, is expressed in visual as well as verbal terms. Graphical images are powerful tools which are often treated by the unenlightened as absolute statements - and sometimes even as nothing more than the product of the imagination of the artist. We intend to show that this is not the case. Any archaeological image is the result of the research and experience carried out by the practitioner and their interaction with their colleagues. The work is as capable of interrogation as any other form of archaeological research.'*[656]

Despite photography and newer technologies, such as 3D digital imaging, accurate scale drawing of objects and sites retains an important place in modern archaeology.

The recording of archaeology by drawing is something anyone with the ability to hold a pencil or tape can engage in but proficiency requires a great deal of patience and practice. Of critical importance is a knowledge of the drawing conventions involved in landscape survey, architectural drawing and the drawing of smaller artefacts and ecofacts.

An excellent resource for the beginner is *A Practical Guide to Drawing Archaeological Sites* published in 2011 by the Royal Commission on the Ancient and Historical Monuments of Scotland which is available as a free download at **www.swaag.org**. Accompanying the publication are four short (5-15 minute) training films made by the RCAHMS Scotland's Rural Past team and available at their website (**www.scotlandsruralpast.org.uk**) and also via YouTube. These cover:

- Site sketching
- Using hand-held GPS
- Tape-and-offset
- Plane tabling

The conventions regarding the drawing of small finds can be found in many sources. A good starting place is the University of Aberdeen's 2002 *Archaeological Illustration* which is an on-line twenty-two page set

---

[656] 'Graphic Archaeology News', Spring 2014, the Graphic Archaeology Group, IfA

of exercises teaching the basics. The activities guide the user through the whole process of making accurate drawings of metal objects, pottery and stonework. This is the link:

www.scran.ac.uk/packs/exhibitions/learning_materials/resources/main-text.pdf

If you want a good book on the subject Lesley and Roy Adkins' *Archaeological Illustration* (Cambridge University Press, 1994) is highly recommended.

## Personal development plans

A good Personal Development Plan (PDP) will include plenty of informed reflection on your academic, experiential and observational research activities. So, don't just describe what you have done but comment on how it has developed your knowledge, understanding and skills. It is also worthwhile reflecting upon how the development of these has enhanced your research experience (e.g. how you are now visiting museums etc. with a new, more sophisticated perspective).

If the PDP is to be submitted for assessment it should be topped and tailed with an introduction that outlines your methodology and the content of your submission, and a conclusion that provides a summary and overview of your personal development (i.e. what you have achieved). It should include some reflection on your future targets in relation to this on-going personal development.

## Careers in the heritage sector

The heritage sector is a major employer of graduates in Britain in the twenty-first century. Heritage workers include:

- Archaeologists
- Archivists
- Heritage managers
- Historic buildings inspectors/conservation officers
- Museum education officers
- Museum/gallery curators

- Museum/gallery exhibitions officers
- Tourism officers
- Tourist information centre managers

Major employers in the sector include:

- CADW: Welsh Historic Monuments
- English Heritage Trust
- Historic England
- Historic Scotland
- National Museum Wales
- National Trust
- National Trust for Scotland

A plethora of less well-known amenity societies provide further opportunities for employment.

Finding work in the sector is a challenge and those best prepared have sound and relevant academic qualifications, very likely at postgraduate level, and practical experience, much of which is likely to have been gleaned as an unpaid volunteer. There are many places, on-line and elsewhere, to look for work. This list is not comprehensive but it will help get you started:

**Museum Jobs** www.museumjobs.com jobs in museums world-wide, both paid and voluntary
**Leicester University Museums Jobs Desk** www2.le.ac.uk/departments/museumstudies/JobsDesk
**The Museums Association** www.museumsassociation.org
**Museum Net** www.museums.co.uk
**art jobster** http://artjobster.com Artworkers jobsite: arts, media, visual arts, gallery, museum, community arts, heritage, theatre, dance, festivals, music, & art therapy jobs.
**24-Hour Museum** www.24hourmuseum.org.uk "the national virtual museum" with news, listings and features from over 3500 museum, gallery and heritage sites.
**Virtual Library of UK museums on the Web** http://museophile.org the Virtual Library site has similar listings for museums in other countries
**Canterbury Cathedral Official Website** www.canterbury-

cathedral.org
English Heritage www.english-heritage.org.uk
The National Trust www.nationaltrust.org.uk
Wordsworth Trust www.wordsworth.org.uk regularly recruits volunteers to work at the Wordsworth museum in the Lake District
The British Museum volunteering opportunities www.britishmuseum.org/join_in/volunteers.aspx
Do-It www.do-it.org search for volunteering opportunities by sector, location etc.

**HERITAGE VOLUNTEERING OPPORTUNITIES**
www.kent.ac.uk/careers/workin/HeritageVolunteering.htm

The study of History, Heritage and/or Archaeology is an excellent foundation for work in many contexts beyond that defined as the 'heritage sector' above. Much of your undergraduate study is skills-based and the skills you develop are 'transferable' - they are relevant to many other contexts and fields of employment such as business management, the public services, education, law, and journalism. As you study it is sensible to build a portfolio of evidence of your personal development (see PDP section above) in relation to these transferable skills – it will prove invaluable when you next need to make a job application or prepare for an interview with a prospective employer.

# 8 Projects

## Desktop survey

A desktop survey begins with an analysis of the Historic Environment Record (HER) for the site. This is a database of information on buildings, archaeological sites and monuments. The HER provides site descriptions, a summary of what is known about the site and references for further research. Where the HER is available as an electronic database historic Ordnance Survey maps and relevant photographs are likely to be available.

Each site is given a code in the HER database. For example, the deserted medieval village site at Discove in the Somerset parish of Bruton is 53618 (OS ref. ST 691 336). A note is provided regarding public access to the site. A summary of what is known about the site follows:

*'Old OS maps show that there were formerly more cottages S of Discove Farm. Several enclosures and areas of earthworks remain, but there are no clear traces of the remains of holloways or abandoned crofts. APs show some disturbance but no clear evidence.*

*Wells and small yards shown on OSAD 6" map at ST69073374, ST69143357 and ST69233345 appear to relate to six buildings collectively called Discove Dairy. The northern group has three buildings, the southern two.*

*Lynchets also on site.'*

The record concludes with a list of references for further research:

1. Mention - *Proceedings of the Somerset Archaeological and Natural History Society* Aston, M. and Murless, B. J. 1978 "Somerset Archaeology 1977" vol. 122, 135
2. Mention - *Medieval Village Research Group Annual Report* 25 (1977) (page 15
3. Detailed records - Ordnance Survey Archaeology Division 1979 ST63SE39 (SCC Planning Department)
4. Map - Ordnance Survey Archaeology Division 1962 6" ST63SE

(SCC Planning Department)
5. Aerial photographs - HSL 71 179 Run 69E 8330. (06/09/1971) Location: Local Studies collection at Somerset Heritage Centre.
6. Detailed records - Ordnance Survey Archaeology Division 1979 ST63SE30 (SCC Planning Department)[657]

A desk-based assessment is likely to involve the analysis of geo-technical investigations and will usually be done in conjunction with a site visit. Desk-based assessments are the starting place for archaeological reports, historic landscape characterisation surveys, planning applications, conservation management plans, cultural heritage environmental statements, and historic building records.

The HER directs the researcher towards historic maps, aerial photographs, historic documentary literature, and grey literature (for example, archaeological reports that have not been formally published). Google Earth and Microsoft MSN Virtual Earth are exceptionally useful for a survey of what can be seen at designated sites from the air.

Archaeological desk-based assessments should conform to the standard defined by the IfA (Institute for Archaeologists):

'Desk-based assessment will determine, as far as is reasonably possible from existing records, the nature, extent and significance of the historic environment within a specified area. Desk-based assessment will be undertaken using appropriate methods and practices which satisfy the stated aims of the project, and which comply with the *Code of conduct, Code of approved practice for the regulation of contractual arrangements in field archaeology*, and other relevant by-laws of the IfA. In a development context desk-based assessment will establish the impact of the proposed development on the significance of the historic environment (or will identify the need for further evaluation to do so), and will enable reasoned proposals and decisions to be made whether to mitigate, offset or accept without further intervention that impact.'[658]

---

[657] Somerset County Council (2014); recorded created October 1984
[658] IFA (2012), *Standard and Guidance for Historic Environment Desk-based Assessment*

The report that follows will contain as a minimum:

- non-technical summary
- statement of research and/or conservation objectives and how they have been addressed by the study
- clear map of study area
- aims and purpose of assessment including the context of development or other land use change
- methodology including sources consulted
- identification of existing heritage or archaeological site management plans that may be in operation in the locality, and where sufficient information about the proposed development is available an assessment of the impacts that new development may have on them
- description of the heritage assets and archaeological potential of the study area
- an assessment of the interest and significance of each asset and its setting, focussing on those aspects which will be affected by any proposed or predicted changes
- assessment of the nature of the effects and options for reducing or mitigating harm. Opportunities for positive effects should be identified as well as negative impacts and mitigation options.
- a description of the area's historic character and the effect of proposed development upon it (where appropriate, this should include options for conserving or enhancing local character)
- conclusion, including a confidence rating and the extent to which the aims and purpose have been met
- supporting illustrations at appropriate scales
- supporting data, tabulated or in appendices
- index to and location of archive
- references[659]

## Local history

[659] IfA (2012), *Standard and Guidance for Historic Environment Desk-based Assessment*

The most important repository of historical evidence for the local historian is the County Records Office. The County Record Office holds original documents, (e.g. tithe maps, enclosure maps and parish registers), hard copies and microfiche versions of the available material. These documents include such things as wills, deeds, electoral rolls, estate papers, industrial investigations, agricultural surveys, charters, census records, and parish registers. Booking prior to a visit is advisable for records office research and materials can be ordered in advance. Obviously it is advisable to access what is available online before committing time to research in a records office. Many trade directories such as Collinson's and Kelley's have been made available as digital versions and can also be found in records offices. Collections of aerial photographs can also be found. The Victoria County History, available at records offices and in libraries is, for many counties, an invaluable resource; this too has been made freely available in a digitised form in many instances.

Sources of information for local historians beyond the records offices include local archaeological and historical societies, museums, universities, archaeological units and trusts, the records of the Royal Commissions, and national heritage bodies such as the National Trust and English Heritage.

Useful online sources include the Heritage Gateway, the Archaeology Data Service, Pastscape, Intute, CANMORE, Access 2 Archives, MAGIC, and Coflein.

**Family history**

Although the terms 'family history' and 'genealogy' have much in common, they do not mean exactly the same thing:

*Genealogy:*
*Establishment of a Pedigree by extracting evidence, from valid sources, of how one generation is connected to the next. (In essence, this means the discipline of the construction of a valid family tree)*

*Family History:*

*A bibliographical study of a genealogically proven family and of the community and country in which they lived. (In essence, this means the writing of a biography of a series of related ancestors of common genealogy. Family History incorporates Genealogy)'*[660]

Family history focuses on hereditary surnames and it is important to note that hereditary surnames for most people in England did not become the norm until the end of the fourteenth century.

In 1911 the Society of Genealogists (SoG) was founded. Its library and education centre are in Clerkenwell in London. The society's purpose is defined in its 'vision' and mission statements:

**'VISION.** *A world in which everyone has convenient, affordable access to records, finding aids, knowledge and skills necessary to conduct authoritative research into family history.*

**MISSION.** *To be the leading national learned Society concerned with family history and genealogy and their associated disciplines*

*1. Promoting recognition of the worth of family history research by:*
*Influencing academic standards*
*Providing education, skills and standards for research*

*2. Assisting members and the public in their research objectives by:*
    *a) Making widely available an expanding Society collection of relevant records, finding aids and other material both*
        * *physically in its library and*
        * *remotely through its publications in any media*
    *b) Providing access through a variety of media to expertise by:*
        * *giving research advice in the library, at external events or remotely*
        * *signposting to material held or published by others*
    *c) Increasing the availability of research material by undertaking projects for:*
        * *transcription and indexing*
        * *digitization*

*3. Being an effective voice campaigning for:*

---

[660] http://www.sog.org.uk/learn/education Accessed 27/05/14

*a) The integrity and preservation of records relevant to current and future research*
*b) Optimum access to such records*

4. *Being the essential contact for appropriate media, commercial and public sector interests*

5. *Co-operating with and providing support for individuals and organisations effectively contributing to the Society's vision. In particular catalysing, coordinating or contributing to transcription, indexing or other group projects or objectives.'*

SoG is especially valuable as a resource for genealogists seeking information that predates the introduction, in 1837, of the civil registration of births, marriages and deaths. It is the repository of the largest collection of parish register copies and nonconformist registers. The library also contains collections of local histories, gravestone inscriptions, trade directories and poll books. It also holds thousands of family histories that have already been compiled; these are all catalogued and the family historian embarking upon new research should always search such archives to check the work has not already been done. The genealogy-dedicated search engine 'Mocavo' helps researchers hunt for what is available on the internet by prioritising material with a family history connection when a name is entered as a search term.

Some of SoG's resources are available on-line in association with the family history website www.Findmypast.co.uk.

Other useful websites for researchers include
    www.Ancestry.co.uk
    www.thegenealogist.co.uk
    www.familyrelaitives.com
    www.origins.net
    www.genuki.org.uk

Genuki, which is a registered charity based at Manchester University, exists to provide key primary sources for free. Its collections are organized on a county by county basis. Plenty of software has been produced to help researchers collate data into family trees.

Opportunities for acquiring DNA information of family members are rapidly expanding.

The Federation of Family History Societies (www.ffhs.org.uk) provides lists of local family history organisations. The FFHS is another charitable trust with the mission to 'support, inform and advise our membership, which consists of family history societies and similar bodies across the world.' The Olympia in London hosts the world's largest annual family history convention.

Important sources for family historians include:

> birth, marriage and death records
> censuses 1841-1911
> wills
> church records
> occupational records
> education and apprenticeship records
> military service records
> tax records
> criminal records
> poor law records
> newspapers
> trade directories
> ecclesiastical licences
> church court records
> tombstones

SoG provides a list of essential principles and standards for family historians:

- Accuracy and honesty of all personal research and of work published, promoted or distributed to others.
- Provision of clear evidence from primary sources to support all conclusions and statements of fact.
- Use of original sources and records (or surrogate images of originals) to gather key information.
- Citation and recording of sources used so that others may also evaluate the evidence.

- Logical and reasoned development of family links with each step proved from valid evidence before further deductions are made.
- Investigation and analysis of all possible solutions and of contradictory evidence with each alternative hypothesis examined and tested.
- Qualification of less certain conclusions as probable or possible so that others are not misled.
- Acceptance of the possibility that a solution may not be found and acknowledgement of circumstances in which this occurs.
- Awareness of gaps in the availability of and information from sources at all levels.
- Receptiveness to new information and to informed comment which may challenge earlier conclusions.
- Acknowledgement and attribution of research done by others and use of such work as a secondary source only.
- Evidence only becomes proof through a reasoned and logical analysis and argument capable of convincing others that the conclusion is valid.[661]

Since 1968 the professional body for genealogists has existed as the Association of Genealogists and Researchers in Archives (AGRA). Information regarding its mission and the services its members provide can be found at **www.agra.org.uk**.

## Oral history

Oral history is a vital aspect of modern historical enquiry. The Oral History Society, based in the Department of History at the Royal Holloway University in London, exists to promote 'the collection, preservation and use of recorded memories'[662] and to assist those involved in this form of research by providing opportunities, guidelines, training, and opportunities to engage with other

---

[661] *Principles of Genealogical Research* www.sog.org.uk/learn/education Accessed 27/05/14

[662] The Oral History Society. http://www.ohs.org.uk/ Accessed May 2014.

practitioners. The society's journal, *Oral History*, details developments and contemporary projects, and provides a platform for public discussion and debate.

The Oral History Association, based in the United States, was founded in 1966, with a mission 'to bring together all persons interested in oral history as a way of collecting and interpreting human memories to foster knowledge and human dignity'.[663] Its on-line journal, *The Oral History Review*, is published by Oxford Journals.

The association's *General Principles and Best Practices for Oral History*[664] documentation is the keystone of academic oral history research in the U.K. The gathering of evidence by this method is not chance recovery but something to which both the oral historian and the interviewee (sometimes referred to as the 'narrator') are fully committed, who both have 'the conscious intention of creating a permanent record to contribute to an understanding of the past'. To this end it is essential that the interviewee is fully informed about the purpose and nature of the project, that they are able to withdraw or withhold information at their discretion, that they retain the copyright over their comments unless these are formally transferred by the interviewee to an individual or institution. It is conventional therefore, if not essential, for the interviewee to sign a consent form prior to interview. Full guidance regarding ethical issues pertinent to oral history research can be located at the Society's website **http://www.ohs.org.uk/ethics.php**, and in a dedicated chapter in Valerie Raleigh Yow, Recording *Oral History: A Guide for the Humanities and Social Sciences*, second edition, London: Sage, 2005.

Since interviewers 'are obliged to ask historically significant questions' the success of the interview greatly relies upon the amount of pre-interview research undertaken. Like an archaeological excavation, an oral history interview produces a unique body of evidence that cannot be replicated - even if the same individual is interviewed on a second occasion and asked the same questions the narration will not be the same as the original. For this reason, as with excavation, an oral history

---

[663] The Oral History Association. http://www.oralhistory.org/about/ Accessed May 2014

[664] http://www.oralhistory.org/about/principles-and-practices/ Accessed May 2014

project should have an archiving and publication policy. The best available recording equipment and modes of preservation should be used.

A number of basic interview principles should be adhered to. These include:

- Identifying an appropriate location for the interview – usually a quiet room.
- The recording of a 'lead' at the start of the session consisting of, at least, 'the names of narrator and interviewer, day and year of session, interview's location, and proposed subject of the recording'.
- The interviewer and narrator agreeing upon the approximate duration of the interview (typically in the region of two hours).

The archive of material generated by an oral history project is likely to include additional items such as photographs and written documents. In addition 'to augment the accessibility of the interview, repositories should make transcriptions, indexes, time tags, detailed descriptions or other written guides to the contents'. Transcription is a massively time-consuming and painstaking process. Ken Howarth, founder of the North West Sound Archive, estimated a one hour interview can take a trained interviewer between seven and ten hours to transcribe.[665] While the transcription should be as accurate as possible, recording every 'er', chuckle and sigh, it is often helpful to annotate (but not edit) the final transcript before archiving: 'Errors in dates can be corrected, placenames inserted, references given, but the transcript should be capable of being read intact without alteration.' However, even the most accurate transcription can never be as valuable as the aural record: 'gone are the inflexions and nuances of language and communication. The interviewee might say something was OK or fine, but by saying it in a certain way, she could mean the exact opposite. Besides actually hearing the voice itself gives the exercise a remarkable quality and makes history live in a meaningful way.'[666]

---

[665] Howarth (1988), p.153
[666] Howarth (1988), p.155

# Archaeological experiments

Plenty of experimental archaeologists who have never excavated a pit in their careers have added as much or more to the record as many of their fellow diggers. In recent times heritage centres, with an emphasis on archaeological experimentation, have sprung up in many parts of the world. The experiments they conduct do not necessarily prove anything beyond what was and is possible.

In the UK Peter Reynolds' (1939-2001) experimental work at Butser Ancient Farm in Hampshire has greatly advanced our understanding of Iron Age farming. In an influential paper entitled *The Nature of Experiment in Archaeology* he began his definition of the approach by explaining what it is not:

> At the outset, it is a fundamental tenet that experiment has absolutely nothing to do with the exercises of 'living in the past', 'dressing in period costume', 're-enactment of past events' or, indeed, the teaching of well understood techniques - which may well have been originally established by the experimental process - like, for example, lithic technology, pottery manufacture or laying mosaics. The former are at best theatre, at worst the satisfaction of character deficiencies; the latter are simple skills which, should they wish to be acquired, require learning. It is extremely unfortunate that these activities have become generally subsumed under the overall title of experimental archaeology since their inclusion militates against the real value of experiment and its acceptance professionally. The labelling of an activity like shaving with a flint flake or even a Roman bronze razor as an experiment rather than exploration is clearly absurd. It advances our knowledge not one iota and serves generally to increase our prejudices of history and pre-history.

> [Experimental archaeology] can be readily appreciated by the following formula. A site is excavated and its product, described as the prime data, is subjected to analysis and interpretation. Rather than use the term 'interpretation' which implies full comprehension, the term 'hypothesis' is substituted. Hypothesis implies a deduced or reasoned conclusion which can and should be further subjected

to test or trial to confirm or deny that conclusion. The method of testing is called an experiment. This is built to the specification of the reasoned conclusion using the prime data as the given evidence.

The experiment, therefore, is not an exercise imagined or concocted on an unconstrained basis by the experimenter. It is quite specific to a particular hypothesis and data resource. Partiality, therefore, is removed in principle. However, bias many still enter especially where sampling contains an element of human choice or estimation. Notwithstanding, the ambition of the experiment is not only to explore the hypothesis to its extremities but even to its destruction.

The requirements of an experiment are also specific. The experiment must satisfy the tenets of the academic or technological discipline within whose remit it falls. For example, an agricultural experiment must be acceptable within the disciplines of agriculture and agronomy. An experiment must be replicable and replicated. An experiment should be designed so that the results may be assessed statistically, otherwise the outcome is again little more than subjective or partial.

[...] The types of experiment are as naturally diverse as the material evidence they seek to examine. It is as well to realise and underline the fact that the data recovered by excavation, despite it being representative of less than one per cent of the original material, is indicative of human activity in all its forms. Therefore, experiment will necessarily draw upon virtually all the sciences in its exploration of hypotheses. In order to simplify the complexity thus implied, it is possible to group experiments into broad categories provided it is clearly understood that these categories are complementary and inter-dependent rather than exclusive. In general terms experiments can be grouped into five categories: the construct, process and function, simulation, eventuality and technical innovation.

[...] Where interpretation is capable of being tested, it should be tested. The testing process itself must be rigorous and should not admit the variables of human motivations. On completion, the test or experiment will provide a positive or negative result. A positive result will validate the interpretation or hypothesis. A negative *result will disprove the interpretation requiring another to be raised in its place. It should not be surprising that the contribution from experiment is most frequently negative. Experiment is necessarily restricted to those hypotheses which are capable of direct examination and have an adequate data base, not only to allow the hypothesis initially but also to formulate the experiment itself. In addition, an experiment must be repeatable, including repetition by other agencies.*[667]

An international experimental archaeology society, EXARC, exists to promote 'the investigation, contextualisation, presentation and interpretation of archaeological and experimental archaeological heritage'.[668] This broad mission statement, with its commitment to presentation and interpretation, accommodates a membership that includes individuals and institutions that have a purely educational purpose. Despite Reynolds' concerns, at EXARC 'living history' and experimental archaeology are regarded as equal partners in pursuit of its goal.

EXARC is affiliated to ICOM (the International Council for Museums) and was founded in Denmark in 2003. Its members, numbering in 2014 almost 200, include re-enactor Roman soldiers, gladiators, and Vikings, together with numerous open-air museums and ancient technology centres in over 30 countries. The EXARC journal helps members keep up to date with developments in the field, including the latest experiments in casting, fletching, cooking, clothing manufacture etc.

Experimental archaeology offers infinite opportunities for students to engage with evidence by forming and testing their own hypotheses. A summary of relatively simple set of experiments conducted by Tom Williams, an undergraduate at Reading University, in 2007/8, provides a good example. His objective was 'to investigate the effectiveness of different types of flint arrowheads from the Neolithic and early Bronze Age periods'.

'The experiments specifically explored:

---

667 Reynolds (1999)

668 EXARC Vision 2013-2017 http://exarc.net/about-us/exarc-vision-2013-2017 Accessed 28/05/14

- The penetration and accuracy of the arrowheads
- The potential for re-use of the arrowheads and the nature of their user-wear and damage
- The relationships between the effectiveness of arrowhead
- types and bow poundage

The experiments used a range of replica arrowhead types knapped by John Lord (barbed and tanged, chisel, oblique, and petit tranchet), hafted with bitumen and nettle fibre rope onto modern shafts with modern fletchings (to reduce the number of experimental variables). The arrows were shot from three modern longbows with different poundage ratings, generating similar draw weights and characteristics to later prehistoric bows. The target was a pig carcass (representing a typical later prehistoric hunted species), with each arrowhead type shot from each of the three longbows over 20 yards range. Arrowhead accuracy (hit/miss) and penetration depths were measured.

The experimental results provided a number of valuable insights into each arrowhead type:

- 25 out of 82 arrows shot hit the target (30% success rate)
- Average penetration was 15.87cm
- The barbed and tanged arrowheads were the most effective (measured by accuracy and penetration) across all three bows

The experiments suggested that barbed and tanged arrowheads were the most effective and represent an 'optimum' later prehistoric design. This supports the concept of evolutionary development in flint arrowhead design and challenges earlier suggestions of the non-utilitarian role of barbed and tanged arrowheads based on funerary associations.'[669]

At an undergraduate level the student's research task does not need

---

[669] Bell, M., Hosfield R., et al (2008), *Experimental Archaeology*, University of Reading

to be 'original' in the sense of never having been approached before. Indeed, for someone engaging in archaeological experimentation for the first time it is sensible to consider following in an expert's footsteps rather than forging ahead alone! Plenty of examples are readily available in print and on-line for experiments in such areas as pottery making, cookery, cordage, the making of shoes, the extraction of birch tar, and the construction of boxes made out of strong leaves or birch bark. Sites such as the Ancient Technology Centre in Dorset and Butser Iron Age Farm in Hampshire sometimes provide opportunities to be tutored by the experts in more ambitious projects such as farming and building experiments.

In designing an experiment it is advisable to adhere, as closely as you can, to the following principles identified by John Coles:

'1. *The materials employed in the experiment should be those considered to be originally available to the society under examination; for example, in making replicas of ancient pottery local clays should be used, and in building copies of ancient houses, do not use plastic thatch.*

*2. The methods used in the work should be appropriate to the society and should not exceed its presumed competence. For instance, in building an earthwork, hand tools and manual labour should be used, and not machinery. But remember that it is unlikely that man can manipulate ancient implements such as stone axes as effectively as his ancestors and even practice may not make perfect.*

*3. Modern techniques and analytical studies should be carried out before, during and after the experiments. So that the results can be fairly assessed it is important to include in the observations the analysis of materials and measurements of stresses and wear. For example, in watching the decay and collapse of a house, or break-up of a boat, it is important to know why it happened, how it happened and when it happened.*

*4. The scale of the work must be assessed and fairly stated. If scale models are used, uncertainties will arise and must be acknowledged; for example, scaled-down earthworks or modern earthworks cannot represent all of the factors of building and erosion of ancient* banks. A full-scale exercise on only a fraction of a structure may not represent the full impact on materials or manpower; for example, to use one timber cut with a stone axe and one hundred others cut with a buzz-saw in building a house cannot but deflect the objectives of measuring workrates, technology, stability or weathering.

5. Repetition of the experiment is important in order to avoid a freak result. For example, the production of a sophisticated flint blade may be achieved by a chance blow so the technique can only be demonstrated by repeated attempts.

Series of experiments, building on the results of previous work, can lead to greater understanding as well as exposing new problems. For example, the way grain was stored in underground pits is now easier to explain because of continued tests which show how pits can be maintained in a fresh condition. The useful life of houses is better understood now that multiple tests have been carried out over 10-15 years.

6. During each experiment certain problems will be examined in the hope of gaining answers. But improvisation should also be considered; and adaptability is of paramount importance. For instance, long distance voyages in untested craft have always required considerable improvisation in handling the boats; firing of pottery in earth kilns has almost always meant last-minute on-the-spot repairs to achieve the appropriate seal.

7. Experimental results must not be taken as proof of ancient structural or technological detail. For instance, it is possible to sail a raft across the Pacific or the Atlantic, but these brave feats do not prove that ancient man made these voyages. In making and hardening leather shields, various methods were found successful. Any of them could have been used in the Bronze Age. But so could a number of other methods. Where a test has eliminated a possible answer, where a presumed function does not work, then the "negative" answer is likely to be a positive one, and that ancient function can be said not to have been performed by that tool. On the other hand, if a certain implement does function successfully in performing a certain act, it need not necessarily mean that the tool was actually used in this way in the past. It may have been used for

*another purpose not considered by the archaeologist. It is not often that absolute proof is claimed, yet in some cases it has. Work on Bushman rock art and their paints and media quite clearly indicated only one positive answer to the media problem. Few other experiments suggest such a clear answer. The work of Heyerdahl is a case in point; although he has been able to show that voyages in reed boats across the Atlantic are possible, he has not claimed that such voyages did take place in the past. His modesty is something that other experimenters might emulate.*

*8. A final test, at least as important as the others, can best be described as "honesty". The experimenter must assess the results of the experiment in the following terms: Were the materials right? Were the methods of using them appropriate? Were mistakes made? Were procedures recorded accurately? Was the experiment affected by personal opinions, idiosyncrasies, preconceived ideas, short-cuts, laziness, tiredness, boredom, over-enthusiasm? All of these must be honestly assessed, and those affecting the experiment should be stated in the publication of the results because experiments with archaeological sites and objects are still sufficiently rare to be eagerly seized upon and used indiscriminately. They are nothing of the sort. For instance, the range of musical notes produced from Tutankamun's trumpet continues to be accepted as an entirely appropriate ancient Egyptian fanfare although serious musicians and archaeologists alike know that the experiment was a complete farce. An honest appraisal of experimental archaeology can go as far as, but no further than: " ... Where history is silent and the monuments do not speak for themselves, demonstration cannot be expected; ... the utmost is conjecture supported by probability ... " (Wise, 1742, p. 5). Experimental archaeology can provide or deny that vital "probability" to the "conjecture" about past human activities.'*[670]

Recent editions of the international *Exarc Journal*[671] provide an interesting indication of the activities of its members and associates. These include reconstructions of a prehistoric fish trap, a medieval rotunda church, an Iron Age horse bridle, a medieval tile kiln, and

---

[670] Coles (1979), pp. 47-8
[671] *Exarc Journal*, 2012-14

Cherokee blowguns and darts, the making of Roman-style fish sauce, lost wax method bronze casting, experimental lime-burning, the testing of a newly built Viking-style log-house in the depth of an Estonian winter, the cremation and radiocarbon-dating of newly burned bone, the forging of Bronze Age style swords, the processing of acorns and their baking into bread, the recreation of a Roman-style hairdo, meat drying experiments, the experimental mummification of dead birds, and spinning wool with a distaff.

## CASE STUDY: Understanding ancient spears and spear-throwers

*Archaeological experiments are not always as ambitious as the earthwork and boat building experiments described in Chapter 5. The scope for conducting small-scale experiments that have equally viable outcomes is vast. In the examples below simple experiments with spears and spear-throwers shed light on ancient technologies.*

Weapons for hunting, inter-personal conflict and warfare have attracted a good deal of attention in the field of experimental archaeology. The oldest known form spear is known as the Clacton type after a spear-point found at Clacton-on-Sea in Essex in 1911. Three Clacton type spears found in a coal mine in Schöningen, near Hannover in Germany have been radio-carbon dated to between 380,000 and 400,000 BP. They were formidable weapons of up to 7.5 foot in length and appear to prove that early man was a hunter as well as a scavenger. A fossilised horse scapula found at Boxgrove in Sussex, dated to c.500,000 BP, was found to have been perforated and a reconstruction of a Clacton type spear produced by experiment an equivalent hole when projected into a fresh bone, thus providing good evidence for the archaeologists that the Boxgrove *Homo Heidelbergensis* hominid associated with the fossil bone find was a hunter. However the experiment could not shed enough light on the issue to determine the mode of hunting: 'As paleoanthropologist Wil Roebroeks of the University of Leiden points out, however, "we still haven't determined whether early man hunted in large groups, or whether they used pits to trap the animals first."'[672]

---

[672] Arlette P. Kouwenhoven, 'World's Oldest Spears' in *Archaeology* Volume 50 Number 3, May/June 1997

Expert flint-knapper, John Lord, was invited by a television company to construct a Clacton spear and described aspects of the project in an article published in 1999.[673] He began by reiterating the value of experimental archaeology: 'The properties and inherent problems possessed by the materials that our ancestors used have not changed significantly, neither have the skills that are required to manipulate them successfully. Through `experimental archaeology' we can therefore often shed light on possible ways in which emergency repair or replacement problems were solved in the past.'

Lord selected a two-and-a-half-inch diameter sycamore sapling from which to create his spear he felled it, using a simple flint chopper of his own making, in about six minutes. Stripping it of branches and bark was easy enough but problems arose when he began to work on giving it a point at one end: 'I started holding the stave with one hand and chopping with the other, the aim being to produce a finely tapering point; but this proved to be too slow and laborious. More would be achieved if a large flake could be used as a draw knife - which is a two handed operation. I initially thought I could clamp the stave between my feet, and weave it through branches in order to gain stability; but these were all vain moves, as the spear became mobile every time that the flake started to bite.' His solution lay in using a vice of some kind and he soon concluded that the stump of the sapling would be ideal. He used a 'cleaver-like flake' to split the stump and 'The stave was then forced down into the newly made split, and sideways movement was now under control.' However 'The same could not be said for forward movement' and, without having someone around to hold the parted stump together he needed string to bind it. For cordage he resorted to a nettle patch nearby. He described the process of making 'prehistoric' string in some detail – an activity that has since become a popular hands-on 'experiment' for visitors to ancient technology centres:

> 'Six long nettles were uprooted and stripped of their leaves, after which the stems were split open and the woody material was peeled from the outer skins. It is the outer skin of the nettle

---

[673] John Lord in *British Archaeology*, 49, November 1999

which contains the strong flexible fibres. Two of the nettle skins were knotted at one end, then while holding the knot with one hand, I used my other hand to roll the two skins which were lying parallel on my thigh. When the knot was released, the two skins plied themselves into a strong cord.

The process was continued by regripping the nettle where the plying had ceased with the `knot hand', and parallel rolling with the other. As each nettle skin neared its end, a fresh skin was introduced until all six stems were used. This process produced a cord about three metres long, but in order to increase its strength, I doubled the cord, gripped it in the centre, then rolled and plied it again to form a shorter, stronger length. From start to finish the cord took about 15 minutes to produce.'

Once the stump was lashed together he could continue with his main purpose of fashioning the spear point: 'To achieve this, I selected a flake which had an obtuse-angled cutting edge, as flakes with acute-angled edges, although initially sharp, soon become chipped and ineffective. The carving was over in less than half an hour, and the vice then became useful for holding the spear firmly while any slight twists were pulled straight.'

The experiment had proven that this is a viable way of making a Clacton type spear. The question that remains unanswered is: 'did this process ever take place in the prehistoric past?'

Numerous experiments have been conducted into the efficacy of the atlatl (spearthrower) as detailed in an interesting article by John Whittaker - 'Weapon Trials: the atlatl and experiments in hunting technology' (2010).

An atlatl can be defined as 'essentially a stick with a hook or socket to engage the spear on one end and a grip for the hand on the other end.'[674] It enables the hunter to project a spear further than when thrown by hand alone. It was common in many prehistoric contexts and predates archery. Compared to archery it has left less of a footprint in either the historical or the ethnological record and thus could be considered an even better candidate for analysis by

---

[674] Whittaker (2010)

experimentation. As a hunting tool the atlatl was rediscovered by western European explorers such as Charles Darwin who recorded its use when his ship, the *Beagle*, arrived at a site near to Bathhurst in Australia in 1936:

> 'at sunset a party of a score of the black aborigines passed by, each carrying, in their accustomed manner, a bundle of spears and other weapons. By giving the leading man a shilling, they were easily detained, and threw their spears for my amusement [...] In their own arts they are admirable. A cap being fixed at thirty yards distance, they transfixed it with a spear, delivered by the throwing-stick with the rapidity of an arrow from the bow of a practiced archer.'[675]

Atlatls of various kinds were identified in prehistoric archaeological contexts at a number of sites in different parts of the world as archaeology 'took off' in the late nineteenth century. Frank Cushing, who excavated atlatls in America, commented in 1895 on the effectiveness of his reproduction of one of these tools and thus he can be described as probably 'the first atlatl experimenter on record'.[676]

Whittaker identifies three archaeological issues confronting atlatl experimenters: '(1) the relationship of spearthrowers to the bow and arrow; (2) the recognition of altlatls in the archaeological record, from projectile point evidence and from atlatl parts themselves, especially stone weights or bannerstones; and (3) the function and capabilities of atlatls.'

Whittaker concludes that, in relation to the first of these issues, 'Any evolutionary relationship between the atlatl and the bow remains speculative and [...] unlikely [since] atlatls and bows work on completely different principles, not through common use of the power of a flexing spring'.

The second issue has prompted much debate regarding the projectile points as to whether these represent archery or spear throwing; the

---

[675] Darwin (1909) in Whittaker (2010)
[676] Whittaker (2010)

simple assumption that light projectile points indicate arrows and heavier ones indicate spears is demonstrably problematic. The discovery of bannerstones could indicate the use of the atlatl; Whittaker describes bannerstones as 'stone objects – drilled lengthwise – with a variety of forms that range from tubular to triangular in cross-section, sometimes with "wings" or other elaboration and often finely made of hard and colorful stone.' In the early twentieth century Charles Willoughby suggested these could be the weights at the distal end of throwing spears, a view that is shared by many modern archaeologists.

Most experimentation with atlatls has focused on the third of the three issues. Whittaker has commented 'our knowledge of how to throw a light spear with an atlatl, both theoretical and practical, comes from ethnographic observation and practical experience.' Experiments have considered in particular the role of weights and bannerstones, attempting 'to measure changes in efficiency, or at least maximum throwing distance.'

Weapon trials 'have shown that atlatl-thrown projectiles can be deadly.' Whittaker highlights the work of George Frison (1989) who 'experimented with the carcasses of culled elephants to demonstrate that a Clovis point on a spear hurled with the aid of an atlatl could make a fatal wound in even the largest animals.' The efficiency of the tool is highly subjective and hence very difficult to quantify – not only do construction decisions impact upon outcome but so too do the skill and physique of the user. Thus 'one of the basic premises of experiments with prehistoric technology is that the experimenter should be competent enough in using the tool to give it a fair.'

Whittaker concludes that experiments with atlatls are especially valuable because 'atlatls are fairly easy to make and to use at an elementary level, even if difficult to master, they are ideal for teaching experimental archaeology and for instilling in students and the public a respect for, and interest in, preindustrial technology.' Like archery, spear throwing has become a popular modern sport in parts of the western World.

Of course, as with the other experiments described in this book, the atlatl experiments have a fundamental limitation, as Whittaker recognizes: 'they create only analogies to prehistoric tool use, a body of hypothetical functions that we know work and ones that we are fairly sure do not.' Furthermore, Whittaker the experimenter acknowledges the advantages of the observations of anthropologists: 'Experiments do not quite substitute for actual observations of a tool in use in its living culture.' Nevertheless replicative experiments are of immense importance to the discipline since, as the atlatl experiments of the past hundred years or so have amply demonstrated, 'they allow us to make much more realistic interpretations of the archaeological evidence and inspire more imaginative ideas that can be tested against further experiments and the evidence provided by the artifacts.'

## Architectural survey

English Heritage (now Historic England) provided some useful 'first steps' guidance for those interested in tracing the history of the property in which they live:

'Before you begin your research try to establish the following key points:

- Whether your house is listed. The National Heritage List for England records a brief overview of the date of construction and significant features of every listed building in England.
- A rough estimate of how old your house is. This can be established through a basic architectural evaluation, by reading up about the local area, and by talking to your neighbours and other members of the local community.
- The date when it was built even be carved on the building.
- What administrative area your house is in. Knowing the names of the county, registration district and parish in which the property stands will help with locating relevant records later on in your research.
- What you know about the area. A general understanding of the area can be useful when you're researching the history of an individual house. Whether it's in a village, a suburb, or right in the heart of a city, you can find such information through published resources such as the Victoria County

*History series or the Survey of London, and on the British History Online website.'*[677]

Maps, photographs and plans help establish a property's architectural history while registers, censuses, directories and other archival material can reveal the history of its inhabitants.

The Vernacular Architecture Group (VAG) 'for all those interested in lesser traditional buildings' was established in 1952. Vernacular houses are defined by English Heritage as 'houses built in the main from locally available materials that reflect custom and tradition more than mainstream architectural fashions'.[678] VAG, of course, is also concerned with other structures such as commercial, industrial and agricultural buildings.

The group's mission is 'to further the study of traditional buildings, originally those of the British Isles'. Its members are concerned with the study of detailed local or regional surveys; studies of particular types of buildings including houses, farms, industrial and urban buildings; building materials; techniques of building, including carpentry and masonry; documentary evidence.[679] Its journal, *Vernacular Architecture*, is, in the group's own words 'the authoritative voice on the subject'.

The Institute for Archaeologists' Buildings Archaeology Group was established in 2003 'to act as a forum for promoting the archaeological analysis, research, interpretation of standing structures'.[680]

The essential starting place for any vernacular architecture recording project is English Heritage's 2006 publication *Understanding Historic Buildings: a guide to good recording practice*, available as a free on-line PDF download in three parts.[681] It contains 'clear, practical guidance on

---

[677] http://www.english-heritage.org.uk/your-home/your-homes-history/how-to-find-out/ Accessed 24/05/14
[678] Anon. (2011), *Vernacular Houses*, English Heritage, p. 2
[679] http://www.vag.org.uk/ Accessed 17/04/14
[680] Buildings Archaeology Group. http://www.archaeologists.net/groups/buildings Accessed 24/05/14
[681] http://www.english-heritage.org.uk/publications/understanding-historic-buildings/understandinghistoricbuildings1.pdf Accessed 24/05/14

the ways in which the wealth of historical evidence embodied in buildings can be gathered and disseminated for the lasting benefit and enjoyment of all' and, fully illustrated with case studies, makes available conventions for architectural survey drawing.

## Investigations and dissertations

*The information below is closely based upon advice and guidance provided for Level 6 History undergraduates by my colleagues at Plymouth University. Much of it is relevant to students at any level undertaking an extended investigation.*

The dissertation, typically around 10,000 words long and a core element of Level 6 / BA (Hons) study, aims to bring together many of the skills developed during the course of the degree, providing an opportunity to put these skills into practice on an extended basis. With the completion of the dissertation, students will have shown their ability to work as autonomous learners, recognising and explaining the possibilities and difficulties of a research programme which they have helped to create.

Planning and writing a dissertation can be very intimidating tasks. The basic challenges which you will encounter include choosing a suitable topic; managing and assessing the volume of material you uncover; and turning this material into a coherent and readable argument.

The main aim of the dissertation is the completion of an in-depth study of an area of special interest, making use of primary sources, academic texts and, where appropriate, experiential learning. It is likely to consider different approaches to, and interpretations of history and/or heritage and/or archaeology.

At the beginning of the process, in a Project Proposal, students will determine their area of study, undertake a literature review and locate the primary sources and/or experiences necessary for their study. By the time of the submission of this assignment, students will be able to critically review the available body of knowledge on a particular topic, and will have enhanced their ability to evaluate sources, to organise their work into a coherent argument, and to support their case with bibliographical apparatus, presented in a scholarly manner.

The completed dissertation should have an introduction (an updated and amended version of the Project Proposal), clearly structured chapters or sections, a conclusion, a comprehensive bibliography. It should be word processed and must conform to scholarly academic style as far as footnoting and bibliographic conventions are concerned. Assessors will pay particular attention to the framing of the project/scope of investigation; knowledge and awareness of relevant historiography and/or professional practice; use of primary source material and/or experiential learning; and the level of interpretation and analysis.

As with other assignments, there is no magic formula for researching and writing a dissertation. Your path from beginning to submission will depend on many different factors: for example, your previous knowledge of the subject, whether or not you have strong views on it, your usual working methods etc. However, whatever route you adopt, you will first need to come up with a suitable area of research. Maybe you have always had a strong desire to cover a particular topic. If not, maybe you have to think carefully about what aspects of History, Heritage and Archaeology you enjoy most, or least.

Whichever of these categories you fall into, here is a checklist of items to consider before you get started:

In order to help you decide whether your idea has the potential for a successful dissertation, always bear in mind in the question: how can the topic be attempted?

Do you have the opportunity and finances to look at required material / visit key sites / engage in the necessary experiential learning?

Within your general area of interest, is there a specific aspect that has not been fully investigated? Can you think of a distinctive angle that would allow you to undertake something more detailed than a coursework essay? You need the right size of topic, neither too ambitious nor too narrow for the word limit.

While your choice of topic is open-ended, remember that you will get the best help from the supervisor helping you if it falls within the established areas of staff teaching and research interests. Choosing a topic outside areas of staff expertise will mean possibly accepting constraints on supervision in certain respects, e.g. advising on the location and accessibility of primary sources.

Be prepared for a certain amount of trial and error: you may go down a few 'dead ends' in doing preliminary reading, but it's vital to end up with a topic which works. Most of all, try to find something that interests and stimulates you - you've got to live with it for several months.

You need to set aside time throughout the academic year to do justice to your dissertation. While there is no exact measurement, you should aim to spend between 300 and 400 hours on your dissertation over the course of a year, with up to half of these spent on primary research. While every individual will have their preferred methods of working, the following 'how to' advice allows you to amend your practice as required.

Start by reading the most obvious books on the subject and work through their bibliographies and footnotes looking for more obscure sources. You can then order these from the library or on Inter Library Loan if they are out of print or not available. If you can't find a book or journal on the shelf, it is always worth asking further questions about it, especially if it is a rare or out of print book. Some items (in the University Library) are on (easy to use) microfilm, on databases, or in remote corners because of cataloguing, space considerations or reasons of rarity.

Sometimes the most helpful thing you can do is to spend a day browsing shelves, noting areas of interest, the dates of books, the key critics' names, and wandering through their arguments. If your subject is a much-researched one, don't be overwhelmed by the mass of material on it. Much of what is said will duplicate arguments from other books, and if you narrow your field of interest as you progress, you will begin to know what to look for in the index or chapter headings of a book and can save time by reading selectively. On the other hand, if there is surprisingly little written about your subject, you have an opportunity to make it your own. Early on in the process, you'll need to plan out in what order you'll tackle the required primary sources (as agreed with your supervisor), undertaking trips to archives and sites as and when time allows.

Note-taking is a key part of writing a dissertation. Always write down everything that you think might be useful. It is best to assume that you will never see the book, article or primary source again and act accordingly. While conventions for referring to secondary sources are clear cut, in the case of primary sources the best advice is to: look at how writers of monographs refer to their sources; ask your supervisor for assistance, given the variety of source available; and use common sense (e.g., if a letter is being cited, then put: x to y, date, name of archive, reference number in archive).

By the time you have read around the subject a little, you will have begun to form a view or hypothesis about your area of research. Take time to think about what you have read, to weigh up different views and to come up with ideas of your own. At this stage you should think about beginning to plan, for example thinking carefully about the structure of the dissertation. With some topics, particular ones linked to work-placements, you need to think carefully about the health and safety aspect of your research.

You should before too long develop an awareness of the debates and 'grey areas' that need further exploration; a notion of some of the questions that need to be asked; and a collection of views quotations which begin to provide a framework for your study.

If you do all the research which you think you need, and only then start to write shortly before the assessment deadline, you will most likely experience unwelcome panic. You can avoid some of the excesses of last minute writing stress if you begin to write early. Plan, draft, re-plan and re-draft until you are happy with what you've done.

Don't try to produce a draft, big or small, for your supervisor every week. This kind of pace will leave you with little time to think and develop your views, and it will exhaust both you and your supervisor. It is best to allow yourself time to mull over new reading. Always read your drafts through before submitting them: you will undoubtedly think of some correction or modification at the last minute.

It's a good idea to construct a bibliography as you write. In that way, you will quickly identify any omissions from your notation of titles, dates, publishers etc. and should be able to remedy them. Writing the bibliography as you go will prevent much last minute searching for works consulted, and the panic of trying to remember in a week everything you've ever read on the subject. ENDNOTE software is available to help with this task if needed.

When you have finished a draft, read and review it. How could you make your points more clearly? Are there any sections which are confused, irrelevant, or deserve more space? How does the dissertation look as a whole? Is its central 'thesis' clear, and are its areas of exploration well-defined?

Rework the argument to make sure that all the material is relevant to the title, and that the introduction and conclusion set out a clear path and describe your destination. Read through the dissertation looking at the start and end of paragraphs. Do they connect to advance your argument a stage further each time?

Presentation of the dissertation is a vital component of its success. Aim to write in a clear and fluent style, with all your work checked by you (and via drafts, with your supervisor) *before* submission, for spelling, grammar and punctuation.

The dissertation is not just a description of your subject and other scholar's critical views of it – it is also your opportunity to develop at length your own critical analysis and argument and to show your skills as a researcher, writer, scholar and debater. Assessors don't expect original discoveries at undergraduate level, but we do expect a thorough investigation of existing material on your topic.

Interest and enthusiasm is the key. Try to write a dissertation which other people will want to read, which will inform and engage them, and which will allow them to recall the main points, sum up the argument and say whether they agree with your interpretation. A dissertation is an extended essay or report which gives you space to develop a view. Adduce many examples to prove and illustrate it, and to say what you think and why you have come to your conclusions on the subject.

## CASE STUDY: A history of a house in Wells, Somerset

*What follows are extracts from a contemporary heritage project carried out by a Level 6 student, Marja Haas, in 2015.*[682] *The analysis of the structure and its fittings, together with documentary evidence, enabled the student to construct a history of the property and to make a significant and original contribution to the historical record. Note the very wide range of approaches identified and applied by the student.*

### Aims and Methodology

The aims of this project are threefold:

- To investigate the history of the physical structure of the building and uncover any distinctly vernacular features of the architecture as well as to identify how long a house may have been extant in this position and when alterations may have been made.
- To trace the ownership of the house, starting from the present day to as far back as can be achieved given the available time and resources.
- To trace the occupants of the house, starting from the present day to as far back as can be achieved given the constraints stated above.

The methodology can be broadly grouped into three categories which reflect the aims of the project:

- The investigation of the structure entailed analysing the physical structure, consulting photographs taken approximately five years ago which reveal structural detail, research in the Wells City Archives (WCA) and Somerset Records Office and consulting various texts relating to vernacular architecture.

---

[682] Marja Haas, submission for *History, Heritage and Archaeology* Module SHHA 302, Strode College in partnership with Plymouth University, 2015-2016.

- The enquiries into ownership were carried out by consulting the title deeds, research at the WCA and independent research utilising tools such as birth, marriage and death records as well as wills and probate records.
- The exploration into occupancy was primarily achieved by researching census data (where available) as well as consulting the WCA for any supplemental information.
- Further information was obtained through interviews with local residents and discussions with personnel at the WCA.

**Historical Background**

Southover, now a single street, is an ancient area of settlement and development within the city of Wells. Archaeological evaluation and observation, carried out between 2000 and 2003 indicate there was once Romano-British occupation in this area, Domesday mentions Southover as one of three clusters of houses within the manor of Wells and Bishop Reginald (1174 – 1191) issued a charter outlining new boundaries to enable growth of the city and this seems to have added Southover to the borough. [683] Southover was also the main route from Wells to Street and the site of the Southover Gate tollhouse (although this was replaced in 1842 by the Keward Gate).[684] The area of Southover is described as working class with a tanner recorded in 1499-1500[685] as well as six beer sellers and a shoemaker recorded in 1635.[686] In 1645 it seems to have been '… the odorous suburb of Southover with its tanners, cobblers and smiths'[687] and this description is echoed by Shaw who believes it contained people of more modest means than other streets such as Chamberlain Street.[688] In addition to these written references, initial discussions with Dr. Julia Wood at Wells City Archives elicited the suggestion that the house 'may well be ancient.'[689]

---

[683] Tony Scrase, *Wells, A Small City*, (Tempus; 2006), pp.16-23.
[684] http://www.turnpikes.org.uk/Somerset%20-%20Wells.htm.
[685] Scrase, *Wells, A Small City*, pp.59-61.
[686] Scrase, *Wells, A Small City*, p.92.
[687] Anthony Nott, *Under God's Visitation: A Study of Wells from the Civil War to the Restoration*, (Anthony Nott; 2010), p.10.
[688] David Gary Shaw, *The Creation of a Community:The City of Wells in the Middle Ages*, (Oxford University Press; 1993), p.40.
[689] Pers Comm, Dr. Julia Wood, Wells City Archivist, 6th October 2015.

## Building Age, Structure and Vernacular Features

Examination of the Title Deeds and associated documents soon established that there has been a house on this site from at least 1814. The current structure is a two storey house; downstairs is a small entrance way, a large front/living room with an open hearth fireplace, and a large kitchen also with fireplace; upstairs comprises a landing, three bedrooms and a bathroom.

Recent documentary evidence shows that a planning application was granted in 2005 for the replacement of the front door.[690] Retrospective planning permission was gained in 1998 for the 'insertion of two doors and six windows'[691] (this is the total number of external doors and windows). This was necessary as permitted development rights in terms of the installation, replacement and alteration of any windows, doors or other openings, were removed in 1992 under the terms of the Town & Country Planning General Development Order of 1988, relating to part of the Wells Conservation Area.[692]

Maps viewed at the WCA show that the house was extended to its current size and shape sometime between 1860 and 1885.[693] These extensions are different in terms of building material with stone being used at the back and brick at the front so it is likely they were carried out separately. A 1788 map of Wells[694] shows buildings on the site and Strachey's map of Somerset[695] suggests that there may have been a building present in 1736. No further documentary evidence relating to the age of the house was uncovered.

Vernacular building materials are in evidence in the thick stone walls,

---

[690] Mendip District Council planning reference 113457/001.
[691] Mendip District Council planning reference 113457/000.
[692] Documentation is held together with the Title Deeds at Bartlett, Gooding & Wheelan Solicitors.
[693] WCC/108/1 Large Scale Sewerage Survey Map of Wells, 1860; WCC/uncatalogued item: First Large Scale Ordnance Survey Map of Wells, 1885/1886 (XLI.5.13).
[694] SRO DD/FS/193 1788 Map of the parish of St. Cuthbert by William White.
[695] SRO T/PH/SAS/C2026/2(d) Wells portion of Strachey's 1736 Map of Somerset.

some measuring two feet;[696] the flagstone floors appear to be blue lias which is typical in this area;[697] and the clay pantiles on the roof, almost certainly manufactured in Bridgewater and common from the eighteenth century onwards. This is in keeping with what could be expected.[698]

The substantial fireplace in the older part of the house may provide a clue to the age of the building as this is not dissimilar to those seen in houses in Westbury-sub-Mendip, some having been tentatively dated to the sixteenth century and may reflect building on a medieval footprint.[699]

Despite the modern bricks the fireplace is clearly an open hearth of the type found in country cottages throughout Somerset although some date to the Victorian period rather than the more distant past.[700] The large breastsummer is characteristic of an earlier build and may indicate the introduction of a smoke hood.[701] This may also explain the large chimney breast which runs the entire width of the hearth. While the breastsummer is large enough to be dated by dendrochronology, this would not provide a reliable date for the hearth as the timber may have been reclaimed from elsewhere.

The blue lias flagstones in the oldest part of the house extend to the exterior edge of what were the exterior walls, indicating that the floor is older than the existing house structure. The quality and size of some of the flagstones in the area adjacent to the fireplace do not seem in keeping with a simple cottage. One flagstone is 75 inches (6'3") long by 42 inches (3'6") wide which is more akin to what may

---

[696] E.H.D. Williams, 'The Building Materials of Somerset's Vernacular Houses', SANHS Proceedings, Vol 135, 1991, pp.123 – 134.
[697] Jane Penoyre, Traditional Houses of Somerset, (Somerset Books; 2005), p.14; Williams, 'The Building Materials of Somerset's Vernacular Houses'.
[698] Penoyre, Traditional Houses of Somerset, p.20; Williams, 'The Building Materials of Somerset's Vernacular Houses'.
[699] Elaine Jamieson, The Historic Landscape of the Mendip Hills, (Historic England; 2015), pp.178-218; W.G. Hoskins, 'The Rebuilding of Rural England, 1570 – 1640', The Past and Present Society, No.4. (Nov. 1953), pp.44-59.
[700] C.W. Green, Country Life in Victorian Somerset vol II, (Friends of the Abbey Barn, Somerset Rural Life Museum; 1979).
[701] Jamieson, The Historic Landscape of the Mendip Hills, p.79; R.W. Brunskill, Vernacular Architecture: An Illustrated Handbook, (Faber and Faber; 2000), pp. 122-123.

be expected of a burial slab. Others are very neatly cut and finished. This is interesting as there is evidence of a medieval (or possibly Anglo-Saxon) chapel in Southover (location unknown)[702] and these flagstones may provide a clue. It is not inconceivable that either the house has been built on the site of the former chapel given the approximate east-west orientation of the flagstones or that the flagstones were reclaimed from the chapel site. The floor in the front room shows evidence of an internal wall having been removed; there is some anecdotal evidence to support this which indicates that this alteration took place post 1990.[703]

Another aspect of the building that is worth further investigation is the wall which adjoins the building next door (possibly late eighteenth century). Unlike the other walls of the house, this is a single brick thick and is apparently shared with the neighbouring property – this may indicate that the house was built as part of that structure or that it was widened at some point; this possibility may also explain the lateral front door way.

**Conclusion**

There has clearly been an occupied house on this site since at least the beginning of the nineteenth century and possibly earlier. The house has been built and extended using vernacular building materials. The large fireplace may prove a useful tool for dating the current structure although the floor seems to be the oldest feature. While the house has served as a family home for this period it also appears to have served as a boarding house when occupied by Mary Hammond, as per the 1891 census returns. There is no evidence to support any other commercial use for the building, although it is feasible that Elizabeth Green's eldest son was carrying out his trade on the premises. There is no evidence to suggest that the house has been in anything other than private ownership.

---

[702] A.J. Scrase, 'A medieval chapel at Southover in Wells, and its possible Anglo-saxon origins'. *SANHS Proceedings*, Vol. 126, 1982, pp. 107-110.
[703] Interview with Brian 'Taff' Ebdon (born 1936) on 9th October 2015. Taff lodged in the house on many occasions after moving to Wells in 1958, often after a 'good night' in the Full Moon public house which is sited across the road from 23 Southover and recalls there having been an internal wall.

**Evaluation**

While this project has met the stated objectives, there are obviously some gaps in the information that has been discovered. This is partly due to the nature of the available resources; records of BMD as well as census records are most suited to family history rather than house history and the census records for Southover are only reliable from 1881. In addition, the ten year intervals in census records can only provide a snapshot rather than an ongoing picture.

To gain a more complete history of the house it would be valuable to undertake wider research into the Southover area and certainly to consider the adjoining houses. It would also be beneficial to carry out more detailed research into all of the people who owned or lived in the house prior to 1963 to gain a better understanding of whether it has been used for commercial activities and to gain a more complete record of occupancy.

A full vernacular architecture survey would be valuable to uncover any further indications of age and associated history. Further research into the location of the early chapel may provide additional information.

This document will be lodged at the WCA where Dr. Julia Wood will add it to the library of existing research material for future reference. Dr. Wood will also be contacting the eminent local historian, Tony Scrase, with regard to the possible connection to the early chapel.[704]

**Bibliography**

Brunskill, R.W., *Vernacular Architecture: An Illustrated Handbook*, (Faber and Faber; 2000).
Green, C.W., *Country Life in Victorian Somerset Vol II*, (Friends of the Abbey Barn, Somerset Rural Life Museum; 1979).
Hoskins, W.G., 'The Rebuilding of Rural England, 1570 – 1640', *The Past and Present Society*, No.4. (Nov. 1953), pp. 44-59.
Jamieson, Elaine, *The Historic Landscape of the Mendip Hills*, (Historic England; 2015).
Nott, Anthony, *Under God's Visitation: A Study of Wells from the Civil War to*

---

[704] Pers Comm, Dr. Julia Wood, Wells City Archivist, 10th November 2015.

the Restoration, (Anthony Nott; 2010).
Penoyre, Jane, Traditional Houses of Somerset, (Somerset Books; 2005).
Scrase, A.J. 'A medieval chapel at Southover in Wells, and its possible Anglo-Saxon origins'. SANHS Proceedings, Vol. 126, 1982, pp. 107-110.
Scrase, Tony, Wells, A Small City, (Tempus; 2006).
Shaw, David Gary, The Creation of a Community:The City of Wells in the Middle Ages, (Oxford University Press; 1993).
Williams, E.H.D. 'The Building Materials of Somerset's Vernacular Houses', SANHS Proceedings, Vol 135, 1991, pp.123 – 134.

**Somerset Records Office**

SRO DD/FS/193  1788 Map of the parish of St. Cuthbert by William White.
SRO DD/SAS/C795/SE/24  Will of William Young dated 1774.
SRO T/PH/SAS/C2026/2(d)  Wells portion of Strachey's 1736 Map of Somerset.

**Wells City Archives**

WCC/uncatalogued item  Maps Showing Land Ownership in Wells up to circa 1825.
WCC/uncatalogued item  First Large Scale Ordnance Survey Map of Wells, 1885/1886 (XLI.5.13).
WCC/108/1Large Scale Sewerage Survey Map of Wells, 1860.
WCC/108/3    Wells Survey Book of Reference, 1860.
WCC/1022/11 List of tenants in 1701 with amendments in 1710.

**Websites**

http://www.ancestry.co.uk
http://www.findmypast.co.uk
http://www.turnpikes.org.uk/Somerset%20-%20Wells.htm

# Research

A vast range of journals is accessible on-line, some of which are also available as hard copies, some of which only exist electronically. Some of those that are relevant to students of History, Heritage and Archaeology and available on-line are:

**Journals**

**HISTORY**

History Today
Past and Present
Journal of Women's History
Journal of Social History
Journal of Economic History
Journal of Contemporary History
Journal of Medieval History
Local History News
The Local Historian: journal of the British Association for Local History
The Oral History Review
The Journal of the History of Childhood and Youth
German History
Twentieth Century British History
Journal of World History
The Journal of Religious History
Economic History Review
The Journal of Modern History
The Journal of Military History
Magic, Ritual and Witchcraft

**HERITAGE**
Journal of Cultural Heritage
International Journal of Heritage Studies
Journal of Heritage Tourism
Museum and Society
Museum International
Museum Management and Curatorship
The International Museum of the Inclusive Museum

**ARCHAEOLOGY**
International Journal of Historical Archaeology
Journal of Maritime Archaeology
Environmental Archaeology
Journal of Field Archaeology
Journal of Anthropological Archaeology
Oxford Journal of Archaeology
Antiquity
Archaeology, Ethnology and Anthropology of Eurasia
World Archaeology
Journal of Archaeological Science

Most of the journals in the list are accessible by subscription only. Many are made available to students by their colleges and universities. Some key journals, such as *Current Archaeology*, do not exist in an electronic form.

Numerous websites provide access to digitised archives. Jisc Historic Books (http://jischistoricbooks.ac.uk/) is the gateway to 350,000 books dating from the late fifteenth century to the end of the nineteenth century, all published in English. It combines three vast collections: Early English Books Online (EEBO), Eighteenth Century Collections Online (ECCO) and 65,000 nineteenth century texts from the British Library. The related Jisc Media Hub (http://jiscmediahub.ac.uk/) provides access to thousands of images, videos and audio files, all of which can be used freely by students for academic purposes.

KnowUK provides access to many contemporary secondary sources including useful reference books such as *The Oxford Companion to British History* and *The Oxford Companion to Family and Local History*.

The following section provides Internet addresses for sites relevant to students of History, Heritage and Archaeology.

**Useful websites**

The Oral History Society
The Oral History Association
National Organisations
Ancient Monuments Society
Architecture.com
Association for Studies in the Conservation of Historic Buildings
British Association for Local History
British Brick Society
Carpenters Fellowship
Castles of Britain
Construction History Society
Council for British Archaeology
English Heritage
Friends of Friendless Churches
The Georgian Group

Historic Chapels Trust
Historic Farm Buildings Group
Historic Houses Association
Institute of Field Archaeologists: Buildings Archaeology Group
Institute of Historic Building Conservation
The National Trust
Regional Furniture Society
The Royal Commission on the Ancient and Historical Monuments of Scotland
The Royal Commission on the Ancient and Historical Monuments of Wales
SAVE Britain's Heritage
Society of Architectural Historians of Great Britain
Society for the Protection of Ancient Buildings
Stone Roofing Association
Cumbria Vernacular Buildings Group
Wealden Buildings Study Group
Yorkshire Vernacular Buildings Study Group
Scottish Vernacular Buildings Working Group
Suffolk Historic Buildings Group
Essex Historic Buildings Group
Domestic Buildings Research Group (Surrey)
Norfolk Historic Buildings Group
Somerset Vernacular Building Research Group
Oxfordshire Buildings Record
East Midlands Earth Structures Society
Wessex Mills Group
Historic Buildings in the Faversham Area
Buildings in Herefordshire
Buckinghamshire Archaeological Society Historic Buildings Group
Vernacular Architecture Forum
AVISTA (Association Villard de Honnecourt for Interdisciplinary Study of Medieval Technology, Science, and Art)
The Timber-Framers Guild of North America
The Vernacular Architecture Society of South Africa
Libraries, Archives and Online Resources
Paul Oliver Vernacular Library
Oxford Society of Architects Collection
A2A - Access to Archives
National Monuments Record

Images of England
Archaeological Data Service
The Oxford Dendrochonology Laboratory dated buildings register
The National Archives
PastScape
Jean Manco's Sources for Building History
Timber Framed Houses
BBC History Online
British Archaeological Jobs Resource
Looking at Buildings
Heritage Gateway
GENUKI - UK and Ireland Genealogy
Explore England's Past
Museums
Avoncroft Museum of Historic Buildings
Chiltern Open Air Museum
Ryedale Folk Museum
Weald and Downland Open Air Museum
IBRA Bee Boles Register
Deliberately Concealed Garments Project
Apotropaios
Victoria County History
Wattle and Daub: Craft, Conservation and Wiltshire Case Study
Ken's Great Barns

### *Primary sources and catalogues*

**British**
www.nationalarchives.gov.uk/
The National Archives, Kew. Includes detailed research guides for locating material on particular topics, and the capacity to order digital copies of some documents.

http://sas-space.sas.ac.uk/4684/
Institute of Historical Research guide to manuscript sources for British history: a guide by R. J. Olney (c. 56 pages)

http://www.history.ac.uk/ihr/Resources/about.html
History online developed by Institute of Historical Research – information about quality resources for historians.

Check the site History Online
http://www.history.ac.uk/projects/digital/history-online

Reviews in History
http://www.history.ac.uk/projects/digital/reviews-history

http://www.british-history.ac.uk/
British History Online, a digital library for primary and secondary sources from medieval to 1900 period. Mostly freely available.

http://www.connectedhistories.org/
Connected Histories (launched on 31 March 2011) is a federated search facility for a wide range of distributed digital resources relating to early modern and nineteenth-century British history.

http://www.historyofparliamentonline.org/
Since 1964, the History of Parliament Trust has been researching and publishing a major source of British historical reference.

http://www.victoriacountyhistory.ac.uk/explore/
Provides free access to reliable local history materials, produced by academics and volunteers. Photographs, paintings, drawings, maps, text, transcribed documents and audio files are organised thematically and by their geographical location.

http://www.spartacus.schoolnet.co.uk/REVhistoryjournals.htm
Links to online history journals, and providing you with a portal into the world of modern Higher Education debates in History.

http://www.artstor.org/index.shtml
A database of over 1 million digital images in the arts, architecture, humanities, and science

http://vos.ucsb.edu/index.asp
Voice of the Shuttle (History): database listing and linking to many online resources for history, both general and specific.

http://www.lib.byu.edu/~rdh/wwi/
World War One document archive

**http://archivegrid.org/web/index.jsp**
A major catalogue of historical documents, personal papers and family history material held in repositories around the world.

**http://archiveshub.ac.uk/**
Archives Hub: national gateway to descriptions of archives of over 180 UK repositories (including Oxford and Cambridge)

**http://ukdataservice.ac.uk/**
Providing access to, or abstracts for, a wide-ranging collection of historical digital resources. Based on material that was previously accessed via the UK Data archive.

**http://www.dango.bham.ac.uk/**
DANGO (Database of Archives of Non-Governmental Organisations): a database of archives of U.K. NGOs since 1945, for a project completed in October 2011.

## Newspapers

**Nexis**
Newspapers and magazines: includes international, national, regional and local titles

**Lexis Library**
UK national, regional and local newspapers going back more than 20 years. Within Lexis you will need to choose the News tab to access.

**Onlinenewspapers.com**
A free website giving access to recent news but does not give full or archive content.

**Times Digital Archive**
Access to the Times online between 1785 - 1985.

**19th Century British Library newspapers**
48 influential national and regional newspapers representing different political and cultural segments of the 19th century British society.

**17th-18th Century Burney Collection newspapers**
Access to 1757-1817 early English newspapers


## Historic books and pamphlets

Googlebooks

**http://www.gutenberg-e.org/**
Gutenberg-e: collaboration between Columbia University Press and the American Historical Association, offering free access to selected e-book titles

**http://www.fordham.edu/Halsall/index.asp**
Internet History Sourcebooks Project: collections of public domain and copy-permitted historical texts presented for educational use.

http://archive.org/details/texts
Internet Text Archive: free online library of over 3 million titles

## British university special collections

http://digital.bodleian.ox.ac.uk/
Bodleian Libraries Special Collections

http://cudl.lib.cam.ac.uk/
Cambridge Digital Library and Cambridge University Library Digital Collections

http://collections.ex.ac.uk/repository/
University of Exeter Digital Collections Online: open access repository.

## British national libraries, museums and galleries

**British Library**
http://www.bl.uk/onlinegallery/index.html
British Library Online Gallery: online access to 30,000 items from the collections; includes collection highlights and online exhibitions

**National Library of Scotland**
http://www.nls.uk/
http://www.nls.uk/digital-resources
Includes online popular music galleries, film, drawings, maps, Post office directories.

**National Library of Wales**
Various digitisation projects and collections, see
http://www.llgc.org.uk/index.php?id=welshjournals

**Copac**
http://copac.ac.uk/
The integrated online catalogues of many major university, specialist, and national libraries in the UK and Ireland.

**British Museum**
http://www.britishmuseum.org/explore.aspx

British Museum: online highlights and capacity to search the database, which covers almost 2 million items, of which over 610,000 have one or more images attached.

**National Gallery**
http://www.nationalgallery.org.uk/
The online collections from the National Gallery in London.

**Victoria and Albert Museum**
http://www.vam.ac.uk/page/t/the-collections/
The online collections from the Victoria and Albert Museum, London.

**Cambridge University**
http://janus.lib.cam.ac.uk/
The combined database of more than 1800 catalogues of archives held throughout Cambridge University colleges.

**National Trust Collections**
www.nationaltrustcollections.org.uk/
Three-quarters of a million itmes on the database.

**BBC 'Your Paintings'**
http://www.bbc.co.uk/arts/yourpaintings/
210, 000 oil paintings online.

*International, European and American*

**International**
http://www.etown.edu/vl/
Guide to resources on international affairs – media sources and various organisations (UN, EU, US Government and more).

www.thecommonwealth.org
Includes references to material on the Commonwealth history

http://ocp.hul.harvard.edu/
*Harvard University Library Open Collections Program. A digital library includes Islamic Heritage Project.*

http://pudl.princeton.edu/collections.php
Princeton University Digital Library: collection of high-resolution digital e.g., Chinese Revolution, Gautemala 1963-2000.

**European**
http://www.theeuropeanlibrary.org/tel4/
http://www.theeuropeanlibrary.org/exhibition/
European Library portal and Exhibitions: online exhibitions of items from European national libraries: paintings, music, films and books from galleries, libraries, archives and museums

http://gallica.bnf.fr/
Gallica Digital Library: digital library of over 1 million books and documents, provided by the Bibliothèque nationale de France

http://www.fordham.edu/halsall/mod/modsbook.html
The site, 'Internet History Source Books Project' comprises collections of public domain and copy-permitted historical texts re European history and American history, as well as in modern Western Civilization and World Cultures.

http://eudocs.lib.byu.edu/index.php/Main_Page
Primary historical documents from Western Europe

**American**
http://www.loc.gov/
The Library of Congress. The online library includes 'American Memory', a gateway to rich primary source materials relating to the history and culture of the United States. The site offers more than 7 million digital items from more than 100 historical collections.

http://docsouth.unc.edu/
Documenting the American South (DocSouth) is a digital publishing initiative that provides Internet access to texts, images, and audio files related to Southern history, literature, and culture from the colonial period through the first decades of the 20th century. Currently DocSouth includes seven thematic collections of books, diaries, posters, artifacts, letters, oral history interviews, and songs.

http://www.hti.umich.edu/m/moagrp/

The Making of America, 19th century American text collection, plus hundreds of journal articles.

http://ocp.hul.harvard.edu/
*Harvard University Library Open Collections Program*. A digital library of 6 subject-specific, web-accessible collections c.2.3 million digitized pages. Also includes non-American history e.g., Islamic Heritage Project.

http://dl.lib.brown.edu/collections.php
Brown University Center for Digital Scholarship
Access to some of Brown University's special collections, includes African American sheet music, alcohol and temperance exhibitions, ethnomusicology, Napoleonic satires, Lincolniana.

http://pudl.princeton.edu/collections.php
*Princeton University Digital Library*: collection of high-resolution digital images of selected materials from Princeton University Library in fields of English restoration, Chinese Revolution, Gautemala 1963-2000, James Gillray, Eighty Years War.

**American National Archives**
http://www.archives.gov/
U.S. National Archives and Records Administration: website of the U.S. National Archives; includes online exhibits (documents, photographs etc).

*Useful databases*

**Arts & Humanities Full Text**

Arts & Humanities Full Text is an indexing and abstracting database covering Art, Architecture, Design, History, Philosophy, Music, Literature, Theatre, Cultural Studies and Women's studies.

**Blackwell Reference Online**

Blackwell Reference Online is a collection of handbooks, reference and companion texts covering the humanities and social sciences.

**BoB (Box of Broadcasts) National**

BoB (Box of Broadcasts) National is an innovative shared online off-air TV and radio recording service for UK higher and further education institutions. BoB enables all staff and students in subscribing institutions to choose and record any broadcast programme from 60+ TV and radio channels. The recorded programmes are then kept indefinitely (no expiry) and added to a growing media archive (currently at over 1 million programmes), with all content shared by users across all subscribing institutions.

**British History Online**

British History Online contains primary and secondary sources for the history of the British Isles.

**British Online Archives**

A disparate collection of primary source archival material including contemporary manuscripts, diaries, private papers, illustrations and more. Available collections:
- Defining Gender: 1450-1910
- Empire Online
- Women in the National Archives
- Nixon Years: 1969-1974
- Perdita Manuscripts
- Mass Observation Online
- India, Raj & Empire
- Victorian Popular Culture
- Grand Tour
- Literary Manuscripts: The Brotherton Collection
- Literary Manuscripts: Berg Collection
- London Low Life
- John Johnson Collection: an archive of printed ephemera

**British Periodicals (ProQuest)**

British Periodicals (ProQuest) provides access to hundreds of periodicals from the late seventeenth century to the early twentieth, comprising millions of high-resolution facsimile page images. Topics covered include literature, philosophy, history, science, the social sciences, music, art, drama, archaeology and architecture.

## Cambridge Companions Online

Cambridge Companions Online provides access to the companion books for many classic texts in literature, philosophy, religion and culture.

## Cambridge University Press Journals

Cambridge Journals (referred to as Cambridge University Press Journals) is a multidisciplinary journal publisher. We subscribe to many, but not all, of the journals available via this website.

## Historical Abstracts (EBSCO)

Historical abstracts (EBSCO) is an indexing and abstracting database for History.

## Historical Texts (JISC)

Includes: EEBO (Early English Books Online) with full-text digital versions of over 125,000 books published in English up to 1700; ECCO (Eighteenth Century Collections Online) a digital collection of all the books published in Great Britain and its colonies during the eighteenth century; and, Nineteenth Century books from the British Library which includes digitised versions of more than 65,000 first editions from the 19th century.

## House of Commons Parliamentary Papers 1688 – 2004

House of Commons Parliamentary Papers 1688 – 2004 includes sessional papers with supplementary material back to 1688.

## JSTOR Arts & Sciences III Collection

JSTOR is a multi-disciplinary journals archive - coverage is particularly strong on the humanities and social sciences. Please note that there is no current content available. Check Primo for current subscriptions.

**Literary Encyclopedia** publishes biographies of major and minor writers; scholarly descriptions of all interesting texts written by these authors, including those often neglected; and a variety of descriptive and critical essays on literary, cultural and historical matters. The vast majority of its contributors are practising academics who teach the subjects they write about in universities across the world.

**Oxford Journals**

Full text access to multi-disciplinary journals published by Oxford University Press.

**Periodicals Archive Online**

Backfiles of scholarly periodicals in the arts, humanities and social sciences providing access to the searchable full text of hundreds of titles. The database spans more than two centuries of content.

**Project MUSE**

Project MUSE is a full text resource particularly useful for Humanities and Social Science subjects. Content includes journal articles and book chapters.

**SAGE journals online**

Sage is a multidisciplinary journal publisher.

**Taylor & Francis Online**

Taylor & Francis and Routledge journals covering a variety of subject disciplines.

**UK Data Archive (UKDA)**

The UK Data Archive is curator of the largest collection of digital data in the social sciences and humanities in the United Kingdom. With several thousand datasets relating to society, both historical and contemporary, this archive is a vital resource for researchers, teachers and learners.

## Major British Archives

For those with the energy (and the money!) to visit national archives further afield, here is a selection of key locations:

**THE NATIONAL ARCHIVES**, Kew, Richmond, Surrey TW9 4DU   Tel: 020 876 3444
This holds government papers – Cabinet, Prime Minister's papers, Treasury and all other departments. 30 year rule applies on access – pencils only!

Includes:
http://www.nationalarchives.gov.uk/a2a/
Access to Archives: combined catalogue of archives held in 418 Record Offices and other repositories in England and Wales, dating from the eighth century to present.

**BODLEIAN LIBRARY**, Broad Street, Oxford OX1 3BG   Tel: 01865 277000
Holds (Conservative Party archive) politicians' private papers and microfilms of cabinet records etc.

**PEOPLE'S HISTORY MUSEUM**, 103 Princess Street, Manchester M1 6DD   Tel: 0161 838 9190
Holds Labour Party archive: NEC, Parliamentary Party, Shadow Cabinet etc.

**CHURCHILL COLLEGE**, Cambridge CB3 0DS   Tel: 01223 336000
Holds the private papers of many leading post-war politicians – contact the Archivist in the 'Archive Centre'.

**NATIONAL NEWSPAPER LIBRARY**, Colindale Avenue, London NW9 5UE   Tel: 020 200515
Holds all the main newspapers – national and local – some only on microfilm.

**INSTITUTE OF HISTORICAL RESEARCH**, Malet Street, London WC2

**NATIONAL REGISTER OF ARCHIVES**, now located in the National Archives, in Kew.

http://www.nationalarchives.gov.uk/nra/default.asp

**E-book Access**

MyiLibrary
Ebscohost e-Book Collection
Dawsonera
Safari Books Collection
All suppliers, with the exception of Safari books, allow you to set up a free account which allows you to make your own notes within the e-book for future reference. You can also print or download several pages within copyright law.

Increasingly, publishers are allowing their titles to be downloaded to a mobile device for reading off campus. Where this is an option follow the on screen instructions from the supplier.

**PhD Theses**

The British Library has set up EThOS, a service which enables individuals to register online at http://ethos.bl.uk and access PhD theses directly without library mediation. EThOS currently provides details of more than 250,000 theses.

**Oxford Dictionary of National Biography**
The DNB (first published in the late 19C) is freely available on-line as a facsimile and transcription of the entire work. The modern ODNB (electronic resource, frequently updated) can be accessed through the university or any public library (for public library card holders).

# Glossary

**Albigensian heresy** Also known as the Cathars, the Albigensians advocated beliefs that were deemed heretical by the Roman Catholic Church. Among other things, they maintained that the physical world was the evil creation of Satan. This theory would help pave the way for beliefs in 'diabolism' (people making pacts with the Devil) and the witch-hunts of the early modern period.

**Annalist** Named after a 'school' of twentieth century French historians who advanced the principle of 'total history'.

**Anthropology** The study of human beings.

**Archaeometry** The scientific analysis of archaeological material.

**Bourgeois** Literally 'of the middle classes'; the term used by Karl Marx to define the business class/middle class that he stated 'owned' the labour of the working class.

**Carlyle, Thomas** (1795-1881), Scottish essayist and historian, wrote *On Heroes and Hero Worship and the Heroic in History* (1841).

**Cartography** The study of maps.

**Clio** The muse of History in Greek mythology

**Cosmology** A world view.

**Counterfactual method** An approach to explaining the past that considers how things might have turned out differently if any one or more factors was absent. By so doing historians can begin to estimate the relative importance of different factors in forming their interpretations for why things happened as they did.

**Counter-revisionist** An argument that challenges the claims of history which 'revises' the traditional view. There is no 'school' of counter-revisionist historians and the term needs to be used with caution.

Glossary

**Cultural history** The history of popular ideas and their expression (e.g. through the arts).

**Demography** The study of population. Those who study population are demographers.

**Dendrochronology** Tree-ring dating technique.

**DMV** Deserted medieval village (historians and archaeologists also identify shrunken medieval villages).

**Determinist explanations** Explanations based on the assumption that events are determined by previous circumstances.

**Durkheim, Emile** Often seen as the 'father' of modern sociology. He published his pioneering sociological text, *Suicide*, in 1897.

**Economic determinism** The theory that the driving force in history is economics.

**Empirical history** History that relies entirely upon the objective 'truth' some consider inherent in every piece of historical evidence.

**Enumerator** Someone who collects data, e.g. a commissioner employed to fill in census information through a house-to-house survey.
**Feminist/women centred history** ' ... above all else, it is about the everyday experience of women, just as feminism itself is' (Sayer (1994), p. 7).

**Freud, Sigmund** (1856-1939), an Austrian neurologist and psychiatrist, is popularly identified with founding the science of psychoanalysis. He identified in the repression of one person or group by another an unconscious human defence mechanism.

**Frontier thesis** The highly influential theory of Frederick Jackson Turner concerning how American institutions and mentalities were shaped by the experience of expanding the frontier of modern America in the eighteenth and nineteenth centuries.

**Fogou** Man-made underground chambers of uncertain function; mostly associated with the Iron Age; found in Brittany, Ireland and Cornwall.

**Gender history** according to Green and Troup, 'arose from women's dissatisfaction with their historical invisibility' (Green and Troup (1999), p. 253). The history of women has become commonplace in university degree programmes since the 1970s.

**Genetic (or historical) relationism** The principle of exploring past events and individual actions in relation to past values and conditions.

**Glorious Revolution** The Glorious Revolution of 1688 overthrew England's king, James II, and replaced him with William of Orange (William III of England).

**Gothic restoration** Destructive architectural fashion of the nineteenth century aimed at restoring churches to their former medieval glory.

**Great Exhibition** 1851 trade fair and celebration of British culture and that of her colonies.

**Great Rebuilding** Era identified by Hoskins spanning the sixteenth and seventeenth centuries in which open hall houses with a central hearth began to be rebuilt as two (or more) storey houses incorporating chimneys; organic materials such as timber, wattle and daub, were largely replaced with stone and brick.

**Historical determinism** The theory that dynamic forces such as economic structures determine historical developments.

**Historiography** The study of historians and their writing about the past. It is the history of history writing and the factors determining historical accounts and interpretations.

**Lidar** Abbreviation for light detection and ranging: a highly effective airborne method of geophysical prospection.

**Liminal location** A location set where one context is juxtaposed with another (e.g. a beach where sea meets land).

**Local or regional history** The 'local' or 'regional' approach to history that investigates the past at a micro level is, arguably, more likely to produce a genuinely 'total' history than the ambitious projects of the first wave of Annalist historians.

**LSE** The London School of Economics (LSE) was founded by a group of reformist, as opposed to revolutionary, socialists known as the Fabian Society. In addition to the Webbs, the society's membership included the famous playwright, George Bernard Shaw. Their aim in setting up the school was to promote research into poverty and other economic issues of social concern. The LSE aimed to provide a socialistic foundation for the training of Britain's future captains of business and industry, and it was an important influence on the shaping of the British Labour Party.

**Macauley, Thomas Babington** (1800-59), Scottish Whig historian, poet and politician, wrote *The History of England from the Accession of James I* (1848).

**Magna Carta** The famous charter imposed by his barons on England's King John in 1215. Although it has been celebrated as a great step towards constitutional monarchy, John never intended to adhere to its excessive terms and conditions which would have destroyed the very foundation of medieval kingship. Nevertheless, although constitutional monarchy would not become a reality until the seventeenth century in England (and much later elsewhere), it is still regarded by some as the foundation of the US and French constitutions.

**Malthusian crisis** Thomas Malthus (1766-1834) is sometimes seen as the founder of the historical approach known as 'demography' (the study of population). The 'Malthusian crisis' marked the moment at which population growth outstripped the supply of food. Nature, he believed, left to its own devices, 'checked' such a crisis by such means as epidemic disease - unfortunate, but ultimately necessary, facts of life.

**'Mappa Mundi'** A map of the world made in England, c.1290.

**Malthusian crisis** Thomas Malthus (1766-1834) is sometimes seen as the founder of the historical approach known as 'demography' (the study of population). The 'Malthusian crisis' marked the moment at which population growth outstripped the supply of food. Nature, he believed, left to its own devices, 'checked' such a crisis by such means as epidemic disease - unfortunate, but ultimately necessary, facts of life.

**Marxist history** Historical approaches and interpretations informed by the theories of Karl Marx concerning the interplay between economic and political developments.

**McCarthyite campaign** Campaign of U.S. Senator McCarthy against suspected communists in America during the Cold War.

**Metanarratives** Literally the 'great stories' that some historians identify to explain aspects of the history of the societies they examine.

**Morphology** The study of the shape ('form') of artefacts.

**National Amenity Societies** A group of seven societies which have emerged since the late nineteenth century, all designed to preserve the artistic and architectural output of past times.

**Petrology** The analysis of stone.

**Polemical sources** Sources that may be controversial.

**Postmodernism** The term is sometimes used to describe new ways of viewing the past that have evolved since the late twentieth century.

**Proletarian** Term favoured by Karl Marx to define the waged working class, whose labour he maintained was controlled/owned by the 'bourgeoisie'.

**Provenance** The history of something – e.g. an object. Provenance in history is concerned with the nature, age, origin and purpose of items of historical evidence.

**Psycho-history** The application of the science of psychoanalysis to historical studies

**von Ranke, Leopold** (1795-1886), German historian who promoted the principle of history writing based on primary sources. He maintained that it is not the historian's 'duty to judge the past, nor instruct one's contemporaries with an eye to the future, but merely to show how it actually was'.

**Reformation** Era of religious upheaval in Europe in the sixteenth century; gave rise to the Protestant churches.

**Regressive method** Attempting to explain the past by 'working backward from the known to the unknown' (F. W. Maitland).

**Renaissance** Era of great cultural developments in Europe between the fourteenth and seventeenth centuries; literally means 'rebirth'.

**Romantic movement** Cultural, intellectual and artistic movement starting in the eighteenth century in Western Europe and continuing into the nineteenth; in part a reaction to the experience of modern industrialisation.

**Social Darwinism** Building on the theory of Charles Darwin (1809-92) that evolution is determined by the success of the 'fittest' in the evolutionary struggle, Social Darwinism applies the idea to the development of human societies. The theory was used as a justification for the claims of supremacy of one ethnic group over another in the first half of the twentieth century in the rightwing dictatorships of western Europe.

**Sociology** The study of society.

**Stratigraphy** The study by archaeologists of the soil layers (strata) in which objects are found.

**Structuralist approach** The assumption that the course of history is determined by structural factors such as a society's economic system.

**Subaltern studies** This defines historical studies that focus on marginalised groups in a political structure, specifically those of the

Indian sub-continent in the 'post-colonial' history that started to be written in the 1970s.

**Suez crisis** In 1956, Egypt's leader, Colonel Nasser, laid claim to the Suez Canal, an important trading route which runs through Egypt and connects the Mediterranean Sea to the Red Sea. Following unsuccessful negotiations with Nasser, the British and French governments secretly backed an Israeli attack on Egypt, providing an excuse for British and French troops to occupy the canal zone in order to keep the canal open. Condemnation of their actions, particularly from the US government, forced a humiliating British and French withdrawal.

**Taylor** A. J. P. Taylor, English historian (1906-90), was well known for his controversial comments on the major events of the twentieth century, including the origins of the Second World War. Sometimes his interpretations seemed to other historians to have been produced merely for the sake of provoking an argument. He became well known later in his career through his hugely popular televised lectures.

**Terminus post / ante quem** Time after which / time before which; used in archaeology for defining the youngest oldest age an object or archaeological context can be presumed to be.

**Top-down history** Studies of the past that focus on the evidence for, and actions of, the social elite.

**Total history** A broad vision of history, associated with the Annalists school of historians, that tapped into the associated disciplines of geography, psychology economics and sociology.

**Trevelyan** G. M. Trevelyan, English historian (1876-1962), like all historians, was influenced by the values of the age in which he was writing. He proved to be a keen advocate of the nationalist spirit in his *Garibaldi's Defence of the Roman Republic* (1907) - a stance that would fall into disrepute as Italy and other countries suffered the consequences of overtly nationalistic government. His *English Social History* (1944) appears to have been written as a patriotic gesture as the storm clouds grew over Europe in the years leading up to the Second World War.

**Typology** The defining of artefacts according to their distinctive attributes.

**UNESCO** United Nations Scientific, Educational and Cultural Organization.

**Vernacular architecture** Ordinary buildings constructed in regional styles using local materials.

**Viking placenames** The suffix -by meant a farmstead while -thorpe indicated a small extra or overflow settlement

**Whig history** 'History that is written either from the point of view of the winners or from an unthinking commitment to progress. The term implies criticism of such an approach.' (Jordanova (2006), p.230)

**World Heritage Sites** Sites nominated by signatory states that meet certain criteria recognised by the World Heritage Committee.

**Zeitgeist** Literally 'spirit of the age'.

# Bibliography

Alcock, L., *'By South Cadbury is that Camelot...' Excavations at Cadbury Castle 1966-70* (Thames and Hudson, 1972).
Allen, M. J., 'Analysing the landscape: a geographical approach to archaeological problems' in Schofield, A. J. (ed) *Interpreting Artefact Scatters: Contributions to Ploughzone Archaeology* (Oxbow Books, 1991).
Alpers, E. A. (1975) 'The impact of the slave trade on East Central Africa in the nineteenth century' in Inikori, J. E., *Forced Migration: the Impact of the Export Slave Trade on African Societies* (Hutchinson University Library, 1982).
Ambrose, T., and Paine, C., *Museum Basics* (Routledge, 2006).
Arnold, B., 'The Past as Propaganda: Totalitarian Archaeology in Nazi Germany' in Preucel, R., and Hodder, I. (eds.) *Contemporary Archaeology in Theory* (Blackwell, 1996).
Arnold, J., *History: a very short introduction* (Oxford University Press, 2000).
Bahn, P., et al, *Dictionary of Archaeolog* (Collins, 1992).
Barker, P., *Techniques of Archaeological Excavation* (Batsford, 1993).
Barry, J., and Davies, O., *Witchcraft Historiography* (Palgrave, 2007).
Barstow, A., *Witch Craze* (Harper Collins, 1994).
Baugh, Brizzi and Baker, 'Otzi's Bow' in *The Bulletin of Primitive Technology*, Spring 2006, issue 31.Beachy, R. W., *The Slave Trade of*

*Eastern Africa* (London, 1976).
Becker, C. and Martin, V. (1982), 'Rites de sepulture preislamiques as Senegal et vestiges protohistoriques' in *Archives Suisses d'Anthropologie generale*, 46 (2): 261-93.
Bell, M., Hosfield R., et al, *Experimental Archaeology* (University of Reading, 2008).
Bell, M., Fowler, P. J., Hillson, S. W., *The Experimental Earthwork Project, 1962-1992* (Council for British Archaeology, 1996).
Bell, M., 'Understanding how earthworks change', *British Archaeology*, 17, September 1996.
Binford, L., *In Pursuit of the Past* (Thames and Hudson, 1983).
Black, J. and MacRaild, D., *Studying History*, Palgrave, 2000, 2007).
Black, J., 'Whig history and lost causes', in *History Review*, December 1995.
Boese, W. (1973) *A Study of the Slave Trade and the Sources of Slaves in the Roman Republic and the Early Roman Empire*. University of Washington: Dissertation (obtainable in book form from University Microfilms, Ann Arbor, Michigan).
Bograd, M. D. and Singleton, T. A., 'The interpretation of slavery: Mount Vernon, Monticello, and Colonial Williamsburg' in Jameson, J. H. (ed), *Presenting Archaeology to the Public* (Sage Publications, 1997).
Bradley, K. R., 'On the Roman Slave Supply and Slavebreeding' in M. I. Finlay, M. I. (1987) *Classical Slavery* (Frank Cass, 1987).
Bradley, K. R., *Slavery and Rebellion in the Roman World, 140 B.C. - 70 B.C.* (Batsford, 1989).
Brailsford, J. W., *Hod Hill: Volume One* (British Museum, 1962).
Carr, E. H., *What is History?* (Penguin, 1961, 1964).
Carretta, V., *Olaudah Equiano: The Interesting Narrative and Other Writings [1789]* (Penguin Books, 1995).
Carver, M., *Sutton Hoo: Burial Ground of Kings?* (British Museum, 1998).
Castledon, R., *The Cerne Giant* (Dorset Publishing Company, 1996).
Cazorla-Sanchez, A., 'The New Cultural History - and you' in *History Review*, March, 2008.
Chadwick, N., *The Celts* (Penguin, 1971).
Chandler, C., *John Leland's Itinerary: travels in Tudor England* (Sutton, 1993).
Cole, R., *A. J. P Taylor: The Traitor Within The Gates* (Palgrave Macmillan, 1993).

Coles, J. M., 'Experimental Archaeology' in *The Proceeding of the Society of Antiquaries*, 1966-7.
Coles, J. M., *Experimental Archaeology* (Academic Press, 1979).
Collis, J. R., 'Markets and Money' in Hill, D., and Jesson, M., *The Iron Age and its Hill-forts* (University of Southampton, 1971).
Collis, J., *The European Iron Age* (Batsford, 1984).
Cowell, B., *The Heritage Obsession: the battle for England's past* (Tempus, 2008).
Crawford, M., 'Republican Denarii in Romania: the Suppression of Piracy and the Slave-Trade' in *Journal of Roman Studies* 67, 1977, 117-24.
Crawford, M., *Coinage and Money under the Roman Republic* (Methuen, 1985).
Cribb, R., 'On-site ethnoarchaeology' in *Archaeological Review from Cambridge*, Vol. 2, 1983.
Cunliffe, B., 'Some Aspects of Hill-forts and their Cultural Environments' in Hill, D., and Jesson, M., *The Iron Age and its Hill-forts* (University of Southampton, 1971).
Cunliffe, B., *Iron Age Communities in Britain* (Routledge and Kegan Paul, 1974, 1978, 1991, 2009).
Cunliffe, B., *Hengistbury Head* (Paul Eleck, 1978).
Cunliffe, B., 'Relations between Britain and Gaul in the First Century B.C. And Early First Century A.D.' in Macready, S., and Thompson, F. H., *Cross-Channel Trade between Gaul and Britain in the Pre-Roman Iron Age* (The Society of Antiquaries, 1984).
Cunliffe, B., *Iron Age Britain* (Batsford, 1995).
Cunliffe, B., *Wessex to A.D. 1000* (Longman, 1993).
Cunliffe, B., *Prehistoric Europe: an Illustrated History* (Oxford University Press, 1994).
Cunliffe, B., *The Ancient Celts* (Penguin Books, 1997).
Curtin, P. D., *Economic Change in Pre-Colonial Africa* (The University of Wisconsin Press, 1975).
Van Dantzig, A. (1975) 'Effects of the Atlantic slave trade on some West African societies' in Inikori, J. E., *Forced Migration: the Impact of the Export Slave Trade on African Societies* (Hutchinson University Library, 1982).
Davis, D. B., *Slavery and Human Progress* (Oxford University Press, 1984).
Dowdy, M., Miller, I., Austin D., *Be Your Own House Detective* (BBC Books, 1997).

Dresser, M., *Bristol and the African Slave Trade* (Bristol City Council, 1997).
Durkheim, E., *Suicide: A Study in Sociology* (Kegan Paul, 1962).
Duval, A. 'Regional groups in western France' in Macready, S., and Thompson, F. H., *Cross-Channel Trade between Gaul and Britain in the Pre Roman Iron Age* (The Society of Antiquaries, 1984).
English Heritage (2012) *PPS5: Planning for the Historic Environment Practice Guide.*
Evans, R., *In Defence of History* (Granta Books, 1997, 2001).
Evans, R., 'Postmodernism and the study of history' in *History Review*, December 1998.
Fage, J. D., *A History of Africa* (Hutchinson, 1978).
Feachem, R. W., 'Unfinished Hill-forts' in Hill, D., and Jesson, M., *The Iron Age and its Hill-forts* (University of Southampton, 1971).
Fines, J., *Reading Historical Documents* (Basil Blackwell, 1988).
Firstbrook, P., *Surviving the Iron Age* (BBC Worldwide, 2001).
Gaffney, C., Gater, J., and Ovenden, S., *The Use of geophysical Techniques in Archaeological Evaluations in Institute of Field Technologists*; Technical Paper Number 9 (University of Birmingham, 1991).
Galliou, P., 'Days of wine and roses? Early Armorica and the Atlantic wine trade' in Macready, S., and Thompson, F. H., *Cross-Channel Trade between Gaul and Britain in the Pre Roman Iron Age* (The Society of Antiquaries, 1984).
Gingell, C., 'The Marlborough Downs in the Bronze Age' in Barrett, I., Bradley, R., *Settlement and Society in the British Later Bronze Age* (Oxford, 1980).
Green, A., and Troup, K., *The Houses of History*, (Manchester University Press, 1999).
Hair, P. E. H., *The Atlantic Slave Trade and Black Africa* (The Historical Association, 1978).
Harris, R., *Discovering Timber-Framed Buildings* (Shire Publications, 1993).
Harris, W., 'Child Exposure in the Roman Empire' in *Journal of Historical Studies*, 84, 1994, 1-22.
Haselgrove, C., 'The Iron Age' in J. Hunter, J., and I. Ralston, I., *The Archaeology of Britain* (Routledge, 1999).
Haselgrove, C., Millett, M., and Smith, I., *Archaeology from the Ploughsoil: Studies in the Collection and Interpretation of Field Survey Data* (University of Sheffield, 1985).

Hawkes, N., 'The folk who lived on the Hill' in *Heritage Today*, December, 1998.
Hayes, P. P., 'Models for the distribution of pottery around former agricultural settlements' in Schofield, A. J., *Interpreting Artefact Scatters: Contributions to Ploughzone Archaeology* (Oxbow Books, 1991).
Henson, D., *Doing Archaeology* (Routledge, 2012).
Henstock, A., *Tracing the History of Your House* (Nottinghamshire Local History Association, 1988).
Hey, D., *The Oxford Companion to Local and Family History* (Oxford University Press, 1996).
Heyerdahl, T. (1984), 'Foreword to the 35$^{th}$ Anniversary Edition' in Heyerdahl, T., *Kon Tiki* (Simon and Schuster, 2013).
Hill, D., and Jesson, M., *The Iron Age and its Hill-forts* (University of Southampton, 1971).
Holgate, R., 'Identifying neolithic settlements in Britain: the role of field survey in the interpretation of lithic scatters' in Haselgrove, C., Millett, M., and Smith, I., *Archaeology from the Ploughsoil: Studies in the Collection and Interpretation of Field Survey Data* (University of Sheffield, 1985).
Hoskins, W. G., 'The rebuilding of rural England, 1570-1640' in *Past and Present*, 1953, 4: 44-59.
Howarth, K., *Oral History* (Sutton, 1998).
Hughes, A., *Horsham Houses* (The Camelot Press, 1986).
Inikori, J. E., *Forced Migration: the Impact of the Export Slave Trade on African Societies* (Hutchinson University Library, 1982).
Iredale, D. & Barrett, J., *Discovering Your Old House* (Shire Publications, 1991).
James, S. and Rigby, V., *Britain and the Celtic Iron Age* (British Museum Press, 1997).
James, S., *The Atlantic Celts: Ancient People or Modern Invention?* (British Museum Press, 1999).
Jenkins, K., *Rethinking History* (Routledge, 1991).
Jordanova, L., *History in Practice* (Bloomsbury Academic, 2006).
Kershaw, I., *Hitler: 1889-1936: Hubris, vol. I* (Penguin, 1998; 2001).
Klein, H., 'The Portuguese slave trade from Angola in the eighteenth century' in Inikori, J. E., *Forced Migration: the Impact of the Export Slave Trade on African Societies* (Hutchinson University Library, 1982).
Klein, H., *The Atlantic Slave Trade* (Cambridge University Press, 1999).
Kouwenhoven, A. P., 'World's Oldest Spears' in *Archaeology*

Volume 50 Number 3, May/June 1997.
Laing, L., and Laing, J., *Celtic Britain and Ireland: Art and Society* (The Herbert Press, 1995).
Langouet, L., 'Alet and cross-Channel trade' in Macready, S., and Thompson, F.H., *Cross-Channel Trade between Gaul and Britain in the Pre Roman Iron Age* (The Society of Antiquaries, 1984).
Levack, B., *The Witch-Hunt in Early Modern Europe* (Longman, 2006).
Lyall, J. and Powlesland, D., 'West Heslerton Parish Project' in *Internet Archaeology*, October, 1996.
Machin, R. (1977) 'The Great Rebuilding: a reassessment' in *Past and Present*, 77: 33-56.
Macready, S., and Thompson, F. H., *Cross-Channel Trade between Gaul and Britain in the Pre Roman Iron Age* (The Society of Antiquaries, 1984).
Madden, J. (1996) 'Slavery in the Roman Empire' In *Classics Ireland*. Vol 3. Dublin: University College.
Martin, P. (1970) 'The trade of Loango in the seventeenth and eighteenth centuries' in Inikori, J. E., *Forced Migration: the Impact of the Export Slave Trade on African Societies* (Hutchinson University Library, 1982).
Martin, S., *Britain's Slave Trade* (Channel 4 Books, 1999).
May, J., *Fogou* (Gothic Image, 1996).
McCann, W.J., '*Volk und Germanentum*: The Presentation of the Past in Nazi Germany', in Gathercole, P., and Lowenthal, D., *The Politics of the Past* (Unwin, 1990, pp. 74-88).
McIntosh, J., *The Practical Archaeologist* (Thames and Hudson, 1999).
Marwick, A., *The Nature of History* (Macmillan, 1970).
Miles, D. (1997) 'The interpretation, presentation and use of tree-ring dates' in *Vernacular Architecture* 28: 40-56.
Millson, D., et al (2010), *Experimentation and Interpretation: the use of experimental archaeology in the study of the past* (Oxbow Books, 2010).
Nash, D., 'The basis of contact between Britain and Gaul in the Late Pre-Roman Iron Age' in Macready, S., and Thompson, F. H., *Cross-Channel Trade between Gaul and Britain in the Pre Roman Iron Age* (The Society of Antiquaries, 1984).
Oliver, R., and Fage, J. D., *A Short History of Africa* (Penguin Books, 1975).
Papworth, M., *The Search for the Durotriges: Dorset and the West Country in the Late Iron Age* (The History Press, 2011).

Peacock, D. P. S., 'Roman Amphorae in Pre-Roman Britain' in Hill, D., and Jesson, M., *The Iron Age and its Hill-forts* (University of Southampton, 1971).
Peacock, D. P. S.,'Amphorae in Iron Age Britain: a reassessment' in Macready, S., and Thompson, F. H., *Cross-Channel Trade between Gaul and Britain in the Pre Roman Iron Age* (The Society of Antiquaries, 1984).
Pearson, S. (1997) 'Tree-ring dating: a Review', in *Vernacular Architecture* 28: 25-39.
Peddie, J., *Conquest: the Roman Invasion of Britain* (Sutton, 1987).
Percival, J., *Living in the Past: a journey back to the Iron Age* (BBC Books, 1980).
Pleuger, G., 'Chance in history' in *History Review*, March, 1992.
Pryor, F., *Farmers in Prehistoric Britain*, (The History Press, 2011).
Ralling, C., *The Kon-Tiki Man*, (Guild Publishing, 1990).
Renfrew, C., and Bahn, P., *Archaeology: Theories, Methods and Practice* (Thames and Hudson, 1996; 2008).
Reynolds, P., *Iron Age Farm: the Butser experiment* (Colonnade, 1979).
Reynolds, P., 'Living in the Past' exhibition notes (Cheddar Exhibition Centre, 1979).
Reynolds, P., 'Pit Technology in the Iron Age' in *British Archaeology*, November/December, 1988.
Reynolds, P., 'Reconstruction or Construct? The Pimperne House' in *British Archaeology*, January/February, 1989.
Reynolds, P., *The Life and Death of a Post-Hole*, paper given to Interpreting Stratigraphy, May, 1995.
Reynolds, P., 'The Nature of Experiment in Archaeology' in Hardin, A. F., et al, *Experiment and Design in Archaeology* (Oxbow Books, 1999).
Richmond, I., *Hod Hill: Volume Two* (British Museum, 1968).
Ritchie, W. F., and Ritchie, J. N. G., *Celtic Warriors* (Shire Publications, 1997).
Salzman, L. F., *Building in England down to 1540* (Oxford University Press, 1952).
Sandell, R., James, R., *Museum Management and Marketing* (Routledge, 2007).
Schofield, A. J., *Interpreting Artefact Scatters: Contributions to Ploughzone Archaeology* (Oxbow Books, 1991).
Severin, T., *The Brendan Voyage* (Arrow Books, 1978).
Sharpe, J., *Witchcraft in Early Modern England* (Pearson, 2001).
Sharples, N., *Maiden Castle* (Batsford, 1991).

Simms, S. R. (1988) 'The archaeological structure of a Bedouin camp' in *Journal of Archaeological Science*, 15.
Souden, D., *Stonehenge Revealed* (Collins and Brown, 1997).
Stanford, S. C., 'Invention, Adoption and Imposition - the Evidence of the Hill-forts' in Hill, D., and Jesson, M., *The Iron Age and its Hill-forts* (University of Southampton, 1971).
Stern, F., *The Varieties of History* (Vintage, 1956; 1973).
Stone, L., *The Past and the Present* (Routledge and Kegan Paul, 1981).
Theroux, P., *The Happy Isles of Oceania: paddling in the Pacific* (Penguin, 1992).
Toivo, R. 'The witch-craze as holocaust: the rise of persecuting societies', in Barry, J., and Davies, O., *Witchcraft Historiography* (Palgrave, 2007).
Tosh, J., *The Pursuit of History* (Longman, 1984; 2009).
Transactions of the Medical Society of London, 1894-1896.
West, S., et al, *Understanding West Stow* (Jarrold Publishing, 2000).
Whittaker, J., 'Weapon Trials: the atlatl and experiments in hunting technology' in Ferguson, J., *Designing Experimental Research in Archaeology: examining technology through production and use* (University of Colorado Press, 2010).

# Further reading

### History

Arnold, J., *History: a very short introduction* (Oxford University Press, 2000).
Black, J. and MacRaild, D., *Studying History* (Palgrave, 2000; 2007).
Jordanova, L., *History in Practice* (Bloomsbury Academic, 2006).
Marwick, A., *The New Nature of History: knowledge, evidence, language* (Macmillan, 2001).
Tosh, J., *The Pursuit of History* (Longman, 1984; 2009).

### Heritage

Ambrose, T., and Paine, C., *Museum Basics* (Routledge, 2006).
Benton, T., *Understanding Heritage and Memory* (Manchester University Press, 2010).
Black, G., *The Engaging Museum: developing museums for visitor involvement* (Routledge, 2005).
Black, G., *Transforming Museums in the Twenty-First Century* (Routledge, 2011).
Corscane, G., *Heritage, Museums and Galleries: an introductory reader* (Routledge, 2004).
Cowell, B., *The Heritage Obsession: the battle for England's past* (Tempus, 2008).
Fairclough, G., Harrison, R., Jameson, J. H., Schofield, J., *The Heritage Reader* (Routledge, 2007).
Graham, B., Ashworth, G.J., and Tunbridge, J. E., *A Geography of Heritage: Power, Culture and Economy* (Arnold Publishers, 2002).
Harrison, R., *Heritage: Critical Approaches* (Routledge, 2012).
Harrison, R., *Understanding the Politics of Heritage* (Manchester University Press, 2010).
Henson, P., Stone, P. and Corbishley (eds), *Education and the Historic Environment* (Routledge, 2004).
Hey, D., *The Oxford Companion to Local and Family History* (Oxford University Press, 1996).
Howard, P., *Heritage: management, interpretation, identity* (Continuum, 2002).
Smith, L., *Uses of Heritage* (Routledge, 2006).

Thurley, T., *Men from the Ministry: how Britain saved its heritage* (Yale University Press, 2013).
West, S., *Understanding Heritage in Practice* (Manchester University Press, 2010).

**Archaeology**

Henson, D., *Doing Archaeology* (Routledge, 2012).
Hunter, J., and Ralston, I. *The Archaeology of Britain: an introduction from earliest times to the twenty-first times* (Routledge, 2009).
Renfrew, C., and Bahn, P., *Archaeology: Theories, methods and practices* (Thames and Hudson, 2012).
Scarre, C., *The Human Past: World prehistory and the development of human societies* (Thames and Hudson, 2013).

**Professional Practice**

Adkins, L. and Adkins, R. A., *Archaeological Illustration* (Cambridge: Cambridge University Press, 1984).
Anon., *A Practical Guide to Drawing Archaeological Sites* (The Royal Commission on the Ancient and Historical Monuments of Scotland, 2011).
Burns, T. and Sinfield, S., *Essential study skills: the complete guide to success at university* (2nd ed.) (Sage, 2008).
Levin, P. and Topping, G., *Perfect Presentations* (Open University Press, 2006).
Menuge, A., ed., *Understanding Historic Buildings: a guide to good recording practice* (English Heritage, 2006).
Race, P., *How to get a good degree: making the most of your time at university* (Open University Press, 2007).
Valerie Raleigh Yow, *Recording Oral History: A Guide for the Humanities and Social Sciences*, second edition (Sage, 2005).

Made in the USA
Charleston, SC
28 August 2016